Virtual Team Collaboration

Jasmin Mahadevan

Virtual Team Collaboration

A Guide for Individual Team Members

Jasmin Mahadevan
Engineering and Management
Pforzheim University
Pforzheim, Baden-Württemberg, Germany

ISBN 978-3-658-44968-1   ISBN 978-3-658-44969-8 (eBook)
https://doi.org/10.1007/978-3-658-44969-8

© The Editor(s) (if applicable) and The Author(s), under exclusive license to Springer Fachmedien Wiesbaden GmbH, part of Springer Nature 2024

This work is subject to copyright. All rights are solely and exclusively licensed by the Publisher, whether the whole or part of the material is concerned, specifically the rights of translation, reprinting, reuse of illustrations, recitation, broadcasting, reproduction on microfilms or in any other physical way, and transmission or information storage and retrieval, electronic adaptation, computer software, or by similar or dissimilar methodology now known or hereafter developed.
The use of general descriptive names, registered names, trademarks, service marks, etc. in this publication does not imply, even in the absence of a specific statement, that such names are exempt from the relevant protective laws and regulations and therefore free for general use.
The publisher, the authors and the editors are safe to assume that the advice and information in this book are believed to be true and accurate at the date of publication. Neither the publisher nor the authors or the editors give a warranty, expressed or implied, with respect to the material contained herein or for any errors or omissions that may have been made. The publisher remains neutral with regard to jurisdictional claims in published maps and institutional affiliations.

This Springer Gabler imprint is published by the registered company Springer Fachmedien Wiesbaden GmbH, part of Springer Nature.
The registered company address is: Abraham-Lincoln-Str. 46, 65189 Wiesbaden, Germany

If disposing of this product, please recycle the paper.

To Peer, Fredrik and Io

Acknowledgements

The author wishes to thank Annabelle Stärkle, Iuliana Ancuţa Ilie, Larissa Dausien, Jule Amelie Vögele, Jasmin Kensington and Angelo Albano for their research and supportive work on this book. Many thanks go to Springer, in particular Ulrike Lörcher and Monika Mülhausen, for their ongoing support and editorial guidance. Further thanks are extended to Gabriella Loveday for proofreading and (in alphabetical order) to Lisa Bacher, Daniel Becker, Jennifer Blaich, Robin Burghardt, Raphael Diehm, Isabelle Dittus, Florian Goedeckemayer, Frederik Goroll, Marvin Hammer, Sven Metzler, Michael Mohaupt, Tobias Reichert and Jakob Steinmann for insights provided and an enriching intellectual exchange.

Contents

1	**Why a Book on Virtual Team Collaboration, and What Makes It Unique?**		1
	1.1	From 'Just Practice' to 'Best Practice'.	1
	1.2	Ten Essential Knowledge-Areas of Virtual Team Collaboration	2
	1.3	A Pedagogical, Problem-Based Learning Focus	6
	1.4	Summary: What Sets This Book on Virtual Team Collaboration Apart	6
2	**Virtual Team Collaboration and the Digital Transformation: Effects of the COVID-19 Pandemic, and a Five-Factor Model.**		7
	2.1	Introduction	7
		2.1.1 Learning Objectives	8
		2.1.2 Opening Case	9
	2.2	Key Concepts: Virtual Team Collaboration	9
		2.2.1 What is a Team?	9
		2.2.2 What Sets Virtual Teams Apart? The Role of Information and Communication Technologies	11
		2.2.3 Virtual Teams as a Global Opportunity: The Relevance of Diversity and Dispersion	12
	2.3	Virtual Team Collaboration as Configuring Key Transformative Dynamics	14
		2.3.1 Key Virtual Team Inputs	14
		2.3.2 Key Virtual Team Dynamics	14
		2.3.3 Key Virtual Team Outputs: Perspectives on Performance and Learning	15
	2.4	The COVID-19 Effect on Virtual Team Collaboration and Flexible Work Arrangements	18
		2.4.1 The Need for Social Distancing and the Emergence of a New Type of Virtual Team	18
		2.4.2 A Trend Towards Flexible Work Arrangements	19

		2.4.3	Global Patterns and Differences in Work-from-home Preferences	20
	2.5	Virtual Teams Today and Tomorrow: Types and Characteristics		23
		2.5.1	Teamness, Virtualness and Remoteness: Three Characteristics of Virtual Teams Today	24
	2.6	Virtual Team Collaboration and the Digital Transformation		26
		2.6.1	Drivers of the Digital Transformation	27
		2.6.2	Phases of the Digital Transformation	27
		2.6.3	Strategic Imperatives of the Digital Transformation	28
	2.7	Summary and Recommendations: Virtual Teamwork as a Configuration Challenge		30
		2.7.1	What Makes Virtual Team Collaboration Succeed (and how can we predict and achieve success)?	30
		2.7.2	A Five-factor Model	32
	2.8	Closing Part		34
		2.8.1	Chapter Summary	34
		2.8.2	Key Points	35
		2.8.3	Review Questions	36
		2.8.4	Opening Case Revisited	36
		2.8.5	Closing Activity: When and how are Virtual Teams Successful?	36
	References			37
3	**Information and Communication Technologies in Virtual Team Collaboration: Configuration Challenges and Solutions**			**41**
	3.1	Introduction		41
		3.1.1	Learning Objectives	42
		3.1.2	Opening Case	42
	3.2	What Are ICTs, and How Do They Influence Virtual Team Collaboration?		42
	3.3	The Relevance of Considering ICT Richness		44
		3.3.1	What is Media Richness?	44
		3.3.2	Considering ICT Richness in Relation to Communicative and Task Complexity	45
	3.4	ICT Richness in Relation to Task Complexity and Communicative Challenge		49
	3.5	Configuring ICTs in Relation to the Constitutive Factors of Virtual Team Collaboration		51
		3.5.1	ICTs in Relation to Team Inputs	53
		3.5.2	ICTs in Relation to Team Processes	54
		3.5.3	ICTs in Relation to Team Moderators	56
		3.5.4	ICTs in Relation to Team Characteristics	56

3.6		Recommendations: How Technology Can Help to Overcome Virtual Team Challenges	60
	3.6.1	Configure ICTs in Light of Task and Team Factors	60
	3.6.2	Create ICT-Based Social Spaces for More Trust and Less Conflict	62
3.7		Closing Part	64
	3.7.1	Chapter Summary	64
	3.7.2	Key Points	64
	3.7.3	Review Questions	65
	3.7.4	Opening Case Revisited	65
	3.7.5	Closing Activity	67
References			68

4 Communication as Enabler of Virtual Team Collaboration: Properties and Best Practices ... 71

4.1		Introduction	71
	4.1.1	Learning Objectives	72
	4.1.2	Reading Requirement	72
	4.1.3	Opening Case	72
4.2		What is Communication? Three Approaches	73
	4.2.1	The Sender-Receiver Model of Communication	74
4.3		Communication as Content and Context	75
4.4		Communication as a Simplification Process: Iceberg, Glasses and Backpack	77
	4.4.1	Communication as an Iceberg	78
	4.4.2	Communication as Glasses	80
	4.4.3	Communication as a Backpack	81
4.5		Virtual Team Communication: Recommendations and Best Practices	84
	4.5.1	The Five Principles of Communicative Action	84
	4.5.2	Acknowledging the Four Sides of Communication	86
	4.5.3	Integrating Communicative Context and Content on Team Level	89
	4.5.4	Reframing Strategies	90
4.6		Recommendation: A Psychologically Safe Climate as a Virtual Team Safety Belt	92
4.7		Closing Part	94
	4.7.1	Chapter Summary	94
	4.7.2	Key Points	95
	4.7.3	Review Questions	95
	4.7.4	Opening Case Revisited	96
	4.7.5	Closing Activity	96
References			97

5 Building Collaborative Cultures in Cross-Functional and Interdisciplinary Virtual Teams: Relationship Management, Project Time Planning and Workspace Organization ... 99

- 5.1 Introduction ... 99
  - 5.1.1 Learning Objectives ... 100
  - 5.1.2 Reading Requirements ... 100
  - 5.1.3 Opening Case ... 100
- 5.2 What is Culture, and How is It Relevant to Virtual Team Collaboration? ... 101
  - 5.2.1 Collaborative Culture as the Ideal Positive Convergence-Divergence Configuration ... 101
  - 5.2.2 The Limitations of ICT-Based Collaboration: A Lack in Richness and Context ... 102
  - 5.2.3 What is the Goal? Configuring Complexity, Remoteness, Teamness and Virtualness ... 103
  - 5.2.4 What Needs to Be Integrated Through Collaboration? Three Levels of Culture ... 104
  - 5.2.5 Why Virtual Team Culture Does Not Simply 'Happen': Divergent Core Cultural Assumptions ... 106
  - 5.2.6 Culture as Communication as a Tool for Integrating Culture Despite ICT Limitations ... 107
- 5.3 The Communication of Relationship Assumptions and Trust Requirements ... 108
  - 5.3.1 Low- and High-Context, and In-Group and Out-Group, in Virtual Team Communication ... 108
  - 5.3.2 Difference in Trust Building Patterns and Requirements ... 111
  - 5.3.3 Achieving Trust and Task Clarity Across Hierarchy, Functions and Disciplines ... 113
- 5.4 The Organization of Space and Work-Life Interrelations ... 115
- 5.5 Project Planning Assumptions and the Organization of Time ... 118
- 5.6 Recommendations for Collaborating Across Hierarchies, Disciplines and Professions ... 122
  - 5.6.1 How to Use the 'Culture as Communication' Perspective? ... 122
  - 5.6.2 How to Become Aware of the Cultural Dimension of Communication ... 124
  - 5.6.3 Designing the Temporal Rhythm of Virtual Team Collaboration ... 124
- 5.7 Closing Part ... 127
  - 5.7.1 Chapter Summary ... 127
  - 5.7.2 Key Points ... 128
  - 5.7.3 Review Questions ... 129

	5.7.4	Opening Case Revisited.............................	129
	5.7.5	Closing Activity..................................	130
	References...		131

6 Organizational Design and Core Technologies for Virtual Collaboration: How to Shape the Conditions Under Which the Team Can Thrive 133

6.1	Introduction		133
	6.1.1	Learning Objectives...............................	134
	6.1.2	Opening Case....................................	135
6.2	The Organizational Dimension of Virtual Team Collaboration........		135
	6.2.1	What is Organization?.............................	135
	6.2.2	Building Blocks of Organization.....................	136
	6.2.3	Virtual Team Members as Organizational Designers.........	137
	6.2.4	Mechanistic Versus Organic Virtual Team Collaboration	139
	6.2.5	How Organizational Design Contributes to Performance	140
6.3	Images of Organization: The Impact of Metaphors on Virtual Team Collaboration		142
6.4	The Organizational Structure of Virtual Team Collaboration		144
	6.4.1	Functional Design	144
	6.4.2	Divisional Organizational Design	145
	6.4.3	Matrix Organizational Design for Virtual Team Collaboration	146
6.5	Organizational Transformation, Technology and Human-machine Interactions...		147
	6.5.1	Virtual Teams as Dynamic Socio-Technical Systems or Networks	148
	6.5.2	The Need to Configure ICTs, and Convergent-Divergent Dynamics.....................................	150
	6.5.3	Summary of the Organizational Transformation Process Achieved by Virtual Teams	152
6.6	Organizational Core Technologies: Three Main Design Options..		153
	6.6.1	Mediating Technologies............................	153
	6.6.2	Long-Linked Technologies	154
	6.6.3	Intensive Technologies.............................	155
6.7	Should Teams Organize for Change or Stability, and How Much Bureaucracy is Required?......................		157
6.8	Closing Part		159
	6.8.1	Chapter Summary	159
	6.8.2	Key Points	160
	6.8.3	Review Questions.................................	161

		6.8.4	Opening Case Revisited	161
		6.8.5	Closing Activity	161
	References			162
7	**Digital Leadership and Virtual Team Collaboration: Options and Success Factors for Industry 4.0**			165
	7.1	Introduction		165
		7.1.1	Learning Objectives	166
		7.1.2	Opening case	166
	7.2	Evolution and Components of Virtual Team Leadership		168
	7.3	Main Leadership Styles, and Their Pros and Cons for Virtual Team Collaboration		174
		7.3.1	Transactional Leadership	175
		7.3.2	Transformational Leadership	175
		7.3.3	Transformational and Transactional Leadership Compared	176
	7.4	Alternative and Complementary Leadership Styles for Virtual Team Collaboration		177
		7.4.1	Pragmatic and Cognitive Leadership: Useful for Expert and Interdisciplinary Teams	177
		7.4.2	Servant and Authentic Leadership: A Means of Counterbalancing Ideology and Power	178
		7.4.3	Shared and Distributed Leadership: A Must-Have of Virtual Team Collaboration	179
		7.4.4	Directive and Passive Leadership: Not Ideal for Virtual Team Collaboration	179
	7.5	Recommendations for Leading Virtual Teams		181
		7.5.1	Leading Virtual Teams Through Change and Crisis	181
		7.5.2	Situational Leadership: Rooting Leadership Practices in Followers' Needs	183
		7.5.3	Virtual Team Leadership: Summary and Best Practices	185
	7.6	Closing Part		189
		7.6.1	Chapter Summary	189
		7.6.2	Key Points	190
		7.6.3	Review Questions	190
		7.6.4	Opening Case Revisited	191
		7.6.5	Closing Activity	192
	References			193

8 Cross-Cultural Management of Virtual Team Collaboration: Cultural Dimensions and Intercultural Competencies for Culturally Diverse Settings ... 197

- 8.1 Introduction ... 197
  - 8.1.1 Learning Objectives ... 198
  - 8.1.2 Opening Case ... 198
- 8.2 What is Cross-Cultural Management, and How is It Relevant to Virtual Team Collaboration? ... 199
- 8.3 Cross-Cultural Differences in Global Virtual Team Collaboration ... 202
  - 8.3.1 The Hofstede Dimensions: First Ideas of 'What is a Team, and How Should It Function?' ... 202
  - 8.3.2 The Cultural Dimensions of Project GLOBE: A More Sophisticated Framework ... 208
- 8.4 Recommendations for Cross-Cultural Management and Global Leadership in Virtual Teams ... 214
  - 8.4.1 What Cultural Dimensions are Useful For ... 214
  - 8.4.2 Cultural Dimensions as Part of the Global Virtual Team Configuration Challenge ... 216
  - 8.4.3 How to Do Reality Justice When Using Cultural Dimensions: Two Considerations ... 217
  - 8.4.4 The Long-Term Goal of Developing Intercultural Competencies ... 219
- 8.5 Closing Part ... 220
  - 8.5.1 Chapter Summary ... 220
  - 8.5.2 Key Points ... 221
  - 8.5.3 Review Questions ... 222
  - 8.5.4 Opening Case Revisited ... 222
  - 8.5.5 Closing Activity ... 224
- References ... 224

9 Global Leadership and English Language Management in Virtual Team Collaboration: Considering Globalization, Digitalization and Power Effects ... 227

- 9.1 Introduction ... 227
  - 9.1.1 Learning Objectives ... 228
  - 9.1.2 Reading Requirements ... 228
  - 9.1.3 Opening Case ... 228
- 9.2 What Are Global Virtual Teams, and What Sets Them Apart? ... 229
  - 9.2.1 Diversity, Dispersion, Power: Three Constitutive Factors of Global Virtual Teams ... 229
  - 9.2.2 ICTs as Key Enabler of Global Virtual Team Collaboration ... 230
  - 9.2.3 The Need to Configure Global Virtual Team Dynamics ... 231

	9.3	The Strategic Dimension of Global Virtual Team Collaboration.	233
		9.3.1 The Digital Transformation in a Global Perspective	234
		9.3.2 Standardization and Differentiation Advantages in Globalization	234
		9.3.3 Glocalization as an Integrative Strategy.	236
		9.3.4 Corporate Internationalization Strategies and Their Digital Transformation Potential	236
	9.4	Specifics of Global Virtual Team Leadership	239
	9.5	English Language Management in Virtual Team Collaboration	242
		9.5.1 Collaborative Challenges of English as a Lingua Franca Communication	243
		9.5.2 English as *the* Global Language	244
		9.5.3 Language Power, Position Power and Expert Power in Virtual Team Collaboration	245
		9.5.4 Overcoming Language Closures: A Virtual Team Checklist.	246
	9.6	Being a Virtual Team Leader on a Global Level	247
	9.7	Closing Part	249
		9.7.1 Chapter Summary	249
		9.7.2 Key Points	250
		9.7.3 Review Questions.	250
		9.7.4 Opening Case Revisited.	251
		9.7.5 Closing Activity	251
	References.		252
10	**Change and Learning, Tacit Knowledge Management and Virtual Team Innovativeness Under BANI Conditions: The Role of Leadership, Organization and Technology**		255
	10.1	Introduction	255
		10.1.1 Learning Objectives.	256
		10.1.2 Reading Requirements.	257
		10.1.3 Opening Case.	257
	10.2	Are Virtual Teams More Innovative?.	258
	10.3	How to Organize Virtual Team Collaboration for Innovation, Learning and Change?.	260
		10.3.1 What is Learning, and how Should It be Implemented?	261
		10.3.2 What is Change, and how can it be Implemented?	262
	10.4	Facilitating Innovativeness: Leadership as Working Towards Safe Belonging During Crisis	264
		10.4.1 Combining Leader Self-identities for Higher Resilience and Adaptability.	264

		10.4.2	Perceived Virtual Team Membership for Overcoming Passiveness..	265
		10.4.3	Virtual Team Performance Norms for Increasing Perceived Virtual Team Membership.....................	267
	10.5	Knowledge Creation and Tacit Knowledge Management in Virtual Teams...		269
		10.5.1	Knowledge Types in Relation to Knowledge Creation in Virtual Teams...................................	270
		10.5.2	Tacit Knowledge Management and Knowledge Conversion by Means of the SECI Spiral	271
		10.5.3	Recommendations for Preventing Tacit Knowledge Loss Because of ICT Limitations............................	272
	10.6	The Technological Dimension of Virtual Team Learning and Change..		274
		10.6.1	Towards an Internet of Things?	275
		10.6.2	Designing Human—Machine Interfaces for Virtual Team Collaboration	277
		10.6.3	The Johari Window	278
	10.7	Closing Part		281
		10.7.1	Chapter Summary	281
		10.7.2	Key Points	281
		10.7.3	Review Questions.....................................	282
		10.7.4	Opening Case Revisited...............................	282
		10.7.5	Closing Activity	283
	References...			283
11	**Digital Ethics, Artificial Intelligence, and Responsible Research and Innovation: Sustainable and Inclusive Virtual Team Collaboration for a Better Future**			**289**
	11.1	Introduction		289
		11.1.1	Learning Objectives..................................	290
		11.1.2	Opening Case..	290
	11.2	The Wider Requirements of Virtual Team Collaboration		292
		11.2.1	Sustainability as a Measuring Rod for Virtual Team Collaboration	292
		11.2.2	The Starting Point: From Shareholder to Stakeholder Value......................................	293
		11.2.3	The Diversity Responsibility of Inclusive Virtual Team Collaboration	294
		11.2.4	What are Virtual Teams and Their Individual Members Responsible for?......................................	296

11.3	The Ethics of Digital Collaboration and Artificial Intelligence		299
	11.3.1	Ethical Principle of Digital Collaboration	299
	11.3.2	The Ethical Principles of Artificial Intelligence	301
11.4	Responsible Research and Innovation		303
	11.4.1	What is Responsible Research and Innovation, and Why do we Need it?	303
	11.4.2	Stakeholder Engagement as a Crucial Process	304
11.5	The Collingridge Dilemma and Technological Assessment		306
	11.5.1	The Collingridge Dilemma	307
	11.5.2	Technological Assessment as a Way of Handling the Collingridge Dilemma	309
11.6	Closing Part		311
	11.6.1	Chapter Summary	311
	11.6.2	Key Points	312
	11.6.3	Review Questions	313
References			314

List of Figures

Fig. 2.1	Diversity and dispersion: the two distinguishing qualities of global virtual teams. *Source* Own figure.	12
Fig. 2.2	Convergent and divergent virtual team collaboration processes. *Source* own figure	15
Fig. 2.3	Teamness, remoteness and virtualness. *Source* own figure	25
Fig. 2.4	A five factor model of virtual team collaboration. *Source:* own figure	32
Fig. 3.1	Richness of Information and Communication Technologies. *Source* own figure	45
Fig. 3.2	The iceberg model of knowledge. *Source* own figure	47
Fig. 3.3	Bringing implicit knowledge to the surface in ICT-based communication. *Source* own figure	48
Fig. 3.4	ICT effectiveness in relation to communicative and task complexity. *Source* own figure, based on Daft and Lengel (1984)	50
Fig. 3.5	Information and Communication Technologies as enabler of virtual team collaboration. *Source* own figure, further developed from Chap. 1	52
Fig. 3.6	ICT requirements in relation to virtual team characteristics. *Source* Own figure, partly based on Martins and Schilpzand (2011)	56
Fig. 3.7	The online accounting team. *Source* own figure	58
Fig. 3.8	The business development team. *Source* own figure	59
Fig. 4.1	The sender-receiver model. *Source* own figure	74
Fig. 4.2	Context and content in communication. *Source* own figure	77
Fig. 4.3	Communication as an iceberg. *Source* own figure	78
Fig. 4.4	Wearing glasses when communicating. *Source* own figure	81

Fig. 4.5	Unpacking and repacking one's backpack in communication. *Source* own figure	82
Fig. 5.1	Three levels of culture according to Schein. *Source* own figure	105
Fig. 5.2	Low- and high-context collaborative roads. *Source* own figure	109
Fig. 5.3	Low- and high-context social relations assumptions. *Source* own figure	110
Fig. 5.4	Low- and high-context social relations, and high-context variations. *Source* own figure	111
Fig. 5.5	Space bubbles (proxemics) according to Hall. *Source* own figure	116
Fig. 5.6	Project time and execution: M-time and P-time assumptions. *Source* own figure	120
Fig. 5.7	The required temporal rhythm of cultural integration. *Source* own figure	126
Fig. 6.1	Functional organizational design. *Source* own figure	144
Fig. 6.2	Divisional organizational design for virtual team collaboration. *Source* own figure	145
Fig. 6.3	Matrix organizational design for virtual team collaboration. *Source* own figure	146
Fig. 6.4	Virtual team collaboration as organizational transformation. *Source* own figure	148
Fig. 6.5	Requirements of virtual team collaboration as organizational transformation. *Source* own figure	152
Fig. 6.6	Mediating technologies: the case of a global sales team. *Source* own figure	154
Fig. 6.7	Long-linked technologies: the case of preparing a presentation across time zones. *Source* own figure	155
Fig. 6.8	Intensive technologies: the case of software troubleshooting. *Source* own figure	156
Fig. 7.1	provides a comprehensive overview on the components of virtual team leadership based on the previous considerations	172
Fig. 9.1	Interrelated global and local drivers of the digital transformation. *Source:* own figure	236
Fig. 9.2	Glocalization and digitalization in an exemplary value chain. *Source:* own figure, based on Porter (1985)	237

Fig. 9.3	The digital transformation potential of internationalization strategies. *Source:* own figure, partly developed from Bartlett and Ghoshal (1998)	239
Fig. 10.1	Lewin's mechanistic model of organizational change. *Source* Hatch with Cunliffe, 2006, p. 309	262
Fig. 10.2	Tacit knowledge management by means of employing the SECI spiral. *Source* own figure	272
Fig. 10.3	Knowledge conversion in virtual teams. *Source* own figure	274
Fig. 10.4	The Johari window for virtual team learning and knowledge enhancement. *Source* own figure, based on Luft and Ingham (1955)	279
Figure Opening Case 11	Levels of vehicle autonomy. *Source* own figure	291
Fig. 11.1	Key principles of ethics in digital collaboration. *Source* own figure	300
Fig. 11.2	Key principles of the ethics of artificial intelligence. *Source* own figure	302
Fig. 11.3	The rationale, pillars and outcomes of the RRI framework. *Source* own figure, based on Lukovics et al. (2020)	304
Fig. 11.4	RRI as a multi-stakeholder collaboration process. *Source* own figure	305
Fig. 11.5	The Collingridge dilemma, pacing effects, and consequences over time. *Source* own illustration, based on Malanowski (2017)	308
Fig. 11.6	The three main phases of the technological assessment process. *Source* own figure	310

List of Tables

Table Application 2.1	Challenges of virtual team collaboration	13
Table 2.1	Responses to the question "And in which of these ways would you prefer to work once the pandemic is over?", in percent.	21
Table 2.2	Responses to the question "Thinking of a time when the pandemic restrictions are lifted, to what extent do you agree or disagree with the following statement? I want flexibility in the amount of time I go into the office.", in percent.	22
Table 2.3	Responses to the question "Thinking of a time when the pandemic restrictions are lifted, to what extent do you agree or disagree with the following statement? Employers should be more flexible in terms of requiring employees to go to an office.", in percent.	22
Table Application 2.3	Virtual team collaboration from home: who loses and who gains, and how?	23
Table 3.1	Checklist for configuring and using Information and Communication Technologies in virtual team collaboration	66
Table 3.2	Examples for the use of Information and Communication Technologies.	67
Table 4.1	Context- and content-orientation in light of each other	91
Table 4.2	Reframing communication across context and content	92
Table 5.1	Summary of the interrelations between communication, relations, time and space	123
Table 5.2	Checklist for creating collaborative cultures across functions and disciplines	125

Table Opening Case 6	Configuration of the global operations team.	136
Table 6.1	Functional organizational design for virtual team collaboration	145
Table Opening Case 7	Leadership in light of volatility, uncertainty, complexity and ambiguity.	174
Table 7.1	Overview of situational leadership	184
Table 7.2	Overview of leadership styles and their suitability for virtual team collaboration	186
Table Closing Activity 7	A personal leadership SWOT-Analysis.	192
Table 8.1	The cultural dimensions by Geert Hofstede	203
Table 8.2	Country scores according to the Hofstede dimensions	205
Table 8.3	Cultural dimensions according to project GLOBE	210
Table 8.4	Societal cultures scores according to project GLOBE.	213
Table 9.1	Overview of key virtual team dynamics	232
Table Application 9.1	Technologies for managing diversity, dispersion and power distortions	233
Table 9.2	GLOBE leadership styles	240
Table 9.3	GLOBE leadership scores for Germany, USA, India, China and France	241
Table 10.1	The perceived virtual team membership model	268
Table 10.2	Relevant definitions of the internet of things	276
Table 11.1	Managing the challenges of autonomous driving via the RRI framework	306
Table 11.2	Tools and methods for technological assessment	311

Why a Book on Virtual Team Collaboration, and What Makes It Unique?

Virtual team collaboration is omnipresent in today's world. Chatting via social media is a low-level collaborative virtual experience, and developing a product across locations, using virtual reality, lies at the other end of the spectrum. The starting point of this development was combined technological advancements and globalization from the 1990s onwards which led to the inception of global virtual teams. The COVID-19 pandemic added new forms of work, such as local virtual team collaboration or extensive work-from-home and has spurred trends towards virtualized and individualized workplace arrangements. Today, we face a world of work that is increasingly team-based, digitalized and flexible, with wide-ranging implications for the skill set required by employees, management and organizations, for how humans are going to integrate work and life, and for how future society, business and ecology will develop.

1.1 From 'Just Practice' to 'Best Practice'

However, while most people have experienced some forms of virtual team collaboration by now—be it at school or university, at work or in their private lives—there is not yet a clear understanding of what differentiates 'just practice' from 'best practice'. Or, in other words: how can you make sure that what you (think you) know about virtual collaboration, how you use technology, and how you self-organize and collaborate in virtual team settings is *truly* state of the art and not just what the world stumbled into recently? Offering the first concise overview since the end of the COVID-19 pandemic, this book provides students, academics and practitioners with a comprehensive and practical guide for mastering today's and tomorrow's virtual team collaboration challenge, in light of the digital transformation and as a contribution to sustainable development. This guidance is relevant for and applicable to every single individual—who, like you, is or will also be a virtual team member at a certain point of their lives and in some context or another, based on the interrelated insights that virtual team collaboration has become omnipresent and that it is the whole team, not merely a single 'leader' formally in charge, who contributes to a high-performance virtual team.

1.2   Ten Essential Knowledge-Areas of Virtual Team Collaboration

Chapter 2 highlights essentials of virtual team collaboration, answering the question: what are virtual teams, and what makes them successful? In order to answer this question, this chapter differentiates between different types of virtual teams, such as global virtual teams or COVID-induced virtual teams, and outlines how and why they have developed. This increases your collaborative awareness and enables you to make more informed virtual collaboration choices. Introducing the five-factor model of virtual team collaboration, this chapter discusses key properties of virtual team collaboration in light of the digitalization of work, industries and businesses, and draws conclusions for high performance virtual team collaboration. By thus understanding how team inputs, characteristics, moderators, dynamics and outputs are interrelated and should be configured, also with regard to digital transformation requirements, you will then be able to contribute to virtual team collaboration in a more structured, and, thus: effective and efficient manner. This is likely to also increase your overall coping abilities or personal satisfaction when finding yourself in any collaborative virtual setting.

Chapter 3 presents the role of Information and Communication Technologies (ICTs) for virtual team collaboration. After having read this chapter, you will know how to choose and configure ICTs for improved virtual team collaboration. To this end, this chapter first discusses the topic of ICT richness, or: the lack thereof, and outlines the consequences of leaner, ICT-based collaboration, in relation to communicative purposes and underlying task complexity. This enables the reader to understand how technology affects key virtual team processes, such as communication, trust or creativity, and to also become aware of the limits of ICT-based collaboration. ICTs are further discussed in light of the constituents, dynamics and moderators of virtual team collaboration so that you know which ICT choice to make and how (not) to use ICTs for which purposes and under which circumstances. The chapter concludes with recommendations for how to configure ICTs for overcoming virtual team challenges and contributing to positive virtual team dynamics and outcomes.

Chapter 4 focusses on team communication as the enabler of all other team dynamics. It begins with outlining communicative properties and purposes. Models of communication, such as the sender-receiver model, or the metaphors of communication as iceberg, glasses and backpack increase your awareness of how communication simplifies—but also sometimes complicates—human interactions. Communication is further differentiated into context and content, and the ability to do so in one's own practice is an essential skill for identifying and overcoming the challenges of virtual and ICT-based communication. Crucial to this skill is the insight that ICT-based communication lacks context and that teams need context to build and maintain trust. To achieve communicative alignment, this chapter concludes with five principles of how to engage in communicative action and to acknowledge the four sides of virtual communication, so that one can better integrate communicative context and content on a team level. It also highlights the relevance of a psychologically safe team communication climate. After having engaged with this chapter, you should be more able to configure virtual communication dynamics positively, in alignment with team purposes and goals and in a way that is psychologically safe for all involved.

Chapter 5 highlights how 'culture' glues teams together beyond formal organizational structures. It also illustrates how 'good' or 'bad' team culture can have real consequences for individual and team-level performance and shows how a 'culture of collaboration' is built. The starting point is the realization that people proceed from different expectations regarding how to establish relations and trust, how to plan time and projects, how to organize space, and how to achieve work-life balance, and that it is essential to integrate these differences, in particular in cross-functional and interdisciplinary teams. To develop this ability, this chapter first focusses on culture, visualized by means of an iceberg, and explains how the 'hidden' parts of the iceberg influence visible communication and behaviour in divergent, often conflicting ways. This leads to an analysis and practical recommendations of how to build and maintain trust despite divergent relationship assumptions, of how to integrate conflicting work-life balance and workspace demands, and of how to streamline project planning and time assumptions. The chapter concludes with recommendations of how to create collaborative team cultures across hierarchies, disciplines and professions. After having engaged with this chapter, you should be able to contribute to a culture of collaboration, in particular in cross-functional and interdisciplinary virtual teams, thus maximizing the contribution of one of the key moderators of positive virtual team dynamics and outcomes, namely culture.

Chapter 6 provides further details on the organizational challenges of virtual team collaboration. It enables the reader to make informed organizational choices and to contribute to a work environment in which the team can thrive and which is the most conducive to high-performance collaboration. The starting point lies in becoming aware of the organizational dimension of work, and to also understand how the images of organization which one has in mind unconsciously shape one's expectations, actions and interpretations. Afterwards, the chapter introduces the main organizational structures available, such as matrix, functional or divisional design, and discusses which of these are more or less helpful for high-performance virtual team collaboration. As virtual team collaboration would be impossible without the contribution of technology, the chapter then highlights the properties and challenges of human–machine or human–technology interaction in socio-technical systems, such as virtual teams. It provides you with three main design options for configuring a virtual team's organizational core technologies and also discusses the question of how much bureaucracy virtual collaboration requires. After having engaged with this chapter, you should be able to make more informed organizational design choices, thus influencing one of the key moderators of successful virtual team collaboration positively and in the most conducive manner.

Chapter 7 focusses on the interrelations between digital leadership and virtual team collaboration under Industry 4.0 conditions. It provides an overview on a variety of leadership styles and discusses their advantages and disadvantages in light of each other. The chapter also highlights why and how leadership in virtual team collaboration needs to be shared and distributed for the team to excel, and provides recommendations for how each team member can strengthen their self-leadership abilities in light of the team's purposes and goals. It concludes with recommendations for leading virtual teams, collectively and individually, in particular, the need to navigate volatility, uncertainty, complexity and ambiguity, for instance, by means of situational or crisis leadership. After having engaged with this chapter, you will be aware that leadership in the age of virtual team collaboration is something entirely different—and much more—than an individual, formal and hierarchical leadership function. You will know what it takes to be a virtual team leader under Industry 4.0 conditions (and why this is difficult). Finally, you will have encountered the models and methods for contributing to the required shared and distributed digital leadership practices in virtual teams, thus leveraging the benefits of yet another moderator of high-performance collaboration.

Chapter 8 introduces the cross-cultural management perspective on virtual team collaboration. Cultural diversity is a characteristic of many virtual teams today. It can become an asset to the team because it might increase creativity and innovativeness—but only if cultural differences do not result in misalignment and mistrust. This chapter enables you to assess and, consequently, overcome and integrate differences in cultural orientations, behavioural styles, and expectations and perceptions, as relevant, for example, in global, cross-functional or interdisciplinary virtual team collaboration. The focus of this chapter lies in the tool of cultural dimensions which is the starting point—but not the end goal—of understanding and integrating cultural diversity. After having engaged with this chapter, you know key cultural dimensions, and how (not) to use them. You will also be more able to positively influence and integrate difference in cultural orientations, this being a crucial moderator of any virtual collaboration involving cultural diversity.

Chapter 9 highlights the role and requirements of global leadership and English language management in virtual team collaboration, thus building upon and adding to your combined knowledge and skills from Chaps. 3 (communication), 6 (digital leadership) and 7 (cross-cultural management). The first theme, global leadership, is specific to those teams that are characterized by global dispersion and multinational cultural diversity, so called global virtual teams. These teams *must* rely on Information and Communication Technologies (see Chap. 3), and, together, these effects place additional requirements on virtual team leaders, require specific, culturally-sensitive leadership styles, and generally make it more difficult to implement the shared and distributed leadership style required for successful virtual team collaboration. After having engaged with this topic, you will

1.2 Ten Essential Knowledge-Areas of Virtual Team Collaboration

better understand the strategic dimension of global virtual team collaboration and how to contribute to strategy by means of global leadership practices that overcome dispersion, diversity and ICT limitations. Again, this will help you to configure virtual team dynamics in more conducive ways. The English language, the second topic of the chapter, is not only the working language of global virtual teams, but also a means of collaboration for other types of teams. If mismanaged, the English language can distort competency and position power, result in language closures and hinder further team development. This chapter enables you to configure the English language as a positive virtual team dynamic.

Chapter 10 covers learning and change, knowledge creation and innovativeness in virtual team collaboration, also in relation to human–machine interface and leadership requirements. This enables you to combine and deepen your learning from Chaps. 2 and 5 (Information and Communication Technologies, and organizing the collaboration of humans and technology), 6 and 8 (digital and global leadership), and 3 and 4 (establishing communication and collaborative cultures). It first highlights the challenges of the post-COVID environment, in which systems are increasingly brittle, in which people suffer from anxieties, and in which problems are increasingly non-linear and often incomprehensible. It discusses when and how virtual teams are more innovative than non-virtual teams, and how change, learning and innovativeness can be facilitated by means of leaders' self-identities and team-performance norms which, together, increase perceived virtual team membership. Next, the chapter focusses on the technological dimension of virtual team learning. Two methods, the SECI spiral for managing tacit knowledge and the Johari window for increasing individual and team awareness are proposed. After having engaged with the chapter you are able to positively configure learning, change and innovativeness as key moderators of virtual team collaboration.

Chapter 11 concludes with a discussion of the wider requirements of virtual team collaboration, such as the need to contribute to sustainable development, the need to collaborate inclusively and ensure the equity of diverse team members, and the need to engage in responsible research and innovation. Team members and leaders need to develop a sense of ethics, work towards a more ethical and responsible organization, leadership and business system, and to also apply ethical considerations to digital technology, artificial intelligence and human-technology interactions for these wider goals to be achieved. A key element is the understanding of how to handle the Collingridge dilemma which describes how humans can never fully control technology, particularly not its unintended consequences by means of various modes of technological assessment. After having engaged with this chapter, you will have brought your virtual team collaboration skills to the next level of inclusive, responsible and sustainable development, and you will know how to contribute to these wider human and technological goals in your everyday work life.

1.3 A Pedagogical, Problem-Based Learning Focus

Uniquely, this book proceeds from a problem-based learning orientation when offering the aforementioned content. This means that knowledge, methods and skills are not discussed and present in abstract terms but developed step-by-step from real-life problems to be solved, which then makes learning more relevant and easier to achieve. To this end, each chapter involves a variety of pedagogical features to ensure that knowledge also becomes skills, i.e.: that you are able to put what you have learned into practice. Each chapter, therefore, begins with an introductory case, and after the end of each sub-section, you will be asked to apply your knowledge by means of a student activity that links theoretical knowledge and methods to the opening case. There are practical examples and helpful features throughout, such as margin definitions, visualizations and maxims. After the full content of a chapter has been presented, key points are summarized and you can check your understanding with the help of review questions. Finally, each opening case is revisited with the help of the full chapter knowledge, and a closing activity enables you to apply and further develop your understanding.

1.4 Summary: What Sets This Book on Virtual Team Collaboration Apart

The COVID-19 pandemic has thrown the world into a global 'remote work' experiment; yet, most people and organizations have not yet reflected systematically upon this experience. In closing this gap, this book is set apart by three features: First, this book enables you to advance from 'just practice', as you are experiencing it now, to 'best practice', based on the insight that virtual team collaboration has become part of our everyday work and lives. This way, you will not only have better work experiences and team contributions, but you will also find higher personal satisfaction and a better work-life balance. Second, this book offers advice not only to team leaders formally 'in charge' but to everyone contributing to virtual collaboration as a team member. This is timely, as leadership and organization are increasingly team-based and built from the shared and distributed practices of all involved. Third, the pedagogical features of this book and its problem-based learning orientation ensure relevance and practicality.

Outlining the contours of ten essential knowledge areas of virtual team collaboration, this book closes a crucial skills and knowledge gap in learning-oriented ways. It enables you—and everyone—to contribute to and further develop the best-practice virtual team collaboration required for today's and tomorrow's society, business and ecology. The content of this book stems from the author's own virtual collaboration experiences since 2004, and her constant research and practical engagement with virtual team collaboration since then, for instance, when facilitating organizational learning and change in distributed technological research and development units, or when leading a research project on COVID-induced virtual teams.

Virtual Team Collaboration and the Digital Transformation: Effects of the COVID-19 Pandemic, and a Five-Factor Model

2.1 Introduction

Virtual and remote work has been on the rise since the COVID-19 pandemic, and being able to collaborate in virtual teams has become an essential workplace skill. This chapter enables you to understand what makes a virtual team successful and thus to contribute to high-performance virtual teams of various kinds by means of a structured overview. To this end, this chapter delineates different types of virtual teams, such as global virtual teams or COVID-induced virtual teams, and outlines how and why these have developed. This way, you can better understand what benefits virtual team collaboration might have for you professionally and personally, for instance, with regard to the work-life balance or work-life integration which you wish to achieve. This chapter then proposes a three-dimensional model for assessing collaborative requirements. Next, it views virtual team collaboration in light of the digital transformation and highlights the five constitutive factors to be configured and managed for high-performance virtual team collaboration. After having read this chapter, you will possess a general understanding of how to assess and, consequently, manage virtual team collaboration of various kinds and for various purposes. You will not yet know the details of each factor and how to configure it. Subsequent chapters will develop this knowledge and related skills in relevant areas, such as Information and Communications Technologies, communication, team culture, relationship management, project time planning, workspace organization, digital and global leadership, cross-cultural and English language management, learning, change, knowledge creation and innovation, sustainability and diversity, and digital ethics, artificial intelligence and responsible research and innovation. This chapter lays the foundational structure for all these subsequent chapters and themes. After having read the whole book, you will have acquired the full knowledge for mastering today's and tomorrow's virtual team collaboration.

> **Background Information: Why Virtual Team Collaboration?**
>
> Virtual teams, variously defined as geographically dispersed, electronically dependent, dynamic, or comprised of diverse members working remotely (Gibson & Cohen, 2003; Griffith et al., 2003; Kirkman & Mathieu, 2005; Martins et al., 2004), are growing in number and importance. Potentially, such teams make it easier to acquire and apply knowledge to critical tasks in global firms (e.g., Madhavan & Grover, 1998; Sole & Edmondson, 2002). Geographic dispersion and electronic dependence can provide access to relevant expertise even when it is scattered around the globe (Kirkman et al., 2002) and can enable a better understanding of global clients, operations, and suppliers (Boutellier et al., 1998; Gluesing & Gibson, 2004). A dynamic structure and diverse participants can facilitate creative and flexible responses to challenging development needs through access to diverse expertise and perspectives on an as-needed basis (Brown & Eisenhardt, 1995; Sole & Edmondson, 2002). Such capabilities are central to innovation, to the collective process of making sense of new and diverse information, and to incorporating new knowledge into novel methodologies, products, and services (Dougherty, 2001; Nohria & Berkley, 1994; Nonaka & Takeuchi, 1995).

2.1.1 Learning Objectives

After having read this chapter, you should

- Understand what virtual team collaboration is characterized by and what makes it special.
- Know how virtual team collaboration has developed and how it is likely to evolve in the future.
- Be able to differentiate between different types of virtual teams, such as global virtual teams, COVID-induced virtual teams or work-from-home virtual teams.
- Be familiar with the phases, drivers and key aspects of the digital transformation.
- Be able to assess virtual team collaboration in light of the digital transformation.
- Be able to differentiate virtual teams with regard to their teamness, virtualness and remoteness.
- Have a first understanding of team performance, and how it is achieved.
- Know the five factors to be configured for high-performance virtual team collaboration, namely inputs, processes and dynamics, outputs, moderators and characteristics.

2.1.2 Opening Case

> **Example**
>
> Imagine that you are employed as a project manager at a German medium-sized company. During the COVID-19 pandemic, you, like virtually all white-collar workers in the company, have been mostly confined to working from home, a measure for distancing socially in order to stop the virus from spreading.
>
> In the beginning, COVID-induced work-from-home had felt like work had been turned upside down and everyone, you included, had to make wide-ranging adjustments: the company was unprepared, employees were inexperienced with virtual technologies and how to use them, and everyone had to make do with the equipment and home-working spaces at their disposal. However, slowly, there were also unexpected learnings and rewards: sometimes, it was easier to integrate work and life demands, there were no more traffic jams when commuting to work, and, at certain points, your performance just surged because no one disturbed you. Yet, there were also times when it was truly depressing to work alone and without meaningful social interaction and when home demands and general circumstances depleted your work energy, and you noticed the same amongst your co-workers. Throughout, it also seemed to be more difficult to communicate and align a team: it was never easy to understand who had done the job, and, if so: how the job has been done, and to identify team obstacles and achievements.
>
> Now, with everyone being back in the office, your manager asks you: "Many employees would like to continue to work from home at least partly, but I am not sure whether virtual team collaboration will be as productive as on-site work. You, too, have experienced COVID-induced work-from-home with your team. What is your opinion on that: shall we shift to flexible and virtual team collaboration in the future, and, if so: how can we make sure that teams perform?"
>
> What do you answer, and what are your reasons for giving this answer? ◄

2.2 Key Concepts: Virtual Team Collaboration

2.2.1 What is a Team?

A **team** is a small number of individuals who share a common goal or purpose and who collaborate to use their complementing skills to achieve it. Previously labelled 'small groups' or 'small work groups', teams are a product and indicator of a corporate change towards less hierarchical and more self-empowered and collaborative work places that began in the 1980s. They are thus a rather 'young' managerial construct (Levine & Moreland, 1990). In general language usage, the word 'team' is older than its business application. It originates from verbs for 'towing' (e.g. draft animals yoked together). Its modern sense usage of 'people acting jointly' seems to have emerged in the sixteenth century (Etymology online, n.d.), and the idea of 'towing' is part of its root, presumably since the nineteenth century (ibid.). Additionally, the word 'team' has been applied to sports, with terms such as 'team spirit' and 'team player',

▶ A **team** is a (small) group of people that collaborate for achieving a common goal and purpose.

The idea behind employing teams is that individuals will perform better if they can complement each other's skills, learn from each other and collaborate. Teams are thus often employed in areas of work which are knowledge-based, but they can also be found in skills-based, manual and blue-collar work. Consequently, task allocation requirements will vary: whereas tasks tend to be unique and unstructured in knowledge-based/white-collar work, they are often repetitive and structured in skills-based/manual/blue-collar work. Out of this then follows the need to employ different managerial styles: whereas a production team is led by means of clear rules, schedules and procedures and a directive leadership style, the work of a research and development team is characterized by a collaborative, team-based leadership style and a mere minimum of formal requirements and guidelines.

Three team processes are assumed to be essential to a well-functioning team across all types of teams. These are cohesion, communication and conflict management.

- **Cohesion** as defined by Shaw (1976) indicates the degree to which members of a team are motivated to remain on the team. Highly cohesive teams tend to have less absenteeism, high involvement in team activities and high levels of coordination during team tasks (Morgan & Lassiter, 1992). Cohesion has also been identified as a critical motivational factor that influences team performance (Weaver et al., 1997).
- **Communication:** Dyer (1987) suggests that factors such as increased listening, openness to suggestions, and prompt, relevant feedback are communication-based indicators of effective team functioning. Easy communication is critical for goal accomplishment and completion of regular, daily team activities (Zander, 1994).
- **Conflict management:** A conflict exists when two or more members of a group, or two or more groups, disagree. A conflict becomes harmful if tensions impede members from collaborating, thinking clearly or making sound decisions (Zander, 1994). However, not all conflicts are harmful. Conflict may be useful if it awakens members to alternative points of view and stimulates creativity in problem solving and decision making (Dyer, 1987; Zander, 1994). Thus, the consequences of the conflict depend on how the team identifies, manages, controls and resolves the problem.

▶ Successful team collaboration requires sufficient cohesion, appropriate communication and conducive conflict management.

2.2.2 What Sets Virtual Teams Apart? The Role of Information and Communication Technologies

A team is *virtual*, if it uses some degree of **Information and Communication Technologies (ICTs)** to collaborate and achieve its goals. Virtual team collaboration was made possible by technological advances in the 1990s, such as the invention of the personal computer, the emergence of the world wide web, or the development of mobile phone technologies and infrastructures (Kirkman et al., 2002). What sets such teams apart is their reliance on ICTs for communication and collaboration.

Due to it being ICT-based, virtual communication is more than 'speaking' or 'writing to each other': it also encompasses the exchange of data, information and knowledge. What sets virtual communication, as defined above, apart, is that it is generally leaner (less 'rich') than non-virtual communication. Richness firstly refers to the **number of communicative modes,** such as voice, text, audio, and so on, which are facilitated by an ICT. For example, facial expressions (non-verbal communication) help understand how spoken messages (verbal communication) are 'meant'. Consequently, a video meeting is richer than a phone conversation. Still, a phone conversation is richer than an e-mail which cannot transmit tone of voice (para-verbal communication). All ICTs mentioned are less rich than face-to-face meetings. **Synchronicity** is the second differentiating element of ICT richness. For example, phone conversations or video meetings flow back and forth between speakers and actors: they are synchronous. Conversely, updating documents on a shared server across time zones is an asynchronous way of collaborating. Different levels of media richness and synchronicity are required for a successful virtual team collaboration depending on **task type and interdependence** and the purpose of the interaction. For example, it is impossible to come to a strategic agreement on the next product innovation via back and forth e-mailing across the globe: The medium is simply too asynchronous and not rich enough for such a knowledge-intensive, highly interdependent task that often involves divergent tacit knowledges.

▶ **Virtual teams** are teams that use Information and Communication Technologies (ICTs) to collaborate and to achieve their goals. ICT-based communication is leaner (less rich) than non-virtual communication.

Link to Practice: The Meta Quest Pro Headset

Reality Labs, a division of Meta (formerly Facebook), has been exploring how their AR and VR technology, for example the Meta Quest Pro headset, can contribute to high information virtual collaborations, to make virtual office spaces more reflective of real life and to decrease the emotional disconnect that can arise from a lack of in person meetings within the corporate world (Meta, 2022). Meta's vice president of People Experience Brynn Harrington stated on the topic that: "Companies need to think about the immersive experiences that will support distributed teams and build culture and connection in a virtual environment" (Yalalov, 2023). The target concept behind the name 'Meta' is the 'Metaverse', a concept which describes a digital space created by the interaction of virtual, extended and physical realities. ◀

2.2.3 Virtual Teams as a Global Opportunity: The Relevance of Diversity and Dispersion

The history of virtual team collaboration started with the inception of so-called **global virtual teams** to make use of the combined opportunities arising from technological advancements and globalization effects (for details, see Chap. 9). These are virtual teams that are distributed on a global scale and enable companies to take advantage of the global business environment. Global virtual teams are *always* characterized by two distinct factors (Maznevski, 2012), namely:

- Diversity: the culture effect
- Dispersion: the distance effect

Diversity (*Who* is the team?) refers to the insight that most global virtual teams work in different cultural environments. Cultures are characterized by certain specifics in relation to each other. For example, in Germany a facts-oriented and assertive communication style tends to prevail, whereas, in France, communication tends to be more emotional (House et al., 2004). Cross-cultural management approaches to virtual team collaboration take this difference in business cultures into account (Chap. 8).

Dispersion (*Where* is the team?) refers to the phenomenon that team members are geographically removed from each other and often work in different time zones. Dispersion also enables the team to take opportunities of access to local customers, suppliers or partners, without individuals having to physically move and travel.

Figure 2.1 visualizes both dynamics.

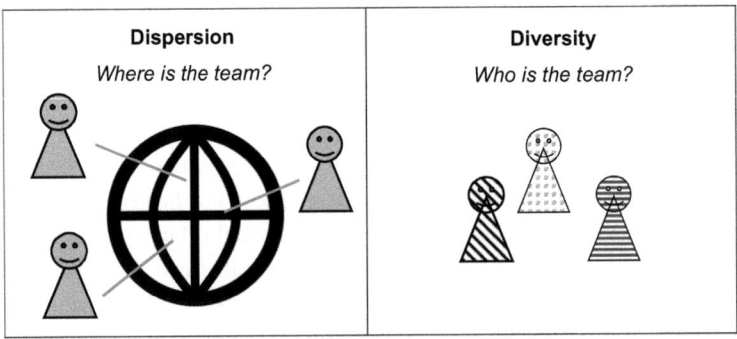

Fig. 2.1 Diversity and dispersion: the two distinguishing qualities of global virtual teams. *Source* Own figure

2.2 Key Concepts: Virtual Team Collaboration

Diversity Variations in individual team members' cultural characteristics, to be assessed and utilized.

Dispersion Team members' widespread geographical locations, to be assessed and utilized.

Dispersion ('where is the team?') and diversity ('who is the team?') can also be found in non-global virtual teams. For example, team members might be culturally diverse with regard to their family relations or countries of origin, though they all live in the same location, and due to individualized flexible work arrangements, even a local virtual team displays certain degrees of dispersion. These conditions can be both beneficial and harmful to teams—depending on how they are configured and moderated. How to utilize team diversity and dispersion in such ways that they are beneficial, and not harmful, to virtual team collaboration, is therefore a key leadership challenge in virtual team collaboration.

▶ Global virtual teams are characterized by physical dispersion and cultural diversity. These two factors also shape non-global virtual team collaboration to varying degrees.

> **Application 2.1: Challenges of Virtual Team Collaboration**
>
> Which challenges of virtual team collaboration have you personally experienced or know about from the stories of others? How should this challenge be remedied, and what are the requirements for this remedy to be doable? Structure your ideas by means of a table, such as the one below. Keep your insights for the further reading of this chapter Table Application 2.1. ◀

Table Application 2.1 Challenges of virtual team collaboration

Challenge	Remedy	Requirements
Feeling disconnected from the team	Regular virtual meetings	Suitable technological infrastructure, team members' willingness to participate, leader's support
Work overload when working from home	Consciously setting a start and end point to the working day	Satisfactory/good self-organization skills and support from the organization/team leader
…	…	…

Source own table

2.3 Virtual Team Collaboration as Configuring Key Transformative Dynamics

A virtual team is a definite, smaller group of people that transforms inputs into outputs by means of certain processes. These processes are enabled via communication, which, in the case of virtual teams, requires the usage of Information and Communication Technologies (ICTs). Moderators are those factors which influence team processes in the best possible way, in order to achieve the desired output (also see Maznevski, 2012). These interrelations are briefly introduced in this section as virtual team fundamentals.

2.3.1 Key Virtual Team Inputs

The conditions and resources from which the team starts its collaborative processes are referred to as **team inputs**. These inputs may emerge from team levels or—as is more often the case—from supra-team levels, such as the organization or its environment. Organizational level inputs are, for example, the number of team members, team members' qualifications, which sites and locations are involved in collaboration, the nature of the task, deadlines and goals, the technological infrastructure provided to the team, and many more factors (see Dulebohn & Hoch, 2017). A team must cope with these factors and make the best out of them, but can hardly influence them. Team dynamics, such as communication, are often a result of these input factors. For instance, some tasks require a high degree of interdependence, and therefore more and simultaneous communication, whereas other tasks can be executed by single members, without significantly affecting other members' workflows (Maznevski, 2012). This then further influences the kind of knowledge that has to be transferred within the team.

Another decisive influence on the processes and dynamics within a team is the corporate culture of the organization. It includes organizational structures and beliefs, such as hierarchies and innovative thinking. Flexibility and encouragement of innovative thinking, for example, are organizational-level input factors which are more conducive to virtual team collaboration than other types of cultures, for instance, those focussed on reliable schedules and plans (also see Chap. 6). Flat hierarchies and more flexible structures, such as matrix or network designs, have a more positive effect on teamwork than conventional, static, structures by means of which people are grouped into functions (Maloney & Zellmer-Bruhn, 2006). Further details on how organizational design contributes to well-functioning team dynamics can be found in (Chap. 6).

2.3.2 Key Virtual Team Dynamics

Successful team collaboration requires that a defined, smaller group of people engage in a common task or purpose. As a rule, this requires that team members subsume their own, personal and task-related interests, under the overall team goals and act accordingly. Team inputs are transformed into team outputs more or less successfully via these processes, such as performance or learning. Communication, which in the case of virtual teams requires ICTs, is the meta-level enabler of all team processes: virtual teams could not collaborate without ICT-based communication. This is why Chaps. 3 and 4 of this book focus on how to configure and manage ICTs (Chap. 4) and communicative team processes (Chap. 5).

Some of the processes that characterize virtual team collaboration, such as e-mail exchange, are fairly stable. However, some of them are not easily structured or foreseen. These more volatile team processes are also referred to as **team dynamics** (Maznevski, 2012).

Team dynamics can be categorized by means of their direction (**convergent or divergent**) and their effect on the team (**positive or negative**). For example, cultural diversity may increase creativity (positively divergent) or diminish trust (negatively divergent). Lack of cultural diversity may increase coherence (positively convergent), yet might also result in 'groupthink', diminishing creativity (negatively coherent). Figure 2.2 provides an overview.

Virtual collaboration usually promotes divergence and complicates convergence (Stahl & Maznevski, 2021). This is evident in both global virtual teams and (local) work-from-home virtual teams, these being the most prominent types of virtual team collaboration.

2.3.3 Key Virtual Team Outputs: Perspectives on Performance and Learning

Performance is one—but not the only—desired output of virtual team collaboration. It describes the immediate outcomes of work efforts, and how they have been reached, and is usually measured by means of key performance indicators. The two classic indicators

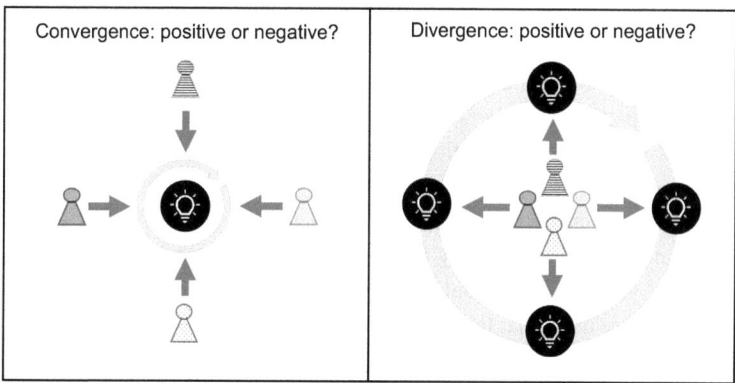

Fig. 2.2 Convergent and divergent virtual team collaboration processes. *Source* own figure

for performance in the narrow, production- or cost-oriented sense, are efficiency and effectiveness.

- **Efficiency** is the input-related dimension of performance: it is the measure for assessing how well an organization uses resources, such as capital, labour, material, technology or people, for creating added value. Or in other words: Efficiency is the ability to make the most out of a defined amount of input factors with the least amount of wasted time, money, effort, skills, competencies and other resources.
- **Effectiveness** is the output-related dimension of performance: it is the measure for assessing the degree to which 'something'—a managerial decision, an investment into a certain technology, the employment of certain people, resources or processes, et cetera—is successful in reaching a goal or end state. Or, in other words: effectiveness is the ability to steer potential performance factors, such as time, money, effort, skills, competencies and other resources, in such a way that the least amount of these factors produces the desired results in the best possible ways.

Effectiveness and efficiency are the relevant measuring rods for companies aiming at digitization. For example, even though the initial costs for digitizing analogue information seem too high at present: if measured against the long-term increase in digital efficiency and effectiveness, they suggest a clear return-on-investment. Or, in other words: if the focus is on cost reduction, then performance in the narrow sense is the right measuring instrument.

▶ From a cost- or production-perspective, performance requires efficiency and effectiveness.

Performance can also be understood as a result of people's abilities, motivation and opportunities. For example, it is a requirement of virtual team collaboration that members are able to use the required ICTs. However, this might not yet mean that they are also motivated to do so. Or, it could be that some members are able to achieve higher technological excellence but are not given the opportunity to do so. 'Performance' is not only outcome but also process-related from this perspective. For instance: how can one further develop team members and how can one facilitate learning so that higher combined levels of ability-motivation- opportunities are reached? Also, looking at team members' abilities and motivations in relation to the opportunities to be provided acknowledges non-technical performance factors such as why people identify with a team and what makes them feel they belong. This then requires a more individualized and differentiated view on individual team members so that they feel valued and recognized for who they are and what they contribute.

▶ From a people's-related perspective, performance emerges from the best possible combination of ability, motivation and opportunity.

> **Pause and Reflect: Are Remote Workers More Productive?**
>
> A 2015 Stanford study headed by Nicholas Bloom found that the productivity of call centre employees at a Chinese travel agency increased by 13% for remote workers. Subsequent analysis of data collected during March 2021 found that 40% of the 30,000 U.S. workers surveyed reported a higher productivity during the pandemic at home, than in the office. The combined research of Stanford, the Mexico Autonomous Institute of Technology and the University of Chicago Booth School of Business concluded that remote work arrangements will increase the overall productivity of U.S. workers by 5% (Stropoli, 2021). At the same time, Elon Musk of Tesla referred to the company's remote workers by saying that they can 'pretend to work somewhere else' (Kaplan, 2022), thus strongly suggesting that those who are not at the offices are not productive. Felix et al. (2023) refer to this quote in their study on remote workers in Brazil. They find that remote work does indeed reduce the productivity of some employees. However, they also identify employees who *could* be equally or more productive from home. Yet, because this group needs to constantly prove their productivity to the organization, they then also become less productive, as 'showing productivity' takes up too much work time and energy. ◀

> **Application 2.2: Virtual Team Performance**
>
> Think back to virtual team collaboration which you yourself have experienced or are currently involved in. Alternatively, or additionally, talk to people and let them describe a virtual collaboration experience of theirs. Find out:
>
> - How do people use ICTs? Which ICTs are used?
> - Do their abilities, e.g. their abilities to use ICTs, meet requirements and, if not: which measures are taken to either advance their skills or to provide them with more fulfilling tasks?
> - How is their motivation affected by working virtually?
> - To what extent do they feel cost and time pressures to work effectively and efficiently? Do they feel exploited by virtual work and, if so: why, and what should be done for a better work experience, and by whom?
> - Is their motivation considered and are they given enough opportunities to be 'seen' and show that they perform, and to also 'feel valued' through their contribution? If not: how does this affect motivation and performance?
>
> Come up with conclusions of which scenarios constitute better or worse practice. Support your assessment with 'data', that is: descriptions from own experiences or statements of your interviewees. ◀

2.4 The COVID-19 Effect on Virtual Team Collaboration and Flexible Work Arrangements

The previously mainly global orientation of virtual team collaboration changed with the onset of the COVID-19 pandemic. Since then, more people than ever before have engaged in remote and virtual collaboration, both globally and locally, and flexibilization of work has increased (Ipsos, 2021). This section briefly summarizes these developments and their implications.

2.4.1 The Need for Social Distancing and the Emergence of a New Type of Virtual Team

The COVID-19 pandemic, caused by a novel type of Coronavirus, spread across the globe from late 2019 onwards, with millions of people falling ill or even dying, and national and global infrastructures being (at risk of being) severely impacted. Social distancing, in order to reduce the spread of infections, wherever possible, soon became an almost worldwide governmental and corporate countermeasure., Remote work and education, wherever possible, emerged as the global premise of the time in the process (Wiles, 2020): schools and childcare facilities were fully or partially closed, and many activities and jobs were reorganized as telework or remote work. A new type of virtual teams came into being, namely **COVID-induced virtual teams** (overview in Mahadevan et al., 2024).

Unlike global virtual teams, COVID-induced virtual teams were not formed out of strategic considerations. Rather, they emerged by 'accident', as a result of an external crisis requirement put on companies and people, namely the need to distance socially. Often, this involved pre-existing teams which were forced to 'go virtual'. Team members were not necessarily trained, skilled or knowledgeable in virtual collaboration, and might have even lacked the required infrastructure and technological equipment. In contrast to previous types of virtual team collaboration, COVID-induced virtual teamwork often took place on local levels and from home, and under very specific circumstances: social life had come to a halt in most societies, and, often schools and childcare facilities were closed. Thus, the boundaries between home and work became more blurred for most, and care work requirements intersected with work requirements much more than used to be the case before.

The first vaccines, becoming available from 2021 onwards, drastically reduced the risk of severe causes of the decease, and potentially also its long-term effects. However, as it turned out, they did not guarantee immunity or not becoming infected. At the same time, the subsequent mutations of the Coronavirus turned out to be more infectious but potentially less threatening. Thus, even when the pandemic became 'endemic' in most parts of the world at about the beginning of 2023, aspects such as considering employees' health and safety, securing the availability of products and services and protecting critical corporate, national and global infrastructure, still remained a topic of relevance. For example, even if their employees did not become critically ill anymore, companies still needed to fear that due to the shear amount of infections and people not being able to come to work, they might not be able to sustain production or other parts of their value chain.

▶ **COVID-induced virtual teams** are teams which were forced to 'go virtual' due to external reasons (the COVID-19 pandemic), without this being part of corporate strategy, under the wider conditions of shutdown and social distancing.

The COVID-19 pandemic also had wider economic consequences: it disrupted, for example, global flows of goods between China and other parts of the world. Global production and value chains were disrupted even further with the Russian invasion of Ukraine at the beginning of 2022, which caused, for example, an almost global rise in the price of gas and oil. Thus, in many countries, it became more expensive to commute to work or to work on-site. Furthermore, healthcare and education systems were still under pressure, and there was a higher likelihood of employees with **care work** responsibilities not being able to come to work. It was also more likely that employees had to stay home because family members or they themselves had contracted the virus (again). As a result, a new type of virtual team, namely (non-global) **work-from-home (WFH) virtual teams**, have been added to the virtual team catalogue by the COVID-19 pandemic (see Mahadevan & Steinmann, 2023).

2.4.2 A Trend Towards Flexible Work Arrangements

The crises experiences of the COVID-19 pandemic and its aftermath made it more and more apparent that **home-sourcing**, **telework** and other types of **flexible work arrangements**, such as work-from-home, **work-from-anywhere** or mobile work, might be profitable for individuals and organizations. The 'workplace' as a fixed locality from which to work by means of fixed equipment has decreased in relevance, at least for knowledge-based, white-collar work, and work-from-home (WFH), in particular, is more widely demanded and employed (Ipsos, 2021). Employees' wishes for a better **work-life integration** are also behind these developments. At the same time, the ways in which individuals seek to combine work and life have become more individualized and diverse, implying that companies need to individualize and diversify the employment options and conditions which they offer to individuals.

Flexible Work Arrangements	Work arrangements or schedules that differ from the traditional working day and week.
Work-From-Anywhere	A type of flexible work arrangement that allows the employee to choose their workplaces.

Work-From-Home	A type of flexible work arrangement that allows the employee to work from a defined home working space.
Care Work	(Unpaid) work in the service of others (family members), such as elderly or children.
Work-Life Integration	(Being given the opportunity of) combining work and life demands in such ways that both may be met (in such ways that fulfilment is achieved).
Home-Sourcing	A business model in which employers hire employees to work from their homes.
Telework	A work model in which the employee works from a non-office site location, such as their homes and communicates with others via information and communication technologies, but is not necessarily geographically remote to their office site (and may come to the office, if required).

2.4.3 Global Patterns and Differences in Work-from-home Preferences

Even though work-from-home seems to be a general trend, it is not as easy as suggesting that everyone everywhere wishes to work from home more after the end of the pandemic. The following survey-based study which was conducted by Ipsos (2021), a multinational market research and consulting firm with headquarters in Paris, provides further insights on who wants to work from home, and where. 12,445 employed adults around the globe were asked about their opinion on work from home. The study found the following patterns and differences between countries.

- Worldwide, 35% of the interviewees prefer to work completely from home or work from home more than they used to. The USA, GB and India exceed this global average with high values (46 and 45%). Germany and France are close to the worldwide average with 35 and 37%, whereas only 27% of the employees in China fit into this category. This is in line with a study by McKinsey (2020) which found that the shift to remote work is often easier in developed countries because of a better infrastructure.
- About a fifth of interviewees in GB, France and Germany answered that remote work is not applicable to the nature of their jobs which they considered to be location-bound (Table 2.1). This value is much lower in the USA (12%), India (3%) and China (9%). These findings (Table 2.1) partly contradict the aforementioned study by McKinsey (2020), pointing to country-level differences in the degree to which jobs are digitalized.
- Concerning the amount of time spent in the office, interviewees in India and China, in particular, wish for more flexibility, with 74 and 70% agreeing at least somewhat

to the statement "I want flexibility in the amount of time I go into the office". Flexibility is the least important in Germany with 48% (Table 2.2). This suggests that culture-specific values, such as 'flexibility' are more or less relevant in different societies, which then also 'run' in more or less flexible ways. For instance, the degree of flexibility offered by schools and day-care facilities, which then changes the ways in which employees align work and care work demands.

- There is also a notable difference in the degree to which employees expect employers to be flexible when it comes to requiring employees to go to an office. Again, India and China exceed the global average the most with 82 and 74% (Table 2.3). Again, this points to a difference in cultural preferences and country-level infrastructures.

Tables 2.1, 2.2 and 2.3 visualize the whole of the study's findings.

> **Application 2.3: Work-life Integration and Virtual Team Collaboration**
>
> Work and life place different demands on individuals, and individuals need to be able to integrate work and life in order to be able to perform at work. Under which conditions will virtual work-from-home be of benefit to a person, what might be the opportunities and dangers of work-from-home (and for whom), and what are the conflicts between different interest groups arising from virtual team collaboration? Imagine that working hours are flexible and subject to negotiation. These are the fictitious individuals that you need to consider:

Table 2.1 Responses to the question "And in which of these ways would you prefer to work once the pandemic is over?", in percent

Response	Global Country Average	USA	France	Great Britain	Germany	India	China
Prefer to work completely from home / work from home more than I used to	35	46	37	46	35	45	27
Prefer to work from home about as much as I used to do	11	9	7	6	10	13	19
Prefer to work completely away from home / work from home less than I used to	33	28	29	22	25	37	42
Other / Don't know	6	6	5	5	10	2	3
Not applicable (the nature of my job means I don't have a choice where I have to work)	15	12	22	21	21	3	9

Remark: Deviations from the Global Country Average with over one percentage point were highlighted in dark grey for scores above average and light grey for scores below average
Source Own table, based on data from Ipsos (2021)

Table 2.2 Responses to the question "Thinking of a time when the pandemic restrictions are lifted, to what extent do you agree or disagree with the following statement? I want flexibility in the amount of time I go into the office.", in percent

Response	Global Country Average	USA	France	Great Britain	Germany	India	China
Strongly agree	28	25	20	31	19	34	23
Somewhat agree	37	35	36	26	29	40	57
Total "agree"	65	60	56	57	48	74	70
Neither	25	28	30	30	38	17	17
Somewhat disagree	6	6	10	7	9	6	3
Strongly disagree	4	5	5	6	5	3	1
Total "disagree"	10	11	15	13	14	9	4

Remark: Deviations from the Global Country Average with over one percentage point were highlighted in dark grey for scores above average and light grey for scores below average
Source Own table, based on data from Ipsos (2021)

Table 2.3 Responses to the question "Thinking of a time when the pandemic restrictions are lifted, to what extent do you agree or disagree with the following statement? Employers should be more flexible in terms of requiring employees to go to an office.", in percent

Response	Global Country Average	USA	France	Great Britain	Germany	India	China
Strongly agree	28	27	26	37	23	34	18
Somewhat agree	38	33	35	32	30	48	56
Total "agree"	66	60	61	69	53	82	74
Neither	25	29	29	24	38	11	22
Somewhat disagree	6	6	7	6	6	5	4
Strongly disagree	4	5	4	2	3	3	0
Total "disagree"	10	11	11	8	14	8	4

Remark: Deviations from the Global Country Average with over one percentage point were highlighted in dark grey for scores above average and light grey for scores below average
Source Own table, based on data from Ipsos (2021)

- a team member with a long commute to work
- a team member who lives near to the offices
- a team member employed part-time who cannot spend more hours at the offices because of their children's school and social schedule

Table Application 2.3 Virtual team collaboration from home: who loses and who gains, and how?

Team member	WFH opportunity	WFH risk	Conflict of interest
New team member	Not that clear	Does not get to know team members and corporate culture	1) With team members whose work-life integration would profit from WFH 2) …
Team members with underage children	Flexibilization of working hours, taking care work breaks in between	Over-exhaustion because of intensified work-home demands	1) With team leader's need for monitoring working hours and performance 2) with team members who require a clear separation of working hours (e.g. daytime) and leisure time (e.g. evening)
…	…	…	…

Source own table

- a team member who lives alone and has no care work obligations
- a team member who takes care of elderly family members
- a team member with a spouse who also works full-time, and has underage children
- a single parent with underage children
- the team leader
- a team member with underage children whose spouse takes care of all home demands
- a team member in a double-income partnership, with no children
- a new team member (no care work obligations) who has just started on the job
- a team member who does not have a home working space at home
- a team member whose internet connectivity from home is insufficient

Structure your insights by means of a table, such as the one below (Table Application 2.3). ◄

2.5 Virtual Teams Today and Tomorrow: Types and Characteristics

Contemporary virtual teams are more complex in their configuration in comparison to the original idea of 'virtual teams', mainly to be employed on global levels. For example, it might well be that members are still located in the same region, but are on different work-from-home schedules, because of different caring commitments. Or, it might be that one or more team members have a 'work-from-anywhere' contract, allowing them to choose and change their location of work whereas others work from office workplaces. Teams might consist of some remote and some non-remote team members simultaneously, and team members even at one location might be culturally diverse with regard to their family history, mobile life decision or countries of origin. Boundaries across these conditions are also shifting and permeable, as many teams alternate between virtual and non-virtual modes of collaboration on a regular basis. Thus, any team that uses ICTs to *some* degree in order to collaborate in certain phases or for certain purposes, is also characterized by 'virtual team collaboration'.

▶
- Virtual teams are not fundamentally different from non-virtual teams.
- Most teams are virtual to some extent.
- Most teams alternate between virtual, non-virtual and hybrid phases.
- Virtual collaboration applies to all teams with some degree of 'virtualness' in any phase.
- When coupled with flexible work arrangements, e.g. work-from-home, virtualness increases individual autonomy, team diversity and variations in work-life configuration.

2.5.1 Teamness, Virtualness and Remoteness: Three Characteristics of Virtual Teams Today

Virtual team collaboration today combines on-site and work-from-home, local and global, and mobile and permanent workplaces, and asks those involved to manage these complexities. Diversity and dispersion no longer adequately describe virtual team collaboration today due to increased complexity. To enable a more systematic approach to contemporary virtual team collaboration, as a phenomenon that may occur *in any contemporary team*, the three dimensions **teamness, remoteness** and **virtualness** (developed by the author from the global virtual team delineations by Martins & Schilpzand, 2011) are helpful. Figure 2.3 provides an overview.

The degrees to which these three characteristics—teamness, remoteness and virtualness—are evident in a certain setting, determine the specifics of virtual team collaboration:

- A certain degree of **teamness**, that is: shared operational processes and goals, is a prerequisite for a certain group of people becoming and being a 'team'.
- A certain degree of **remoteness**, that is: remoteness and being removed from work and each other, is a prerequisite for a team having to rely on Information and Communication Technologies (ICTs) to achieve teamness. Remoteness also determines the specifics of teamness and virtualness. For example, global virtual teams need to consider differences in culture, national environments, languages and time zones

2.5 Virtual Teams Today and Tomorrow: Types and Characteristics

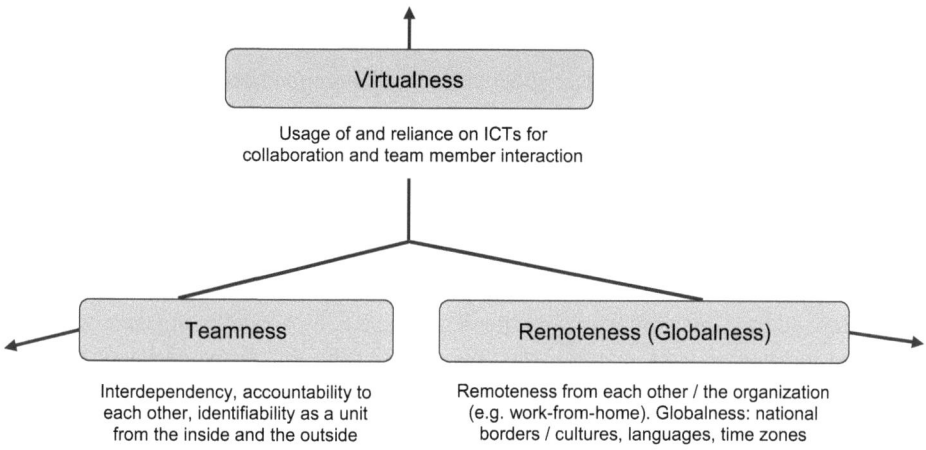

Fig. 2.3 Teamness, remoteness and virtualness. *Source* own figure

whereas local virtual teams are not influenced by these factors. **Globalness** is thus a specific sub-component of remoteness that is specific to virtual teams operating across multiple countries and time zones (global virtual teams).
- A certain degree of **virtualness**, that is: reliance and usage of ICTs for communication and collaboration, is a prerequisite for a team becoming and being 'virtual'.

Virtual team tasks and task types are closely intertwined with team characteristics in the following ways:

- The **degree of task interdependence** directly determines the degree of teamness: the more interdependent the tasks are, the more teamness is required for success.
- The **type of task**—routine or exceptional/innovative, skills-based or knowledge-based—determines the type of teamness which is required. For example, more routine tasks can be allocated and executed by means of pre-prepared manuals and specifications whereas exceptional and innovative tasks required frequent team exchange, lessons learned and a more active way of collaboration.
- The type of knowledge required for executing the task—**explicit or tacit**—determines whether and how easily knowledge may be shared across individuals. Explicit knowledge refers to knowledge that can be put into words ('explain how') whereas tacit knowledge is embedded in action and needs to be 'shown' ('do how'). Consequently, it is easier to transfer explicit knowledge virtually than tacit knowledge.

▶ Teamness, virtualness and remoteness are key characteristics of virtual teams.

> **Application 2.4: Key Characteristics of Virtual Team Collaboration**
>
> Talk to people and let them describe a virtual collaboration experience of theirs. Find out:
>
> - What are their specific workplace arrangements? Where do they work and who makes that decision?
> - What are their working hours? Which freedom do they have over working hours and how much control over working hours is exercised?
> - How do they integrate work and life demands, e.g. by how they organize work and the location or work and how they plan time? Who makes the decision, and how much freedom or control is exercised?
> - How do they describe the workplace and time planning arrangements for the wider team, group or organization of which they are a part? Are these arrangements unified or diverse? How are they aligned and integrated?
> - How do they assess their experiences with regard to the team's cohesion, communication and conflict processes?
>
> Come up with conclusions of which scenarios constitute better or worse practice. Support your assessment with 'data', that is: descriptions by your interviewees. ◀

2.6 Virtual Team Collaboration and the Digital Transformation

Virtual team collaboration has developed and is still evolving against the background of the so-called **digital transformation** which is defined as:

> "*a change in how a firm employs digital technologies, to develop a new digital business model that helps to create and appropriate more value for the firm*" (Verhoef et al., 2021, p. 889; referring to Kane et al., 2015; Liu et al., 2011; and Schallmo et al., 2017).

This term is related to a general turn from physical economic (and other) transactions to virtual interactions supported by technology which has fundamentally altered people's behaviour and experiences at work and beyond. In an overview on how businesses have been transformed by technology, Venkatraman (2017, p. 1) states that "(t)echnology has changed the way consumers shop, communicate and consume media so profoundly, we feel like we are already living in the future". However, he also expects that "this is only the first wave of digital business transformation" (ibid.). The COVID-19 pandemic has further accelerated this change in many aspects, for instance by further affirming the trend towards online retail. As Verhoef and colleagues (2021, p. 889) write:

2.6 Virtual Team Collaboration and the Digital Transformation

> *"Digital transformation and resultant business model innovation have fundamentally altered consumers' expectations and behaviours, pressured traditional firms, and disrupted numerous markets".*

Virtual team collaboration is one way in which businesses reposition themselves in light of the digital transformation.

2.6.1 Drivers of the Digital Transformation

Commonly known **drivers of digital transformation** are the emergence and global adoption of the World Wide Web and related Information and Communications Technologies (ICTs). This new technological infrastructure then changed the scope of action for business participants such as countries, companies and individuals. For example, companies had the means to reach out to far away markets, consumers could access locations elsewhere, and competition diversified. This implies from a strategic perspective:

- Virtual teams should only be employed in those organizational units for which needs of strategic importance can be identified, such as: being nearer to the customer, identifying a new market entry strategy, designing a new product, conducting research, and so on. Additionally, virtual teams may be employed to achieve cross-functional organizational integration (e.g. interdisciplinary teams) or to pursue special projects.
- Team members should be specially selected for working in virtual teams, based on their unique competencies which cannot be found at a single location or which cannot be utilized solely in the offices (e.g. because of flexibilization needs). Many virtual teams are thus a unique combination of locations and individuals that are only brought together by means of technology for achieving a certain, special goal. These team members often need to be further trained and their competencies and skills be further developed.
- It might not be worthwhile investing in less knowledge-intensive teams of lesser strategic importance: the combined coordination, integration and development costs of having them work virtually would simply be too high and the return-on-investment too low.

2.6.2 Phases of the Digital Transformation

As Verhoef et al. (2021) summarize in their literature review, companies undergo three phases, namely (1) digitization, (2) digitalization and (3) digital transformation when reacting upon the aforementioned drivers of the digital transformation. They find that the first two are prerequisites of the third (ibid., p. 891).

- **Digitization** means to change from analogue to digital tasks (Sebastian et al., 2017), to integrate IT into existing tasks, and to encode analogue information in a digital format so that it may be stored and processed by means of computer hardware and software programs (Li et al., 2016). For example, starting to use SAP, instead of paper, for managing accounts and clients, requires the digitization of analogue account and client information. Virtual (team) collaboration is unfathomable without this first step. Digitization is thus often the initial hurdle which companies face when wishing to turn towards virtual collaboration: if the company has been based on analogue modes of work before, this then simply requires a huge additional amount of time and effort to even become operational, and companies might shy away from this step for too long. The paradox here is that digitization is mainly implemented in order to save costs, however, in order to take advantage of this cost reduction, one first has to invest in the change.
- **Digitalization,** the next step, refers to how the company exploits digital technologies, and ICTs, to enable novel modes and processes of business, work and collaboration (Li et al., 2016). The focus is no longer solely on cost reduction, but also on making use of new opportunities. The possibility of implementing virtual team collaboration starts with this phase.
- **Digital transformation,** which is impossible without having completed the previous two steps, means to change the core business model of the company through the use of digital technologies (Li, 2020). For example, during the COVID-19 pandemic, many companies realized that remote work was more fruitful than they had initially expected. They might then choose to transform their operations into that direction, e.g. allow for more work-from-home than previously.

2.6.3 Strategic Imperatives of the Digital Transformation

Companies need to follow certain strategic imperatives for implementing the digital transformation. based on which phase of the digital transformation they are in.

- **Digital resources and leadership qualities**: the company requires sufficient *digital assets*, such as computer hardware, ICT infrastructure and technologically versatile people, as well as *digital agility*, that is the ability to exploit the advantages associated with digital technologies, for instance by means of certain digital leadership qualities (Chap. 7). For example, if virtual team members do not know how to use existing ICTs and are furthermore sceptical towards digitalization, then digital transformation is impossible. This means to network with other teams, inside and outside of the organization on a collective level, to figure out which of one's own practices and technological solutions are 'best practice' instead of a mere 'just practice'. Especially during the COVID-19 pandemic, when virtual teams were working in isolation from each other, such an exchange and benchmarking did not take place, neither within nor

2.6 Virtual Team Collaboration and the Digital Transformation

across organizations. However, digital learning is essential in order to transform this COVID-19 virtual experience into new digital opportunities (Chap. 3).

- **Organizational design choices**: companies wishing to achieve the digital transformation need to make organizational design choices that are conducive to the envisaged digitalization change (Chap. 6). For example, if a company is based on hierarchical structures, it is less likely that virtual team collaboration is implemented successfully (Maznevski, 2012). The company thus needs to be organizationally agile (Chap. 7).
- Finally, companies should have a clear understanding of what they wish to gain by transforming digitally, and how success can be measured (**strategic digitalization goals and metrics**), and be able to communicate their digital development strategies to their stakeholders, that is: those internal and external actors and groups who have an interest in corporate operations (**strategic stakeholder involvement in digitalization**). For example, a company wishing to provide improved customer services by means of flexible work arrangements needs to make sure that employees are also oriented towards this goal and do not misunderstand flexible work arrangements, for instance, as a cost reduction measure. Otherwise, customer experience and employee experience are misaligned and, consequently, customer service will suffer. The company should also consider digital ethics, and the ethics of Artificial Intelligence, and engage in responsible research and innovation (Chap. 11). Referring to market-oriented aspects of digital growth, Verhoef et al. (2021) furthermore find the creation and management of digital platforms, and the management of platform partners as a key requirement for digital transformation. Further information on the leadership dimension of digital strategy can be found in (Chap. 7).

> **Application 2.5: Virtual Team Collaboration in Light of the Digital Transformation**
>
> Think back to virtual team collaboration which you yourself have experienced or are currently involved in. Alternatively, or additionally, talk to people and let them describe a virtual collaboration experience of theirs. Find out:
>
> - Which drivers of the digital transformation underlie this virtual team collaboration?
> - At which stage of the digital transformation is the company or organization?
> - Is this stage the right stage for this virtual team collaboration to be successful? If not: what needs to be changed—either on the level of virtual team collaboration or on the level of strategy, or both.
>
> Come up with conclusions of which scenarios constitute better or worse practice. Support your assessment with 'data', that is: descriptions from own experiences or statements of your interviewees. ◄

2.7 Summary and Recommendations: Virtual Teamwork as a Configuration Challenge

As the previous sections have outlined, virtual team collaboration underwent key developments over the last decades which can only be understood in light of a far-reaching and ongoing digital transformation. What is so fascinating about virtual team collaboration in a business context (and also beyond) is therefore the question:

2.7.1 What Makes Virtual Team Collaboration Succeed (and how can we predict and achieve success)?

Answering the question of what makes a virtual team succeed is difficult—and, thus: interesting, because each team is different in its circumstances, organizational boundary conditions, team members, workplace conditions, and so on.

For example, a highly dispersed virtual team in which members work all across the globe is impacted by time zone differences whereas a less dispersed virtual team in which members work from home in the same location is not. Even if all those factors remained the same, then team tasks and goals would make a difference: if a highly dispersed team has to engage in frequent discussions to solve problems, then time zone differences become an issue. However, if the same team is challenged with a task such as inputting information, then time zone differences become an asset because they enable 24/7 work.

Virtual team collaboration in general tends to be more divergent than convergent, but the root causes differ for global and non-global virtual teams. For example, cultural diversity, as a condition promoting divergent processes, impacts both types of teams differently.

Divergent collaboration processes are encouraged in the case of global virtual teams because team members work within different national cultural contexts and often also originate from different societal cultures (e.g. Stahl et al., 2010). For example, the business styles of countries such as China, Germany and the USA differ from each other, and this then influences how members communicate, interact and approach shared goals and tasks. Conversely, in the case of less globally dispersed teams, such as work-from-home virtual teams, diversity-induced divergence is often caused by a lack of cohesion in organizational culture: because team members work from home, they do not share a common work culture and this might induce diversity effects despite team members' similarities in national and social cultures.

Likewise, divergence-promoting dispersion effects might originate from different conditions. Divergence is induced by dispersion on a global level in the case of global virtual teams: because team members work, for example, in different time zones, it might not be possible for them to engage in rich synchronous communication as often as required, which then impacts negatively upon collaboration and trust. Secondly, the dispersion effect is induced by the need to use (cost-efficient) ICTs most of which are less rich than face-to-face communication. The dispersion effect in the case of work-from-home virtual teams is mainly related to the difference in work-from-home conditions, such as technological infrastructure and equipment or different time planning requirements for combining work and home demands.

Diversity and dispersion effects can lead to a combined effect in all types of teams. For example, non-diverse teams tend to be more coherent because members are more alike. If team members also work at the same location, coherence is further strengthened. However, this is not always positive for the team: if team members are too alike, they might become complacent and not challenge each other's work-related ideas and processes anymore and thus develop 'groupthink'. As a known team phenomenon, in particular in teams that have worked together for longer, groupthink involves high personal trust (rooted in people's likeness) but also strong work-related blind spots (no team member thinks and acts outside of the collectively accepted box anymore), and new and different views are blocked or left out altogether (Stahl et al., 2010). This then implies that the likelihood of creativity is higher in a diverse or at least a newly-formed team.

How to manage virtual team collaboration is thus not a checklist that applies to all teams. Rather, it is a **configuration challenge** that is specific to each and every team, in a certain stage of the team's lifecycle. Configuration refers to using those factors that shape team collaboration in the most conducive way. Some of these factors can be influenced by team members and team leaders, whereas other factors cannot be changed. For example, the overall performance goal is often given to the team, but what the team can then decide upon is how to split up the task in the best possible way and how to approach tasks, given the specific characteristics and working conditions of the team.

▶ **Configuration** Here: Influencing the performance factors of virtual team collaboration in the most conducive way.

Technology adds additional variables to the question of what makes a team excellent, such as:

- technological boundary conditions
- the Information and Communication Technologies (ICTs) chosen and employed for interacting and working together
- technological infrastructure and the availability of technology
- people's versatility in using technology and ICTs

Again, some of these technological factors can be influenced by the team, whereas others cannot. For example, team members may be trained in using ICTs but neither the team nor the organization can change the available internet bandwidth in a certain location.

Together, this implies that the right factors need to come together in exactly the right ways in order to enable high-performance virtual team collaboration. The next section sheds further light on this insight.

2.7.2 A Five-factor Model

To understand and, consequently, manage the virtual team configuration challenge, five factors need to be considered (e.g. Maznevski, 2012). These are: team inputs, team processes, team outputs, team characteristics and team moderators (see Fig. 2.4).

Team inputs, such as team tasks, team members and their composition, or the technologies being allocated to the team, are the starting point for any team process. Some of these factors can be configured by the team (and then become 'moderators', see below), some of them are fixed external factors which are set for the team.

Team processes, such as creativity, cooperation, alignment or decision making, are the means by which a team converts input into output. This involves both divergent and convergent team processes, and, in order for team collaboration to be successful, the positive convergent and divergent processes must outweigh the negative ones.

Team outputs, such as products, services, ideas or innovations, are what the team delivers after collaborating. The major output factor of any team is **performance**. The choice

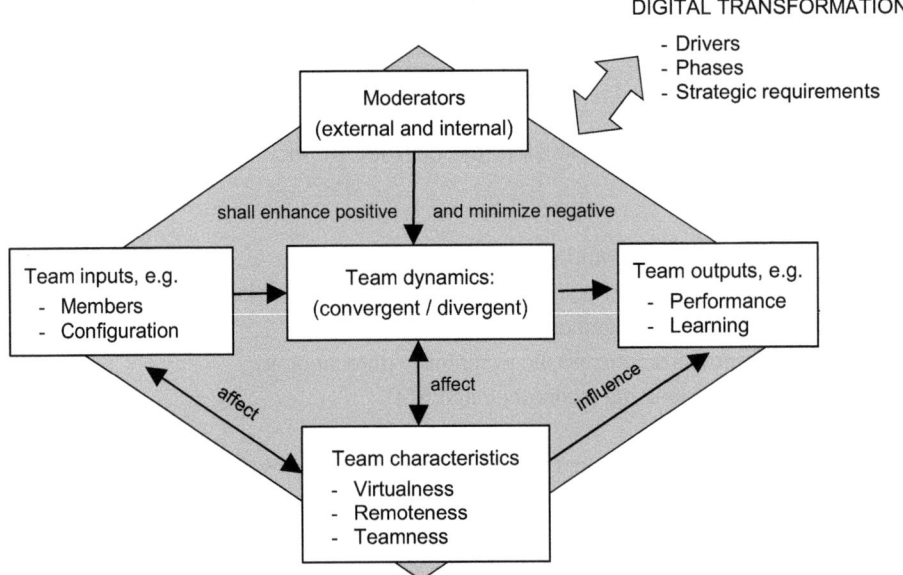

Fig. 2.4 A five factor model of virtual team collaboration. *Source:* own figure

to be made is how to define performance: in the narrow or in the wider sense, or in a cost-oriented or people-oriented way.

Together, inputs, processes and outputs, shape **team characteristics**, such as a team's degree of virtualness, remoteness and teamness (see before). For example, a more distributed team (location as an input factor) might result in lower trust and cohesion, which then impacts negatively upon communication (a team process) and hinders performance (a team output).

Moderators are those aspects by means of which one may influence team processes and -dynamics, and, consequently, outputs and performance. For example, creativity is a positive divergent process in virtual team collaboration—depending on which team members are brought into the team and which ICTs they use to collaborate, creativity can be hindered or supported. Some moderators are configured on team levels (**internal moderators**), some moderators are set on wider, organizational levels (**external moderators**), and some moderators are a combination of internal and external factors.

Finally, there are **boundary conditions** to virtual team configuration. These are digital transformation drivers, the company's digital transformation phase, and the strategic requirements emerging from the combination of both. **Digital transformation** is not part of the virtual team configuration challenge because it cannot be influenced on team levels. However, virtual team collaboration can only be successful if the five factors and their boundary conditions are aligned (s. Fig. 1.4).

Internal and external moderators, and the team's boundary conditions are always interrelated, and the key to high-performance virtual team collaboration lies in shaping these interrelations in the best possible way (and to also define what this 'best possible' way is). For example, organizational culture, an external moderator, also influences team communication, an internal moderator. Chapters 6 and 4, respectively, focus on organizational design and communication, and, integrating both, Chap. 5 highlights the role of team culture for gluing members together and instilling a sense of organizational belonging. Also, how the company positions itself in terms of English language usage influences global leadership opportunities and whether the English language is beneficial or detrimental to the team (Chap. 9). Likewise, the degree of digital leadership readiness on higher organizational levels, an external moderator, also influences the leadership styles that are possible and practiced on team levels (Chap. 7). Similarly, corporate ethics influence the degree to which virtual teams act responsibly, also regarding how to develop and interact with technology, but, at the same time, each team member is responsible for the outcomes of their work and has to develop their own sense of ethics (Chap. 11).

Therefore, any assessment of virtual team collaboration has to take the wider circumstances into account, but at the same time also needs to proceed from the insight that it is every single member who *makes* the team, based on what they identify as their responsibilities and how they act upon these insights. Further chapters will deepen your understanding and ability to manage and configure the internal moderators of virtual team collaboration in light of the external boundary conditions, and you can then fill in the five-factor model with further knowledge. For now, it suffices that you are aware of these interrelations, and ensuing responsibilities.

▶ Team dynamics need to optimize the relations between team inputs and team outputs for **high-performance virtual team collaboration**. To achieve this goal, team characteristics (teamness, virtualness and remoteness), and external and internal moderators, have to be assessed and configured in the most conducive ways. This requires using ICTs in ways that fit task requirements and complexity. Configuration needs to be in alignment with digital transformation drivers, and corporate digital transformation phase and strategic requirements, and needs to consider wider responsibilities.

Seeking balance between trust and conflict, in particular, is essential for high-performance virtual team collaboration: Trust, as a positively convergent team dynamic, is mainly built from shared experiences, which can be task-related or relationship-related. The team thus needs to set up synchronous and sufficiently rich ICT-channels (like video calls) for more shared task-related experiences (Jarvenpaa & Leidner, 1999). If possible, team members should also be enabled to meet in person, as face-to-face interactions help build relationship-oriented trust, which can then speed up initial team-building processes (Gluesing & Gibson, 2004). Relationship (and sometimes task) conflict, as a potentially harmful divergent team process, can negatively impact upon team effectiveness (Maznevski, 2012). It is therefore essential that team members do not make task conflict personal, and, when facing conflict of any kind, apply appropriate conflict management techniques. For example, team members should rather speak about their perspective ('I do not know what to do next…') than putting blame on another team member ('You did not explain this well…'). Explicating oneself and respecting others' positions, and also the difference across both, is therefore an indispensable prerequisite for bridging team diversity and dispersion, and for building teamness from remoteness, under the condition of virtualness.

> **Application 2.6: Five Factors of Virtual Team Collaboration**
>
> Think back to virtual team collaboration which you yourself have experienced or are currently involved in. Alternatively, or additionally, talk to a person and let them describe a virtual collaboration experience of theirs in depth. Visualize what they told you by means of the five-factor model. ◀

2.8 Closing Part

2.8.1 Chapter Summary

This chapter has highlighted the essentials of virtual team collaboration, thus providing a first answer to the question: what are virtual teams, and what makes them successful? It has also delineated different types of virtual teams, such as global or COVID-induced

2.8 Closing Part

virtual teams, and has outlined how and why these have developed. It then focussed on three main qualities by means of which one can assess the requirements of any given virtual team, namely teamness, remoteness and virtualness. The chapter also places these developments and qualities of virtual team collaboration in the context of the ongoing digital transformation. Three digital transformation phases need to be differentiated for configuring virtual teams, namely 1) the emergence of external drivers stimulating digital transformation; 2) the actual phases by means of which a company transforms digitally; and 3) digital transformation becoming a strategic corporate imperative. Introducing the five-factor model, this chapter highlighted the five constitutive factors to be configured and managed for high-performance virtual team collaboration, in relation to the digital transformation phase in which the company finds itself. After having engaged with this chapter, you are now better able to assess virtual team collaboration in light of professional and personal requirements, to configure its moderators, and thus to contribute to high-performance dynamics and outcomes. What you do not yet know in detail is how to fill in the five-factor model with specific knowledge, models and practical tools: this learning will be provided in the subsequent chapters of this book, each of which is dedicated to a crucial theme and its requirement for mastering virtual team collaboration today and tomorrow.

2.8.2 Key Points

1. A team is a (small) group of people that collaborates for achieving a common goal and purpose, and virtual team collaboration means to rely on Information and Communication Technologies for doing so.
2. Most contemporary work is team-based, and most teams rely on ICTs at a certain point, thus engaging in virtual team collaboration at least partially.
3. Being able to assess and contribute to 'best practice' virtual team collaboration is therefore an essential workplace skill of any present or future employee, you included—not only for work-related reasons but also for achieving a better work-life integration.
4. Virtual team collaboration today takes different shapes: it can be employed globally and/or locally, and it can involve different corporate locations but also work-from-home and remote-work conditions.
5. The COVID-19 pandemic has further accelerated trends towards virtual collaboration, and has also added new types of teams and member requirements.
6. Virtual team collaboration is characterized by key convergent and divergent dynamics, each of which can be positive or negative. The key to success is to configure these dynamics in such ways that the positive ones are supported and the negative ones are minimized.

7. Achieving ideal collaborative dynamics requires configuring virtual team moderators in light of team inputs, team characteristics, team outputs, and the ongoing digital transformation.
8. Diversity and dispersion are the two classic distinguishing factors of virtual teams.
9. Assessing a team's degree of teamness, remoteness and virtualness is helpful for those settings in which virtual team collaboration is not the only collaborative mode.
10. Virtual team collaboration demands across all types of teams can be assessed by means of the five-factor model.

2.8.3 Review Questions

1. What differentiates *virtual* team collaboration from non-virtual team collaboration, and which opportunities and challenges are associated with this difference?
2. How did the trend towards virtual team collaboration begin and what were key further developments into that direction?
3. Which types of virtual teams are you aware of, and what are their opportunities and challenges in light of each other (and for whom and under which circumstances)?
4. What are the key dynamics of virtual team collaboration and how do these manifest similarly or differently in different types of contemporary virtual team collaboration?
5. By means of which three characteristics can you assess any type of team?
6. What is the digital transformation and what are its drivers?
7. What are the phases of the digital transformation and how do they differ?
8. Based on the digital transformation phase an organization is in: what are the strategic imperatives for a successful implementation of virtual team collaboration?
9. What is the five-factor-model, and what does it imply for virtual team collaboration?
10. What makes virtual team collaboration succeed, and how can one predict and achieve success?

2.8.4 Opening Case Revisited

With the full knowledge of this chapter in mind: How would you answer the question which you are being asked by your manager in the opening case? Structure your answer with the help of the concepts, models and considerations of this chapter.

2.8.5 Closing Activity: When and how are Virtual Teams Successful?

Based on your reading of this chapter: Choose a virtual team collaboration which you have experienced in the past or are currently involved in. Try to answer the question: When and how is this virtual team collaboration successful?

Differentiate your considerations into

- team inputs
- team processes
- team outputs
- team characteristics
- team moderators
- digital transformation drivers, phases and strategic requirements

Note, which of these elements are required, and how should they be aligned, configured and managed, to have a positive effect upon the team.

References

Boutellier, R. O., Grassman, O., Macho, H., & Roux, M. (1998). Management of dispersed product development teams: The role of information technologies. *R&D Management, 28,* 13–26.

Brown, S. L., & Eisenhardt, K. M. (1995). Product development: Past research, present findings, and future directions. *Academy of Management Review, 20,* 343–378.

Dougherty, D. (2001). Re-Imagining the differentiation and integration of work for sustained product innovation. *Organization Science, 12,* 612–631.

Dulebohn, J. H., & Hoch, J. E. (2017). Virtual teams in organizations. *Human Resource Management Review, 27,* 569–574.

Dyer, W. G. (1987). *Team building.* Addison-Wesley.

Etymology online. (n.d.). Team. In *Etymology.* https://www.etymonline.com/word/team. Accessed 13 Dec 2022.

Gibson, C. B., & Cohen, S. G. (2003). *Virtual teams that work: Creating conditions for virtual collaboration effectiveness.* Jossey-Bass.

Gluesing, J., & Gibson, C. B. (2004). Designing and forming global teams. In M. Maznevski, H. Lane, & M. Mendenhall (Eds.), *Handbook of cross-cultural management* (pp. 199–226). Blackwell.

Griffith, T. L., Sawyer, J. E., & Neale, M. A. (2003). Virtualness and knowledge in teams: Managing the love triangle of organizations, individuals, and information technology. *MIS Quarterly, 27,* 265–287.

House, R., Hanges, P., Javidan, M., & Gupta, V. (2004). *Culture, leadership, and organizations: The GLOBE study of 62 societies.* Sage.

Ipsos Group. (2021). *Return to the workplace 2021 global survey. A 29-country Ipsos survey* [PDF]. https://www.ipsos.com/sites/default/files/ct/news/documents/2021-07/Global%20Advisor%20-%20Return%20to%20Workplace%20Survey.pdf. Accessed 4 Sept 2022.

Jarvenpaa, S. L., & Leidner, D. E. (1999). Communication and trust in global virtual teams. *Organization Science, 10*(6), 791–815.

Kane, G. C., Palmer, D., Philips, A. N., Kiron, D., & Buckley, N. (2015). Strategy, not technology, drives digital transformation. *MIT Sloan Management Review and Deloitte University Press, 14,* 1–25.

Kirkman, B. L., & Mathieu, J. E. (2005). The dimensions and antecedents of team virtuality. *Journal of Management, 31,* 700–718.

Kirkman, B. L., Rosen, B., Gibson, C. B., Tesluk, C. B., & McPherson, S. O. (2002). Five challenges to virtual team success: Lessons from Sabre, Inc. *Academy of Management Executive, 16*(3), 67–79.

Levine, J. M., & Moreland, R. L. (1990). Progress in small group research. *Annual Review of Psychology, 41*(1), 585–634.

Li, F. (2020). The digital transformation of business models in the creative industries: A holistic framework and emerging trends. *Technovation, 92–93,* 102012.

Li, F., Nucciarelli, A., Roden, S., & Graham, G. (2016). How smart cities transform operations models: A new research agenda for operations management in the digital economy. *Production Planning & Control, 27*(6), 514–528.

Liu, D. Y., Chen, S. W., & Chou, T. C. (2011). Resource fit in digital transformation—Lessons learned from the CBC bank global e-banking project. *Management Decision, 49*(10), 1728–1742.

Madhavan, R., & Grover, R. (1998). From embedded knowledge to embodied knowledge: New product development as knowledge management. *Journal of Marketing, 62*(4), 1–12.

Mahadevan, J., Reichert, T., Steinmann, J., Stärkle, A., Metzler, S., Bacher, L., Diehm, R., & Goroll, F. (2024). COVID-induced virtual teams: A phenomenon-based framework and methodological advice for studying novel events. *Central European Management Journal* (ahead of print). https://doi.org/10.1108/CEMJ-12-2022-0244. Accessed 20 Feb 2024.

Mahadevan, J., & Steinmann, J. (2023). Cultural intelligence and COVID-induced virtual teams: Towards a conceptual framework for cross-cultural management studies. *International Journal of Cross Cultural Management, 23*(2), 317–337. https://doi.org/10.1177/14705958231188621. Accessed 20 Feb 2024.

Maloney, M. M., & Zellmer-Bruhn, M. E. (2006). Building bridges, windows and cultures: Mediating mechanisms between team heterogeneity and performance in global teams. *Management International Review, 46*(6), 697–720.

Martins, L. L., Gilson, L. L., & Maynard, M. T. (2004). Virtual teams: What do we know and where do we go from here? *Journal of Management, 30,* 805–835.

Martins, L. L., & Schilpzand, M. C. (2011). Global virtual teams: Key developments, research gaps, and future directions. In A. Joshi, H. Liao, & J. J. Martocchio (Eds.), *Research in personnel and human resources management* (pp. 1–72). Bingley.

Maznevski, M. L. (2012). State of the art: Global teams. In M. C. Gertsen, A. –M.Søderberg, & M. Zølner (Eds.), *Global collaboration: Intercultural experiences and learning.* Palgrave Macmillan.

McKinsey. (2020). Future of work. https://www.mckinsey.com/featured-insights/future-of-work/whats-next-for-remote-work-an-analysis-of-2000-tasks-800-jobs-and-nine-countries. Accessed 1 March 2024

Meta (2022). The future of VR - top trends for 2023? *Workplace.* https://www.workplace.com/blog/the-future-of-vr. Accessed 12 Feb 2024.

Morgan, B.B. Jr, & Lassiter, D.L. (1992). Team composition and staffing. In R. W. Swezey & E. Salas (Eds.), *Teams: Their training and performance* (pp. 75–100). Ablex.

Nohria, N., & Berkley, J. D. (1994). The virtual organization: Bureaucracy, technology, and the implosion of control. In C. Heckscher & A. Donnellon (Eds.), *The post-bureaucratic organization: New perspectives on organizational change* (pp. 108–128). Sage.

Nonaka, I., & Takeuchi, H. (1995). *The knowledge creating company.* Oxford University Press.

Schallmo, D., Williams, C., & Boardman, L. (2017). Transformation of business models—Best practice, enablers, and roadmap. *International Journal of Innovation Management, 21*(8), 1740014.

Sebastian, I. M., Ross, J. W., Beath, C., Mocker, M., Moloney, K. G., & Fonstad, N. O. (2017). How big old companies navigate digital transformation. *MIS Quarterly Executive, 16*(3), 197–213.

Shaw, M. E. (1976). *Group dynamics: The psychology of small group behavior.* McGraw-Hill.

Sole, D., & Edmondson, A. (2002). Situated knowledge and learning in dispersed teams. *British Journal of Management, 13,* 17–34.

Stahl, G. K., Mäkelä, K., Zander, L., & Maznevski, M. (2010). A look at the bright side of multicultural team diversity. *Scandinavian Journal of Management, 26*(4), 439–447.

Stahl, G. K., & Maznevski, M. L. (2021). Unraveling the effects of cultural diversity in teams: A retrospective of research on multicultural work groups and an agenda for future research. *Journal of International Business Studies, 52,* 4–22.

Stropoli, R. (2021). *Are We Really More Productive Working from Home?* Chicago Booth Review. https://www.chicagobooth.edu/review/are-we-really-more-productive-working-home. Accessed 16 Feb 2024

Venkatraman, V. (2017). *The digital matrix: New rules for business transformation through technology.* LifeTree Media.

Verhoef, P. C., Broekhuizen, T., Bart, Y., Bhattacharya, A., Dong, J. Q., Fabian, N., & Haenlein, M. (2021). Digital transformation: A multidisciplinary reflection and research agenda. *Journal of Business Research, 122,* 889–901.

Weaver, J. L., Bowers, C. A., Salas, E., & Cannon-Bowers, J. A. (1997). Motivation in work teams. In M. Beyerlein, D. Johnson, & S. Beyerlein (Eds.), *Advances in interdisciplinary studies of work teams* (pp. 167–191). JAI Press.

Wiles, J. (2020). *With coronavirus in mind, is your organization ready for remote work?* https://www.gartner.com/smarterwithgartner/with-coronavirus-in-mind-are-you-ready-for-remote-work/. Accessed 4 Sept 2020.

Yalalov, D. (2023). *How augmented reality will transform the workplace of the future.* Metaverse Post. https://mpost.io/how-augmented-reality-will-transform-the-workplace-of-the-future/. Accessed 12 Feb 2024.

Zander, A. (1994). *Making groups effective.* Jossey-Bass.

Further Reading

Ipsos Group (2021): Return to the workplace 2021 global survey. A 29-country Ipsos survey. https://www.ipsos.com/sites/default/files/ct/news/documents/2021-07/Global%20Advisor%20-%20Return%20to%20Workplace%20Survey.pdf. Accessed 1 May 2024.

The study highlights how the COVID-19 pandemic has changed people's workplace and work arrangement preferences in selected countries all over the globe.

Information and Communication Technologies in Virtual Team Collaboration: Configuration Challenges and Solutions

3.1 Introduction

Virtual team collaboration would be impossible without **Information and Communication Technologies (ICTs)**. At the same time, many of the challenges and opportunities of working in virtual teams arise from ICT infrastructure, choices and usage. Thus, understanding the impact of ICTs in relation to communication, teamness, purpose and tasks, and being able to make informed ICT-related choices, is essential for successful virtual team collaboration. This chapter provides the required knowledge and skills for making informed technological decisions for virtual team collaboration and for assessing the team's ICT-related boundary conditions with regard to their collaborative impact upon the team. To this end, ICTs are differentiated with regard to their richness, that is 1) the number of communicative modes and 2) the synchronicity of the communication which they enable. Next, the choice of ICTs is related to the complexity of the message, the knowledge to be transmitted, and the specific configurations of the virtual team using ICTs. Recommendations for how to configure ICTs in ways that are the most conducive to virtual team performance follow out of the combined insights from ICT richness and the complexity of the message to be transmitted and the specifics of a team's configurations. This includes the need to design ICT-based social spaces which overcome the communicative leanness and dispersion experienced by individuals collaborating virtually.

▶ **Information and Communication Technologies (ICTs)** The variety of digital collaboration tools employed for virtual collaboration.

3.1.1 Learning Objectives

After having read this chapter, you should.

- Know how and why ICTs have developed.
- Understand what differentiates the available ICTs, also in relation to other team factors.
- Be able to choose ICTs in relation to task complexity and communicative purpose, and in relation to team properties.
- Know how to configure ICTs in relation to virtual team inputs, characteristics, boundary conditions, dynamics and outputs, and also as befitting the team's lifecycle stage.
- Know how to build social spaces by means of ICTs in order to create and maintain trust.

3.1.2 Opening Case

> **Opening Case**
>
> Imagine that you work in a virtual team. You are now tasked with developing the Information and Communications Technologies (ICT) configuration for this team. This involves choosing ICTs and also making informed suggestions as to when, and how often, the team should collaborate by means of ICTs. This also implies that you need to figure out which ICTs are suitable for which team- and task-related purposes, and when, how often, and by whom they should be used. How would you approach this task? ◄

3.2 What Are ICTs, and How Do They Influence Virtual Team Collaboration?

Information and communication technologies (ICTs) is the generic term for all technologies applied in a virtual environment with the purpose of reducing task complexity (Daft & Lengel, 1984). This means that they are media for conveying a message and the way in which the message is conveyed is relevant to how well a task is understood and, consequently, executed. In such ways, ICTs enable communication and exchange processes across locations and people which could not take place otherwise. Or, in other words: without ICTs, collaboration across distance (and sometimes also across time zone differences) would be impossible or at least too time consuming and cost intensive, and thus neither feasible nor profitable.

ICTs are both an internal and external factor of virtual team collaboration. For example, virtual teams require the creation of the right kind of technological infrastructure for communicating and exchanging information (an external factor), and the training of team members in using the appropriate ICTs and feeling comfortable in doing so (an internal factor). Most of the time, external and internal ICT determinants go hand in hand: for example, the tools used for virtual collaboration can be chosen by the teams themselves to some extent, and each team member may contribute suggestions and best practices. Yet, teams are also constrained in their choices, for example, by the technological options provided by the company or organization, or by the general corporate attitude towards technology and digitalization. Nonetheless, if virtual teams provide feedback to higher levels concerning the ICT infrastructure which they need, even presumably 'external' organizational ICT dimensions might be influenced. Still, some technological boundary conditions, such as the availability of high-speed internet, are beyond the team's and the organizational scope of action: here, teams and organizations are dependent on wider infrastructures and general levels of technological development and may only reflect upon whether these given technological circumstances are sufficient for executing the required tasks and reaching the intended goals. Thus, even though team members can usually decide for themselves which ICTs they use for communication and knowledge transfer, they are dependent on the technologies available in the company and the wider technological infrastructure and policies of a country or region. Therefore, ICTs are usually classified as organizational level inputs, even though some of them may, indeed, be chosen and configured by the team (Dulebohn & Hoch, 2017).

> **Link to practice: The rise of Zoom**
>
> The need to hold meetings virtually due to COVID-19 restrictions and stay at home orders have led to a high demand for video conferencing technology as a means of communication. For example, the daily users of Zoom increased from 10 million in December 2019 to over 300 million in April 2020 (Karl et al., 2022). ◄

ICTs are only of use to virtual team collaboration on a large scale in terms of their feasibility if they are not too cost-intensive and do not require too much expert knowledge. For example, even though virtual, augmented and extended realities are an option for virtual team collaboration in general, they are still too cost- and sometimes also knowledge-intensive. However, as soon as the cost–benefit-ratio of this ICT changes, virtual team collaboration might take a very different shape, much like the public availability of the world wide web transformed global communicative patterns. In such ways, the ICTs in use are both relatively new and still continuously developing: an ongoing reconfiguration of how virtual teams collaborate.

▶ ICTs may not be too cost-extensive and must be easy enough to handle in order to be applicable to virtual team collaboration on a larger scale.

> **Application 3.1: Technologies for virtual teamwork**
>
> Technologies for virtual teamwork are constantly evolving. Think back to your first interaction with such technologies and consider how they have evolved to the present day. Which of these new technologies do you find particularly useful and why? ◄

3.3 The Relevance of Considering ICT Richness

3.3.1 What is Media Richness?

ICTs as the media for reducing task complexity are usually differentiated in terms of their richness (Daft & Lengel, 1984). Media richness is determined by two factors, namely 1) the degree of communicative synchronicity achieved by means of this ICT and 2) the number of communicative modes enabled by the respective ICT. For example:

- An e-mail offers only one mode of communication, namely text. A video conferencing tool, on the other hand, allows for video, audio, and text messages to be transmitted and therefore facilitates multiple modes of communication.
- Telephone, audio and video conferencing, instant chat, and text messaging are synchronous modes of communication: the exchange of information and communication takes place in real time. Conversely, e-mail, voicemail, fax, shared drives, and web bulletin boards are asynchronous modes of communication: here, the processing of tasks is not aligned across people; it takes place at different times and at different paces.
- Augmented and extended realities, such as virtual and 3D environments, are currently the richest ICTs available.

Figure 3.1 classifies well-known ICTs with regard to their synchronicity and the number of communicative modes facilitated by them.

Besides these objective criteria, it is furthermore relevant to understand that richness is much more a perception than an objective quality, as it ultimately depends on the user and how they experience the media in use (Martins & Schilpzand, 2011).

> ▶ The higher (the perceived) ICT richness, the more synchronous modes of communication are facilitated.

3.3 The Relevance of Considering ICT Richness

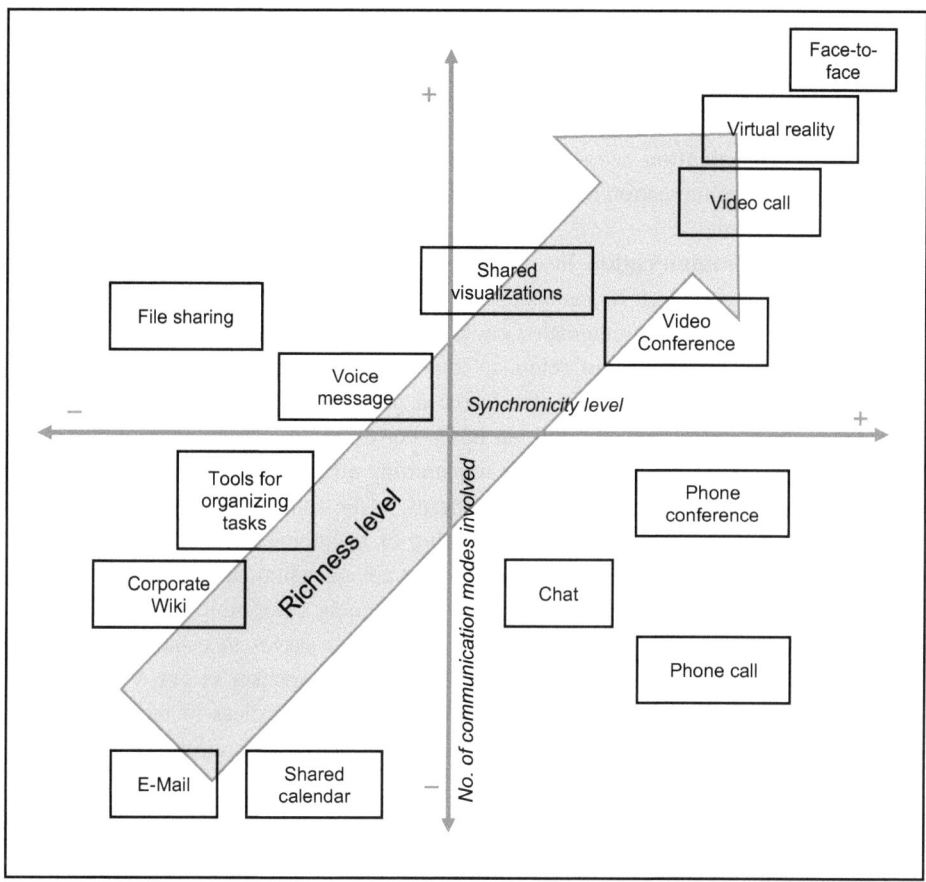

Fig. 3.1 Richness of Information and Communication Technologies. *Source* own figure

3.3.2 Considering ICT Richness in Relation to Communicative and Task Complexity

Making appropriate ICT choices is one of the key challenges of virtual team collaboration. The goal of making these choices is optimizing communication within the team and therefore enabling a type of collaboration that is efficient and effective (Jonsen & Gehrke, 2014). The best option depends on several factors, such as the complexity of the message, the nature of the task to be handled, the type of knowledge involved, the work cultures of team members, team size, or simply the cost of communication (Martins & Schilpzand, 2011).

The communicative task to be facilitated via ICTs can be differentiated into verbal, non-verbal and implicit, para-verbal and tacit elements, it also involves both content and context. These qualities of communication are more or less conducive to being transmitted by means of ICTs, and considering these patterns is part of the virtual ICT configuration challenge.

- **Verbal communication** encompasses spoken and written communication. It was the first type of communication to be transported via early ICTs, such as the telegraph or, later, the telephone.
- **Non-verbal communication** involves gestures and facial expressions which early ICTs could not transport. It was only when photo and video technology became available that this type of communication could be transported as well.
- **Para-verbal communication** refers to messages that are transmitted via the tone, pitch, and pacing of voice, and also to the degree of overlap between speakers. All of these are not easily transported via ICTs. For example, communication via phone or video call, even though potentially transmitting all aspects of para-verbal communication also change 'natural' speech patterns in the sense that overlap needs to be minimized in order to ensure the functioning of technology and to transport verbal messages. Thus, potential para-verbal messages are cancelled out.
- **Context** refers to the boundary conditions influencing communicative content, such as the place, people and time framing a message. It serves to establish meta-level communicative information, such as whether to trust a speaker or not. Context communication is almost impossible to transfer virtually, regardless of the ICT chosen, and is thus a major communicative issue in virtual team collaboration.

The following rule applies concerning the message to be transmitted: the less complex the message to be transmitted is, the easier it is transferred via ICTs. Or, to reverse the logic: the more complex the message to be transmitted is, the more difficult it is to be transferred via ICTs. It is helpful to differentiate message into its content and context components for establishing whether a message is more or less complex: ICTs can better enable content-oriented communication and often fail to facilitate context-oriented communication. Rich ICTs are required for transferring complex messages, whereas leaner media suffice for simple, rule-based task communication.

Verbal communication	Communication via words.
Non-verbal communication	Communication by means of gestures and facial expressions.
Para-verbal communication	Wider communicative aspects such as pace of speech or overlap between speakers.
Communicative context	The boundary conditions and influencing factors framing how messages are transmitted and perceived.

The knowledge to be transported via ICTs can be differentiated into three types, as visualized in Fig. 3.2:

3.3 The Relevance of Considering ICT Richness

Fig. 3.2 The iceberg model of knowledge. *Source* own figure

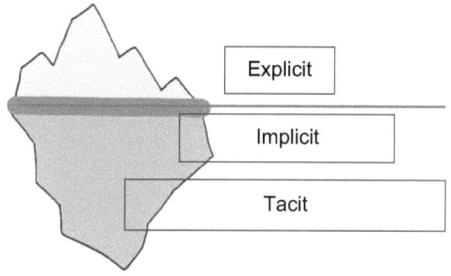

- **Explicit knowledge** ('what to do') is any communicative content that can be put into words and/or text and can therefore be formalized by means of schedules, procedures and rulebooks.
- **Implicit knowledge** is any communicative content that is communicated alongside with words, without people necessarily being aware of it. It is 'right below the surface'.
- **Tacit knowledge** is any communicative content of which people are unaware and which they could not put into words, even if they were aware. It generally involves 'how to do' knowledge, such as 'how to operate a certain machine or interact with customers', that is personalized and rooted in experience. If one understands knowledge as an iceberg, tacit knowledge is the part which is 'below' the surface and which is unique to every person and situation.

Explicit knowledge	'What to do' knowledge that people can put into words.
Implicit knowledge	Knowledge of which people are only partially aware and that is 'right below the surface'. It can potentially be put into words, but is normally not.
Tacit knowledge	'How to do' knowledge of which people are unaware and that is personalized and rooted in experience, so that it cannot be explicated, even if people *were* aware.

It is essential to assess and differentiate these types of knowledge in virtual team collaboration, as their communicative requirements and effects differ.

- Explicit knowledge can be transferred relatively easily via ICTs because it can be recorded and written down.
- Implicit knowledge is the context-based knowledge that *can* potentially be put into words, but is normally not. For instance, in a non-virtual meeting, you can 'read the room' and this gives you information about how to interpret what others say and how to react. In a virtual meeting, this information—which is crucial to communicative success—does not simply come to you. Therefore, you will need to consciously explicate implicit context-related knowledge. This requires that team members consciously share information about the situation and the boundary conditions to what they com-

Fig. 3.3 Bringing implicit knowledge to the surface in ICT-based communication. *Source* own figure

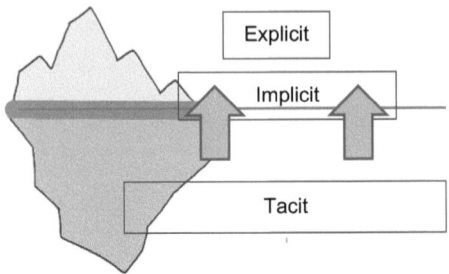

municate so that they enable each other to better interpret the message. Figure 3.3 visualizes the required virtual explication process.

- As Fig. 3.3 also shows, tacit knowledge is almost impossible to transfer virtually. The underlying problem is that tacit knowledge cannot be formalized and is generally difficult to pass on, even if people are physically present in the interaction. It is thus the biggest problem of ICT-based communication, and this is why Chap. 10 is dedicated to tacit knowledge management to a large extent. For now, the most you can do is to always share more information 'around the task' than you believe to be relevant for others, thus increasing the portion of implicit knowledge that is transferred and minimizing the tacit part as much as you are aware of.

▶   Team members in ICT-based collaboration must bring implicit knowledge to the surface by means of explication as much as possible.

Background information: Is virtual reality the ICT solution of the future?

Virtual reality, as the currently richest ICT available, could potentially solve issues of context and tacit assumptions, as it allows people to experience and manipulate the environment as if it was the real world. This is achieved by an increasingly powerful graphics hardware and innovative tracking technologies (Wolfartsberger et al., 2020). Head-mounted displays and sensors that track head and body movements facilitate a person's entry into the virtual world (Sonalkar et al., 2020). This makes it possible to connect with someone in the same room at the same time, regardless of the physical location. Therefore, virtual reality enables significantly richer communication between virtual team members. Facial expressions, gestures and voice make it possible to better understand the emotions and intentions of one's counterparts. Virtual reality is also the richest technology available for transmitting tacit knowledge. For example, how to operate a machine (tacit 'how to do knowledge') cannot be transported via words and text but it can be shown and experienced—thus: transmitted and received via action—in virtual realities. Nonetheless, virtual realities also eliminate context, compared to face-to-face

> interactions. This is even one of their strengths when it comes to the execution of tasks, as distractions can be eliminated in the virtual space, enabling people to focus even more on work. This then makes it possible to increase people's attention span compared to video calls (Rogers, 2019). However, because this highly data-, bandwidth- and memory-intensive technology requires a very advanced infrastructure worldwide, as well as people being comfortable and skilled in using it, it is still not an option for virtual team collaboration on a larger scale, not to mention the costs of this technology.

▶ Lack of context is a major problem when communicating via ICTs:

- Explicit communication can easily be transmitted via most ICTs.
- Implicit communication requires specific, selected ICTs.
- Communicating tacit knowledge virtually is impossible, except for the 'richest' of ICTs.
- Virtual reality might be a solution to this dilemma in the near future.

Application 3.2: Information and Communication Technologies, and their richness

Which technologies do you use in your daily life to communicate, and to share, distribute and acquire information? Note them down and classify them in terms of their richness (number of communicative modes which they enable and degree of synchronicity). ◀

3.4 ICT Richness in Relation to Task Complexity and Communicative Challenge

The main recommendation of media richness theory is to use rich media for complex information, and leaner media tools for simple and explicit, rule-based information (Daft & Lengel, 1984). An interaction via ICTs is considered successful, when there is an appropriate fit between the complexity of the communicative task and its medium. Conversely, if ICT richness and communicative task complexity do not match, communicative effectiveness is compromised (see Fig. 3.4).

The more complex the message to be transmitted or the task underlying it, the richer the ICTs one should use. For example, as a comparably lean technology, e-mails are insufficient for decision making: they oversimplify the message. Also, e-mailing does not allow for the exchange of relational messages and can lead to isolation. If misread, e-mails can cause distrust, and copying everyone on e-mails creates an information overload. Furthermore, e-mails do not suffice as a repository of team knowledge, as both search and storage options are limited. Thus, the only thing that e-mails *can* do is to

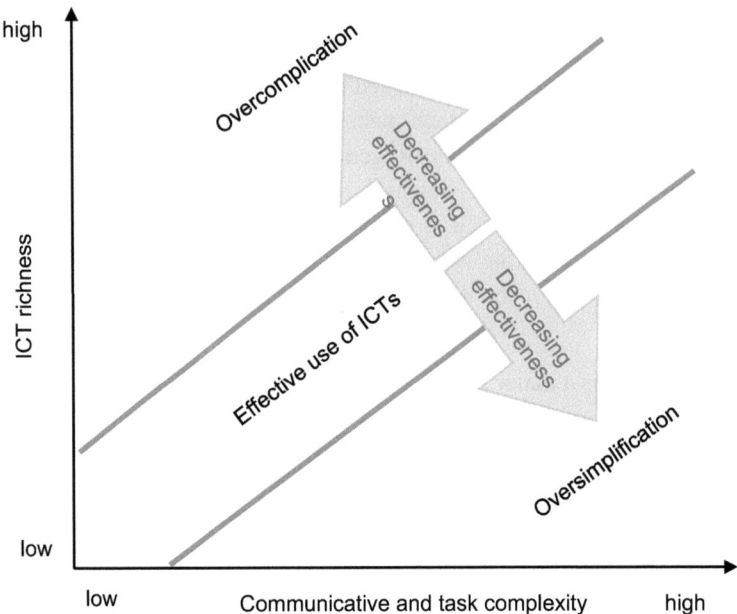

Fig. 3.4 ICT effectiveness in relation to communicative and task complexity. *Source* own figure, based on Daft and Lengel (1984)

transmit information that does not require a direct response and that is not intended to prevent the recipient from performing other tasks at the time.

To jointly develop solutions and clarify conflicting viewpoints, one needs telephone or video conferencing, that is: richer media in real time (Martins & Schilpzand, 2011). File shares, in which members make their ideas, processes and work outcomes available for peer review, are the suitable media for collaborative work on documents (Lindner, 2020). Instant messaging technology, such as chats, encourages social interaction during work and prevents isolation (Breuer et al., 2020).

However, rich communication might also overcomplicate collaboration, for instance, as it requires more resources and coordination. For example, if a team relies solely on synchronous video calls for collaboration, then the flexibility advantage of members working on different schedules is lost and team members might get the feeling that their working hours are not spent effectively and efficiently. Thus, the guideline for making ICT choices is: as low-tech as possible, and as rich as necessary. Still, the issue remains that even the richest ICTs are comparably lean when viewed in light of 'real-life' interactions.

▶ Technological richness needs to match the complexity of the underlying task or communicative purpose. Complex tasks and purposes *must* have ICT richness.

> **Application 3.3: The problem with e-mailing**
>
> You have certainly used e-mails in work-related contexts before. Based on what you now know about ICT configuration: Would you say that you and others have used e-mails well? Why (not)? How would you use e-mails differently when collaborating virtually in the future, and what other media would you use alongside e-mails, and for what purposes, and why? ◄

3.5 Configuring ICTs in Relation to the Constitutive Factors of Virtual Team Collaboration

It is highly debated whether virtual communication is more positive or negative than face-to-face communication. According to Maznevski (2012), virtual communication is more difficult than communicating face-to-face. Challenges include lower richness, the lack of social information, and the danger of misunderstandings due to asynchronous tools. On the other hand, there are also advantages associated with virtual communication, such as a better access to knowledge and expertise, and a higher flexibility in responding to messages. What is agreed upon is that one cannot judge virtual communication per se but rather has to create the conditions under which virtual communication can thrive in the best possible way. Making appropriate ICT choices in relation to a specific team and task is essential for achieving this goal. Based on the work of Maznevski (2012), Martin und Schilpzand (2011) and others (Chap. 2]), the five constitutive factors of virtual team collaboration are:

- **Team inputs**, such as team members and team configurations (e.g. team members' locations and workplaces)
- **Team processes**, which can be convergent and divergent and positive or negative. For example, trust is a positive convergent process, and creativity is a positive divergent process. Groupthink is a negative convergent process, and conflict is a negative divergent process.
- **Moderators**, such as leadership, training and/or ICT usage, are those measures taken to support positive team dynamics and minimize negative ones.
- **Team outputs**, understood as what is achieved and delivered by means of virtual team collaboration, e.g. performance, learning or creation of products and services.
- **Team characteristics**, such as the team's degree of virtualness, teamness and remoteness.

ICT choices, usage and requirements need to be aligned with these five factors. For example, if learning is a key goal of a research and development team, then there must be a knowledge database to facilitate, exchange and document such learning. Likewise, without a virtual meeting tool, convergent team dynamics are impossible to achieve and characteristics such as teamness cannot be established. If this condition is in conflict with the team's overall goal, for example, because individual tasks are interdependent and in need of verbal explanation (which makes virtual meetings a key process requirement), then ICTs function as a negative moderator, as they do not support the required team dynamics. Consequently, the desired team outputs cannot be achieved. The key—and ongoing—ICT configuration challenge in virtual team collaboration is thus: how shall inputs, processes, outputs, moderators and characteristics be enabled by means of ICTs in the best possible way? Figure 3.5 visualizes these interrelations.

▶ **Wichtig**

The benefits and limitations of a specific Information and Communication Technology for virtual team collaboration are determined by:

1. The ICT's richness (degree of synchronicity and number of communicative modes).
2. The complexity of the communicative task.
3. The five constituent factors of virtual team collaboration (team inputs, processes, outputs, moderators and characteristics).

All three aspects need to be aligned when choosing and using ICTs.

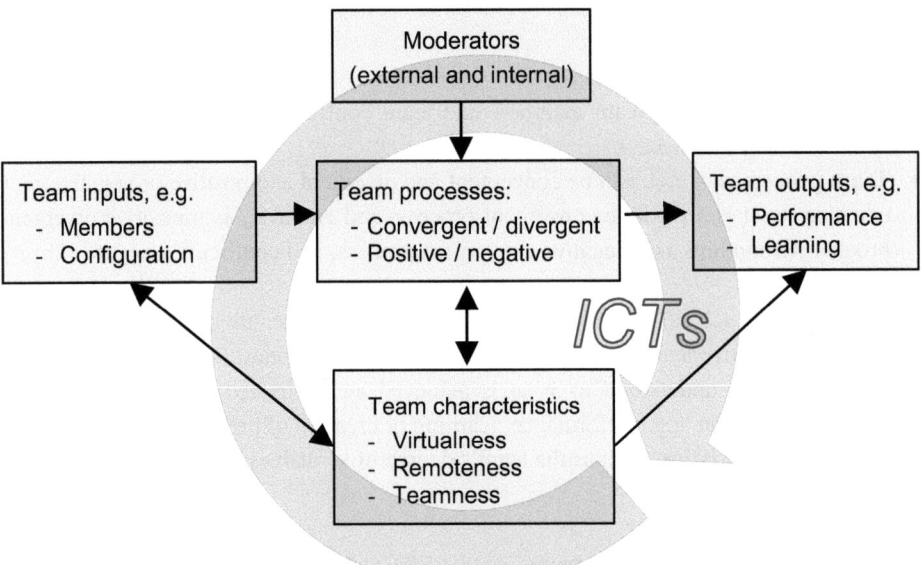

Fig. 3.5 Information and Communication Technologies as enabler of virtual team collaboration. *Source* own figure, further developed from Chap. 1

3.5.1 ICTs in Relation to Team Inputs

The most relevant team inputs are its team members, and the team's configuration in terms of members' locations and workplaces. It is essential that team members are sufficiently qualified for collaborating via ICTs. What is particularly harmful to virtual team collaboration is a digital divide within the team, that is: huge differences in how technologically versatile team members are. Secondly, because ICTs are subject to rapid technological change, team members need to be sufficiently motivated to constantly invest in their technological competencies and skills. For example, every virtual meeting tool user knows the experience of entering the tool after a few days, sometimes a mere few hours of pause, and, suddenly, an update is required that, sometimes, seems to have fundamentally changed the user surface and, potentially, also the functionality. This means that one needs to invest time to actually inform oneself what has changed and to keep track of the updates and new possibilities offered by any ICT used. It is thus essential from a team leaders' perspective to also give team members the space and time they need to engage in this learning, e.g. by setting the norm that everyone enters the team's regular virtual meeting a few minutes early and by also doing so themselves. This way, everyday technological learning becomes part of the team's performance norms and also serves a secondary purpose, namely the exchange of implicit knowledge (see before), prior to the start of the actual, formal, meeting. Thirdly, team members' attitude towards digitalization and technology in general also tends to influence how they interpret benefits and outcomes of ICT-based collaboration. For instance, because attitude influences experience, a technologically versatile team member who is simply 'sceptical' towards digitisation might find ICT-based collaboration unsatisfying and lacking, even though they perform well.

The biggest challenge to virtual team collaboration with regard to ream configurations is ICT-related distortions linked to location and workplaces. For example, if a virtual team collaborates long-distance, potentially even globally, then the infrastructure at some sites is better or worse than at others. If this then coincides with formal or knowledge hierarchies, e.g. if headquarters' or 'the experts' location' is also the one with a better IT infrastructure, better equipment, a better connectivity or, very simply, without power shortages, then it becomes more difficult to 'see' the competencies and skills of team members at the technologically disadvantaged site. The same can happen in the case of a work-from-home virtual team: in many countries, it is not a given that all localities, in particular rural ones, have equal access to reliable high-speed internet. This might then impact negatively upon a team members' performance while working from home, or, in case they cannot sustain this mode of work due to incommensurable technological obstacles, resulting in diminished work-life integration opportunities.

Finally, special attention needs to be paid to imbalances in team members' locations and workplaces. For instance, if only one or two team members are located at remote sites, and the overwhelming majority of members is co-located at one or only a few main sites, this then creates knowledge- and relationship hierarchies across sites: the minority sites will always be worse off, unless all team members consciously engage in additional ICT-based communication in order to make up for configurative imbalances.

3.5.2 ICTs in Relation to Team Processes

Team processes can be either convergent or divergent, with each of them having the potential of influencing the team's output in positive or negative ways. Communication is the enabler that steers the direction of team processes, and how these processes impact the team. The first insight is that virtual communication requires more conscious awareness than communicating face-to-face. Challenges include media leanness, the lack of social information, and the danger of misunderstandings due to asynchronous tools. For instance, lacking clues for interpreting body language and tone of voice, and fewer feedback opportunities increase the risk of misinterpretations (also see Chap. 4). Therefore, teams need to find ways to verbalize implicit knowledge (see before).

Still, the same conditions are also beneficial to certain types of teams: It has been found that short-term teams with heterogenous participants tend to perform better virtually than in a face-to-face setting (Crisp & Jarvenpaa, 2013). This is mainly due to the leaner collaborative technologies (e.g. e-mail) which reduce social interaction. This then makes it less likely that personal conflicts, e.g. as based on diverse values or other differences, occur, and it is then easier to execute decision making tasks. Furthermore, because virtual communication supports divergence, a virtual setting could lead to a higher performance when it comes to idea generation and innovation. Thus, it is not despite but *because* team members do not get to know each other on a personal level that these types of virtual teams perform better in the short run.

However, the picture changes when virtual teams are not newly formed or are asked to work together more long term. In this case, the swiftly built task-related trust of the newly formed virtual team is insufficient for sustaining the team for a longer period of time: long-lasting relationship-based (personal) trust would be required (Jarvenpaa & Leidner, 1999), and, as relations are not easily communicated by means of ICTs, this kind of trust usually requires face-to-face interactions. Most researchers thus recommend that virtual teams meet face-to-face once in a while in order to replenish their long-term trust reserves.

ICTs play an ambiguous role in these wider team processes. On the one hand, they enable a better and more 'democratic' access to knowledge and expertise, also when responding to messages. Therefore, more participants may contribute and share more unique information (Mesmer-Magnus et al., 2011): a positive divergent effect. At the same time, the usage of ICTs also tends to reduce the general openness for information sharing, especially, if team members are induced into a passive information overload by the technologies in use: this happens if team members are so exposed to ICTs and have to constantly be available to them that they lose the energy to actively engage in team collaboration: a negative divergent process. If this happens, ICTs might then result in lower levels of individual commitment, or increased 'absenteeism'—a team member is no longer actively involved in collaboration, despite the available ICTs registering them as 'active'.

Trust and control are key issues to be balanced in virtual team collaboration. For example, some technologies allow for managers and peers to track team members' status, such as 'active', 'non-active' and 'in-between'. If this is used as a medium for controlling performance, team members then start to devise ICT-based means of escape. For example, they might set their status to 'active' *and* schedule fictitious meetings which then makes them unavailable again. This then makes it impossible to get hold of them for knowledge- and information sharing: a culture of control resulting in a loss in convergence and a decrease in team outputs. Thus, ICTs also project images of 'productivity' which are seldom the full picture. Therefore, what virtual team collaboration requires is that ICTs are not used as means of total control but rather that leaders establish trust-based modes of alignment so that team members do not feel forced to pretend to be productive via ICTs which, in the end, then only impacts negatively upon the team's productivity.

ICTs also enable higher flexibility in responding to messages, for instance, one does not need to respond immediately to an asynchronous message such as an e-mail. Team members can thus be on different schedules and in different time zones. However, what is essential for trust to emerge across this time-related team diversity, is shared performance norms concerning responsiveness. The issue is not that team members need to be available 24/7 but rather that standards are set and adhered to when and how one wishes individual team members to respond in communication and action. These standards do not have to be the same for all team members, rather, they need to be aligned with the team's overall and individual tasks and goals, as well as with the type of knowledge to be transferred, and they also need to be aligned with the team's characteristics and configurations. Furthermore, all team members have to share a sense of fairness regarding the standards set. Ideally, these norms would not be prescribed top-down but be developed collaboratively by the team.

Finally, it is more difficult for team members to discern organizational and professional roles when communication is mainly virtual. Therefore, it is essential to make team members aware of their own role and the role and contribution of others, for instance, prior to discussing tasks in a virtual meeting. As communication theory suggests (see Chap. 4), the content of the message is framed by the relations of those involved in the communication, or, in other words: if these relations and subsequent role expectations remain unclear due to the leaner communicative environment, then the content of the communicative process is compromised.

3.5.3 ICTs in Relation to Team Moderators

Moderators refer to all impulses given to the team, such as leadership (see Chaps. 7, 9), knowledge management, learning and innovation techniques (see Chap. 10) or organizational structures (see Chap. 6). The purpose of these impulses is to support positive team dynamics and minimize negative ones. This section highlights those moderating aspects which are directly related to ICTs.

3.5.4 ICTs in Relation to Team Characteristics

The main characteristics by means of which virtual teams may be classified is the team's degree of virtualness, teamness and remoteness (own conceptualization, based on Martins & Schilpzand, 2011). Figure 3.6 provides an overview.

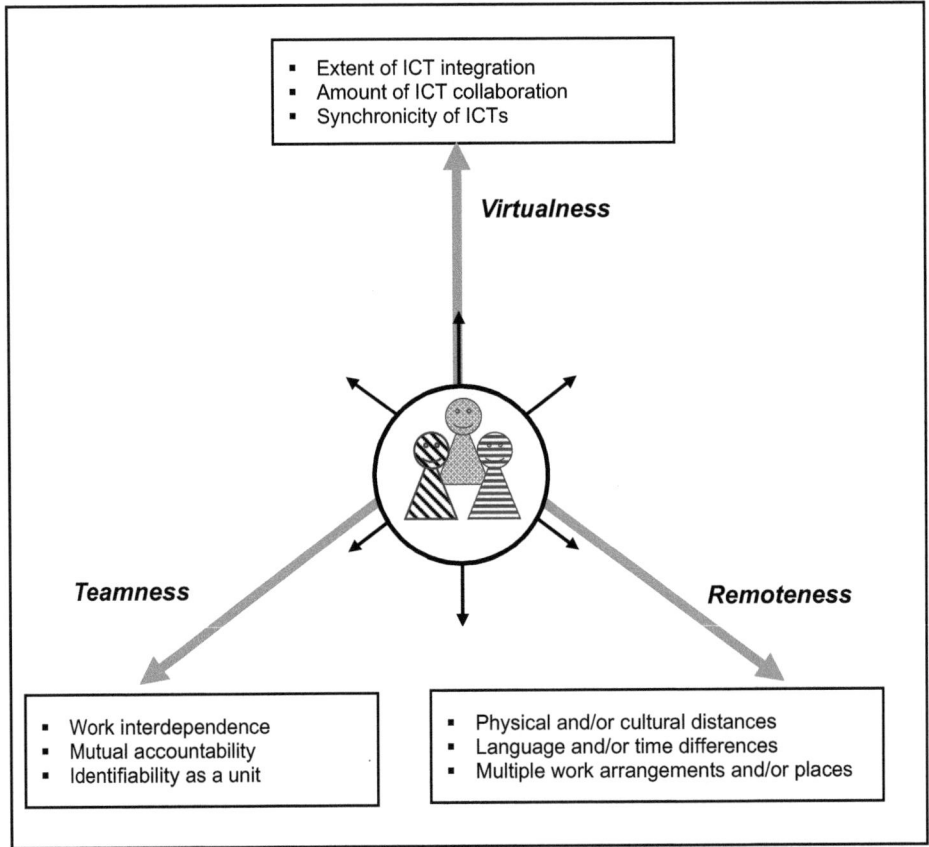

Fig. 3.6 ICT requirements in relation to virtual team characteristics. *Source* Own figure, partly based on Martins and Schilpzand (2011)

3.5 Configuring ICTs in Relation to the Constitutive Factors …

As Fig. 3.6 shows, remoteness refers to any aspects which let team members experience remoteness, such as geographical or time zone differences, cultural and linguistic diversity, and the differences induced by different work arrangements and work places (also work-from-home). Virtualness covers the degree of ICT integration and synchronicity, as well as the amount of collaboration which takes place via ICTs. Teamness describes the degree to which work packages and tasks are interdependent, to which there is mutual accountability and dependency and to which the team is identifiable as a unit from the outside.

Tasks are closely intertwined with teamness in the following ways:

- The **degree of task interdependence** directly determines the degree of teamness: the more interdependent the tasks are, the more teamness is required for success.
- The **type of task**—routine or exceptional/innovative, skills-based or knowledge-based—determines the type of teamness which is required. For example, more routine tasks can be allocated and executed by means of pre-prepared manuals and specifications whereas exceptional and innovative tasks require frequent team exchange, lessons learned and a more active way of collaboration.
- The type of knowledge required for executing the task—**explicit or tacit**—determines whether and how easily knowledge may be shared across individuals. Explicit knowledge refers to 'knowledge that can be put into words' ('explain how') whereas tacit knowledge is embedded in action and needs to be 'shown' ('do how'). Consequently, it is easier to transfer explicit knowledge virtually than tacit knowledge.

Assessing teams by means of these three dimensions is helpful for assessing whether a certain ICT set-up fits the needs of a specific team. How a team is characterized by these three aspects is thus highly relevant for making ICT collaboration choices, as the following comparison of two example teams highlights.

Example 1: The online accounting team

The online accounting team is characterized by the following collaboration patterns:

- Individual tasks are assigned during weekly face-to-face meetings in the offices.
- Members work flexibly and execute tasks by the next meeting, either on-site, at home or from anywhere, as fits their schedule and needs.
- Normally, there is no need for further task-related clarification.
- Exchange between colleagues is limited and, if occurring, takes place via e-mail.
- Team members handle accounts all over the world.
- Accounts are assigned to individual team members based on their respective cultural and country expertise.

As this assessment suggests, example team 1 is characterized by a higher, but not extraordinarily high, remoteness and low levels of both teamness and virtualness

(Fig. 3.7). Teamness is low because work is assigned and executed by individuals who, despite their frequent meetings, are not engaged in social interactions. Thus, they are more remote from each other than the team's frequent on-site presence might suggest at first glance.

Out of this follows the fact that the team can make do with basic levels of ICT infrastructure and user knowledge, as ICTs are neither required for creating high levels of teamness via positive convergent dynamics such as trust, nor necessary for executing individual team members' tasks. What needs to be made sure of is 1) the clarity of task-related non-virtual communication during regular and frequent face-to-face meetings and 2) sufficient connectivity for executing individual team members' tasks. Team members are and remain remote from each other, as they are distant in terms of the tasks to be executed and diverse in terms of their countries of origin. However, this does not impact negatively upon virtual team collaboration. Overall, this thus looks like a stable and suitable ICT configuration. However, should task requirements change towards higher integration, ICTs would need to be reconfigured in such ways that they better support team members' positive convergence and task execution. Most likely, richer ICTs and a stronger ICT integration would be required.

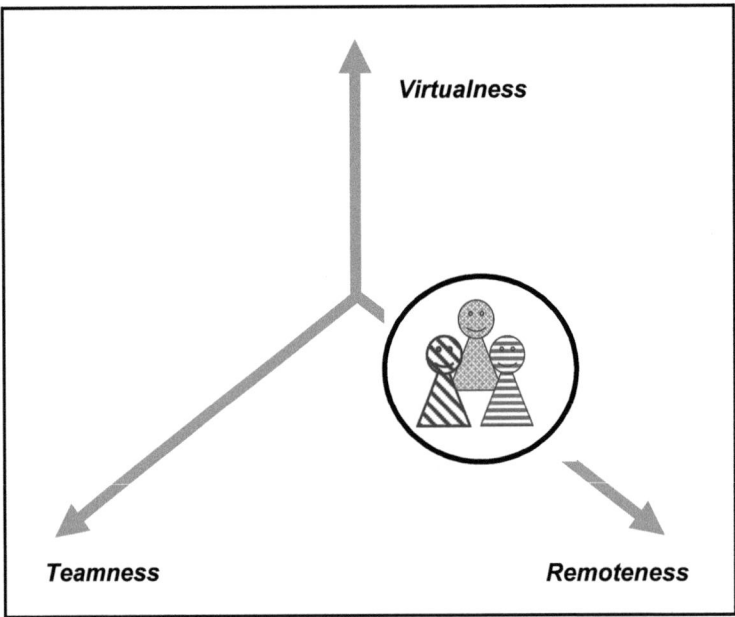

Fig. 3.7 The online accounting team. *Source* own figure

3.5 Configuring ICTs in Relation to the Constitutive Factors ...

Example 2: The business development team

This business development team is characterized by the following collaboration patterns:

- Pre-COVID, work was done on-site.
- There is a lot of contact, even friendship, among members and a strong sense of togetherness.
- Since COVID, members have made intensive use of the new work-from-home option.
- Virtual collaboration among team members takes place via instant messaging or video calls, which are also used for 'office talk' and for exchanging personal information.
- Meetings and brainstorming sessions are held online.

Together, this means that the team exhibits high levels of virtualness and teamness, and a low level of remoteness, as team members do not feel 'remote' from each other, even though they in fact are in some aspects (Fig. 3.8).

As this is an established team, members have already created relationship-based, personal trust with each other. As long as the tasks are stable, this trust may thus be assumed to also sustain the team virtually. However, should tasks change and require higher innovativeness and novel approaches, the team might suffer from the negative side effect of high cohesion among members who feel alike, namely groupthink. In this case, it is highly relevant to introduce rich ICTs to the team that stimulate creativity, such as shared visualization boards coupled with synchronous communication technologies such as online meeting tools. Furthermore, novel virtual social interaction should be stimulated,

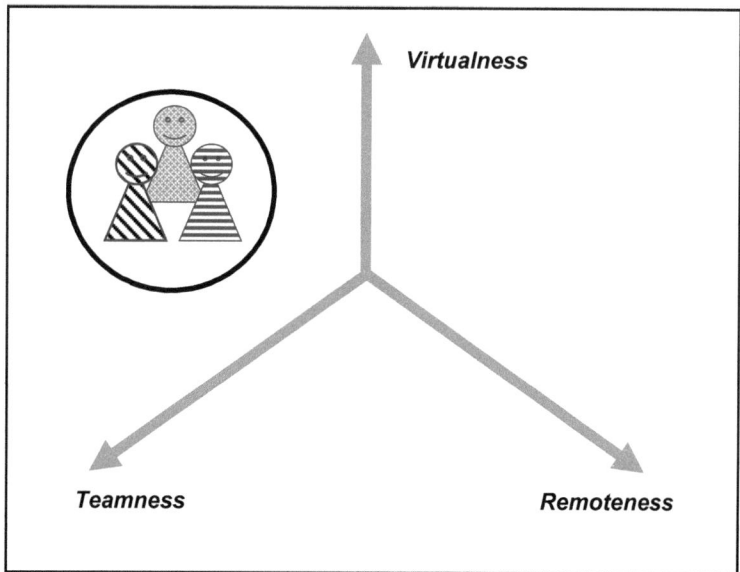

Fig. 3.8 The business development team. *Source* own figure

e.g. via re-grouping the team or via assigning more than one individual to a specific sub-task, so that collaboration is encouraged.

> **Application 3.4: Absenteeism and commitment in ICT-based collaboration**
>
> Some collaborative ICTs allow for tracking a person's status, e.g. as absent, occupied or available. Also, within an organization, e-mail programs let others know whether a person is available or not when they try to schedule a meeting. Some people might thus schedule fictitious meetings for themselves in order to be tracked by their superiors and peers. Based on your present understanding of how ICTs function, try to answer the following questions:
>
> - Is such behaviour good or bad for the team?
> - Would you make such an assessment categorically, or does it depend on circumstances?
> - If the assessment is circumstantial: please provide details on when and how such behaviour would be good or bad.
>
> Next, reflect: Is it not understandable that people do not wish to be 100-percent transparent to everyone when it comes to how they spend their time at work? Also, due to their lack of richness, ICTs might not adequately represent a person's status at work. For instance, a team member might wish to schedule intensive work time for themselves and not wish to be interrupted by calls and meeting requests. Therefore:
>
> - Which other means besides ICT-based time control might there be for aligning schedules and securing commitment in a virtual team?
> - What other control mechanisms besides actual 'control' can you think of? ◄

3.6 Recommendations: How Technology Can Help to Overcome Virtual Team Challenges

3.6.1 Configure ICTs in Light of Task and Team Factors

There is no absolute right or wrong in how to use ICTs in virtual team collaboration: it is a **configuration challenge** that is ongoing and specific to each team and task. The previous sections have outlined how the factors which are in place in every virtual team collaboration need to be assessed with regard to their specifics and, next, be put together in such ways that ICTs facilitate the highest possible team performance.

For example, richer communication technologies give teams an advantage in managing their project, sharing information, and making decisions, and using e-mail and richer technologies in parallel can result in higher satisfaction and less information loss.

However, there is also the requirement to use ICTs that are as lean as possible and rich as necessary, in order to neither overcomplicate nor to oversimplify the task: **media richness and communicative complexity** thus need to be considered in light of each other.

The choice and use of ICTs must also be adapted to crucial aspects of the **task environment**, such as availability of technology and infrastructure, the need to consider security issues, members' experience with technology and budget. Further **task-related ICT requirements** are:

- ICT-based collaboration is particularly suitable for knowledge sharing and structured and/or detailed tasks.
- The ICTs used should be more synchronous with increasing task complexity or urgency. and enable team collaboration in real time.
- Different technologies are more or less suited to different types of tasks: synchronous ICTs should be used for decision making, and asynchronous ICTs should be used for more complementary tasks, such as information sharing and assessment.

It has also been found that ICTs contribute to task-related conflict under certain circumstances. First, high access, one-to-many media such as e-mail allow for large volumes of communication on concurrent tasks, and this might lead to information overload (DeSanctis & Monge, 1999). People need to not just provide relevant information but also receive feedback on their message for effective communication. However, the use of asynchronous electronic media such as e-mail tends to delay feedback (Brennan, 1998). This lack of immediate feedback can bring about task conflict when communicating parties ascribe the wrong meanings to instances of silence from the other end (Cramton, 2001).

Furthermore, ICT configurations also depend on **members' preferences**. For example, as Martins and Schilpzand (2011) find, members with higher levels of temporal focus (i.e., engagement, attention, and task focus) prefer asynchronous technologies, whereas members with higher levels of temporal dispersion (i.e. not focused on maintaining a sense of time, multitasking) might prefer synchronous technologies.

Additionally, the **team's lifecycle** needs to be considered for ICT configuration, in particular in relation to trust as one of the key success factors for virtual team collaboration. For example, team trust is positively correlated with team-related attitudes, team information processing, and team performance—but almost impossible to be established virtually (Breuer et al., 2020). This can be temporarily remedied by means of so-called swift trust, that is: impersonal, action-based trust between people who had not worked together before (Crisp & Jarvenpaa, 2013). The challenge is then to quickly build a deeper form of trust (Maznevski et al., 2006). To achieve this, steps should be taken early in the team's life. Rich technologies are required in order to get to know one another as rapidly as possible without face-to-face meetings. In addition, team members might stay in contact during the work on a joint project via instant chats and to continuously share the progress via shared documents and folders. Transparency early in the team's life is a key factor here (Maznevski, 2012). Also, the exchange of relevant information through interactions provides members with the opportunity to form a common background, which is an important prerequisite for trust. It is also helpful to use shared visualizations or agile techniques to facilitate collaboration and knowledge sharing. Rich technologies with high synchronicity can then be replaced in latter stages of the team's lifecycle by leaner technologies with low synchronicity. Finally, when sufficient trust is built, members can work on their tasks individually and make their work processes and outcomes, as well as contact information and data, available on a shared drive. As a caveat, however, tacit knowledge tends to resist full explication of such kind.

Team size is another determining factor for making ICT choices. Synchronous technologies are generally suitable for collaboration for smaller teams, while larger teams tend to use asynchronous tools for collaboration. Members usually tend to be more involved, committed and satisfied in small virtual teams. There tends to be a better understanding about team goals and other team members (role, specific expertise, communication style, and personal circumstances), which often results in less coordination requirements. To compensate for this, Martins and Schilpzand (2011) suggest that larger teams use both rich (video calls) and less rich (e-mail) technologies (depending on the subtask) in parallel, in order to achieve a similar level of satisfaction and workflow effectivity.

Finally, ICT requirements are also influenced by leadership styles and expectations, as well as by the 'nature of the audience' (Martins & Schilpzand, 2011), that is: the level of formality expected in interactions. For example, it is known that less hierarchical and more flexible organizational structures enable a more collaborative virtual team experience and that strict and top-down organizational structures rather hinder virtual team performance (see Chap. 6). Likewise, digital leadership styles and leadership expectations might also be more or less conducive to high performance virtual team collaboration (see Chap. 7).

3.6.2 Create ICT-Based Social Spaces for More Trust and Less Conflict

ICTs increase team members' freedom by creating flexible infrastructures and by reducing the dependency on time (e.g. office hours) and place. If combined with work-from-home, work-from-anywhere and other forms of telework and flexible work arrangements, they enable individuals to better balance work, home and life demands and furthermore reduce several types of corporate and individual costs. The main challenge associated with knowledge transfer and management is that tacit (that is: experience-based, implicit) knowledge is almost impossible to be transferred via ICTs. The only solution to this dilemma is to use the richest ICTs possible, and to select tools, such as digital whiteboards or team blogs that allow for collaborative thinking processes to be transferred to the digital world.

Also, what is lacking, is the proverbial 'coffee machine exchange' by means of which relational and personal trust are built. Thus, teams who are purely or almost exclusively virtual need to figure out how to use ICTs in such ways that they create spaces of social exchange for the team—even though this might feel artificial at first. Because it is somewhat counter-intuitive to understand ICTs as tools for creating and maintaining social spaces, this aspect thus emerges as the second crucial recommendation for configuring and using ICTs for virtual team collaboration.

For instance, if it is common practice in a company that project leaders have a weekly lunch or coffee break together, then it makes sense to also do this virtually: just to sit at one's respective desks or potentially move into the kitchen or the coffee area (either on-site or at one's home), and to eat or have coffee together while the camera is on: because the social ritual is known to both participants, it will attune them to a more personal, trust building and relationship creating, exchange, even though the setting is socially 'artificial'. Of course, this strategy works best with people who are already familiar with the job and/or have worked in this setting, potentially even together, for longer.

However, there is also the possibility of building new teams virtually, as many teams learned during the COVID-19 pandemic when work-from-home was mandatory or highly recommended in order to stop the virus from spreading and/or to minimize the number of infections. For example, if one wants to re-create events such as a team gathering or an 'end of the year project' celebration virtually, one could have the same items delivered to every team member, be it food, beverages or gimmicks, organize some input—a show, a tour, a speaker, and then let team members participate virtually. One would need to create a virtual setting that is social for this to work, e.g. not just one virtual meeting space, but many, in which participants can mingle but also be in smaller groups. For example, one could have one meeting space in which food is consumed, one in which the show takes place, one in which team members can get a closer look at the finished products (potentially even using virtual reality), one in which everyone can look at pictures or whiteboards from the last project—as would be the case if the event had taken place in the 'real world'.

Of course, there are costs associated with creating such rich and social virtual collaboration spheres, but the costs of low trust levels are also high, and one needs to keep in mind that the overall costs of virtual, potentially even work-from-home, collaboration are usually much lower than those of on-site collaboration. Furthermore, control in the sense of monitoring the team and team members' performance is much more difficult to achieve in a virtual setting (Breuer et al., 2020). Establishing trust coupled with setting shared performance norms might, very simply, be the only feasible mechanism of 'control' in today's and tomorrow's virtual team collaboration.

Application 3.5: Creating virtual social spaces

Imagine that you are working in an exclusively virtual team that works on highly complex tasks which are also interdependent, and thus needs to achieve high degrees of teamness for success. How would you create and maintain virtual social spaces? ◄

3.7 Closing Part

3.7.1 Chapter Summary

Facilitating collaboration where otherwise there would be none, Information and Communication Technologies (ICTs) are the meta-level requirement and enabler of every virtual team process and outcome. The challenge is to configure ICTs in such ways that they fit team purposes and goals in the best possible way. One needs to assess ICTs in a structured manner for meeting this challenge, so that one can foresee, manage and, if required, adjust their effects on the team. Firstly, the different ICTs can be categorized according to their degree of richness. The degree of technological richness is defined by the degree to which the technology offers 1) synchronous communication and 2) multiple communicative modes. Furthermore, one needs to consider members' perceptions of ICT richness and communicative and task complexity. Together, these aspects help determine which ICTs to choose, and for what purposes. Secondly, ICT configurations need to be assessed in light of the constitutive team factors, such as the degree of virtualness, remoteness and teamness. Together, these factors shape how effectively one may positively influence collaborative team dynamics by means of ICTs (see Fig. 3.5). For example, the ICTs supplied to and used by the team influence the efficiency and effectiveness with which the desired team outputs may or may not be reached. ICTs are also a key enabler of positive team dynamics, such as knowledge sharing and trust, and, when configured appropriately, can deliver certain outputs, such as learning and performance, for instance, when used to build social spaces. This means that ICTs are predominantly a configuration challenge which every individual team member, and the whole team, need to live up to. After having engaged with this chapter, you now know how to choose and configure ICTs for more positive virtual team dynamics and better collaborative outcomes.

3.7.2 Key Points

1. ICTs are the meta-level enabler of team collaboration.
2. Different ICTs can be categorized according to their degree of richness.
3. The degree of technological richness is defined by the degree to which the technology offers 1) synchronous communication and 2) multiple communicative modes.
4. The degree of ICT synchronicity and the number of communicative modes facilitated by an ICT determine communicative effectiveness and may help to positively moderate team dynamics.
5. When configured appropriately, ICTs can deliver key outputs, such as learning and performance
6. ICTs can be used to build social spaces.
7. In virtual team collaboration, it is essential to choose and configure ICTs in relation to team inputs, dynamics, characteristics and outputs.

3.7 Closing Part

8. Boundary conditions, such as organizational-level ICT inputs, or digitalization strategy and infrastructure, cannot be influenced by the team but nonetheless shape the effects which ICTs have on the team.

3.7.3 Review Questions

1. What are ICTs, and how do they influence virtual team collaboration?
2. Why is it relevant to consider ICT richness for virtual team collaboration?
3. How are ICT richness, communicative purpose and task complexity interrelated?
4. Which communicative elements are easy, which ones are difficult to transmit via ICTs?
5. What types of knowledge need to be exchanged via ICTs, and how is this problematic?
6. How can you bring implicit knowledge to the surface when collaborating virtually?
7. What are the problems of oversimplification and overcomplication in virtual collaboration, and how can they be avoided by means of ICT configuration?
8. How are ICT requirements and the constitutive factors of virtual team collaboration interrelated?
9. How can you configure ICTs in light of task and team factors?
10. Why is it relevant to build social ICT spaces, and how can this be done?

3.7.4 Opening Case Revisited

You have been asked to choose the best possible ICT configuration for your team in the opening case. You now know that, in order to reach this goal, you first need to understand ICT richness (synchronicity and number of modes which are transmitted), in relation to task and communicative complexity, and in relation to the type of knowledge to be exchanged. Next, you need to assess the team in relation to its five constitutive factors, in particular with regard to its teamness, virtualness and remoteness. You will also need to consider the team's lifecycle stage when choosing and configuring the right type of ICTs for the team. You are by now aware that, at the beginning of the team's lifecycle, you need to build upon swift trust and use synchronous and social ICTs to develop deeper, more long-lasting and relationship-oriented types of trust—unless this is a short-term, innovation-oriented team that needs to capitalize upon its diversity. Throughout, you need to be careful to limit e-mail exchange only to the purposes which it serves and, during latter stages of the team's lifecycle, make sure to use ICTs for data sharing and asynchronous exchange. You will also need to consider that the team's communicative climate needs to be psychologically safe for all members so that these goals can be achieved.

What is required is thus the conscious configuration and use of ICTs, so that practice becomes best practice. Table 3.1 serves as a further checklist for configuring and using ICTs for high-performance virtual team collaboration.

Table 3.1 Checklist for configuring and using Information and Communication Technologies in virtual team collaboration

Guiding question	Sub-questions
What is the task?	• What is the goal (trust building, decision making et cetera)? • How can we measure and assess task achievement? • Who needs to contribute, and in what ways? • How to make sure that everyone understands? • When do we/I need to change something (early warning)?
Who is the team?	• How large or small is the team? • Have team members collaborated before? • How high is the trust level, and what is the optimum level? • What degree of teamness needs to be achieved? • When do we/I need to change something (early warning)?
Where is the team?	• Where are the team members? • How many team members per location? • Do members work at offices, from home or from anywhere? • How remote are team members from each other? • What are indicators for negative remoteness (early warning)?
When is the team?	• At which stages of their lifecycle is the team? • How long and for what purposes do we need to collaborate? • To what degree are team members' daily schedules aligned? • What kind of responsiveness is required? • When do we/I need to change something (early warning)?
How often is contact required?	• How large or small is the team? • What task requirements of contact need to be considered? • What trust requirements of contact need to be considered? • When and how would team dynamics benefit from contact? • When do we/I need to change something (early warning)?
Which type of contact is required?	• Which type of contact is required for task execution? • Which type of contact is required for building trust? • What are the team and trust requirements of contact? • When and how do team dynamics benefit from contact? • When do we/I need to change something (early warning)?
What technology can help here? (status quo)	• Which ICTs could be a solution to the problems above? • Are we skilled enough to find the best ICT solution ourselves? • What kind of ICT training, if any, does the team/do I need? • In what ICT-related areas do we/do I need external help? • When do we/I need to change something (early warning)?
Are existing ICTs contributing to performance? (continuous improvement)	• Where are we already excellent (and what are the indicators)? • What key aspects are presently missing? • Which technologies can contribute to further improvement? • When do we/I need to change something (early warning)?

Source own table

The idea is that team members, individually and collectively, ask these questions for a higher individual and team ICT awareness. It is also recommended that these questions become part of regular performance evaluation cycles of individuals and teams, thus bringing them to the next level of ICT-related competencies and skills.

3.7.5 Closing Activity

First consider Table 3.2 for this task. It summarizes some of the key challenges faced by virtual teams, and how these can be countered with the help of ICTs.

Table 3.2 Examples for the use of Information and Communication Technologies

Virtual team requirements for collaboration	How to use ICTs to achieve this purpose
Preventing isolation	• Regular virtual meetings and video chats for task exchange and task-related alignment • Telephone and chat for continuous updates and personal conversations • …
Building and maintaining trust	• During early stages of the team's lifecycle: frequent virtual meetings coupled with video chats • Use of a corporate wiki • Use of shared calendars and file sharing • …
Minimizing misunderstandings	• Presenting and exchanging ideas, tasks and work-related assumptions with the help of shared visualizations • Documenting work process and outcome via file sharing • Conversations via synchronous media such as telephone • Use of corporate wiki to establish shared meanings and align understanding in the team • …
Ensuring and maintaining quality of communication	• Adapt the media to the complexity of task or message • Use email for general information or less urgent updates • Use video calls for decision making • …
Ensuring and maintaining task overview and goal alignment	• File and calendar sharing • Decision making via synchronous, richer media (video call and telephone), not asynchronous, lean media (e-mail) • …

Source own table

Complete and extend Table 3.2 as much as possible by considering the following questions:

- Which ICT-based countermeasures can you add to the stated challenges?
- Which other challenges of virtual team collaboration are you now aware of and how would you counter them with the help of ICTs?

First, amend the table on your own. Next, exchange with others to complete it more fully.

References

Brennan, S. (1998). The grounding problem in conversations with and through computers. In S. Fussell & R. Kreuz (Eds.), *Social and cognitive approaches to interpersonal communication* (pp. 210–225). Lawrence Erlbaum.

Breuer, C., Hüffmeier, J., Hibben, F., & Hertel, G. (2020). Trust in teams: A taxonomy of perceived trustworthiness factors and risk-taking behaviors in face-to- face and virtual teams. *Human Relations, 73*(1), 3–34.

Cramton, C. D. (2001). The mutual knowledge problem and its consequences for dispersed Collaboration. *Organization Science, 12*(3), 346–371.

Crisp, C. B., & Jarvenpaa, S. L. (2013). Swift trust in global virtual teams: Trusting beliefs and normative actions. *Journal of Personnel Psychology, 12*(1), 45–56.

Daft, R. L., & Lengel, R. H. (1984). Information richness: A new approach to managerial behavior and organizational design. *Research in Organizational Behavior, 6*, 191–233.

DeSanctis, G., & Monge, P. (1999). Introduction to the special issue: Communication processes for virtual organizations. *Organization Science, 10*(6), 693–703.

Dulebohn, J. H., & Hoch, J. E. (2017). Virtual teams in organizations. *Human Resource Management Review, 27*, 569–574.

Jarvenpaa, S. L., & Leidner, D. E. (1999). Communication and trust in global virtual teams. *Organization Science, 10*(6), 791–815.

Jonsen, K., & Gehrke, B. (2014). Global Team Collaboration. In B. Gehrke (Ed.), *Global leadership practices: A cross-cultural management perspective* (pp. 118–131). Palgrave Macmillan.

Karl, K. A., Peluchette, J. V., & Aghakhani, N. (2022). Virtual work meetings during the COVID-19 pandemic: The good, bad, and ugly. *Small Group Research, 53*(3), 343–365.

Lindner, D. (2020). *Virtuelle Teams und Homeoffice. Empfehlungen zu Technologien, Arbeitsmethoden und Führung*. Springer.

Martins, L. L., & Schilpzand, M. C. (2011). Global virtual teams: Key developments, research gaps, and future directions. *Research in Personnel and Human Resources Management, 30*, 1–72.

Maznevski, M. L. (2012). State of the art: Global teams. In M. C. Gertsen, A.-M. Søderberg, & M. Zølner (Eds.), *Global collaboration: Intercultural experiences and learning*. Palgrave Macmillan.

Maznevski, M. L., Davidson, S. C., & Jonsen, K. (2006). Global virtual team dynamics and effectiveness. In G. K. Stahl & I. Björkman (Eds.), *Handbook of research in international human resource management* (pp. 364–384). Edward Elgar.

Mesmer-Magnus, J. R., DeChurch, L. A., Jimenez-Rodriguez, M., Wildman, J., & Shuffler, M. (2011). A meta-analytic investigation of virtuality and information sharing in teams. *Organizational Behavior and Human Decision Processes, 115*(2), 214–225.

References

Rogers, S. (2019). The role of technology in the evolution of communication. *Forbes*. https://www.forbes.com/sites/solrogers/2019/10/15/the-role-of-technology-in-the-evolution-of-communication/. Accessed 2 Feb 2022.

Sonalkar, N., Mabogunje, A., Miller, M., Bailenson, J., & Leifer, L. (2020). Augmenting learning of design teamwork using immersive virtual reality. In C. Meinel & L. Leifer (Eds.), *Design Thinking Research Investigating Design Team Performance* (pp. 67–76). Springer.

Wolfartsberger, J., Zenisek, J., & Wild, N. (2020). Supporting teamwork in industrial virtual reality applications. *Procedia Manufacturing, 42*, 2–7.

Further Reading

Rogers, S. (2019). The role of technology in the evolution of communication. *Forbes*. https://www.forbes.com/sites/solrogers/2019/10/15/the-role-of-technology-in-the-evolution-of-communication/. Accessed 2 Feb 2022.

This article provides a practical overview on how technology and communication have evolved in relation to each other.

Communication as Enabler of Virtual Team Collaboration: Properties and Best Practices

4.1 Introduction

This chapter focusses on team communication as the enabler of all other team dynamics. Virtual team communication is transported by means of ICTs (Chap. 3). Building upon and adding to previous knowledge, this chapter deepens your understanding of what communication actually *is,* how it makes people feel, and how it can be managed. The starting point is an overview of communicative properties and purposes. Models of communication, such as the sender-receiver model, or the metaphors of communication as iceberg, glasses and backpack increase your awareness of how communication functions to simplify—but also sometimes complicates—human interactions. Communication is further differentiated into context and content, and the ability to do so in one's own practice is an essential skill for identifying and overcoming the challenges of virtual and ICT-based communication (see Chap. 3). Crucial to this skill is the insight that ICT-based communication lacks context and that teams need context to build and maintain trust. This chapter also highlights the relevance of a psychologically safe team communication climate, and how to build it. This chapter proposes three approaches for achieving communicative alignment. These are the "five meta-axioms of communication" by Watzlawick et al. (2000), the "four-sides model" by Schulz von Thun (1981) and key techniques that help reframe communicative context and content, thus: the task and relationship aspects of how people interact.

To achieve communicative alignment, this chapter concludes with five principles of how to engage in communicative action and the need to acknowledge the four sides of virtual communication, so that one can better integrate communicative context and content on team level. After having engaged with this chapter, you should be more able to configure virtual communication dynamics positively, in alignment with team purposes and goals and in a way that is psychologically safe for all involved. You should also be able to assess the virtual team communication which you take part in, and to further develop your communicative skills from your own experience. These learning processes and skills go beyond virtual teamwork, and are also applicable to non-work-related and non-virtual communicative contexts.

This way, this chapter lays the groundwork for a later, detailed consideration of cultural integration (see Chap. 5) and English language effects on virtual team collaboration (see Chap. 9) in subsequent sections of this book.

Team	A small number of individuals who collaborate in a task and/or to reach a goal.
ICTs	Information and communication technologies.
Virtual team collaboration	Working together as a team by means of ICTs.
Configuration	Here: Designing and managing virtual team communication in ways that fit and support the team's tasks and goals.

4.1.1 Learning Objectives

After having read this chapter, you should

- Be aware of what communication involves and how it happens.
- Know the difference between communicative content and context.
- Be able to reflect upon communicative interactions with the help of models such as the sender-receiver model, and the metaphors of communication as iceberg, backpack and glasses.
- Understand what kind of communicator you are and be able to identify this in others.
- Know the five principles of communicative action and how to implement them in practice.
- Be able to acknowledge the four sides of communication when interacting with others.
- Know key communicative reframing strategies.
- Be able to integrate communicative context and content.
- Understand when and how a psychologically safe communicative climate functions as a virtual team 'safety belt'.

4.1.2 Reading Requirement

You should have read Chap. 3 of this book.

4.1.3 Opening Case

> **Example**
>
> Jacob is an intern in a Swiss precision engineering company that specializes in watches and medical equipment. He is supporting the manager of a global team

tasked with product innovation in the area of high-end watches. Every three months, the team meets at another site, in person, for an in-depth innovation workshop. The team communicates virtually, via e-mail, chat and video meetings between these meetings. There is also a shared virtual location in which information, status reports and other documents are safely stored. Jacob has already observed that virtual communication is different from non-virtual communication, and that choice of language plays a role. "But what *is* communication, actually?", Jacob wonders, "and what exactly makes virtual communication differ from non-virtual communication?". ◀

4.2 What is Communication? Three Approaches

Communication is the vehicle by means of which team collaboration and team development and, consequently, team performance is achieved. Generally, communication is an act to exchange on some aspect (what needs to be communicated) which is represented by certain other means (the signs used to represent what needs to be communicated). For instance, a person might be angry and thus shout: "Ahhh—this project!". 'Shouting' (the sign) signifies something invisible, namely 'anger' (the signified). However, it is only communication, if another party also understands it this way. Communication is thus something that happens between actors: often, humans, but increasingly so, also technology.

Communication on abstract levels consists of three elements

- **Syntax**—the 'logic' and 'rules' of the communicative means (signs) used. For example, the words: "Ahh—this project!" are syntactically incorrect. It is more precise to shout, for example, "I hate this project!", and a person focussing solely on syntax would only understand the second exclamation.
- **Semantics**—what helps people to determine the meaning to be found, or, in other words: to understand how signifier and signified are related. As an example, most people would understand "Ahh—this project!", even though it is not grammatically correct and syntactically incomplete—it is semantics which enables them to do so.
- **Pragmatics**—what enables people to establish the 'correct' or, at least, the most likely meaning, in the situation. Examples are: the specific project that the exclamation 'this project' might refer to, how the speaker's role in the project might explain his anger, and, also how one—being in certain relations to project and speaker—should react to this statement now.

Together, these properties underlie how communication is *done by people in a situation*.

Three models of communication simplify this understanding. These are:

- Communication takes place between people: the **sender-receiver model**
- Communication involves content within context: the **content-context model**
- Communication is simplification: the **iceberg**, **glasses** and **backpack model**

4.2.1 The Sender-Receiver Model of Communication

Communication takes place between people. It involves a **sender** and a **receiver**, and a **message** to be transmitted. The transmission process is considered successful, if

- The **sender encodes** the message in such a way that
- The **receiver decodes** the message as it was intended by the sender

Usually, the receiver then responds to the sender—sends a new message back—from which the sender may deduce whether their message was understood or not. This process of 'sending back' is usually referred to as feedback. The original sender of the first message may then acquire the information from feedback for sending the next message, and so on and so forth. Figure 4.1 visualizes this process.

Sender   A person or technology from which a message originates.
Receiver A person or technology which is the target of a message.
Message   A communicative unit in writing, in speech, or by signals.
Encoding The (conscious and/or unconscious) communicative choices made for a message to be sent.
Decoding The (conscious and/or unconscious) communicative choices made for a message to be received.

Technically, there is also the differentiation between analogue and digital communication.

- **Analogue communication** involves a continuous flow of signals, as, for example, transmitted via a telephone call.
- **Digital communication** involves 'either-or' signals, such as those transmitted by computers and other digital (0 and 1) devices.

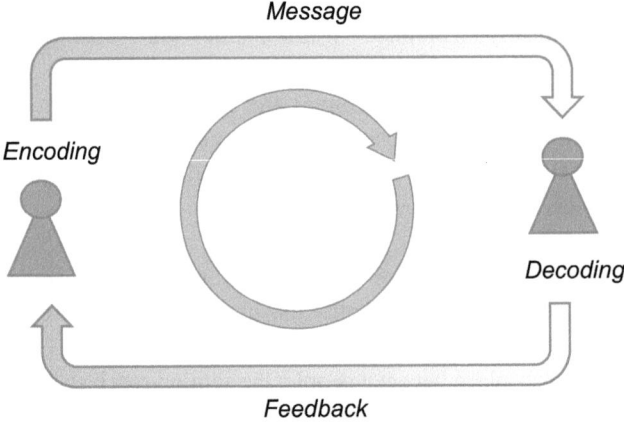

Fig. 4.1 The sender-receiver model. *Source* own figure

> **Application 4.1: Purposes of communication and communicative modes**
>
> Look back onto virtual and non-virtual communication, as you practice and experience it. For which purposes do you use virtual communication, such as e-mailing? For which purposes do you use non-virtual communication, such as talking to a person? For which purposes would you *not* use one or the other, and why? ◄

4.3 Communication as Content and Context

When interacting, people have different modes of communication at their disposal:

- **Verbal communication** encompasses spoken and written communication.
- **Non-verbal communication** involves gestures and facial expressions.
- **Para-verbal communication** refers to messages that are transmitted via the tone, pitch, and pacing of voice, and also to the expected degree of overlap or expected pauses between speakers.
- **Virtual communication** refers to communication that is not in person and mediated by digital technologies.

▶ There are verbal, non-verbal and para-verbal modes of communication.

Communication can be differentiated into content and context. **Content** involves the factual message to be transmitted and received. **Context** refers to the frame or the boundary conditions into which a certain communicative content is placed. For example, a seemingly simple question such as "How are you?" means different things depending on when, where, by whom and towards whom it is asked. If a manager asks their subordinate in a formal meeting, then the subordinate will understand the question and, consequently, answer differently than if asked by a friend whom they run into on the street. Also, the answer will differ with regard to whether one has not seen each other for longer or not, whether one is in a hurry or not, whether one is on good or bad terms with each other and so on.

▶ **Context** The frame or boundary conditions into which a certain communicative content is placed, such as: when, where and between whom communication occurs (time, place, people).

Communicative context influences communicative content. Consequently, the degree to which people orientate themselves to content or context, respectively, changes the message and how it is transmitted, and also determines what is listened to.

- The lower the context-orientation of an individual, the more they will express themselves verbally and will also listen to verbal communication the most: "Listen and answer to what I say, and *only* to what I say".
- The higher the context-orientation of an individual, the more they will listen to non-verbal and para-verbal communication and will also express themselves by these means: "Read between the lines and answer to what I do *not* say".

▶ Communication is a process within certain boundary conditions. These boundary conditions are called context. Context (e.g. place, time, people) influences communicative content.

For example, when being asked "How are you?", an individual may interpret the content of the message: "Someone wishes to know about my health and wellbeing" and answer truthfully on content level: "I am very ill". Or, they may interpret the context of the message: "Someone wishes to start a conversation, and this is simply the opener for doing so." and answer truthfully on context level: "Well, alright, so great to see you, how are you?" to keep the conversation going. Likewise, the sender of the message might have expected a content-related answer (how the receiver *really* feels) or a context-related message (how good it is to see each other). Similarly, a conversation about the weather is sometimes about the weather and sometimes just a small-talk topic, that is: a topic that functions as the opening context for a further, content-related, conversation. The latter then implies that there only need to be a few sentences about the weather, and then everyone moves on with the actual content of the conversation, and that one should not engage others in a half-an-hour actual discussion about certain weather phenomena.

Figuratively spoken, the sender decides (often unconsciously) what to send and how to send it, and which of the two to focus on more (see Fig. 4.2).

- The content of the message is the core of what shall be communicated: it is the gift to be given.
- The context of the message is whether and how elaborately the gift is wrapped.
- To focus on content means to care more about the gift and less, if at all, about wrapping.
- To focus on context means to wrap the gift elaborately and to care about the wrapping.

Likewise, the receiver decides (often unconsciously) what to receive and how, and what to focus on more: the gift or the wrapping (see Fig. 4.2).

- Focussing on content means to unwrap the gift unceremoniously and to get to the gift as quickly as possible.
- Focussing on context means to unwrap the gift elaborately and to also pay attention to how the gift has been wrapped and to how it is unwrapped.

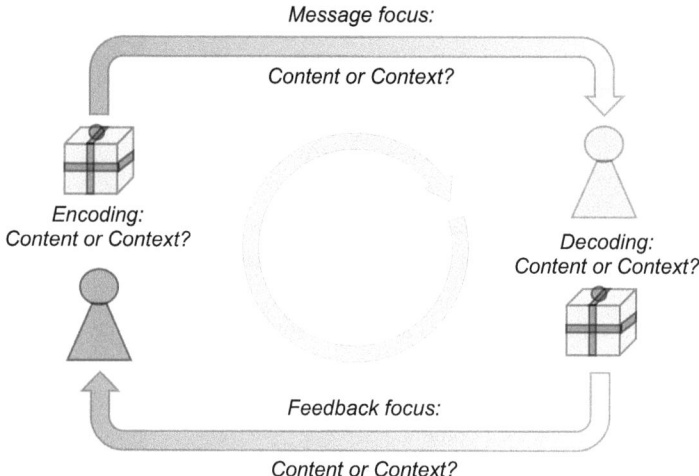

Fig. 4.2 Context and content in communication. *Source* own figure

As one may imagine, differences in context- and content-orientation can create huge misunderstandings between individuals and within teams. These topics will be further discussed in Chap. 5.

Application 4.2: Miscommunication

Miscommunication refers to a message being decoded in other ways than it was intended to be by those encoding it. Based on this understanding, reflect: What do you normally do in order to prevent miscommunication when collaborating with others? Write down your key strategies, and when, how and under which circumstances you have (not) applied them successfully in the past. Exchange with fellow team members, students or co-workers. ◀

4.4 Communication as a Simplification Process: Iceberg, Glasses and Backpack

Communication transports a content that is more complex than its vehicle. This firstly implies that there is no single way in which a message may be encoded or decoded. Secondly, any communicative code is incomplete: it can never cover the whole complexity of the content to be transmitted and the context wherein the transmission takes place. Third, individuals bring different communicative experiences to a situation and thus use different templates for interpreting the same message. Three pictures, **communication as iceberg, glasses and backpack**, illustrate these properties of communication and will be outlined in the following.

4.4.1 Communication as an Iceberg

Communication is like an iceberg in the sense that some part of it is above the surface, but most of it is below the surface. This means that communication needs to be differentiated into explicit, implicit and tacit elements (see Fig. 4.3).

- **Explicit communication**: What is above the surface and what can be put into words and be heard or read. Verbal or written communication is thus the explicit component of communication.
- **Implicit communication:** What is above the surface, thus: visible, but what is not put into words or text directly. For example, pauses or the degree to which eye contact is made are part of implicit communication as they change what the message 'means' without changing its explicit content.
- **Tacit communication**: The type of communication that is invisible, unspoken, inferred or implied, and of which people are not aware when communicating (the 'blind spots' of their communication). For example, people are generally not aware why and how they focus on the content of context of a message. Nonetheless, they communicate these assumptions tacitly.

Further examples of tacit communication are the expected pauses between speakers or the interactive distance to be kept which are part of para-verbal communication (see Chap. 3): those involved will tacitly feel interrupted by another person (too much

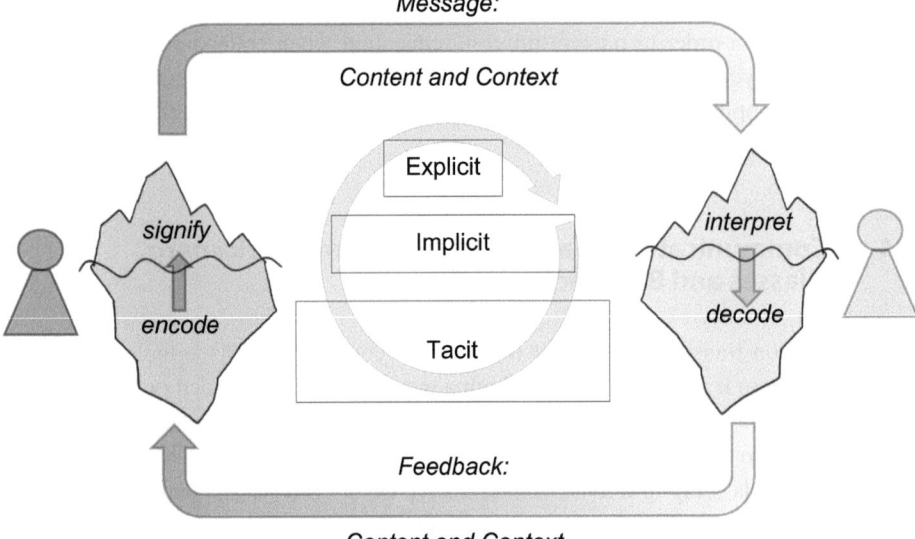

Fig. 4.3 Communication as an iceberg. *Source* own figure

overlap) or ascribe a lack of interest (too much pause). Or, they will perceive another person as intruding upon themselves (not enough distance is kept) or as disinterested (too much distance). Yet, they will most likely not be able to identify the root cause of their feelings (they are not aware of what is being communicated) and, even if they do, they will not be able to advise the other person explicitly ("leave x seconds pause" and "keep y centimetres distance so that I feel comfortable"). This means that tacit communication needs to be converted into implicit and explicit messages in order to be sent, received and understood.

Tacit communicative aspects are often a reason for why people misunderstand each other. For example, the question "How are you?", innocently asked by a friend (the sender), may nonetheless trigger deep emotions if the receiver—unbeknownst to the sender—is currently experiencing a severe health crisis. This means that the sender *interprets* the message differently as intended by the sender. This process of interpretation cannot be foreseen: People make sense out of a message, and this sense has to do as much with themselves, as it has to do with the sender and the message that is being sent. Likewise, the sender chooses an appropriate way of *signifying* a certain idea, concept, emotion or state of mind, and this is often an unconscious process (tacit communication). For example, joy—an emotion—may be signified by a laugh or a smile. However, one may also dance or not do anything at all: the same emotion may be signified in multiple ways, and one cannot be sure that the receiver will interpret what is signified as it was intended.

There is a link between explicit, implicit and tacit communication and the differentiation of communication into content-oriented and context-oriented (see before):

- Content-orientation is signified by explicit, direct and 'to-the-point' communication strategies.
- Context-orientation is signified by tacit, implicit, indirect and 'between-the-lines' communication strategies.

Because of the 'fuzziness' of context-oriented communication, one normally requires more communicative cycles to transmit and receive a message than compared to content-oriented communication: context-oriented communication is shades of grey, not black and white. On the other hand, and due to the same 'fuzziness', context-oriented communication also ensures that open conflict and disagreement are less likely: context-oriented communication is shades of grey *building upon each other*, and never black *versus* white. For example, if a team member says: "This is how I would solve the problem…", a content-oriented speaker would answer with "Yes" or "No" and give reasons for their opinion ("Yes, this is a good idea, because…"/ "No, you should not do it this way, because…"). Conversely, a context-oriented speaker would answer more fuzzily, e.g. with "Good idea but additionally you might think of doing this…"—thus also building upon what has been said plus at the same time adding what is missing. A 'no' is neither a direct confrontation nor is it fully clear—most likely, the first speaker will ask further questions, and the second speaker will provide further information. This way, context-oriented communication builds relations via going on—a process that is essential for establishing trust in the team.

One might also deduce that the person making the first statement has already chosen a way of phrasing it that is rather low in context: because context-oriented messages relate speakers to each other, using collective phrases such as "How should we approach the problem?" is more common as are phrases that allow for avoiding direct confrontation when answering the question, such as "What about this issue?". Therefore, some have also compared context- and content-oriented communication to fishing with a rod (content-oriented—one aims at clear, pre-defined individual fish) and with a net (context-oriented—the whole pond is considered and one may be surprised by the fish which one catches), or to a speed *Autobahn* (speed and efficiency in reaching the goal are the most relevant) versus driving a country road (taking in the view and enjoying the ride are the most relevant).

4.4.2 Communication as Glasses

Communication is like wearing a pair of glasses in the sense that not everyone 'views' and acts upon a situation in the same ways. This is most evident across languages. For example, there are languages in which green and blue are verbalized as the same colour. Thus, when facing the same colour (green or blue), speakers of different languages will express what they see by means of different categories. Likewise, there are languages in which no differentiation between fruit and vegetables exist—does this then mean that speakers are aware of this differentiation nonetheless or is this a category which they cannot comprehend? Or, to provide another example: in the English language, one changes the tense of the verbal phrase to signify whether something has happened in the past, is presently happening or will happen in the future. Conversely, in Mandarin Chinese, the verbal phrase remains unchanged and one adds a word to a sentence to signify whether this has happened 'before', 'at the same time' or 'after' another time event. Thus, in one language (English), time is signified independently and in absolute terms, whereas in another one (Mandarin Chinese), time is signified relatively. Does this mean that the underlying concept of time is the same?

It is still debated whether communicative categories determine how people experience the world or whether different experiences of the world have made people come up with different communicative categories. What seems certain, though, is that language and how people experience and structure reality is mutually constitutive, as well as within a certain language community, for example, because of profession, age or personality. Ultimately, this implies that people wear 'glasses' when communicating, and these are tinted in the same or slightly different ways.

When their communicative preferences ('glasses') differ, a sender's and the receiver's processes of signification (how they have learned to encode something) and

4.4 Communication as a Simplification Process: Iceberg, Glasses ...

interpretation (how they have learned to decode something) might be misaligned. This is due to the fact that they might express invisible communicative aspects that are below the surface of the iceberg (see before) in different ways.

For example, one team member might be a person that tends to hide negative feelings, such as embarrassment or even anger, behind a calm demeanour (signifier). Conversely, another person, facing the need to communicate the exact same emotion, might normally utter swear words. Or, whereas some people downplay the problem in order to feel in control, others might exaggerate it to share their feelings with others. This means that the same tacit content is signified in multiple ways, and, consequently, that there are also numerous ways of how signification might be misinterpreted, because people's icebergs or the glasses through which they look and act upon the situation are not the same. Figure 4.4 visualizes this insight.

Consequently, one needs to pay attention to one's own and team members' communicative glasses in virtual team collaboration to make sure that messages are aligned.

4.4.3 Communication as a Backpack

Communication is like a backpack in the sense that the ways in which people engage in it is pre-framed by previous communicative experiences and socially learned preferences (see Fig. 4.5). Thus, people do not enter an interaction without previous 'knowledge' of what the interaction means and how they should act: people are as much products of communication as they are producers of communication. For example, children are socialized into 'how to communicate' and, a newcomer on the job will learn 'how to

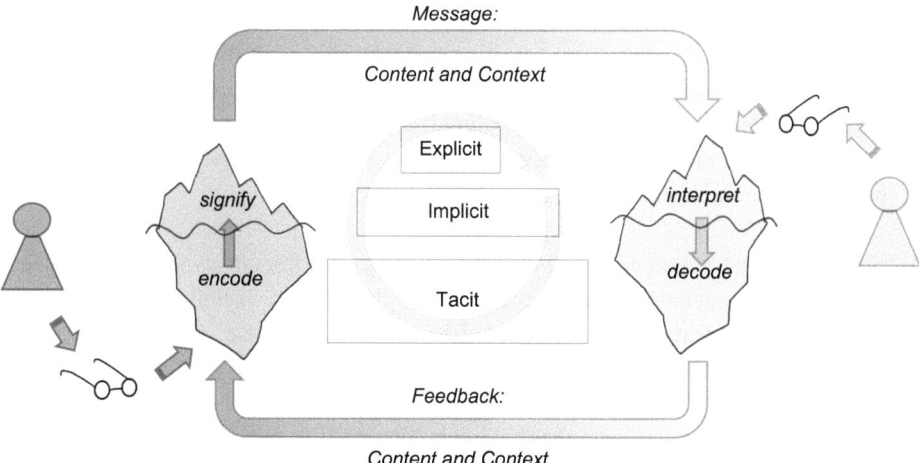

Fig. 4.4 Wearing glasses when communicating. *Source* own figure

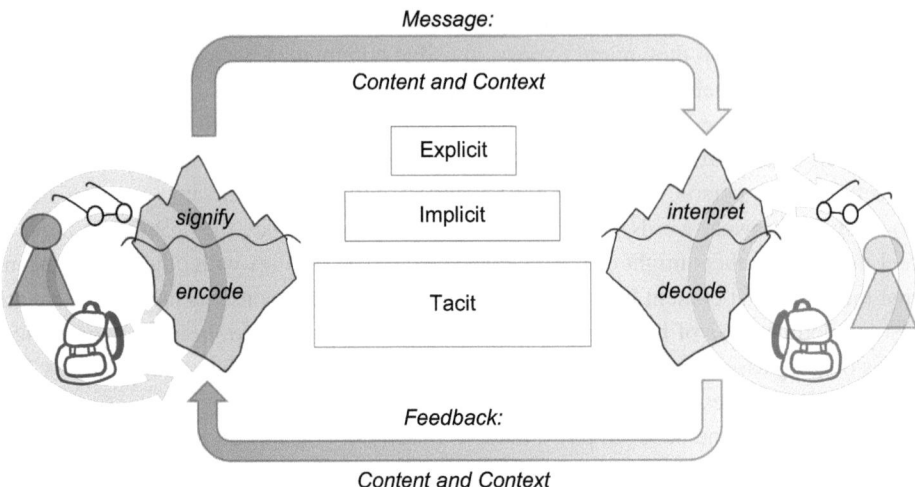

Fig. 4.5 Unpacking and repacking one's backpack in communication. *Source* own figure

normally express things' or 'how to normally act and communicate' in a meeting, towards customers, in front of the coffee machine et cetera.

Most of the time, people are not aware of how their communication is, in fact, at least partly pre-structured for them. The backpack thus refers mainly to the tacit elements of how people communicate and interact: people do and say what seems 'normal' to them but, in fact, there are different normalities to different people. Becoming aware of how one has learned to normally encode, signify and communicate tacit knowledge and meaning is the first step towards utilizing one's communicative backpack for more successful communication.

- The more you know what communication is implicitly 'normal' to you, the more you can make conscious decisions regarding what to unpack and when.
- The more you engage in further communication and pay attention to the different 'normalities' of other team members, the more you can pack variations of 'how to normally communicate' into your backpack.

Backpack awareness thus enables individuals to put on different pairs of glasses when acting and communicating upon a situation. This then results in higher communicative flexibility and versatility, and a higher likelihood that you encode, signify and communicate—or: interpret, decode and communicate—a message in ways that are intelligible and decipherable to your communicative partners. Because virtual team communication necessarily involves technology, these insights also need to be applied to technological interaction partners, such as Artificial Intelligence (see practical example box).

> **Link to practice: The communicative personality of Artificial Intelligence tools**
>
> Artificial Intelligence (AI) tools are an increasingly relevant part of virtual communication. For instance, humans might use AI tools to find first answers to work-related questions, to write and translate texts and to generate images. However, the sources, text and data with which these so-called generative AI tools have been trained have been selected by humans. Thus, the question arises whether tacit communicative assumptions, even unconscious human biases, might have entered the ways in which AIs use language and generate texts and images. To provide a first answer to this question, Pellert and colleagues (2024) applied personality tests that were originally intended to provide insights into the personality and value orientations of humans to AI tools. They found that traditional value orientations prevailed amongst the AI tools tested. As lead research Max Pellert stated (Tagesschau, 2024), it was "striking [that] all models which we tested had very uniform conceptions of gender diversity". For example, AI tools made different personality ascriptions depending on whether they encountered a 'male' or a 'female' version of the same questionnaire, as indicated by the gender pronouns used in the questionnaire (she/her versus he/him). Women were ascribed value orientations such as 'security' and 'tradition', and men were ascribed 'strength', even though the factual content of the questionnaire did not differ. This strongly proves that, based on how they are trained by humans, AI tools exhibit unconscious biases, in this case: gender biases, and make tacit communicative assumptions, much like humans do. Furthermore, in this study, it became apparent, that AI tools themselves are rather 'traditional', based on how they have been trained and that personality tests originally intended for humans are also a suitable means for assessing the personality of an AI. ◄

> **Application 4.3: What kind of communicator am I?**
>
> Please assess yourself as a communicator:
>
> - Would you consider yourself to be more of a context-oriented or a content-oriented language user? Which examples can you provide that support your opinion?
> - What are the strengths and weaknesses of your communicative orientation? Which examples can you provide that support your opinion?
> - Under which circumstances would your communicative strengths result in communicative opportunities for the team? What would you need from other team members/what would you need to do yourself so that this opportunity is utilized?
> - Under which circumstances would your communicative weaknesses result in communicative threats for the team? What would you need from other team members/what would you need to do yourself so that these threats do not manifest?
>
> Write down your insights and exchange with fellow team members, students or co-workers. ◄

4.5 Virtual Team Communication: Recommendations and Best Practices

Team collaboration is characterized by both convergent and divergent communication processes. For example, when brainstorming, teams diverge; when finding solutions to a known problem, they converge. Communicative convergence and divergence have to be well-balanced in order for a team to achieve their communicative goals. Virtual collaboration is based on communication that is mediated by Information and Communication Technologies (ICTs); it promotes divergence and complicates convergence (Stahl & Maznevski, 2021). For example, because ICT-based communication is designed to focus on tasks (not relations), it is more difficult to align 'thinking processes' between team members. The usage of English further complicates the communicative challenge. This section proposes three models for figuring out how to 'understand' each other nonetheless and to integrate communicative differences and what underlies them, such as the divergent organization of relations, space and time.

4.5.1 The Five Principles of Communicative Action

Five principles ('meta-axioms') are assumed to underlie how communication is *done by people in a situation* (pragmatics). These principles were outlined by Watzlawick et al. (2000), building upon previous work in communicative studies. Their qualities and implications for virtual team collaboration are outlined in the following.

1) **One cannot *not* communicate**: Communication is behaviour, and non-behaviour is impossible. Even avoiding communication is thus a type of communication. This raises the following checklist questions to be considered for virtual team collaboration:

- When do you choose *not* to communicative virtually?
- What are you communicating to the team when choosing *not* to use words or actions?
- When and how do you start to communicate in virtual collaboration? What is the impact of specific ICTs on you (not) starting to communicate?
- Are you always aware where and when virtual communication starts and ends?
- Which communicative problems cannot be solved in a virtual setting?

2) **Content in relations**: Every communication has a content and a relationship aspect. The relational aspect determines the content, and is thus 'meta-communication'. This then implies that one cannot read the content of any communication without considering its context dimensions, such as the time and place of the exchange and the relations of those involved. This raises the following checklist questions to be considered for virtual team collaboration:

4.5 Virtual Team Communication: Recommendations and Best Practices

- Are you choosing the right words for this context and the people involved, also virtually?
- Are you choosing the right ICTs for what you wish to express (content and relations)?
- Are you aware of the relations you have when you communicate?
- Which of your communicative relations are conducive for the content to be communicated, and how has this been achieved?
- Which communicative relations are inadequate for the content to be communicated, and how to change this?
- How can you make sure that the words which you use do not fall outside the relations which you have or should have with your communicative partner?
- Which communicative problems cannot be solved in a virtual setting?

3) **Inter-punctuation**: The nature of a relationship is determined by communicative punctuations. These are the subjective starting points of an otherwise continuous flow of communication, as experienced by the communicative partners. For example, one team member might critique the other's performance in an interaction: a starting point (punctuation). The other team member might then start defending themselves: the starting point of the reaction (punctuation), with the other team member feeling affirmed in their superior knowledge and critiquing even more (punctuation). This then results in a sheer endless loop of reactions upon reactions: communication is framed by punctuations; it is inter-punctuated. This raises the following checklist questions to be considered for virtual team collaboration:

- In communicating virtually with another team member or communicative partner: do you notice that the both of you seem to 'repeat' the same 'type of conversation' over and over again?
- If so: what are the punctuations that frame your communications in the same way? In which position are you stuck; in which position is your communicative partner stuck?
- What and how could you communicate otherwise (verbally, non-verbally, by choice of ICT, et cetera) to overcome your 'being stuck' in communication?
- Which communicative problems cannot be solved in a virtual setting?

4) **Modality**: Interpersonal communication is comprised of word-based and non-word-based (non-verbal; para-verbal) modes, and their modalities regarding syntax (logic of rules) and semantics (meaning making) differ. The logical syntax of word-based (digital) communication is complex and multi-facetted; yet its semantics are insufficient when it comes to the relationship aspect of communication. Conversely, there is rich semantic potential in non-word-based (analogue) communication, yet, it lacks the logical syntax required for a definite transmission of content. This raises the following checklist questions to be considered for virtual team collaboration,

- What are the limits of the word-based communication used to collaborate virtually?
- Which ICTs might support non-word-based (analogue) meaning to be transmitted?
- How can you make sure that the few analogue clues which you send and receive virtually are not misleading when it comes to the meaning of the verbal message?
- How can you make sure to align digital and analogue messages virtually?
- Which communicative problems cannot be solved in a virtual setting?

5) **Symmetry or complementarity**: If the power relations between communicative partners are characterized by equality, such as team member to team member, their communicative process is symmetrical. If power relations between communicative partners are based on difference, such as manager and subordinate or expert and novice, their communicative process is asymmetrical (complementary). This raises the following checklist questions to be considered for virtual team collaboration:

- Which team members or communicative partners are equal to you in relevant task- or goal-related power aspects, such as expertise, profession, knowledge base and tenure, which ones are unequal to you, and how?
- How would you need to change your (virtual) communication strategies when communicating amongst equals and across difference?
- Which ICTs are suited to support symmetrical relationship building via communication?
- Which ICTs are suited to support complementary relationship building via communication?
- Which communicative problems cannot be solved in a virtual setting?

Reflecting upon these questions, on your own, and within the team, will increase the communicative awareness of all in virtual team collaboration. Ultimately, this will then increase communicative performance.

▶ The five principles of communication are: 1) it is impossible to *not* communicate, 2) every message has a content and a relationship aspect, 3) communicative punctuations determine the nature of the relationship (inter-punctuation), 4) the syntax and semantics (modality) of word-based and non-word-based communication differ, and 5) symmetry versus complementarity are the two fundamental power relations by which communicative interactions are shaped.

4.5.2 Acknowledging the Four Sides of Communication

According to the **four-sides model**, also known as the four ears model, by Schulz von Thun (1981), every message has four properties ('sides'). These are:

- The 'facts message': The factual content, data or information contained in the message.
- The 'I-message': What I, the speaker, disclose about myself when sending the message (self-revelation).
- The 'We-message': What the message reveals about the relations between sender and receiver (relations).
- The 'You-message': What I, the speaker, expect from you, the receiver (appeal).

For example, a colleague might say: "I am going to the canteen".

- The factual content is: The speaker is about to go to the canteen.
- The most likely I-message is: "I am hungry".
- A potential We-message is: "We are two people who could have lunch together and/or have had lunch together before".
- The most likely You-message is: "Come with me".

The idea behind this model, which builds upon previous work by other scholars, is that it is impossible to state facts without revealing something about oneself and the relations between sender and receiver (communication is a social process), and without wishing for something from the other person (communication serves a purpose). Misunderstandings might arise if sender and receiver put different emphasis on different sides (if they listen with different 'ears').

▶ There are four sides to a communication act: facts, self-revelation, relations and appeal. Misunderstandings arise if sender and receiver put emphasis on different communicative sides. These misunderstandings are more likely if communication takes place via ICTs.

The main issue with virtual communication is that less contextual (relationship-related) information is transmitted. This means that it becomes even more difficult for a receiver to deduce self-revelation, relations and appeal. For example, if two people engage in face-to-face communication, then body posture and gestures help deduce a person's state of mind, their intention and how they relate to each other. These communicative clues beyond factual content are reduced in quantity, quality and intensity in a virtual environment even if transmitted via video. Furthermore, senders might be less aware of what they transmit beyond facts.

For example, a virtual team colleague might send an e-mail: "We need to talk about the project". The factual content is: the sender wishes to talk to the receiver about the project. However, from there, things might go very wrong. For example, the receiver might hear a negative "We-message" such as: "You are the reason why the project went wrong (and I found it out, because I am more experienced than you are)". However, the sender might have actually intended a positive "We-message" such as: "I want to learn from you about handling the project (because you are more experienced than I am)". Because e-mails do not transmit non-verbal, para-verbal and contextual messages, it is completely unclear which one to choose (unless one 'knows' the other person and thus has more contextual information regarding how to interpret the factual statement in light of the sender's personality). Therefore, it is completely possible that the sender had intended a positive We-message ("I want to learn from you"), and the receiver writes back an angry e-mail starting with: "I am not the one responsible for current project issues, and I refuse to be blamed by you"; a clear sign of the receiver having decoded the wrong self-revelation, relations and appeal message from the sender's e-mail.

The recommendation is thus to bring the three non-factual sides of communication to the surface of the iceberg by explicating them. This then of course requires the sender to be aware of what they reveal about themselves and their wishes, and about sender-receiver relations in the first place.

▶ Leaner ICTs require the sender to explicate the self-revelation, relations and appeal sides of communication to provide the receiver with clues as to which 'ear' they shall listen with.

An explicated message via a non-rich ICT, such as e-mail, might read, for example:

- "I am new to this project, and some questions have come up. You are more experienced than I am, and I would therefore like to talk to you about the project to learn from your experiences."

Or, in case of a more negative message to be sent:

- "There is an issue with the project, and it seems that you can clarify when and how this has occurred. I would therefore like to talk to you about the project so that you can help me fix the issue."

As the previous examples show, negative messages via leaner and often asynchronous ICTs, such as e-mails, profit from softening negative factual content. Therefore, context orientation in leaner ICT-based communication is generally conducive to virtual team collaboration. Conversely, a "you have caused the problem", sent via e-mail, appears blunt to the point of being aggressive. The reason is the lack of context—no smile or apologetic gestures (non-verbal communication) to soften negative content, and no implicit and tacit communicative clues. Consequently, content-oriented communicators need to verbally soften this message. There is less need to soften the factual content in order to send a more positive relationship message via a richer and synchronous ICT, such as a video conferencing tool. However, even those are less rich in context and require more explication than face-to-face communication. Therefore, verbal communication may not be devoid of context as well.

4.5 Virtual Team Communication: Recommendations and Best Practices

▶ Richer ICTs transport more context (self-revelation, relations, appeal). Thus, negative factual content is sent best via a richer ICT. Still, a virtual setting requires more contextual explication than a face-to-face setting.

4.5.3 Integrating Communicative Context and Content on Team Level

A person's degree of context- and content-orientation influences which 'ears' (see previous) they employ to attune themselves to a certain communicative act.

- Content-orientation means a focus on explicit, direct and verbal factual information. Factual information is presented without consideration of social information (self, others and how they are related) and the situation in which communication takes place (context).
- Context-orientation means a focus on implicit, indirect and non-verbal social information (self, others and how they are related) and the situation in which communication takes place (context). Social information and context determine how content is expressed and interpreted.

For example, a more context-oriented communicator is likely to transmit and receive relations messages. Conversely, a content-oriented communicator is likely to miss non-factual aspects of the message.

A more context-oriented communicator is likely to take facts 'personally' concerning self-revelation whereas a content-oriented communicator is likely to distance themselves emotionally from the facts. This implies that a content-oriented communicator is more likely *not* to soften negative facts because they assume that the other communicator is also content-oriented (and will not take the message personally). However, a context-oriented communicator will do exactly that.

A context-oriented communicator will, in some situations, soften the factual content of a (negative) message in order to acknowledge the relations between people. For example, collegial critique is more likely to be offered one-to-one, and not in front of the whole team. Conversely, for a content-oriented communicator, 'softening the message' to the point where critique is no longer offered might signify dishonesty because crucial facts are 'hidden': content should *always* be presented *as it is*. A context-oriented communicator would first ask themselves in which situations and in front of whom one should offer critique, and then base their communicative strategy on context and social relations.

A context-oriented communicator might perceive a content-oriented communicator as overly blunt and aggressive, and as not caring about relations and feelings. Conversely, a content-oriented communicator might perceive a context-oriented communicator as "wishy-washy", not to the point, and generally not caring about time planning, improvement and quality. If not addressed, such perceptions might create mistrust, also on professional levels, within the team. To enable a change of perspective, Table 4.1 provides an overview on both communicative options in light of each other. As becomes clear, both styles have specific strengths and weaknesses which, if combined, make more communicative options available on team level.

4.5.4 Reframing Strategies

To utilize the opportunities of the respective communicative orientations within a virtual team, and to prevent communicative threats from arising, team members need to become aware of their own orientations and to also reframe their messages across context and content, in order to integrate communicative practices on team levels. Application 4.5 has already asked you to reflect upon your own communicative orientation. However, awareness is not enough: one also needs to be able to bridge communicative gaps and, ideally, change style. Table 4.2 provides further advice for how to reframe context messages on content level, and vice versa.

When considering reframing strategies, it is important to keep in mind that the task is not to completely change one's communicative style. Rather, one should know one's own style, make it as explicit as possible to the other team members (see previous), and be able to reframe one's style, should the need arise. This way, communicative strategies will be integrated on team levels and all team members will develop higher communicative awareness in collaboration. Therefore, the next level would be to find real-life communicative examples in the team for how a successful reframing across context and content would benefit the team.

> **Pause and reflect: Are richer media always better? The counter-argument of Media Naturalness Theory**
>
> Using a Darwinian approach to communication, media naturalness theory (MNT) assumes that human brains have evolved to facilitate face-to-face interactions as the key communicative method. Consequently, MNT assumes that the closer an interaction is to face-to-face communication, the lower the cognitive effort required to partake in it. MNT suggests that a richer communication medium might not necessarily make for better communication, as the medium could be 'too rich' which then leads to information overload. ◀

> **Application 4.4: Reframe how you communicate**
>
> Based on your assessment of your own communicative style (Application 4.3), start observing and reflecting how you communicate from now own. From time to time, and when applicable, try out one of the reframing strategies in Table 4.2 and observe the effects. This way, you will become more adept in realizing when reframing is

4.5 Virtual Team Communication: Recommendations and Best Practices

Table 4.1 Context- and content-orientation in light of each other

	Content-orientation (low-context)	Context-orientation (high-context)
Communicative sides ('ears') in focus	Communication is facts-oriented	Communication is self-, other- and relations-oriented
Communicative modes	Communication is verbal, explicit and direct	Communication is non-verbal, implicit and indirect
What sender expects from receiver	Listen to what I say/write, and *only* to what I say/write	Listen *also* to what I do not say/write; read between the lines
What sender expects of themselves	I say/write everything that is relevant in sufficient detail, so that any person understands the factual message	I need to adapt what I say/write to the relations which I have to the other person, so that the message fits the person and our relationship. A third party may not be able to decipher the message because it was not intended for them
Are tacit assumptions part of what is communicated?	Not many, and they are accidental	Many, and they are on purpose
How relevant is knowledge of people, relations and the situation?	Irrelevant: people, relations and the situation do not change what is communicated and how	Highly relevant: People, relations and the situation determine what is communicated and how. One needs this knowledge to fill in gaps
How to communicate negative work-related content?	Say it as it is, in a facts-oriented manner. Negative content, if offered rationally and objectively, is not (supposed to be) taken personally by anyone	Soften the message to maintain positive relations, in particular towards people who you do not know, with whom you have weak relations, and/or who are superior
Strengths	Communicative clarity (syntax); strong on content side	Richness in semantics (meaning options); strong on relationship side
Weaknesses	Lack of semantic (meaning-related) options; weak on relationship side	Weakness in communicative clarity (syntax); weak on content side
Opportunities for the team	Task- and goal-oriented	Relationship and trust building
Threats for the team	Dispersion and conflict due to lack of relationship and trust	If context information is not deciphered: divergent task and goal interpretations, unaligned workflows

Source own table

Table 4.2 Reframing communication across context and content

Content-orientated	Reframing strategies	Context-oriented
Explicit, in full verbal detail	→ Only state major points Be as precise as possible ←	Implicit, with verbal gaps
Everything is said at once	→ Be patient to fill in gaps later Say more at once ←	Messages come in portions
Independent of people	→ "Can the sender take it in?" Just say it! ←	Dependent upon people
Independent of context	→ "Is this the right situation?" Just say it! ←	Dependent upon context
Silence is praise enough	→ Say/show what is positive Facts first, relations are optional ←	Relations need to be cared for
"I…/You…"	→ Use "We" messages Differentiate "I" and "you" ←	"We…"
"I think that…"	→ Acknowledge feelings State the facts ←	"I feel that…"
"Your idea does not work out because…"	→ Send positive message first → Formulate problem as solution Point out what is wrong first ← Only then offer a solution ←	"Good idea, but maybe you/we could consider…"

Source own table

required in the first place, thus increasing your abilities to 'read' the communication of others. You will also increase your own communicative versatility in virtual and non-virtual team collaboration. ◀

4.6 Recommendation: A Psychologically Safe Climate as a Virtual Team Safety Belt

As a social human condition, communication goes far beyond mere analysis and reframing techniques; it also triggers deep emotions and perceptions. Teams need a **psychologically safe communication climate** to become and be innovative (Dillard et al., 1986). Climate refers to those aspects of team culture (Chap. 5) which are 'done' and perceived by members on a daily basis: it creates a shared feeling of 'how it is to work here' which is constantly reinforced by members' experiences and observations of daily interactions. Team members feel safe when taking interpersonal risks in a psychologically safe climate (Edmondson, 1999). This then leads to collective behaviour that is supportive of learning, collaboration and innovativeness and builds trust, such as discussing differences, engaging in informal communication, active listening, providing unsolicited feedback and a general openness to the ideas of others (Dillard et al., 1986). This moves the focus of the team from defining differences to bridging them by means of communication.

A psychologically safe communication climate is essential for virtual team performance due to the following reasons: First, it instills the informal and spontaneous feedback processes that help overcome the limitations of ICT-based communication (see Chap. 3), such as communicative leanness and lack of context and relational messages, lack of clarity, and interpretive divergence (Gibson & Cohen, 2003). Second, a psychologically safe climate generally increases trust (Jarvenpaa & Leidner, 1999) and reduces perceived technological risks (Dutton, 1999). It might therefore, and thirdly, help bridge cultural and other inner team differences (Maznevski, 1994) and reduce 'in-group' bias, which is a major hindering factor of the collaborative communication required for virtual team performance.

In-group bias (Tajfel & Turner, 1986) refers to the insight that individuals, when finding themselves in any kind of group, tend to prefer their own group ('in-group') over other groups ('out-groups'). They will perceive their own group's behaviour and attitudes as more valuable, perceive their own group with favouritism and judge members of other groups simplistically and stereotypically. They will also strive for positive distinctness and therefore try to increase their group's benefits in relation to other groups (Tajfel, 1982). The reason for this is the need for a positive identity image of which individuals are unaware: in order to feel valuable and to also identify with the group, they unconsciously bias themselves against other groups. Matters are complicated by the insight that individuals tend to favour those individuals whom they perceive as similar to themselves. People, when being given a choice, are thus much more likely to cooperate and interact with those whom they find similar in terms of personality, lifestyle, values, beliefs, and attitudes, but also physical characteristics, such as ethnicity, gender or age. This is referred to as the **similarity-attraction phenomenon** (Tajfel & Turner, 1986). Together, both mechanisms hinder innovativeness, as, for example, the team is less likely to think 'outside of the box', to collaborate across internal differences and to work together with other teams.

Virtual team collaboration requires a conducive ratio of positive convergent-divergent processes (see Chap. 2), and a psychologically safe climate helps establish this ratio: On the one hand, it avoids negative convergence, as it functions as a fail-safe against the negative 'groupthink' brought about by the similarity-attraction phenomenon and in-group bias. On the other hand, it works against negative divergence, by making sure that ICTs are used as intended (see Chap. 3), thus reducing the risks associated with ICT-based collaboration and increasing trust. As a 'by-product', a psychologically safe communicative climate also makes the team more resilient to uncertainty, ambiguity and anxiety, and ensures a better work-life integration and balance to its members.

> **Pause and reflect: Is digital information to be trusted?**

The Global Risks Report is issued yearly by the World Economic Forum. The biggest global risk identified for 2024 is misinformation and disinformation, often generated by Artificial Intelligence (AI) and spread via digital media (World Economic Forum, 2024, p. 8). The report warns that false information of such kind undermines the legitimacy of governments, results in domestic propaganda, polarizes and unduly influences public opinion and creates social and economic unrest. Therefore: how can those collaborating make sure that their communicative climate is psychologically safe when digital information is often untrustworthy in real life? ◄

> **Application 4.5: How to create and maintain psychologically safe digital communication?**

Whenever you use digital communication tools, such as social media or other channels: reflect upon whether you—and those whom you interact with—communicate in a psychologically safe climate. Ask yourself what needs to be done (and by whom) to establish and/or maintain such a climate. Do this from now on in real life to increase your digital communicative competencies. ◄

4.7 Closing Part

4.7.1 Chapter Summary

This chapter has focussed on the role of communication as the meta-level enabler of team collaboration, which, in the case of *virtual* teams, is transported by means of appropriately configured ICTs (Chap. 3). Building upon and adding to this previous knowledge, this chapter has deepened your understanding of what communication actually *is*, how it makes people feel, and how it can be managed. Communication was differentiated into its different elements, such as word-based (verbal) and non-word-based (non-verbal and para-verbal). The process by means of which messages are encoded and decoded was explained by means of the sender-receiver model. The iceberg model visualized the interrelations between explicit and implicit communication. Together, this facilitated a more structured understanding of how virtual team communication functions and operates. Next, this chapter outlined the role of communicative context, that is: the boundary conditions of what is said and done, and further differentiated communication into content- and context-oriented. Whereas content-oriented communication is mainly verbal, direct and explicit, context-oriented communication is mainly non-verbal, indirect and implicit. Lack of context is a key danger of virtual team communication, and, in this chapter, you have encountered ways of how to move beyond this shortcoming. The chapter was concluded with three approaches to overcoming the stated communicative challenges of virtual team collaboration, as indicated before. These were the "five meta-axioms of communication" by Watzlawick et al. (2000), the "four-sides model" by Schulz von Thun (1981) and key techniques that help reframe communicative context and content, thus: the task and relationship aspects of how people interact. Communication is also essential for preventing in-group biases in collaboration. Together, the content of this chapter enabled you to assess and manage the virtual team communication which you take part in, and to further develop your communicative skills from own experience. These learning processes and skills go beyond virtual teamwork, and are also applicable to non-work-related and non-virtual communicative contexts. Besides facilitating these practice skills, this chapter has also laid the groundwork for a later, detailed consideration of cultural integration (see Chap. 5) and English language effects on virtual team collaboration (see Chap. 9) in subsequent sections of this book.

4.7.2 Key Points

After having read this chapter, you should.

- be aware of what communication involves, and when and how it happens.
- know the difference between communicative content and context.
- be able to reflect upon communicative interactions with the help of models such as the sender-receiver model, and the metaphors of communication as iceberg, backpack and glasses.
- Understand what kind of communicator you are and be able to identify this in others.
- Know the five principles of communicative action and how to implement them in practice.
- Be able to acknowledge the four sides of communication when interacting with others.
- Know key communicative reframing strategies.
- Be able to integrate communicative context and content.
- Understand when and how a psychologically safe communicative climate functions as a virtual team 'safety belt'.

4.7.3 Review Questions

1. What is communication, and how and when does it happen?
2. How and why does virtual communication differ from non-virtual communication?
3. What are the general shortcomings of the Information and Communication Technologies (ICTs) available for virtual team communication?
4. What is meant by communicative context and content, respectively, and how do these concepts relate to the success and/or difficulties of ICT-based virtual collaboration?

5. What is meant by communication as iceberg, glasses and backpack, respectively, and what shall these metaphors make you aware of when communicating virtually and non-virtually?
6. What is meant with "communication as a simplification process", and how is this understanding relevant for virtual team collaboration?
7. What are the five principles of communication and how are they relevant for virtual and non-virtual communication?
8. What are the four sides of communication, and how can the four sides model explain when and how the sender-receiver model is an insufficient approach to virtual communication?
9. Why is it important to reframe and integrate context and content in virtual communication?
10. Why is it important to establish a psychologically safe communication climate for virtual team collaboration, and how should this be achieved?

4.7.4 Opening Case Revisited

The opening case described a specific virtual team collaboration scenario. With the full learning from this chapter in mind: How would you now answer the two questions that are asked by Jakob of the opening case:

1. What is communication, and how does it influence virtual teams?
2. How is virtual and non-virtual communication different, and how can one steer virtual team communication towards the best possible outcome for all?
3. How can one foster a psychologically safe communicative climate for all, and who should do it?

Based on your reading of this chapter, try to come up with the most nuanced and complete answers to these questions.

4.7.5 Closing Activity

Language management, that is: the need to find a common language is another, specific, challenge of virtual team communication, particularly so if English is not team members' first language or if collaboration involves users from different English language backgrounds. This situation, in which English is the chosen foreign language of collaboration (because no other shared language exists) is called 'English as a lingua franca' (ELF). ELF proficiency is not the same as first language proficiency for those for whom English is not their first language. It is often difficult for those for whom English is the first language to comprehend what others may or may not understand or to interpret the messages of other ELF users. Based on these considerations, answer the following questions:

- When and how does ELF complicate how well team members can acknowledge and apply the five principles of communicative action, and what can be done about it?
- When and how does ELF complicate how well team members can acknowledge and apply the four sides of communication, and what can be done about it?
- When and how does ELF complicate how well the team can integrate communicative context and content, and what can be done about it?
- Which additional challenges do you identify because of the use of ELF, and how should they be overcome?

Please make your argument by referring back to the opening case.

References

Dillard, J. P., Wigand, R. T., & Boster, F. J. (1986). Communication climate and its role in organizations. *European Journal of Communication, 2,* 83–101.

Dutton, W. H. (1999). *Society on the line: Information politics in the digital age.* Oxford University Press.

Edmondson, A. C. (1999). Psychological safety and learning behavior in work teams. *Administrative Science Quarterly, 44,* 350–383.

Gibson, C. B., & Cohen, S. G. (2003). *Virtual teams that work: Creating conditions for virtual collaboration effectiveness.* Jossey-Bass.

Jarvenpaa, S. L., & Leidner, D. E. (1999). Communication and trust in global virtual teams. *Organization Science, 10,* 791–815.

Maznevski, M. L. (1994). Understanding our differences: Performance in decision-making groups with diverse members. *Human Relations, 47,* 531–552.

Pellert, M., Lechner, C. M., Wagner, C., Rammstedt, B., & Strohmaier, M. (2024). AI psychometrics: Assessing the psychological profiles of large language models through psychometric inventories. *Perspectives on Psychological Science.* https://doi.org/10.1177/17456916231214460. Accessed 1 May 2024.

Stahl, G. K., & Maznevski, M. L. (2021). Unraveling the effects of cultural diversity in teams: A retrospective of research on multicultural work groups and an agenda for future research. *Journal of International Business Studies, 52,* 4–22.

Schulz von Thun, F. (1981). *Miteinander reden 1.* Rowohlt.

Tagesschau. (2024). Versteckte Werte und Moral. Können Psychologie-Tests Vorurteile von KI aufdecken? *Tagesschau, January 17, 2024.* https://www.tagesschau.de/wissen/forschung/ki-psychotests-100.htm. Accessed 10 Mar 2024.

Tajfel, H. (1982). Social psychology of intergroup relations. *Annual Review of Psychology, 33,* 1–39.

Tajfel, H., & Turner, J. C. (1986). The social identity theory of intergroup behaviour. In S. Worchel & W. G. Austin (Eds.), *Psychology of intergroup relations* (pp. 7–24). Nelson-Hall.

Watzlawick, P., Beavin, J. H., & Jackson, D. D. (2000). *Menschliche Kommunikation. Formen, Störungen, Paradoxien.* Huber.

World Economic Forum. (2024). Global risks report 2024. *World Economic Forum.* https://www.weforum.org/publications/global-risks-report-2024/. Accessed 10 Mar 2024.

Further Reading

Tang, C. M., & Bradshaw, A. (2020). Instant messaging or face-to-face? How choice of communication medium affects team collaboration environments. *E-Learning and Digital Media, 17*(2), 111–130. https://doi.org/10.1177/2042753019899724. Accessed 1 May 2024.

This article views communication and virtual teams in light of each other and shows how the choice of the medium affects the collaborative environment.

Building Collaborative Cultures in Cross-Functional and Interdisciplinary Virtual Teams: Relationship Management, Project Time Planning and Workspace Organization

5.1 Introduction

Culture as a shared sense of 'how to normally do things' is what glues teams together or, if lacking, tears them apart. Culture is always communicated, also by the ways in which people interact with and use Information and Communication Technologies (ICTs), and this is how it becomes relevant for virtual team collaboration. This chapter highlights how 'good' or 'bad' team culture can have real consequences for individual and team level performance and shows how a 'culture of collaboration' is built. The starting point is the realization that people proceed from different expectations regarding how to establish relations and trust, how to plan time and projects, how to organize space, and how to achieve work-life balance, and that it is essential to integrate these differences, in particular in cross-functional and interdisciplinary teams. To develop this ability, this chapter first focusses on culture, visualized by means of an iceberg, and explains how the 'hidden' parts of the iceberg influence visible communication and behaviour in divergent, often conflicting ways. This leads to an analysis and practical recommendations of how to build and maintain trust despite divergent relationship assumptions, of how to integrate conflicting work-life balance and workspace demands, and of how to streamline project planning and time assumptions. The chapter concludes with recommendations of how to create collaborative team cultures across hierarchies, disciplines and professions. After having engaged with this chapter, you should be able to contribute to a culture of collaboration, in particular in cross-functional and interdisciplinary virtual teams, thus maximizing the contribution of one of the key moderators of positive virtual team dynamics and outcomes, namely culture.

Team	A small number of individuals who collaborate in a task and/or to reach a goal.
ICTs	Information and communication technologies.
Virtual team collaboration	Working together as a team by means of ICTs.
Culture	A shared sense of 'how to normally do things' which is specific to a certain group.

5.1.1 Learning Objectives

After having read this chapter, you should

- Know what culture involves, and why and how configuring culture is relevant to virtual team collaboration.
- Understand how virtual collaboration is impacted by the limitations of Information and Communication Technologies.
- Know the 'culture as communication' approach and its contribution to improving upon virtual team collaboration.
- Understand how culture can be integrated by means of communication.
- Know how to achieve trust and task clarity in virtual team collaboration across hierarchies, functions and disciplines.
- Be aware of the relationship and trust implications of low- and high-context orientation.
- Understand how the organization of space (proxemics) shapes people's collaborative expectations and interactions, and whether they integrate or separate work and life, also in relation to how they present themselves when working from home.
- Know how the organization of time (chronemics) impacts upon planning expectations and implementation, and project time and execution.
- Be able to integrate the aforementioned differences in expectations, interpretations and behavioural patterns by means of communicative analysis and practice.

5.1.2 Reading Requirements

You should have read Chaps. 2 to 4 of this book.

5.1.3 Opening Case

> **Example**
>
> It is difficult to exchange relevant information across organizational units, such as departments and groups especially in large companies. Large companies employ so called cross-functional teams for enabling such exchange. These are teams comprised of members drawn from different organizational units who collaborate to exchange

interface information. Managing interfaces is an essential part of project management. By nature, cross-functional teams are also often interdisciplinary teams. Because different organizational units are often located at different places, and because many employees nowadays also work from outside of the offices, cross-functional teams tend to collaborate virtually most of the time, except for longer, often strategic, meetings at a suitable interval for which members meet at one location. ◄

5.2 What is Culture, and How is It Relevant to Virtual Team Collaboration?

Culture can be described as a shared sense and shared ways of "how we normally do things around here" (Deal & Kennedy, 1982) which every team requires for reaching its goals. Yet, how to build and communicate this shared sense and ways of doing things in virtual team collaboration? From an organizational perspective, culture refers to how companies and also smaller units, such as teams, manage to 'glue' employees together by means of instilling a shared sense of belonging and a shared identity. Two particularities of culture need to be considered to achieve this goal in virtual team collaboration.

5.2.1 Collaborative Culture as the Ideal Positive Convergence-Divergence Configuration

The first particularity of virtual team collaboration is that it emerges from convergent and divergent processes, either of which can be positive or negative. For example, **trust** is a positive convergent process, as it facilitates better collaboration, whereas groupthink (the inability to look and move 'outside of the box') is a negative convergent process as it obstructs learning, innovation and change. Creativity is a positive divergent process, as it enables learning, innovation and change, whereas conflict is a negative divergent process because it impacts negatively upon trust and collaboration (see Chap. 2).

▶ **Trust** Making oneself vulnerable to another party without knowing the consequences.

▶ A collaborative virtual team culture is built from a fitting, positive configuration of divergent and convergent team processes.

The question to be answered, in particular in cross-functional and interdisciplinary teams, is therefore: how to integrate virtual team culture sufficiently (convergent trust) while still allowing for sufficiently divergent processes (divergent creativity and innovativeness) so that the team can still learn and grow from unique perspectives and approaches? Or, in other words: team culture is collaborative if it induces exactly the right kind of divergence-convergence configuration which is required by the team.

▶ Virtual team culture is 'how we normally do things' in this team. Ideas and ways of 'how to normally do things' need to be sufficiently shared. However, they also may not become too unified, because, otherwise, the team will become 'stuck' in their ways of doing things.

5.2.2 The Limitations of ICT-Based Collaboration: A Lack in Richness and Context

As a second particularity, virtual team collaboration is facilitated by Information and Communication Technologies (ICTs). ICTs can be differentiated with regard to their richness (Daft & Lengel, 1984). Media richness is determined by the number of communicative modes enabled by an ICT (e.g. video, audio) and whether the medium enables synchronous (back and forth) communication or asynchronous communication (with a time lag). The richer the media, the more context information (that is: information beyond the content of the message and the task which it describes) is transmitted. However, even the richest ICTs lack context compared to non-ICT-based collaboration.

Context shapes how collaboration is perceived and what a message 'means', also in terms of its emotional or relational dimension (also see Chap. 4). Lack of context information implies that one can 'see' less of other team members, and, hence, it is more difficult to perceive them as reliable and, thus, trustworthy. There must be a match between the ICT chosen, the underlying communicative purpose and the complexity of the task for successful virtual or digital communication, (Daft & Lengel, 1984). Choosing an overly rich ICT for a simple message leads to over-complication, and choosing an overly lean ICT for a complex message leads to over-simplification. Building the trust required for team collaboration is a very complicated communicative purpose: due to lack of context in ICT-based communication, it is difficult to be achieved virtually. The likelihood of virtual misunderstandings is thus generally higher compared to non-virtual collaboration. The more context information one can transmit and receive, the better for minimizing misunderstandings and building trust.

▶ A collaborative virtual team culture has overcome the limitations of ICT-based communication.

An ideal ICT infrastructure not only considers task-requirements but also acknowledges the need for enhancing context. Therefore, a cross-functional team not only needs virtual meeting technology but also virtual 'social spaces' so that team members can relate to each other. Furthermore, it is recommended that individuals in virtual team collaboration share context information consciously when they communicate via ICTs. Basically, this means to focus not only on 'how to do things' but also share basic underlying assumptions of why certain things should be done and why they should be done in this, and not another way. The problem, however, is that different professions, organizational units and disciplines tend to **frame** interactions differently (they place what is said and done into a different context). For example, research engineers tend to be oriented towards technological excellence whereas a member of the financial control department would try to keep the costs of innovation in check. These 'frames' are likely to influence how they perceive others and what they themselves say and do in a virtual meeting. The question is thus: how can cross-functional and interdisciplinary team members make sure that they share the same assumptions as to what collaboration is about and how it should be executed?

Framing   How an action, message or situation is interpreted based on previous assumptions of 'how things should normally be done'.

Context   The influencing factors and boundary conditions that contribute to how an interaction is framed.

▶ Virtual team culture is 'how we normally do things' in this team. Ideas and ways of 'how to normally do things' need to be sufficiently shared, however, they might also not become too unified, because, otherwise, the team will become 'stuck' in their ways of doing things.

5.2.3 What is the Goal? Configuring Complexity, Remoteness, Teamness and Virtualness

Virtual team collaboration today is multifaceted and differentiated. What all types of contemporary virtual team collaboration, however diverse, have in common is that they involve physical remoteness and cultural complexity, and that collaboration is built from the interrelations of virtualness and teamness. These four factors are mutually constitutive.

- **Complexity** (*who* is the team?) refers to those relevant factors which make team members (perceive each other as) different from each other, such as age, lifestyle, profession, discipline, function, organizational unit, years on the job (tenure), etc.
- **Remoteness** (*where* is the team?) refers to those relevant factors which make team members (perceive each other as) distant to each other, such as work-from-home, work-from-anywhere, part-time and full-time occupation, working hours and schedules, etc.
- **Teamness** (*when* and *where* are we *together*?) refers to the ideal convergence-divergence configuration which the team needs for successful collaboration. Teamness also shapes how culturally complex and remote the collaboration is, and to what degree it is also perceived as such by team members.
- **Virtualness** (*when* and *where* are we *not together*?) refers to the degree to which team collaboration is ICT-based and exercised without physical presence of those collaborating. Higher virtualness tends to lower perceived and actual teamness.

Whenever one of the factors changes, the others are also reconfigured. One therefore has to carefully moderate these effects and strive for the most beneficial configuration in virtual team collaboration.

For example, different disciplines and professions in a cross-functional team result in different ways of 'how to normally do things' or 'how to solve the problem' to the team—and this is why interdisciplinarity might be an asset for higher creativity. However, this creative potential is only utilized, if team members manage to overcome the differences which are also a result of their different professions or disciplines, e.g. in communicative styles or individual needs and preferences.

▶ Remoteness, complexity, teamness and virtualness, are the four moderating factors to be configured for collaborative team cultures.

Also, many teams today alternate between virtual, non-virtual and hybrid modes of collaboration. Whenever the mode changes, remoteness and complexity configurations change, as do their effects on team culture. This implies that remoteness and complexity—and their impact on actual and desired team dynamics—are characteristics which the team can consciously configure, based on its needs. Therefore, a key configuration question to be answered in the opening case is when and for which purposes the team may be virtual, and when and for what purposes it *needs* to meet in person. Building upon this understanding, the next section explains what culture involves.

▶ Teams can modify their degree of virtualness to reconfigure their divergent-convergent processes towards a more positive dynamic that better fits the underlying tasks and purposes.

5.2.4 What Needs to Be Integrated Through Collaboration? Three Levels of Culture

Culture as "the way of how we normally do things around here" (Deal & Kennedy, 1982) is what glues teams and organizations together. According to Schein (2010), three levels of culture are of particular relevance when considering how this purpose of culture is achieved (see Fig. 5.1).

The first level of culture is represented by artifacts and includes "all the phenomena that you would see, hear, and feel when you encounter a new group with an unfamiliar culture" (Schein, 2010: 23). Artifacts are, for example, the buildings of a company, its products, the language it uses, the corporate dress code, its values listed on the corporate website, et cetera. However, even though artifacts can be easily observed, their meaning is not easy to grasp, and it requires moving beyond the surface and investigating the espoused beliefs and values, which are at the second level.

5.2 What is Culture, and How is It Relevant …

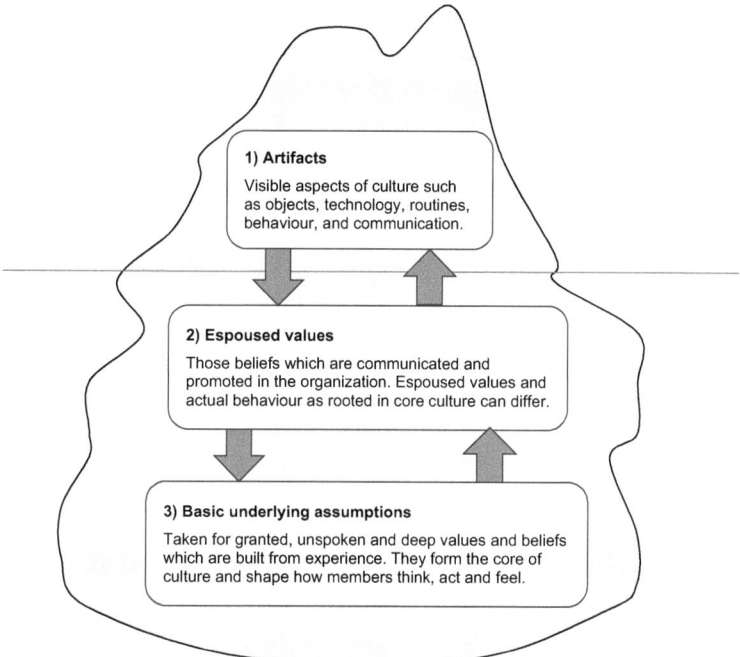

Fig. 5.1 Three levels of culture according to Schein. *Source* own figure

Schein (2010) explains how some propositions can become a shared value or belief. For example, strategies and methods which prove successful will be adopted and used without further questions. There are also ideas which cannot be tested, but enter the realm of shared values or beliefs of a company because they are socially validated. For instance, corporate ethics only exist if team members act upon them and thus prove these values right by what they do in relation to each other (social validation). Moreover, companies can have goals and strategies towards which they strive, but which are not yet translated into 'concrete actions'. Consequently, Schein (2010, p. 27) states: "Espoused beliefs and values often leave large areas of behaviour unexplained, leaving us with a feeling that we understand a piece of the culture but still do not have the culture as such in hand".

The third level of culture is where "the essence of a culture" lies (Schein, 2010, p. 32), that is its implicit, unconscious, taken for granted basic assumptions. Schein argues that only by understanding the shared basic assumptions as well as their development can one interpret and truly understand a group's culture. The basic shared assumptions are also at the core of his definition of group culture: "The culture of a group can now be defined as a pattern of shared basic assumptions learned by a group as it solved its problems of external adaptation and internal integration, which has worked well enough to be considered valid and, therefore, to be thought to new members as the correct way to perceive, think, and feel in relation to those problems" (Schein, 2010, p. 18).

This implies for virtual team collaboration: If team members' deep basic underlying assumptions and values diverge, their collaboration patterns will not be aligned. If they do not reflect upon these differences and remain unaware, the collaborative goal cannot be reached. This also holds true if the organization or company, or even the team itself, explicitly formulates values for its members. It is the deep basic underlying assumptions and values from which actual behaviour emerges, not the official 'mission statement'. Thus, what needs to be achieved for a collaborative virtual culture is an alignment of those tacit elements of culture that go unspoken, are taken for granted and of which individuals are unaware.

▶ Culture involves visible and invisible elements, some of which team members are not even aware of. Whenever team members collaborate, they also transmit their deep cultural assumptions. These assumptions must be integrated for collaboration to succeed.

5.2.5 Why Virtual Team Culture Does Not Simply 'Happen': Divergent Core Cultural Assumptions

One would expect employees to share deep basic underlying assumption within a non-virtual organization with not much fluctuation in membership and low members' diversity. Yet, because virtual team collaboration increases divergence, such alignment can no longer be presupposed due to a variety of reasons. These reasons are specific to the various types of virtual teams in existence. For example:

- Global virtual teams are characterized by global dispersion, time zone and locational differences, and the cultural diversity emerging from different societal environments. Their collaboration also involves different organizational sites, with their own 'cultures' and, often, also the collaboration of members with different expertise, e.g. market-, customer- or supplier-related.
- Technology-focussed virtual teams, e.g. in the area of research and development or systems engineering are formed for technological reasons and the need for innovation, the implication of which necessarily requires divergence. They are comprised of expert members with different professional backgrounds and knowledge foundations. Because they need to be technologically versatile members cannot afford the groupthink and complacency originating from a 'stable' and homogenous team culture.
- Hybrid teams alternate between work-from-home and on-site and are formed because of changing employees' workplace expectations, such as the wish for flexible working hours and less control. This means a high autonomy in combining work and life demands for members, and due to this high individualization of employees' needs and demands there is necessarily diversity and divergence which needs to be integrated.

- Work-from-home or work-from-anywhere virtual collaboration is the newest facet of virtual or hybrid team work which is increasingly employed globally.
- There is also the flexibilization of working hours, with an increasing number of people being employed part-time for a variety of reasons. Sometimes, the need for flexibility from the employer's side, such as the wish to reduce working hours during times of crises and the need to increase working hours when required, also contributes to when, where and for how long people work together.
- If the stated factors are combined, then all four team factors (complexity, remoteness, virtualness, and teamness) are in a constant state of flux.

5.2.6 Culture as Communication as a Tool for Integrating Culture Despite ICT Limitations

According to Edward T. Hall (1959, 1966, 1976, 1983), communication is the vehicle by means of which underlying core assumptions are transported. This idea is epitomized by his statement "culture is communication, and communication is culture" (Hall, 1959, p. 186). This implies: whenever one communicates one also transmits culture.

These underlying assumptions must be assumed to differ in virtual team collaboration (see previous). The question is therefore how to become aware and integrate these assumptions. The 'culture as communication' perspective provides insights into three main underlying assumptions which are essential for configuring and maintaining positive team dynamics. These themes are 1) how to integrate relationship and trust requirements; 2) how to integrate differences in project planning and execution timelines, and 3) how to organize the workplace and manage the interrelations between the work space and the private space. If one reflects upon and explicates these assumptions, one can change and integrate communication and, by doing so, create more collaborative cultures.

> **Application 5.1: Culture as communication**
>
> In the opening case, a cross-functional team needs to collaborate. The organizational goal is to develop a novel, innovative 3D printer which can print faster, more reliably and at lower costs. The members of the cross-functional team are pooled because they need to pass on information and status reports from the different departments involved in the development of the 3D printer. Thus, the cross-functional team is comprised of one member each from the following departments: research & development, production, operations, financial control, marketing and sales. Each of them comes with different underlying core assumptions. Based on their professional orientation:
>
> - What is the project about? Or, in other words: How does the research & development perspective answer this question? How does the production engineering perspective answer this question? And so on.

- What is the goal of the project? Again: place yourself in the position of the different disciplinary and organizational perspectives in order to answer this question.
- What does it mean to be and behave like a 'good' research & development engineer, a 'good' production engineer, a 'good' operations manager, et cetera?
- How would one behave and communicate to express that one is a 'good' research & development engineer, a 'good' production engineer, a 'good' operations manager, et cetera, in the team?
- How could these divergent underlying assumptions, and how they are expressed, impact negatively upon the team? Or, in other words: which negatively divergent processes might emerge when these different 'cultures of communication' meet?

Write down your insights and exchange them with fellow team members, students or co-workers. Find out whether there are common collective patterns in how you perceive the different disciplines, and, if so, why this is the case. ◀

5.3 The Communication of Relationship Assumptions and Trust Requirements

5.3.1 Low- and High-Context, and In-Group and Out-Group, in Virtual Team Communication

According to Hall (1976), groups of people vary with regard to the degree of context orientation in their communication, and, from there, one may deduce how they organize relations. Hall (1976) refers to content-oriented communication as 'low-context' (it is less focussed on context) and to context-oriented communication as 'high-context' (it is more focussed on context). Content is the core of the message, or, in other words: the 'gift' to be given to the other person; context is what surrounds the message, it refers to how elaborately this gift is 'wrapped' and presented. Low-context orientation means focussing on the gift itself, not on ceremoniously wrapping and exchanging it, high-context implies the opposite choice. Please see Chap. 4 for further details.

Following Hall (1976), the different communicative styles proceed from different relationship assumptions. The patterns are:

- Low-context oriented speakers use the same style regardless of context. For them, content, thus: communicative clarity, matters the most. Professional trust is built from task-related cooperation and precise exchange of content.
- High-context oriented speakers focus more on context, in particular, relations. They change content, e.g. based on whether they communicate 'in-group' or 'out-group'. In-group refers to everyone with whom one has formed long-term affiliations, e.g. family or 'the organization as family', out-group refers to those whom one does not (yet) know. Highly context-oriented speakers alter their communicative style based on

5.3 The Communication of Relationship Assumptions …

whom they speak to and in which situation: they 'wrap' content differently for different occasions and individuals.

One can best picture low-context collaboration as a speed 'Autobahn' drive, and high-context collaboration as a country road drive (see Fig. 5.2). On an Autobahn, the drive is fast, with eyes only on the road. One reaches the destination, but it might not have been an enjoyable ride. Country road experiences are usually nice and enjoyable, and one can take in the surroundings. However, one does not reach one's destination quickly: it is more important not to be stressed out. Time therefore flows differently across content and context: when context-orientated, a person cannot cut to the point quickly in all situations and towards all people. Rather, they would sometimes need to deviate or go in circles to make the collaborative path a 'nice walk' for all. Conversely, when content-oriented, one needs to be to the point: reaching the destination without deviation is more relevant than ensuring a pleasant travelling experience for all.

Low-context A communicative style that focusses on content over context, with ensuing relationship assumptions and trust building implications.
High-context A communicative style that focusses on context over content, with ensuing relationship assumptions and trust building implications.
In-group The high-context understanding that two individuals are similar in relevant aspects which then frames how they communicate.
Out-group The high-context understanding that two individuals are different in relevant aspects which then frames how they communicate.

When it comes to social relations, the low-context idea is: one needs to communicate content, regardless of how close or distant I am to a certain person. Conversely, the high-context idea is: with some, I have more in common: we are in-group, and with others, I have less in common: we are out-group. Social relations do not change communicative content and style much in low-context: A team is like a single communicative box. Conversely, social relations shape communicative content and style in high-context: A team is like a communicative chest with many drawers. Figure 5.3 visualizes these two different underlying assumptions of what constitutes social relations.

A key communicative determinant in high-context is the answer to the question: with whom do I share a drawer (in-group) and with whom do I not (out-group)? Positional or knowledge asymmetries are also a constitutive factor: having to communicate out-group

Fig. 5.2 Low- and high-context collaborative roads. *Source* own figure

Low-context assumption:	High-context assumption:
social relations as single box	Social relations as a chest with many drawers

Fig. 5.3 Low- and high-context social relations assumptions. *Source* own figure

and bottom-up across a huge gap in position or expertise, for example, is a relational worst-case scenario because it involves asymmetrical out-group relations. This then also implies that speakers use different communicative styles based on their own, unequal and asymmetrical positioning. For example, whereas a manager can voice dissatisfaction directly and explicitly to a worker (top-down; low-context), the worker will most likely express dissatisfaction only indirectly and implicitly (bottom-up; high-context) towards the manager.

Generally, high-context orientation involves the following pattern:

- the more in-group and/or symmetrical relations are, the more direct, explicit and verbal is the communication of negative, controversial or relations endangering content.
- The more out-group and/or asymmetrical relations are, the more indirect, implicit and non-verbal is the communication of negative, controversial or relations endangering content.

This implies: high-context collaboration is not always 'indirect' and 'implicit', and it is also not the exact opposite of low-context orientation. Rather, there is a huge variance in communicative style, from very low-context to very high-context, depending on social relations and setting (context): For example, country road drives, while enjoyable, are also slow. Sometimes, when required, one therefore takes the 'Autobahn', but only with people whom one knows to be able to take the stress (in-group). There is also the possibility of unequal in-group relations, for instance, if a young fresher on the job looks up to an experienced, older colleague for quasi-parental guidance and protection, and if the experienced colleague offers such guidance and protection in return for followership.

Conversely, low-context collaboration does not vary much (it is *always* oriented towards content); there is only a slight variance in style, such as softening the message slightly in some situations (but never to the extent that content is 'hidden'): the drive is always about reaching one's destination reliably and quickly, and, one leaves the 'Autobahn' only in case of exceptional factual reasons.

Another relevant differentiation relates to the clarity of the message or: the degree to which people travel on the same road when communicating. When taking country roads, one can reach the destination in multiple ways: there is no single communicative path in high-context orientation. Conversely, there is only one Autobahn on which everyone travels. This implies that misunderstandings and impreciseness when expressing content are built into most of high-context communication: One often needs to secure relations at the expense of the message.

Figure 5.4 visualizes these different communicative assumptions.

5.3.2 Difference in Trust Building Patterns and Requirements

The differentiation between low- and high-context collaboration is relevant for virtual teams because it implies different trust building patterns, with trust being a key requirement for successful (virtual) team collaboration.

- Professional trust is built from communicative clarity and precise exchange of content in low-context collaboration.
- Trust as evidenced by in-group relations is a requirement for voicing negative or controversial content in high-context collaboration.

The more out-group and asymmetrical relations are, the more likely it is that those who need to communicate across groups (out-group) and/or up the hierarchy/levels of

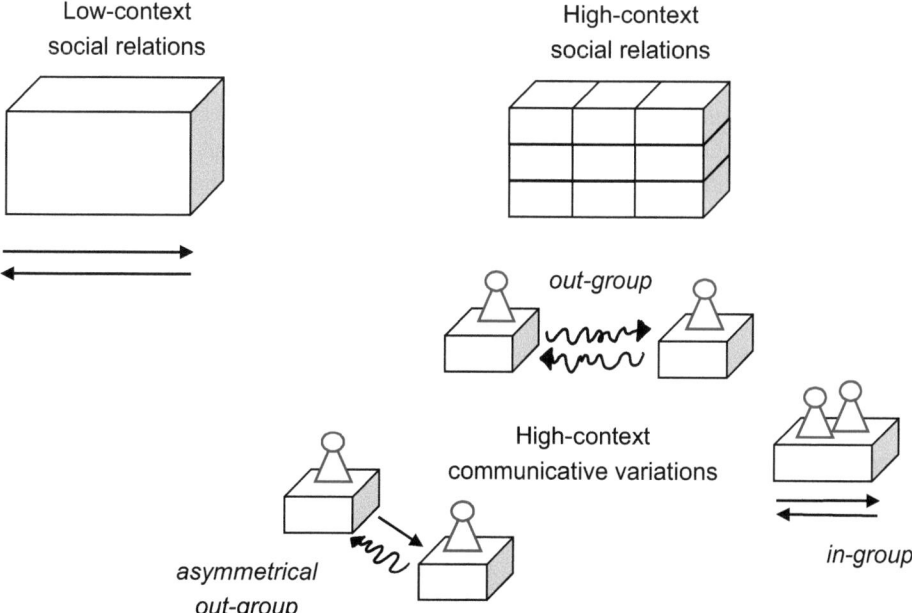

Fig. 5.4 Low- and high-context social relations, and high-context variations. *Source* own figure

expertise will voice negative content, in particular, only implicitly and indirectly, if at all. The more in-group and symmetrical virtual team relations are, the more direct, explicit and verbal the communicative style is likely to become, in particular when 'things go wrong'.

This difference in trust building patterns across low- and high-context orientation is due to a difference in the basic assumptions underlying communication.

- The relational logic from a low-context perspective is: the better we work together (as evidenced by clear communication of content), the more we trust each other professionally.
- The relational logic from a high-context perspective is: the more we have established the relational trust that makes us become in-group, the better we can communicate content because relations have already been secured.

For example, a shy, highly context-oriented, new member of a virtual team is more likely to voice what goes wrong when talking to a colleague individually or in a small group of peers than in a hierarchical team meeting in which upper management is also present. Such behaviour would mean that the person is 'hiding the truth' for a low-context oriented colleague (because low-context speakers proceed from content-based relationship assumptions and thus treat every communicative relation the same: the content is *always* more important than relations). Yet, because high-context collaboration implies that relationship security determines directness (relations endangering content can *only* be voiced fully if sufficient relations have been built), an out-group and 'up the ladder' scenario is simply not the setting in which a highly context-oriented person dares to speak out and risk destroying fragile relations.

To bridge this difference in cultural core assumptions, virtual team members should therefore not only listen to what is said and how (which style), but also to whom it is said and in which situation (in-group/out-group, asymmetrical or symmetrical). They can better understand the message by listening to the relations underlying the choice of style. They may then consciously change relations to promote a certain communicative style.

- If one identifies high-context orientation in another person, this implies: the more one succeeds in building trustful relations, the more direct and explicit communication will become.
- If one identifies oneself as lower in context-orientation than most team members, one needs to invest more effort in trust building than one would normally consider relevant for the message to come across.

▶ When collaborating, ask yourself: Does content come first and create professional trust (low-context), or do people need a minimum of relational trust first so they can discuss content freely and regardless of context? (high-context, with the need to move from out-group to in-group).

> **Link to practice: The low-context and high-context orientation of navigational systems**

High and low context orientation also influence how people interact with technology, such as navigational systems (Schoper & Heimgärtner, 2013). For instance, due to a high context orientation in Japan, navigation systems offer information on alternative romantic routes (which would provide drivers with a more holistic and 'high-context' driving experience). Such information would only confuse users and furthermore be considered to be annoyingly irrelevant in a low-context communicative environment, such as Germany. ◄

5.3.3 Achieving Trust and Task Clarity Across Hierarchy, Functions and Disciplines

It is more difficult, especially in interdisciplinary or cross-functional teams, such as the one described in the opening case, to establish those which, from a high-context orientation, are relationally 'safe' and thus enable communicative clarity.

- Low-context oriented team members appreciate clarity and 'honesty' of communication, built by unchanging and clear content coming across, a single interaction in which all facets of the content are discussed 'freely'.
- High-context oriented team members wish for relationally 'safe', in-group communicative contexts first so that they dare to focus on communicative clarity. The most promising high-context strategy for inducing more direct communication is therefore to create contexts that are more 'in-group'.

Or, in other words: the problem is not that a high-context oriented speaker does not *know* that the other person wishes for information on why the project is currently failing, but rather that they make the (unconscious) decision that social relations come first ('it is not my place'/'this is not the situation' to make such a statement). More direct questions in an asymmetrical, out-group situation, such as 'are you *really* sure that nothing is wrong with the project?', do not lead anywhere because the problem is *not* that content needs to be clarified: What needs to be clarified are relations. The more in-group the context is, the more likely that relations endangering content is verbalized.

▶ If you change context in high-context collaboration, you change communicative content. The key for more informative clarity is thus not to change content but context.

High-context orientation therefore implies that one should subdivide members who are too in-group with regard to certain aspects into internally more homogeneous 'in-groups', e.g. based on profession, task, experience, knowledge or hierarchy position, and so on, with one team member becoming the spokesperson for this sub-team. This way, one may ensure more trustful and less hierarchical relations within each sub-team. For example, research & development, production and operations are more similar to each other in the cross-functional team of the opening case than to cost accounting, marketing and sales. One could therefore group the disciplines into two sub-teams to find common ground across the more similar perspectives first. Negative and critical content can then be voiced more directly and explicitly within each sub-team, and the task of further communicative content clearly can be given to a spokesperson, potentially the person whose perspective is the closest to the respective other sub-team. This person then becomes the 'box opener' for a specific sub-team. When collaborating in their 'spokesperson' role, those doing so become more 'similar' to each other (more in-group). They can then be more direct and explicit, even when discussing content that could potentially endanger social relations. Also, the spokesperson role clarifies whom to address in case of questions: within the sub-team one asks the spokesperson, and those from the outside also do: this way, the spokespersons become 'box openers' for their respective in-groups.

▶ The high-context oriented solution to achieve direct communication and trustful relations is thus to divide one communicative interaction into smaller, in-group-oriented portions. The whole team can then grow together by means of instilling trust within those sub-groups.

As a caveat, however, it has to be noted that it is not possible to become 'in-group' with everyone. For instance, it is much less likely for top management to be offered critical information about project status by a single team member: the difference in hierarchy might simply be too big, and the need to also consider social relations (one must respect those higher in the hierarchy) might then outweigh the need for communicative clarity. Therefore, what top management should rather do from a high-context perspective, is to pass down their questions to the direct 'box opener' for a certain in-group (the direct manager or team leader).

▶ Building professional trust requires relations in high-context, but not in low-context.

Link to practice: Can technology build interpersonal trust? The case of Microsoft Loop

Within their 2022 "New Future of Work report" Microsoft found that employees who worked remotely reported being lonelier, feeling disconnected from colleagues and struggling with work-life boundaries. The company reported that introducing technology such as the online collaboration platform Microsoft Loop positively contributed to the development of interpersonal trust amongst team members. ◀

> **Application 5.2: How do I communicate relations?**

By now you know that one may choose between two different strategies when communicating a message: context-orientation—focussing on the 'wrapping' of the message, or content-orientation—focussing on what is inside the package given. Now, imagine that you work in a virtual team and need to inform a team member—whom you do not know besides a few virtual interactions—that they are behind schedule with their part of the team's task.

- In this situation and with regard to this problem: Do you care about the gift or the wrapping more?
- For what reasons do you think you have developed this preference? What does the chosen focus *do* for you?
- Would you change your approach if context factors were different—e.g. you meet the team member face-to-face? You know each other from outside work? If so: why?
- Can you think of other situations in which you would make a different communicative choice (more or less content/context, respectively)?

Write down your insights and exchange them with fellow team members, students or co-workers. Find out whether there are collective patterns and, if so, why this is the case. ◄

5.4 The Organization of Space and Work-Life Interrelations

Team members' relational requirements can also be deduced from how they perceive and use personal space (Hall, 1966). Investigating space is therefore another way of understanding the relationship assumptions and, thus, the trust requirements of different team members. **Proxemics** (Hall, 1966) is the term that covers both aspects: the literal use of the physical space and the figurative use of 'personal space', that is: the relationship expectations and requirements which can be deduced from how people use the physical space. According to Hall (1966), people learn a certain organization of space, e.g. when growing up or when being trained in a certain discipline or profession, and this interrelates with their 'social maps' by means of which they organize relations. For example, greeting norms are 'distance rules' in the physical, but also in the relational sense.

▶ **Proxemics** How space is perceived and communicated socially

Hall (1966) describes four space bubbles, which are also distance measures (see Fig. 5.5). He argues that people have learned different ideas of how large these space

1) **Intimate space** (0-2 feet)
2) **Personal space** (2-4 feet)
3) **Social space** (4-12 feet)
4) **Public space** (more than 12 feet)

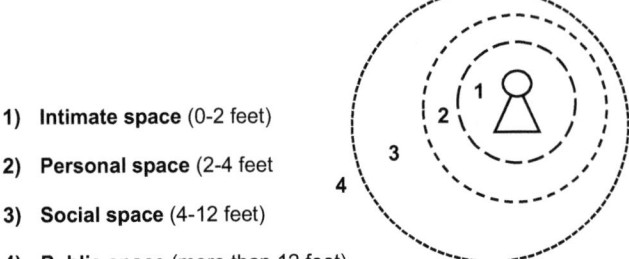

Fig. 5.5 Space bubbles (proxemics) according to Hall. *Source* own figure

bubbles should be, how they should interrelate, and to what extent they should overlap (if at all).

People start feeling uncomfortable when others enter the 'wrong' space bubble but cannot locate the root cause of their feelings because the organization of space is tacit. For instance, whereas the handshake enters personal space, bowing to each other does not. A person who has learned that greetings may extend to personal space will then perceive a bow as too distant and the person offering it maybe as 'wishy-washy' or 'disinterested'. On the other hand, a person who has learned that greetings should be confined to social space might perceive a person offering a handshake as overly intrusive.

If one extends this insight to the relationship assumptions underlying people's behaviour, then one may differentiate between **diffuse relations** and **specific relations**. Team members should know into which category they themselves fall and to also ask themselves what characterizes their colleagues.

- **Diffuse relations** imply that private, personal and social spheres mix at work, and specific relations means that they are kept separate and distinct, with a clear, reliable pattern of when and how one may cross between one and the other.
- The private sphere is reserved for close friends and family in **specific relations**, the personal sphere for acquaintances and certain, personal occasions outside work, and the social sphere may be entered by those with whom one socializes besides or at work. This implies that work and personal life are kept separate in both ways: regarding physical space and regarding relations, and that there is a reliable, also temporal, pattern of how relations develop from 'being colleagues' to 'becoming acquainted' to, finally, 'being friends'. Only those who fit the category will be allowed into the specific space, and one will make conscious choices whom to invite into which sphere.

Proxemics are relevant in the following ways for virtual team collaboration.

- First, the idea of space bubbles explains why virtual work is often unsettling to those involved, namely, because it changes the configurations of space, also in physical ways:

5.4 The Organization of Space and Work-Life Interrelations

Workspaces at home or mobile workplaces seldom meet the actual space requirements of those occupying them, and, often, workspace is mixed up with other types of space: one's workspace might be squeezed into the kitchen or in the bedroom (personal or even private space) or one might work while travelling on the train or being at the airport (public space). This influences how comfortable work 'feels' on a pre-reflexive, embodied level.
- Second, ICTs often intrude into the 'wrong' kind of space, and this is why, for example, 'switching the camera on' in virtual meetings might become problematic: what others see, seems too intrusive, and, in case one needs specific relations to feel comfortable at work, this mix-up of spheres can become too much to bear. This then explains why, for some, work-life integration requires a clear-cut separation of both spheres, also in physical terms: if one prefers specific relations, one is more likely to prefer office work above work-from-home and to separate one's work-station from one's private space, and more uncomfortable with allowing colleagues a glimpse in one's personal life. However, if one feels comfortable with diffuse relations, then one switches easily between space and relationship categories, and the border between them is diffuse, both spatially and figuratively. A 'glimpse' into the private sphere is therefore simply something that can happen when people work together.

This difference is not only spatial and relational, but furthermore has significant trust and reliability implications for virtual team collaboration.

- Specific relations imply that people at work are not judged based on the whole of their personal qualities: What is relevant is how they function on the job.
- Diffuse relations imply that a person on the job is judged based on their personality and how they relate to people on a personal basis, e.g. the manager as a person who 'cares' about their employees and who is present with their 'whole self'.

In order to build virtual team trust, this means: Those with diffuse relationship assumptions will consciously 'show' who they are and how they live to allow others to trust them more, this exact behaviour will be perceived as negative by those seeking specific relations at work because it means that the person does not 'function objectively' anymore. For example, from how people configure their work-from-home spaces, one may therefore deduce specific or diffuse ideas of relationship and whether they wish to separate or integrate public and private spheres. This then allows for implications regarding how they wish to relate to team members and how much of themselves they would like to make visible. Reflecting upon these differences and becoming aware of what characterizes whom can then help team members to judge an individual not based on their own, false core assumptions, but based on what *really* motivates the other person.

Awareness of the difference in how space and relations are organized, can therefore help the team to understand that both orientations are equally valuable and that none of them has direct implications on how 'competent' or 'trustworthy' the other person is.

Team members can then instill higher trust and move beyond initial differences in how to organize space and relations by explicating their previously tacit assumptions together.

> **Application 5.3: Work-life integration or work-life separation?**
>
> How would you personally organize your workplace and your relations at work.
>
> - Would you integrate or separate work and private sphere?
> - Do you prefer diffuse or specific relations at work?
> - When, and how, could your preferences become problematic in virtual collaboration?
>
> Write down your insights and exchange them with fellow team members, students or co-workers. Find out whether there are collective patterns and, if so, why this is the case. ◄

5.5 Project Planning Assumptions and the Organization of Time

The final aspect of what people communicate besides relations and space is how they organize time (**chronemics**). According to Hall (1983), the time-orientation underlying communication can either be monochronic (**M-time**) or polychronic (**P-time**).

- M-time (monochronic time-orientation) is characterized by doing 'one thing at a time' and a preference for clear sequence or steps, events et cetera. Team members who are on M-time apportion time, e.g. into 'work time', 'lunch time', 'leisure time', which means that one can run out of one portion of time: time needs to be planned for by humans and can stress them out. The main goal is thus to 'keep time', which implies a focus on schedules, procedures, tasks and goals, as well as on planning activities. Tasks are executed with a narrow focus on one task or action at a time. M-time is related to a communicative style that is 'to the point' (low-context) and, potentially, also to a preference for specific relations.
- P-time (polychronic time-orientation) implies a preference for 'juggling time': From this perspective, time is just there, and someone who is on M-time fills it with activities: humans are immersed into time. This often means synchronous, holistic actions (more than one thing at a time, with a wider focus beyond the action). It can also take the shape of responding to a number of demands or people simultaneously or to establish connections between previously unlinked demands or people. P-time is linked to a communicative style which considers the multiple influencing factors of a situation and pays attention to the relations between people (high-context).

5.5 Project Planning Assumptions and the Organization of Time

Chronemics How time is perceived and communicated socially
M-time The understanding that time needs to be portioned, and that these portions need to be put into a sequential order without much overlap, which means that one can 'run out' of a specific portion.
P-time The understanding that time exists and that humans juggle with time to make all tasks, relations, requirements, activities, and so on, 'fit' time, which implies multi-tasking and flexibility.

Time-orientation is thus a relevant aspect for virtual team collaboration in particular when it comes to the organization of schedules and meetings.

- Because M-time is content-based, actions are scheduled one after the other, and also in meetings, one plans for a linear, sequential process of topics. Once a topic has been discussed to the end, one expects it not to show up again, unless there are exceptional or unforeseen circumstances. One would bring everyone who is relevant to the specific content, tasks or action, together in a meeting so that every opinion, expertise and perspective may be offered and discussed for this goal to be reached.
- P-time is relations-based. This implies that one tends to start every interaction, sequence or meeting with those topics, actions or themes that are the least confrontational and thus have the highest relationship and trust building potential. Speakers tend to voice the most positive and integrative aspects first, with the most confrontational and negative ones to be reserved for the end. Project time is therefore circular: Content shows up again and again, based on how secure relations are. Topic recur during meetings and project phases: these occurrences are no repetitions because their relationship aspect has changed. The more in-group the interaction is, the quicker one may proceed for relations endangering themes, and this implies that one needs to include context factors such as breaks, break-out sessions and group composition, as well as where to meet, into one's planning considerations: this way, one may change content.

▶ M-time is linear and associated with a low-context communicative style; its sequence and rhythm are dictated by content. P-time is circular; and recurrence of themes and communicative variations are influenced by context, trust levels and relations.

It is furthermore relevant to understand that M-time and P-time have strong ties to low-context and high-context, respectively. Context-oriented P-project time pays attention to hierarchy and status, and to relationships and trust levels across individuals, whereas content-orientated M-project time is largely independent of interpersonal relations.

When on M-time, content dictates project planning and execution. Ideally, topics come up only once and are then clarified conclusively. The expectation is that, at this point, everyone voices their opinion and contributes. One plans by means of project phases and allocating responsibilities. Action items, if closed, indicate the conclusion of a project phase. If a topic is raised again at a later point in time, then it is because work could not be executed as planned, and now needs to be reclarified. More agile versions of this approach, such as 'scrum', also work with the M-time assumptions of task-orientation, pro-active communication and information clarity.

However, if time flows from relations, as it is the case with P-time, then context trumps over content. One therefore needs to integrate relations (from out-group to in-group) first: only then will one have created the situation in which critical and controversial input can be shared. Or, in other words one speeds up the project by building relations and by considering in-group requirements. P-time project planning is thus non-linear and can be best visualized as a 'funnel' into which everyone needs to be integrated for tasks to be executed. Topics are ordered from non-conflicting to conflicting, and thus come up several times, as befits team relations in their present state. Figure 5.6 visualizes both basic underlying time assumptions of how projects should be planned and executed.

In particular, this difference is highly relevant in cross-functional teams. For instance, the production line runs on M-time, whereas sales involves the 'sales funnel', that is: the understanding that there are different communicative types of customers and that one needs to communicate the advantages of a product in such a way that this specific potential customer enters the 'sales funnel' so that the sale is concluded successfully. To align M-project time with P-project time, those involved in collaboration, therefore need to reflect upon their own style and take integrating steps to also meet the requirements of the respective other style.

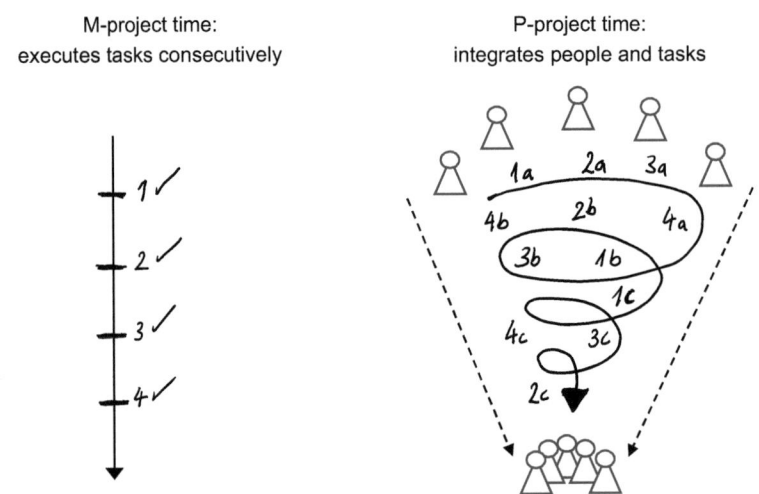

Fig. 5.6 Project time and execution: M-time and P-time assumptions. *Source* own figure

Those on M-project time

- should configure context, not content: People will move down the relationship funnel more quickly if not the whole, hierarchical, unequal and different project team discusses everything in the whole group. Rather, what one needs is a combination of in-groups with 'box openers' who can then integrate diverse in-groups (see before).
- should reserve time for relationship building.

Those on P-project time

- should understand that clarity of information, precise messages and speedy communication instill trust and dare to communicate content regardless of context.
- should be aware that relations are specific and that socializing and work will be kept separate on M-time.

As Fig. 5.6 also visualizes, P-time is not necessarily slower than M-time if one takes a more long-term outlook beyond a single project., Project team members become more in-group via the P-time process of relational integration, thus, what the funnel achieves is that it can speed up time, for instance, when the next project needs to be executed: if people already know each other, then they do not start from the entry point of the funnel anew. In such ways, P-time project execution can be faster than M-time project execution. P-time projects, like the country road experience, are often more about community than the immediate goal. For example, there is the idea of the 'customer lifecycle' in sales which needs to be managed beyond the single sale of a product.

▶ P-time is slower than M-time when executing a project together for the first time, in particularly in the beginning, but faster when executing consecutive projects in the same team.

Application 5.4: Project planning

Imagine that you are in charge of overall time planning in a virtual team, including the work package of a team member who is behind schedule. Your teamleader points out in the weekly team-meeting that you have executed your time planning responsibilities poorly.

- What kind of communication would you wish for? How much content/context do you need, and what do you need it for, in this situation?
- What difference would it make if the team leader pointed out this issue in a 1:1 meeting, and not in front of the team? Which conceptual explanation lies behind choosing this strategy?

Write down your insights and exchange them with fellow team members, students or co-workers. Complement your answers with what you learn from others. ◀

5.6 Recommendations for Collaborating Across Hierarchies, Disciplines and Professions

5.6.1 How to Use the 'Culture as Communication' Perspective?

Hall's (1959) 'culture as communication' approach is based on the insight that people cannot grasp the entirety of culture. Therefore, they should focus on what is visible and can be observed (communication) and deduce deep cultural assumptions regarding relations, time and space from there. This way, team members can prevent negative team dynamics, overcome the limitations of ICTs and create collaborative cultures based on a fitting positive divergence-convergence configuration.

Hall (1959) had originally developed his 'culture as communication' perspective for training individuals for interacting with representatives of other nationalities abroad. Therefore, he proposed that it is the country-specific business cultures from which differences in communicative style originate. Germany, for example, is low in context-orientation in the Hall model, speakers from Latin America, France, Spain and the UK are assumed to be more context-oriented (with Romanic and Latin American communication also being more emotional), and several Asian countries, such as India and China, are described as highly context-oriented. According to Hall (1966) Germany is also characterized by specific relations whereas the USA are characterized by diffuse relations. This then implies that German business most likely runs on M-time.[1]

Hall's country-based differentiations are derived from experience, not from empirical data, as the focus was mainly on how individuals would *perceive* each other when interacting, thus: on the learning from individual experience, not on predicting country-wide behaviour. Therefore, applying the 'communication as culture' perspective is not about 'the data' but about deducing patterns which increase the number of communicative clues available. For example, one may assume that engineering or other 'rational' disciplines are rather low in their context-orientation when compared to other, more relational disciplines, such as corporate communications or sales, in the same country. Production engineering is likely to run on M-time more than sales which also involves P-time elements, for instance, when it comes to customer relationship management. Because larger organizations develop more bureaucratic practices, they tend to involve more specific relations compared to small- and medium-sized enterprises, let alone start-ups, in the same country, industry or profession.

These basic underlying assumptions are hypotheses to be tested upon a situation, they are not definitive 'proof' of difference. The task is therefore not to define borders between people but rather to ask whether a certain basic underlying assumption might

---

[1] For African countries, Hall did not make many assumptions as these countries, at that time, seemed negligible from a business perspective (which, from a contemporary perspective, shows a certain attitude of Western superiority and is also a serious neglect).

create negative divergence in a certain situation. This way, conflict becomes less 'personal', professional expertise and integrity is less doubted, and people are enabled to trust each other more. Those involved in virtual collaboration, also within one country or region, should therefore observe themselves and each other when communicating, based on the understanding that what is *actually* communicated is relationship, space and time assumptions and expectations.

Identifying more communicative clues beyond what is immediately visible and known is highly relevant for ICT-based collaboration. The main limitation of ICT-based communication is that it lacks context, and this limitation cannot be overcome even by the richest ICTs (see background information on context and ICT collaboration). Any team collaboration that involves a virtual component therefore needs to bring members' divergent cultural assumptions to the surface. The 'culture as communication' perspective is an ideal tool for doing so. It enables team members to deduce more context information, such as relationship requirements, time planning approaches and how people organize space, from virtual communication. This way, it provides both sender and receiver with more communicative feedback than could be obtained otherwise. Table 5.1 summarizes the major interrelations between communication, relations, time and space.

Table 5.1 Summary of the interrelations between communication, relations, time and space

Concept	Source	Definition and virtual team implications
Content-orientation (low context) vs. Context-orientation (high context)	Hall (1976)	Degree to which communication is content-oriented, that is: direct, explicit and verbal (low-context) versus the degree to which communication is context-oriented, that is: indirect, implicit and non-verbal (high-context). In high-context, content is determined by relations (in-group/out-group differentiation). Style determines whether all information is transferred regardless of relations (low-context) or whether secure relations are required for conveying negative or controversial messages (high-context)
Diffuse vs. specific relationships	Hall (1966)	Personal and public sphere overlap (diffuse) versus a private sphere that is reserved for close friends (specific). Influences whether trust is instilled by means of personality (diffuse) or function (specific), and what ICT intrusion into personal and private spheres 'means' for those involved
Monochronic (M-time) vs. polychronic (P-time)	Hall (1983)	Singular and sequential time (M-time) versus time as many parallel flows (P-time). Influences to how work and relations are organized, and whether project time lines are linear (M-time) or circular (P-time). P-time implies high-context orientation, and M-time implies low-context orientation (Hall, 1983). Thus, relations organize P-time, and content organizes M-time

Source own table

5.6.2 How to Become Aware of the Cultural Dimension of Communication

Becoming aware of how culture is communicated requires that one not only listens to the content of a message, but also to how relations are communicated and to what the speaker expresses about themselves and the person they are addressing (Schulz von Thun, 1981, see Chap. 4). Therefore, a statement such as 'you need to meet the deadline' is never solely a content-related message: it also expresses what the speaker thinks about themselves (e.g. 'I have understood the importance of the deadline'), what they think of the other person (e.g. 'You might not have understood the importance of the deadline'), and it also says something about the relations between them (e.g. 'I know better than you'). Because people enter communication with potentially divergent underlying assumptions, they might frame what is said in different ways, which then leads to misunderstandings and conflict.

Based on the five fundamental properties of communication (Watzlawick et al., 2000, see Chap. 4), in combination with the 'culture as communication' perspective, one can derive main checklist questions for how to create collaborative cultures across differences, in particular across functions and disciplines. Table 5.2 provides an overview.

Trust means to make oneself vulnerable to another party without being able to know with certainty whether the other party will exploit this vulnerability or not, and there are different requirements for 'daring to trust'. The benefit of the 'communication as culture' approach is that it brings these invisible requirements to the surface. If team members send or obtain more context information on their deep cultural assumptions, and how these differ, they can overcome negative divergence and build more positive team dynamics. Secondly, by giving these differences a 'name tag', the 'culture as communication' perspective makes them less personal. Team members reflecting upon deep differences together, can then better understand that no individual consciously undermines the team or 'hides' information but that they are simply different in what they need to trust the team. This way, professional trust in each other, as a key requirement of high-performance virtual teams, can be built faster and more successfully across these relational differences.

5.6.3 Designing the Temporal Rhythm of Virtual Team Collaboration

The final aspect of how to create cultures is to consider when and how one needs to move beyond a merely virtual and ICT-based collaboration, because the alignment of purpose (people's 'frames') and trustful relations cannot be achieved otherwise. Ideally, this means to alternate between face-to-face interactions and virtual interactions in a way that fits requirements.

Table 5.2 Checklist for creating collaborative cultures across functions and disciplines

Communicative principle	Checklist questions for creating collaborative cultures
One cannot *not* communicate	• Which hidden assumptions of relations, time and space are communicated, and by whom, and how do they differ, in this situation? • Which communicative limitations cannot be overcome in a virtual setting?
Every communication has a content aspect and a relationship aspect	• What are the underlying relationship assumptions of you and others in this situation? • Which communicative relations are inadequate for the content to be communicated, and how to change this (and who should do it)? • How can you make sure that the words which you use do not fall outside the relations which you have or should have with your communicative partner? • Which communicative limitations cannot be overcome in a virtual setting?
The communication of relations has a beginning and end	If the same relational patterns are communicated again and again: • In which position are you stuck; in which position is your communicative partner stuck? • How do relationship, time and space assumptions contribute to this 'being stuck'? • How do your basic underlying assumptions need to change to overcome 'being stuck'? • Which communicative limitations cannot be overcome in a virtual setting?
Digital modes of communication inadequately transport relations	• Which analogue relationship, time and space assumptions need to be transmitted? • Which communicative limitations cannot be overcome in a virtual setting?
There are symmetrical (equal) and asymmetrical (unequal) communicative relations, such as in-group, symmetrical out-group and asymmetrical out-group	• Which team members or communicative partners are equal to you in relevant aspects, such as expertise, profession, knowledge-base, tenure, language proficiency, which ones are unequal to you, and how? With whom do you have symmetrical and with whom do you have asymmetrical relations due to any or more than one of these factors? • Which relationship, time and space assumptions create assumptions of equal, unequal and asymmetrical communication, and what should be done about it? • How would you need to change your (virtual) communication strategies when communicating amongst equals and unequals, and as involving symmetrical or asymmetrical relations? • Which ICTs can support symmetrical relationship building? • Which communicative problems cannot be solved in a virtual setting?

Source own table

- More complex task- and relationship-related issues, such as generating commitment, aligning purpose or building relationship, require face-to-face interactions.
- Less complex, often task-related aspects of execution, can well be transmitted via naturally leaner ICTs.

Rich face-to-face interactions align the team in terms of its underlying core assumptions, such as relationship requirements, time planning, and workplace organization (why and how to do, and with whom). If this alignment has happened, procedures and task (what to do) can be executed virtually. However, at a certain point, core underlying assumptions will start to diverge again, with the danger of negative team divergence. Then, the team needs to meet again and induce a new loop of positively convergent processes (see Fig. 5.7).

Unfortunately, the longer the virtual team has not met, the more of the previously built alignment of purpose and teamness fade away, and it becomes fuzzier and fuzzier why a certain task should be executed in certain ways, and why with those people. A key challenge is therefore to recognize when the team need another face-to-face interaction in order to align tasks, people and purpose again. All prevalent orientations—high- and low-context, diffuse and specific relations, and P- and M-time—need to be considered for making the right call, as enabled by the checklist in the previous section.

> **Application 5.5: Creating a collaborative temporal rhythm for the team**
>
> Revisit the cross-functional team of the opening case, and its configuration and purposes (see previous applications).
>
> - Which temporal rhythm would you propose for the cross-functional team of the opening case, and why? Or, in other words: for which tasks would they have to meet in person? For which tasks do virtual interactions suffice?

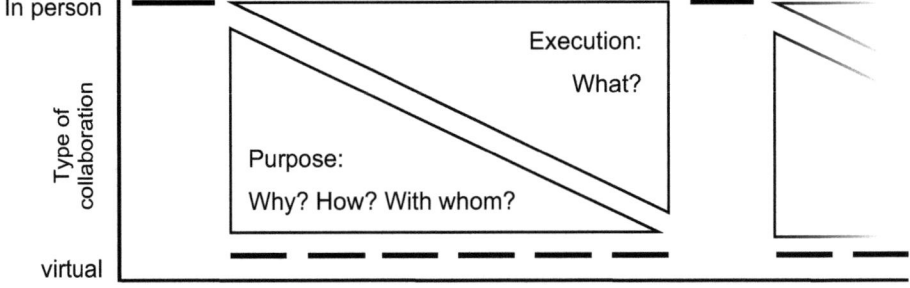

Fig. 5.7 The required temporal rhythm of cultural integration. *Source* own figure

- What could be 'critical incidents' from which you could deduce that the team is no longer culturally integrated, and how do you propose to counteract them?
- What does the cross-functional team 'need' from the company to develop the best possible temporal rhythm, and what does it need from its members in terms of abilities and motivations so that this rhythm can be developed and sustained?

Write down your insights and exchange them with fellow team members, students or co-workers. Complement your answers with what you learn from others. ◀

5.7 Closing Part

5.7.1 Chapter Summary

Culture as a shared sense of 'how to normally do things' is what glues virtual teams together or, if lacking, tears them apart. Culture shapes, for example, how people manage relations, plan time and organize space. These assumptions tend to diverge, in particular in interdisciplinary and cross-functional virtual teams and projects. For a more collaborative teamwork, virtual team members and leaders need to integrate cultural requirements and expectations, and this can be best done if one reflects upon, observes and—when required—changes communication. This chapter provided you with the concepts and tools for building collaborative team cultures for high performance, with a focus on communication and ICT usage.

The starting point was the realization that people proceed from different expectations regarding how to establish relations and trust, how to plan time and projects, how to organize space, and how to achieve work-life balance, and that it is essential to integrate these differences, in particular in cross-functional and interdisciplinary teams. To develop this ability, this chapter first focussed on culture, visualized by means of an iceberg, and explained how the 'hidden' parts of the iceberg influence visible communication and behaviour in divergent, often conflicting ways. As the iceberg model suggests, people's actual cultural behaviour does not emerge from corporate mission statements concerning 'culture' but from their own, basic underlying assumptions which they enact and communicate at work. These basic underlying assumptions must be assumed to diverge, especially in cross-functional and interdisciplinary virtual team collaboration. Furthermore, ICT-based communication is always lower in context-orientation than non-virtual communication, and this contributes to an increased likelihood of communicative and collaborative misunderstandings. It then becomes more difficult to trust each other, with trust being a major requirement of successful (virtual) team collaboration.

A collaborative culture is the means which enables virtual teams to succeed nonetheless. It is built from configuring divergent-convergent virtual team processes. Its best configuration emerges from the constant monitoring and, if required, from altering the four constitutive virtual team factors remoteness, complexity, teamness and virtualness in a way that befits tasks, purposes and the ICTs by means of which the team collaborates.

However, a collaborative virtual team culture can only be achieved if people become aware of the basic assumptions underlying their behaviour. The 'culture as communication' perspective, originally intended for preparing individuals for intercultural interactions abroad, enables such awareness. You may therefore identify how people build trust, plan time and organize space by reflecting upon and by analysing the communication and collaborative patterns of yourself and others.

The chapter concluded with recommendations of how to create collaborative team cultures across hierarchies, disciplines and professions. It provided you with practical recommendations of how to build and maintain trust despite divergent relationship assumptions, of how to integrate conflicting work-life-balance and workspace demands, and of how to streamline project planning and time assumptions. After having engaged with this chapter, you should be able to contribute to a culture of collaboration, in particular in cross-functional and interdisciplinary virtual teams, thus maximizing the contribution of one of the key moderators of positive virtual team dynamics and outcomes, namely culture.

5.7.2 Key Points

- Culture as a shared sense of 'how we normally do things around here' is what glues teams together, or, if lacking, tears them apart.
- ICT-based collaboration lacks richness and complicates trust.
- A collaborative team culture is the means by which the challenges of virtual communication and the limitations of ICT-based collaboration can be overcome.
- A collaborative virtual team culture is built from configuring divergent-convergent dynamics in the most conducive ways.
- Culture can be visualized by means of an iceberg, and it is people's basic underlying cultural assumptions that shape their expectations, interpretations and behavioural patterns of 'how to normally do things' in ways of which they are often unaware.
- Members basic underlying cultural assumptions tend to differ, in particular, in cross-functional and interdisciplinary teams and projects.
- The 'culture as communication' perspective proposes that people communicate their basic underlying cultural assumptions.
- Key basic underlying cultural assumptions which people communicate concern how to establish relations and trust, how to plan time and projects, how to organize space, and how to achieve work-life balance.
- One can build more collaborative cultures by reflecting upon and changing communication.
- For a collaborative culture, one needs to reflect upon and integrate low- and high-context relationship and trust assumptions, to pay attention to in-group and out-group dynamics, to differentiate between work-life separation and integration, to consider M-time and P-time in project planning and to design the temporal rhythm of collaboration accordingly.

5.7.3 Review Questions

1. What is culture, and how is it relevant to virtual team collaboration?
2. What are the limitations of ICT-based collaboration, and how do these affect virtual team collaboration?
3. What are the three levels of culture and how are they relevant to virtual team collaboration?
4. What is a collaborative team culture, and how is it achieved?
5. What is meant by the 'culture as communication' perspective, and how is it relevant to building and maintaining collaborative virtual team cultures?
6. How do the relationship- and trust assumptions differ across high- and low-context orientation, and how can these differences be integrated?
7. What is meant by in-group and out-group and how are these concepts relevant for achieving trust and task clarity across hierarchy, functions and disciplines in virtual team collaboration?
8. What are proxemics, and how is the concept relevant for understanding how people combine work and life in virtual team collaboration?
9. What is meant by M-time and P-time, and what are the implications of these concepts for how (virtual) team projects are planned, executed and timed?
10. Based on the previous insights: how should one design the temporal rhythm of virtual team collaboration?

5.7.4 Opening Case Revisited

The opening case describes a cross-functional team which is comprised of one member each from the following departments: research & development, production, operations, financial control, and marketing & sales.

Now, assume that this team is based in Germany and consists solely of members who grew up and have been educated and professionally trained in Germany. The company wherein they work is a multinational company, but its origins and headquarters are in Germany. Imagine that the team has developed a 'German' style of doing things, that is: low-context, specific relations, M-time. Now, the 3D project is internationalized, which means that members from other countries enter the team. These members come from the research & development, production, operations, financial control, and marketing & sales departments of other corporate sites. Assume that most of them, despite their professional heterogeneity, are more used to high-context, diffuse relations, P-time teamwork.

Based on your learning from this chapter:

- What are the blind spots of a low-context, specific relations, M-time team orientation, also regarding the team's degree of innovativeness?
- What could the existing team learn from the new members with a high-context, diffuse relations, P-time team orientation?
- What needs to happen so that this learning also takes place and does not result in conflict?

Write down your insights and exchange them with fellow team members, students or co-workers. Complement your answers with what you learn from others.

5.7.5 Closing Activity

Revisit your learnings from this chapter and reflect upon your own basic underlying assumptions regarding work.

- What is work *about*? What does it *mean* to work? Or, in other words: what are your basic underlying assumptions as to why you work and how you should work?
- Are you a low-context or high-oriented person at work, and how do you come to this assessment? Which strengths and weaknesses are associated with this orientation? What do you need to keep in mind so that your orientation becomes an opportunity to a team, and not a threat?
- Do you prefer specific or diffuse relations at work, and how do you come to this assessment? Which strengths and weaknesses are associated with this orientation? What do you need to keep in mind so that your orientation becomes an opportunity to a team, and not a threat?
- Are you on M-time or P-time when you organize work, plan projects and schedule meetings, and how do you come to this assessment? Which strengths and weaknesses are associated with this orientation? What do you need to keep in mind so that your orientation becomes an opportunity to a team, and not a threat?

Write down your insights and exchange them with fellow team members, students or co-workers. Do not forget to provide descriptive examples of situations from which your orientation becomes visible to others. Find out whether there are common patterns and, if so, why this is the case.

References

Daft, R. L., & Lengel, R. H. (1984). Information richness: A new approach to managerial behavior and organizational design. *Research in Organizational Behavior, 6,* 191–233.

Deal, T. E., & Kennedy, A. A. (1982). *Corporate culture: The rites and rituals of corporate life.* Addison-Wesley.

Hall, E. T. (1959). *The silent language.* Doubleday.

Hall, E. T. (1966). *The hidden dimension.* Doubleday.

Hall, E. T. (1976). *Beyond culture.* Doubleday.

Hall, E. T. (1983). *The dance of life: The other dimension of time.* Doubleday.

Schein, E. H. (2010). *Organizational culture and leadership.* Jossey-Bass.

Schoper, Y., & Heimgärtner, R. (2013). Lessons from intercultural project management for the intercultural HCI design process. In A. Marcus (Ed.), *Design, user experience, and usability. Health, learning, playing, cultural and cross-cultural user experience* (pp. 95–104). Springer.

Schulz von Thun, F. (1981). *Miteinander reden 1.* Rowohlt.

Watzlawick, P., Beavin, J. H., & Jackson, D. D. (2000). *Menschliche Kommunikation. Formen, Störungen, Paradoxien.* Huber.

Further Reading

Hacker, J. V., Johnson, M., Saunders, C., & Thayer, A. L. (2019). Trust in virtual teams: A multi-disciplinary review and integration. *Australasian Journal of Information Systems, 23.* https://doi.org/10.3127/ajis.v23i0.1757. Accessed 1 May 2024.

This article provides an overview on the literature regarding how to create and maintain trust in virtual teams. You can draw cultural and communication implications from there.

Organizational Design and Core Technologies for Virtual Collaboration: How to Shape the Conditions Under Which the Team Can Thrive

6.1 Introduction

Virtual team collaboration needs to be organized, and this means asking and answering questions such as: How to allocate tasks most efficiently and effectively? How to integrate team members? How to ensure performance? How to maintain these conditions? When and how to change them? The term "organizational design" has been coined for the insight that organization does not exist 'just like that' but needs to be constantly configured. Those collaborating in virtual teams are therefore also in the role of organizational designers, and how well they organize work and technology influences how well the team performs.

Because virtual collaboration is mediated by technology, this always involves making informed technological choices.

To enable virtual team members to take up the role of organizational designers, this chapter first introduces the building blocks of organization. This way, you will gain a better understanding of which fundamental organizational choices need to be made. Ideally, you will not make these choices instinctively, but with the full awareness of why a certain way of organizing seems a good choice to you. Images ('metaphors') of organization facilitate such awareness which needs to be coupled with a patterned understanding of team characteristics and configuration requirements. This enables you to weigh up pros and cons, for example, of mechanistic and organic organization, in light of each other. The next step concerns organizational process, namely the question of how the virtual team may transform input into output in the best possible ways. Because technology, such as artificial intelligence, is increasingly developing into an actor of its own, both human and non-human interfaces have to be considered for designing organizational processes. To this end, this chapter introduces three core organizational technologies—mediating, long-linked and intensive—by means of which human and non-human interfaces may be organized and discusses which core technology fits which type of virtual team. Furthermore, organizational design requires building and maintaining organizational structures, and this chapter discusses and weighs up the available options, such as functional, divisional, matrix and network design. It also ponders whether organizations could over-structure, for instance, by burdening a virtual team with bureaucracy. Finally, because organizational environments and their demands constantly change, one needs to know when to reorganize and to organize for change instead of stability.

In summary, the organizational design perspective on virtual team collaboration implies that virtual team members and leaders should constantly seek to improve upon how work is organized, and how it is perceived and what it stands for, and to aim for the ideal change-stability interrelations in light of the specific circumstances. After having read this chapter, you should be able to make informed organizational design choices, to assess organizational technology, and to contribute to virtual change. Together, this will enable to you to better shape the conditions under which a virtual team can thrive.

Team	A small number of individuals who collaborate in a task and/or to reach a goal.
ICTs	Information and communication technologies.
Virtual Team Collaboration	Working together as a team by means of ICTs.
Organizational Design	The conscious activities by means of which individuals create the processes and structures for allocating tasks to people and for exchanging the required information across distinct responsibilities.

6.1.1 Learning Objectives

After having read this chapter, you should.

- Be able to analyse virtual team collaboration from an organizational design perspective.
- Know the properties and building blocks of organization, also in relation to technology.
- Know which design choices create mechanistic and organic organization, and how well these fit specific types and requirements of virtual team collaboration.
- Understand how humans and technology interrelate in virtual team processes.
- Know different types of organizational core technologies—mediating, long-linked and intensive—by means of which human and non-human interfaces might be organized.
- Know key types of organizational structures—functional, divisional, matrix and network—and their advantages and disadvantages for specific types of virtual team collaboration.
- Be aware of how metaphors influence managers in their organizational design choices, but also enable higher organizational awareness, if reflected upon and combined.
- Understand how bureaucracy emerges, and why it can be dangerous to virtual team collaboration.

6.1.2 Opening Case

> **Example**
>
> Davide is a graduate of medical engineering who recently started to work in a global operations team in a multinational company that manufactures pharmaceuticals, with production sites in India and Mexico, headquarters in Germany and France, and main logistics and customer service hubs in Singapore and the USA. The global operations team members are located at all these sites (see Table); the overall company is divided into regional divisions, with certain strategic functions running across them. Most global operations team members are thus responsible to their regional managers and to the head of global operations manager. Additionally, some are also responsible to the function from which they were drawn (e.g. global logistics, global customer experience management). As the newest team member, Davide is to assist the head of global operations at the German site in their daily business. ◄

6.2 The Organizational Dimension of Virtual Team Collaboration

6.2.1 What is Organization?

Organization is the means by which people try to reach a goal or purpose that is impossible for a single individual to achieve. For example, if a boulder is blocking a road, organizational efforts are required to remove it. In other words: organization emerges because people have needs that cannot be fulfilled without it (Hatch, 2011). What is intriguing about organization is that people do it all the time, yet, seldom notice and reflect about why they have chosen to 'organize' in these, and not in other ways. 'Noticing' organization is therefore the first step towards identifying and, consequently, configuring the conditions under which virtual team collaboration can thrive. Therefore: what exactly needs to be done for the boulder to be removed, what are the options, and which choices fit the challenge the best? Out of such **awareness** follows the ability to design **processes** and **structures**, and to know when to organizationally **learn,** and **change and transform**, what no longer meets requirements. This process by which groups of people, e.g. virtual team members, intentionally create and change organizational processes and structures to increase performance is referred to as **organizational design** (Cunliffe, 2012).

> ▶ **Organizational design** is the sum of the conscious choices by means of which people create and change organizational processes and structures.

Table Opening Case 6 Configuration of the global operations team

Corporate Site	Site responsibility	Global operations team: members and responsibilities
German site	Headquarters	Head of global operations
		Assistant to head of operations
		Production expert
		Supply chain management expert
French site	Co-headquarters, production for Europe	Co-head of global operations
		Assistant to head of operations
		Regional production manager
		Global logistics manager
Indian site	Production for Asia, Oceania and Africa	Global production manager
		Regional logistics manager
		Regional customer support manager
Mexican site	Production for Americas	Regional production manager
Singaporean site	Global logistics and supply chain management	Global logistics manager
		Global supply chain manager
		Global customer experience manager
US-American site	Logistics for Americas	Regional logistics manager
		Regional customer experience manager

Source: own table

6.2.2 Building Blocks of Organization

Organization is as much a process ('organizing') as it is the outcome of this process ('organization') which then becomes an identifiable entity ('*the* organization'). All three properties of organization are mutually constitutive. **Organizational design** is **effective** if it focusses the attention of each employee on the tasks for which they are responsible *and* if it promotes the integration among all the activities of the organization. **Organizational design** is **efficient** if it minimizes the time, effort and resources required (inputs) for achieving the overall organizational goals (outputs) in the best possible way.

What is tricky about implementing and maintaining organizational effectiveness and efficiency is that four contradictory forces need to be balanced out. These are: differentiation versus integration, and cooperation versus competition.

First, one needs to achieve sufficient **differentiation.** There are two main types of differentiation, namely vertical and horizontal: **vertical differentiation** refers to levels of hierarchy (formal authority: the team leader), **horizontal differentiation** describes the division of labour (task and knowledge authority: the professional experts). Differentiation is directed towards roles and functions. A **role** is what an individual represents in an organization; it may be formal or informal, assigned or self-assigned. Examples are: team leader or professional expert. Usually, a role interrelates with **organizational function**: what needs to be done and achieved by means of this role, or, in other words: the task and responsibilities assigned to an individual. Thus, there need to be specific tasks and responsibilities assigned to each role, and these tasks and responsibilities have to be clear to those involved.

▶ A **role** is what a person stands for in the organization. A **function** is the task or responsibility formally assigned to an individual in the organization. Role and function may, but do not have to, overlap. For example, a person might be assigned the role of integrator whenever there is team conflict, even though their formal function is something different entirely, such as coding expert. On the other hand, leadership role and function are often, but not always, united in the person who is also formally in charge of the team. Function is assigned whereas role is 'lived'.

Differentiation enables people to focus on the task, yet, might make it more difficult to communicate critical information across distinct functions, roles, hierarchical levels and knowledge areas. Differentiation thus needs to be counterbalanced by **integration**. Integration refers to all means used to overcome the organizational gap caused by differentiation: for instance, as soon as people are split into separate organizational units, such as departments, there is no incentive for communicating across departments. This, of course, is critical (imagine production not talking to the sales department anymore), and therefore, one needs to design processes and structures, such as regular meeting patterns or reporting structures, that make people communicate across otherwise separate units. However, whenever people collaborate in a differentiated organization, such as a virtual team, there is also **internal competition**, as the best team member might be promoted to team leader. Furthermore, there is **external competition**: another organization might hire the best team member or team leader. Both dynamics thus counteract the collaboration required for integration. This means that organization necessarily involves trade-offs.

▶ Organization of virtual team collaboration is successful when tasks are allocated to functions, and when critical information across tasks and functions is successfully exchanged, both internally and externally. This requires balancing out the contradictory demands of collaboration and coordination, and differentiation and integration, and to strive for the highest possible effectiveness and efficiency. Effectiveness means to find the best integration-differentiation ratio, and efficiency means to optimize input–output relations.

6.2.3 Virtual Team Members as Organizational Designers

There is no template for which organizational design choices to make for the best possible virtual team collaboration. For instance, the ideal ratio between differentiation and integration, and cooperation and competition, will depend on aspects such as the nature of the task, the costs of communication and coordination, and on team members and team member distribution and diversity. Virtual team members thus need to constantly ask which patterns underlie how people organize in their role as organizational designers. To this end, this section introduces key aspects by means of which virtual team members may increase their **organizational awareness**.

▶ Virtual team members in the role of organizational designers need to be aware of how team characteristics interrelate with organizational demands and choices.

Key design choices to be made are:

- **Centralization** versus **decentralization**: should only one person (team leader, expert) or the whole team be involved, for instance, in decision making? The more unique, interdependent, knowledge-based and/or complex the task is, the higher the demand for decentralized decision making.
- **Formalization**: to what degree should the virtual team use formal (written) rules, procedures and communication channels, as opposed to informal ones? Formalization increases reliability, yet might limit the discretion (freedom of choice and action) of the individual team members when doing their job, in particular, in interdisciplinary and knowledge intensive, often novel and innovative collaboration.
- **Standardization** versus **discretion**: shall standard procedures and regulations govern virtual team collaboration or should individual team members be allowed to make their own decisions depending on the circumstances and as they see fit? One would need to allow for more or less discretion depending on the degree of expertise and creativity expected of individual team members and the degree to which tasks are unique and non-repetitive. Generally, higher demands on expertise and creativity coupled with unique and non-repetitive tasks require more discretion.
- **Specialization** versus **generalization**: should individual team members perform narrow, thus specialized tasks, or should individual team members perform tasks located in a wide area of knowledge and expertise? The more interdependent the tasks are and the more knowledge exchange is required across them, the more generalized individual knowledge-areas should be.
- **Grouping decisions**: by means of which criterion should people be further differentiated into sub-groups? For example, a larger virtual team might further group members based on product responsibility, disciplinary function or market orientation.

▶ Making organizational design choices for virtual team collaboration means to find conclusive answers to the following questions:

- To what degree shall decision making and control be centralized?
- How shall integration be achieved?
- To what degree shall rules, procedures and communication channels be formalized?

- To what degree shall tasks be standardized?
- To what degree shall individual and collective tasks and responsibilities be specialized?
- By which criteria, if any, shall people be further grouped?

> **Link to practice: Temporal brokerage as a way of bridging the virtual team divide**
>
> The so-called temporal divide, that is: a condition in which virtual team subgroups are dispersed and operate in distinct time zones without overlap, can result in major coordination and communication issues, in particular in case of high task complexity or interdependency. Temporal brokerage is a practical way of increasing the team's ability to effectively take on complex tasks and projects (overview in Mell et al., 2021). It means to assign an additional organizational role—the one of the 'temporal broker'—to one or more team members, with the purpose of bridging subgroup activities and perspectives across time zones. This creates a higher workload for the broker but also increases individual and collective team outputs, especially if the broker has experience with multicultural and virtual communication. ◀

6.2.4 Mechanistic Versus Organic Virtual Team Collaboration

Some virtual teams emerge as more mechanistic or organic based on the choices made. Each design has its specific advantages and disadvantages.

- **Mechanistic organization** is characterized by centralized control (only a few or only the team leader are involved in decision making), and formalized communication and interaction (meetings are planned, conducted with an agenda and involve formal procedures, such as time planning and tracking of action items. People's tasks are standardized as much as possible (because this achieves formalized communication and centralized control). Specialization is high, people are further grouped based on function, and only sub-group leaders and management meet for formalized exchange. The strengths of mechanistic virtual team organization are clear, efficient and effective reporting relationships. Orientating organization towards these strengths is the most conducive to virtual team collaboration, if task interdependence is low, if tasks can be easily standardized, and if the knowledge required for executing the task can be formulated explicitly.
- **Organic organization** is characterized by decentralized control by many (the team leads the team) and exchange of information by everyone on a needs basis (often informally). Sub-groups are formed based on differentiating criteria, such as functions, with the sub-group reporting to a leader. The strengths of organic virtual team organization are flexibility, adaptability to the environment and the capability of rapid change. This generally fits better to teams with innovative and knowledge-based tasks and to interdisciplinary teams, which are the majority of virtual teams.

Of course, the logic also works the other way: team members who find themselves in a certain virtual team can now better understand which organizational principles underlie this team's collaboration patterns. This way, they can come to more informed conclusions as to whether the present patterns fit the team's purposes and goals or as to whether they need to be changed and reorganized for higher team effectiveness and efficiency.

▶ Key design choices are a way to investigate and, if required, change present collaboration patterns in light of the required organizational excellence *and* to organize new virtual teams effectively and efficiently.

6.2.5 How Organizational Design Contributes to Performance

Ideally, organizational design choices contribute to team **performance** as the ultimate goal of any team collaboration. Performance is often defined as the ideal combination of people's job-related abilities and motivation, and of the job-related opportunities provided to them: performance is a function of ability, motivation and opportunity. To maximize team performance, team members' abilities and motivations need to be utilized and developed, and team members need to be given the organizational opportunity to contribute to the team with their abilities, or to further develop them, in order to be and remain motivated. Organization, in the sense of making appropriate and effective organizational design choices in relation to the aforementioned poles, is one means of improving upon the interrelations between ability, motivation and opportunity in the team. The other facilitator is leadership (see Chap. 7), and organizational design and leadership are always intertwined.

▶ **Performance** A function of ability, motivation and opportunity, to be maximized, for instance, by effective and appropriate organizational design choices.

Further characteristics that differentiate successful from unsuccessful organization (Hatch, 2011) are:

- Formulating a strategic vision that motivates members to achieve organizational goals.
- Structuring roles and relationships between members in such a way that they contribute to implementing this strategy.
- Using technologies in such a way that performance is enhanced.
- Creating a culture that 'communicates' how things should get done to people.
- Designing work spaces in such ways that the desired processes and goals are supported.

Based on the design choices made in light of team characteristics and purposes, one or more of these bullet points become more or less relevant.

▶ From an organizational perspective, performance always includes the human factor, also in case of most mechanistic designs.

Application 6.1: Organizing the global operations team

Operations management has been described as "the art and science of transforming ideas into actions" (City University Hongkong, 2023). It focusses on allocating, managing and optimizing certain resources in light of the global environment. Global operations management is thus a central function that guarantees the optimization of the corporate value chain. The main focus lies on analysing and continuously improving upon production processes, and on training executives and managers in implementing these improvements in industrial settings, such as the one described in the opening case. Typical responsibilities are:

- Continuously analysing and optimizing processes regarding quality, costs, productivity, inputs and outputs, time efficiency and so on.
- Further developing the corporate portfolio (products and/or services).
- Designing business flows and processes to improve upon cost efficiency, organizational responsiveness and operational flexibility.
- Financial control and reporting to higher levels.
- Optimizing production with regard to its 'leanness' and operational excellence, potentially also its sustainability.
- Co-creating value with customers via support, process alignment and other measures.

With regard to the purposes and goals of global operations management and this specific configuration of the team described in the opening case, consider:

- Which is the right ratio between the conflicting building blocks of organization, such as decentralized and centralized decision making, for this specific team?
- Does the way in which roles and responsibilities are presently allocated in the global operations team seem conducive to the team's collaboration processes and goals? If not: what would you change?
- What kind of communication channels would the team need to make sure that people orientate themselves towards their roles and responsibilities, but also pass critical information across functions and hierarchical levels? ◀

6.3 Images of Organization: The Impact of Metaphors on Virtual Team Collaboration

Whenever people organize work, they have images of 'what organization is about and what an organization should look like' in mind when doing so. The ideas of organization which they have in mind influences how they organize and, ultimately, how the organization functions and how people experience work. To make managers and professionals aware of how their assumptions influence their doings and experiences, Morgan (1986/2006) put forward key metaphors of organization. Metaphors are pictures or images of reality that are easily accessible and malleable, but nonetheless transport complex ideas and knowledge about this reality: metaphors make complex, abstract problems small and tangible via a fairly 'simple' analogy for a complex phenomenon. This text focuses on six key metaphors that help organize virtual team collaboration, namely: machine, organism, culture, psychic prison, instrument of domination and brain.

- Managers and professionals who understand **organizations as a machine** are focussed on the internal workings of the organization. They wish to figure out how to organize the parts of the machine the best way possible and aim for order, standardization, measurement and control. This approach can only work well in knowledge extensive teams with low task complexity that focus on execution. What those organizing a machine neglect is the environment and the human dimension of organization, and—because its internal operations have been optimized—an organization running as a smooth machine is not well-suited for adaptation, change and learning.
- Managers and professionals who understand **organizations as an organism** focus on growth, synergies and adaptation: much as the different parts of an organism, such as the human body, cannot explain system-level phenomena such as 'personality', the different parts of an organizational organism, when interacting, create something that is more than the sum of its parts (such as innovative ideas). The purpose of organisms is to adapt to a changing environment, and, if they fail, they fall ill. Organisms also give birth, they grow, die and evolve, and only the fittest will survive: these are relevant considerations for a virtual team to excel. What those organizing an organism neglect is the question of what actually holds the different parts of the organism together and how the borders between organisms and environments may be blurred.
- Managers and professionals who understand **organization as culture** focus on creating a climate that makes people believe in an organization. They focus on establishing shared ideas, values or motivations that glue the organization together and wish to prevent divisive cultures. Often, this involves desired ideologies or shared organizational traditions and rituals Virtual team collaboration needs to be organized by means of culture for creating and maintaining trust and positive teamness. What those organizing for culture neglect is the question when ideology becomes suppressively 'cult-like' (the dark side of culture), and of how organizations might be more

diversity-oriented, innovative and creative if their culture is less cohesive, and how one also needs 'machine-like' aspects for an organization to function well.

- Managers and professionals who understand **organizations as a psychic prison** focus on freeing employees from the pressure of the machine and the ideological oppression (the 'dark side') of culture. They pay attention to how organizations control the subconscious and lead people to self-exploit. They aim at overcoming these effects via trust and learning. Knowledge intensive and innovative virtual team collaboration, in particular, needs to be free of psychic prison effects to reach its goals *and* be sustainable for those involved.
- Managers and professionals who understand **organizations as an instrument of domination** lead by force and charisma; they wish to be 'on stage' and are often uncontrolled in their claim to power. They might thus 'hijack' the organization and create psychic prisons for their employees. This is often disastrous for high-level outcomes of virtual team collaboration, such as innovation or development.
- Managers and professionals who understand **organizations as brains** are focussed on how to configure the nodes between different (human and technological) actors in the virtual team so that they 'fire' like the neural nodes of a brain, thus connecting, processing and spreading information. They enable learning, collaborative organizing and parallel innovation, distribute control, and do not judge team members except for their intelligence, knowledge and networks. Such an approach is particularly suited to knowledge-based, innovative types of virtual team collaboration in which team members are technology- and task-focused (e.g. software developers). What this approach neglects is the self-exploitative capacity of the brain, and that, if learning is a 'must', it might easily become a psychic prison and also a power structure in the team. This is thus the main risk of the ideal of the 'self-motivated' knowledge worker who simply loves to 'think ahead' and improve upon technology 24/7.

Thus, as the previous considerations highlight: what managers and professionals believe in becomes the organizational reality they experience. Therefore, organizing virtual team collaboration starts with consciously reflecting upon what one assumes the properties and goals of organization to be. As each assumption has its blind spots and shortcomings, the best possible organizational design of virtual team collaboration would therefore be one that bridges and combines organizational metaphors for the highest situational and long-term outcomes.

▶ **Metaphor** An image or figure of speech which transports a complex concept that is not directly accessible, not easy to comprehend or involves tacit assumptions and feelings, and which functions to make the concept more accessible, also beyond rational thought.

> **Application 6.2: What organization is about**
>
> Metaphors of organization visualize unconscious or pre-reflexive images of organization which you, too, are likely to have in mind. Therefore:
>
> - What do you believe that organization is about?
> - What does 'good organization' look like and what should be achieved by it?
> - What does 'bad organization' look like, and why is it bad?
> - Which metaphor of organization seems to underlie your expectations, and what are the advantages and potential blind spots of how you would like to organize? ◄

6.4 The Organizational Structure of Virtual Team Collaboration

Organizational structure is a way to regulate organizing and to channel it into certain desired, directions. However, because organizations are always changing, organizational charts can never depict the ongoing process of organizational design. Nonetheless, they are useful because they help people orientate towards the common goal, thus improving upon organization. Virtual team collaboration may take place within the following organizational social structures:

6.4.1 Functional Design

Functional designs are the simplest form of differentiation in organizations (see Fig. 6.1). People and activities are grouped based on the similarities of their tasks (e.g. production, sales, purchasing, engineering, et cetera). Communication and collaboration within functions are facilitated in this structure, yet, become more difficult across functions.

Virtual teams can either be implemented within one of the functions or be designed as a functional team themselves. For instance, there might be a virtual team in production focussing on a certain aspect of production. Alternatively, there might also be a cross-functional virtual team tasked with digitalization across the company. Table 6.1 provides

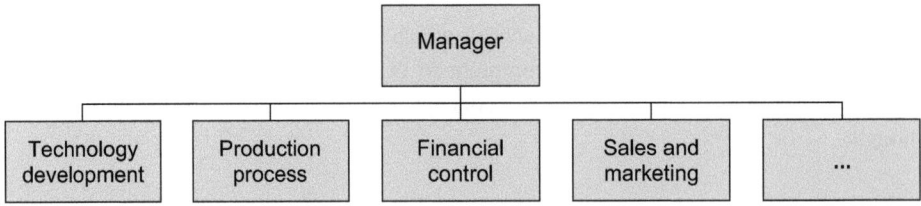

Fig. 6.1 Functional organizational design. *Source* own figure

6.4 The Organizational Structure of Virtual Team Collaboration

Table 6.1 Functional organizational design for virtual team collaboration

Pros	Cons
Practical solution for small teams	Too simple for large teams or interdependent tasks
Economies of scale (from specialization) are maximized	Integration and critical information exchange across functions is difficult. Virtual innovativeness is hindered.
Team members identify with their tasks and function	Team members' identification with the overall goal of the team might be weakened. Difficult to achieve virtual cohesion and teamness.
Transparency of tasks and functions, and how they are allocated	Low encouragement of innovativeness and creativity beyond established task-based and functional borders, low interdisciplinarity. Required trust becomes difficult to establish.
Centralized control  Decision making is easy to implement	Team leader might become overburdened with the control and information node function. Single-person control and information node function might be impossible in a virtual environment. If team leader quits, the team lacks information.

Table: own figure

an overview on the main pros and cons of functional design, also in relation to virtual team collaboration.

6.4.2 Divisional Organizational Design

An organization is structured into sub-units (divisions) in divisional design, and it is the heads of these divisions that bundle control and information (see Fig. 6.2). There are three classic ways in which to build divisions:

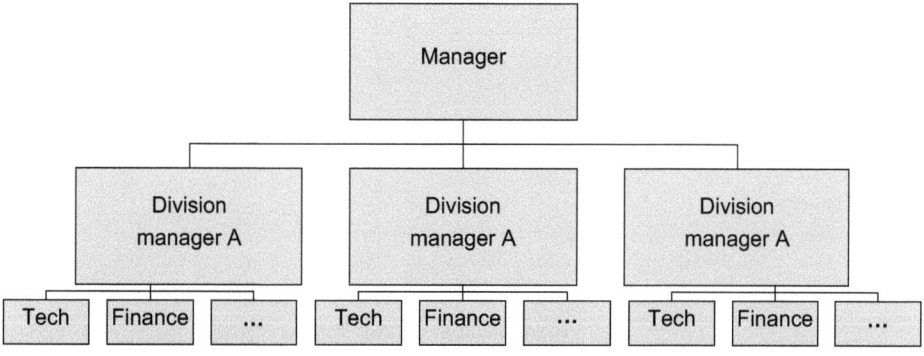

Fig. 6.2 Divisional organizational design for virtual team collaboration. *Source* own figure

- According to similarities in products, services, technologies or processes.
- According to customer, client or user type.
- According to the geographical location of the activity.

The advantages of divisional organizations are that they can grow larger than functional ones. However, because divisional organizations build redundant structures, they are generally less profitable. The only way in which one could think of running a virtual team by means of multi-divisional design is, if the divisions (sub-teams) compete against each other, for instance, when it comes to developing new innovative solutions or processes. Otherwise, the increased costs of coordination and redundancies would offset any potential strategic and operational benefits.

6.4.3 Matrix Organizational Design for Virtual Team Collaboration

Matrix designs balance the contradicting demands of efficiency and flexibility. This is achieved via constantly allocating suitable individuals from different functions to projects. A matrix thus has two structures: functional and project-based (see Fig. 6.3). There are separate responsibilities for each structure, carried out by different individuals. This then means that employees have two superiors: a permanent, functional manager, and a project manager for the duration of a specific project. Matrix designs can also take the shape of a global matrix: in this case, an additional regional dimension is added to projects. For instance, there would be a global project manager for project A, and the project

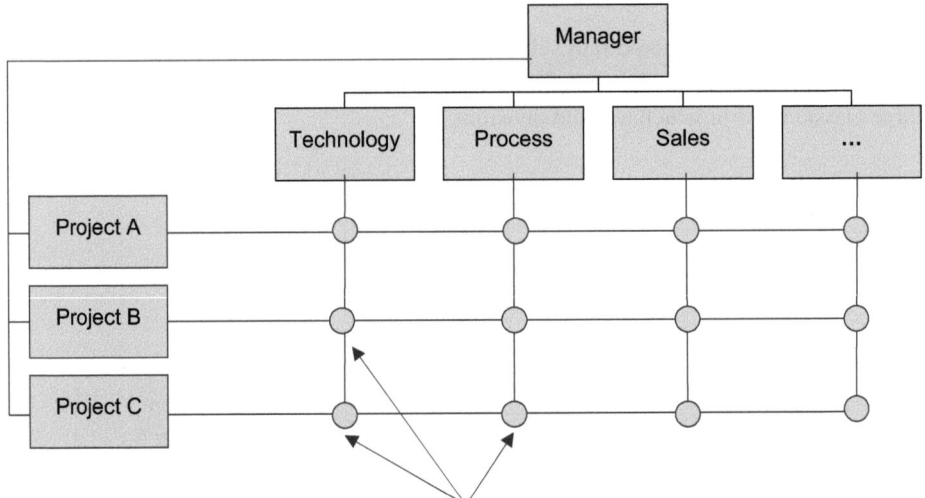

Fig. 6.3 Matrix organizational design for virtual team collaboration. *Source* own figure

would then be further sub-divided in regional project managers who run their own sub-teams. Most virtual teams, especially those with more complex and interdependent innovative and unique tasks, are implemented within matrix organizations.

Matrix designs are generally flexible: whenever there are new requirements, or a change in the organizational environment, a new project is taken on to respond to new opportunities and demands. Matrix designs thus have the unique ability to maximize the value of expensive specialists. However, those working within a matrix are subjected to dual, in the case of a global matrix: triple lines of authority. This increases pressure and workload, as high quality is expected by the different functions and as project time is tightly scheduled. Sometimes, matrix advantages are also weakened by political scheming. This occurs when some individuals and task assignments are preferred over others or when some projects are allocated more resources than others.

In practice, most organizations are characterized by **hybrid designs**. This means that managers choose the best structure for achieving the desired organizational configuration required in this specific setting. Nonetheless, the differentiation into organizational structures helps people become aware and to better manage the processes and outcomes of organization.

> **Application 6.3: Identifying the organizational structure of the global operations team**
>
> Based on what you already know about the global operations team of the opening case (also see Application 6.1):
>
> - Which organizational design (functional, divisional, matrix, hybrid) characterizes this team?
> - Does this type of organizational structure do the realities of global operations management justice? Why (not)?
> - What, if anything, would you change about the team's organizational structure so that it can perform even better? ◄

6.5 Organizational Transformation, Technology and Human-machine Interactions

Organizations transform inputs into outputs. For example, hospitals transform ill people into healthy ones, and universities turn lesser qualified people into more qualified ones, and the organizational success is measured against the effectiveness and efficiency of the transformation processes. The sum of the human, technological and other means used for transforming input into output is referred to as **organizational core technology** (see Fig. 6.4).

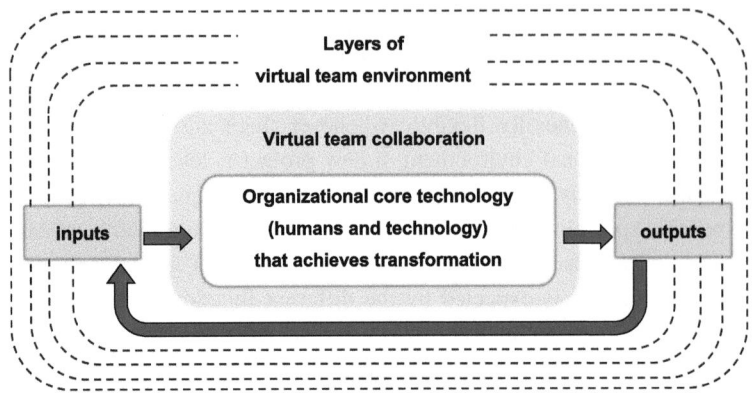

Fig. 6.4 Virtual team collaboration as organizational transformation. *Source* own figure

▶ **Organizational Core Technology** The tools, software and equipment employed for transformation, *and* the craft or knowledge it takes to produce and operate them, and those who possess this craft and knowledge.

The following section describes what makes the organizational transformation process that is achieved by means of virtual team collaboration unique. Three aspects are relevant: First, there is the role of technology as an actor in its own right, which requires a socio-technical systems or network perspective. Second, organizational design needs to take the unique convergent and divergent dynamics of virtual team collaboration into account. Third, because collaboration is necessarily based on the use of technology, organizational design needs to choose the right technology for the right virtual collaboration process.

6.5.1 Virtual Teams as Dynamic Socio-Technical Systems or Networks

The organizational transformation process achieved by means of virtual team collaboration is unique because it necessarily involves information and communication technologies (ICTs) and other technologies to organize the collaboration of humans. Virtual teams can therefore also be understood as **socio-technical** systems or networks. A **system** is a sufficiently distinct entity from an organizational perspective in which different parts come together, sometimes creating synergies from complementarity, to achieve a certain transformation. Humans and technology closely interact in a socio-technical system or network to transform inputs from the organizational environment into outputs for the organizational environment.

6.5 Organizational Transformation, Technology …

The more complex a socio-technical system becomes, the less those acting within it can picture the whole of the system. Rather, what they focus upon is the nodes they are responsible for and which are visible to them. For example, when developing the code of complex application, each individual developer is responsible for their own part, yet also pays attention to how changes in their code affect the functionality of the code parts 'next to them'. However, no developer can picture the final application 'as a whole' and no manager can fully control it.

Technologies such as Artificial Intelligence (AI), are therefore more than merely subject to human manipulation. Rather, technology, even though created by humans, becomes an actor of its own, and this is why organization has become increasingly understood as **actor networks** (Actor-Network Theory, ANT, based on Latour, 1996), with 'actors' standing for a variety of contributors, such as machines, software, AI, humans, and further material. Picturing virtual teams as socio-technological networks, with a variety of actor-technology interfaces and experiences, thus helps identify and make the required organizational design choices.

> **Link to practice: The evolution of Artificial Intelligence**
>
> The ongoing evolution of Artificial Intelligence (AI) brings about new application areas (Kretschmer, 2024). These can illustrate how technology has become an actor in its own right, and how humans and technology are interconnected as socio-technical networks. For example, cars are steered by software and, if permission is given, interact with other technologies and can be centrally administered. For instance, one can update systems remotely. Researchers have now developed and experimentally tested an AI application which alerts diabetics to hypoglycaemia (Troendle & Schmidt, 2024). First, diabetics—supervised by medical personnel and on a test drive—drove the car while exhibiting normal blood glucose levels. Then, they were given insulin to make their blood glucose levels drop, and the data and visuals from these drives were recorded. The researchers found out that hypoglycaemia changes people's head and eye movements, and how they interact with the car, for example, how they operate the steering wheel. This data was then inputted into an AI tool which was able to monitor hypoglycaemia by means of a camera and via analysing changes in human-machine interactions. One can therefore imagine a future in which a car not only serves the purpose of physical movement but is also an interconnected medical device. ◄

If the borders of a socio-technical system become blurred and are integrated with other organizational purposes and units, one speaks of **socio-technical networks** (instead of systems). For instance, when influencers market a product online, the boundary of which 'organization' sells the product becomes blurred. In this case, it is more appropriate to speak of a socio-technical **network** than of a socio-technical system. The network perspective acknowledges that virtual teams are embedded in multiple environments, that the 'borders' between 'team' and 'environment' are often blurred, and that the virtual team relies on internal and external network partners for inputs and outputs, and for achieving transformation. For example, the Internet of Things (see boxed content) connects objects and devices into a technological network of which virtual team collaboration is also a part.

Socio-Technical System	Systems, such as a virtual team, in which humans, and material and immaterial technologies, closely interact for organizational transformation.
Actor-Network Theory (ANT)	Here: the idea that virtual team collaboration is shaped by human and technological actors, with the need to align these actors via effective and appropriate organizational design choices.
Network	The idea that organization is not limited to a fixed and distinct 'organizational unit' but emerges from interaction nodes involving internal and external partners.

6.5.2 The Need to Configure ICTs, and Convergent-Divergent Dynamics

Virtual team collaboration is more dynamic than non-virtual team collaboration (also see Chap. 2). These dynamics can either be convergent or divergent, and their impact on the team can be positive or negative. For instance, trust is a positive convergent process whereas groupthink is a negative convergent process. Likewise, innovativeness and creativity are positive divergent processes whereas lack of trust or conflict are negative divergent processes. Too much convergence is as harmful to virtual team collaboration as is too much divergence: part of the organizational design challenge is thus to contribute to the ideal balance between convergence and divergence, and to support the positive dynamics and minimize the negative ones by means of conducive organizational awareness, processes and structures.

Virtual team collaboration furthermore involves the usage of information and communication technologies (ICTs) (also see Chap. 3). Media richness is thus a crucial influencing factor of organizational design. Media richness refers to the number of communicative modes (audio, video, virtual reality) facilitated by ICT and whether it allows for synchronous exchange (virtual meeting) or asynchronous exchange (e-mail). The higher the number of synchronous communicative modes, the richer the ICT (Daft & Lengel, 1984). The ICTs chosen need to fit the communicative and task-related purposes of collaboration. For instance, if one uses an ICT that is too rich for the communicative purpose (reading out financial numbers on an excel sheet report in a virtual meeting), this leads to over-complication (an e-mail would have sufficed). Yet, if one tries to establish strategy via e-mail, this is prone to fail because this lean and asynchronous ICT oversimplifies the matter. Further influencing factors are team task, team members' location and qualification, and team interdependence.

Out of this follows the fact that the organizational design choices to be made are specific to each virtual team. For instance, a global research and development team needs to be creative (a positive divergent dynamic), yet, this divergence must be integrated by means of trust (a positive convergent dynamic) so that the team does not lose cohesion. A different cooperation-competition, and differentiation-integration ratio is required compared to a product sales team in which team members are assigned to different markets and in which only the respective market sales matter for performance: divergent dynamics must lead to cooperation and integration in the research and development team. Thus, the team-internal organizational transformation process needs to be more aligned and requires richer ICTs. Divergent dynamics may remain competitive and differentiated in the product sales team. Thus, the team-internal organizational transformation process may remain fragmented, and leaner ICTs suffice, as it is only on higher levels (global product portfolio and sales strategy) that integration and cooperation are required. In summary, one needs to align the design choices for successful organizational transformation with the specifics of virtual team collaboration. This then implies:

- Mundane goals and simple, repetitive tasks can be easily organized by means of specifications, procedures and schedules. This then results in lower task interdependence between team members. Consequently, functions are more differentiated, which leads to lower degrees of teamness. Because the goal is mundane, and the task is simple and repetitive, high levels of competition between team members are unlikely. Thus, higher levels of teamness are not required for the team to perform well.
- The more complex or unique the task, the more it involves tacit knowledge, that is: knowledge which is rooted in a person's experience and cannot be put into words ('how to do' knowledge such as 'riding a bike'). Tacit knowledge complicates virtual organization because something needs to be 'shown' to transfer it (explanations do not suffice), and 'showing how' is generally difficult across locations. One thus needs higher levels of task integration, and, because tacit knowledge is rooted in individuals, task integration can only be achieved via teamness. Because collaboration is virtual, this teamness needs to be built by means of rich communication media, that is: ICTs which allow for synchronous exchange and multiple modes of communication, such as written and spoken communication as well as video transmissions.
- Complex activities, coupled with exceptional goals, always require rich ICTs in order to build the required high degree of teamness. However, because these are also activities by means of which an individual can excel and become visible in the organization, managers need to watch out for negative competition and balance it, for instance, by means of their leadership style or by means of creating a strong team culture.

▶   Organizational ICT choices are related to questions such as:

- Should a certain virtual team collaboration happen spontaneously or be planned?
- Is the virtual team directed towards mundane or exceptional goals?
- Is the virtual team tasked with simple or complex activities?

6.5.3 Summary of the Organizational Transformation Process Achieved by Virtual Teams

Figure 6.5 summarizes the factors that are specific to the organizational transformation process achieved by means of virtual team collaboration based on the previous considerations.

> **Application 6.4: Virtual team collaboration as organizational transformation**
>
> Based on what you know about the global operations team and organizational transformation:
>
> - What transformation shall be achieved by means of the global operations team, or, in other words: what kind of organizational technology is the global operations team?
> - How do humans and technologies come together in the transformation process?
> - With which internal and external partners does the global operations team have to network, and how should this be done? ◄

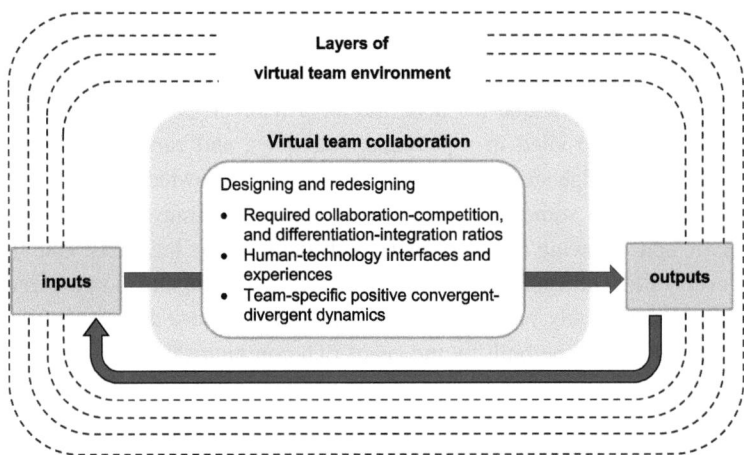

Fig. 6.5 Requirements of virtual team collaboration as organizational transformation. *Source* own figure

6.6 Organizational Core Technologies: Three Main Design Options

This section sheds further light on the organizational transformation process. It introduces three main core technologies by means of which organizations may transform input into output. Or, in other words: when virtual team members design organization, they need to make sure that the core technologies which they choose fit virtual team collaboration purposes and goals. There are three main organizational core technologies based on Thompson (1967), namely mediating, long-linked and intensive. All three differ in how they allocate tasks to people (differentiation) and how they enable the exchange of critical information across functions and roles (integration). Some of them are therefore more or less fitting to certain, but not other, types of virtual teams. Choosing the right kind of technology is thus part of the required organizational awareness but also part of the process and structures by means of which organizational goals are reached. Again, team members may evaluate and, if required, change existing organization with the knowledge of organizational core technologies *or* make sure that they design new teams in the best possible way.

6.6.1 Mediating Technologies

Mediating technologies bring parties—thus: the combination of tasks and people—together for an exchange. For example, an e-learning system integrates lecturers and students. The technological system thus provides each user with a customized technological experience and entry cockpit: lecturers see their respective lectures from a trainer's point of view (involving different configuration rights), and students see those courses which they have enrolled in (across lecturers) from a student's point of view (with limited configuration rights). Mediating technologies require limited coordination. However, they need rules and standard procedures in order to make it clear how decisions should be made and how work processes should be performed. Interdependence is pooled, because individuals (in this case: the lecturers) work independently from each other. Nonetheless, their combined output contributes to the group's or organization's overall goals. An example would be a virtual sales team in which each team member is responsible for certain products that uses a sales tool in which customers can place orders for the whole of the team's product range (inputs). The sales tool then sorts these orders per product and assigns orders per product to each team member; however, the client receives a multi-product shipment, as per order placed. Thus, technology mediates between input and output (see Fig. 6.6).

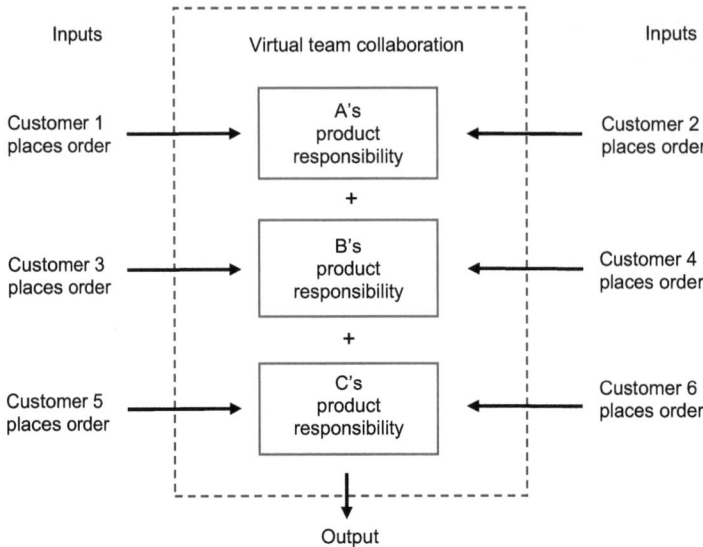

Fig. 6.6 Mediating technologies: the case of a global sales team. *Source* own figure

When should one choose mediating technology as the organizing principle (core technology) for managing how a virtual team transforms input into output?
Mediating technologies are suitable for teams that are loosely knit (low in teamness). For example, the individual sales managers of the aforementioned case work independently of each other, yet the total profit generated by the whole team is measured at the end of each fiscal year. Such teams can thus afford high levels of virtualness and global remoteness during times of execution without this being harmful to the functioning of the team and the overall goal. The main coordination mechanisms are **rules and procedures**. However, whenever a new strategy needs to be rolled out, these types of teams would have to meet in person or collaborate by means of the richest ICTs available to make sure that strategic requirements for the next executive phase are aligned, and also fit all team members and clients.

6.6.2 Long-Linked Technologies

Long-linked technologies align tasks and people in a fixed sequence; with the assembly line, for instance, in automotive production, being the classic example. The overall output is split into discrete, repetitive tasks of small range (high specialization), and, often people work hand in hand with technology to execute these tasks. Because inputs, outputs, and the transformation process itself need to be standardized, long-linked technologies require coordination via scheduling tasks and workers, and **time planning** is imperative. Kanban cards are an example for such a coordination mechanism.

6.6 Organizational Core Technologies: Three Main Design Options

Because long-linked technologies require a linear interdependence of tasks (C builds upon B, which builds upon A), they are not a very good way of structuring virtual team collaboration; they can only be employed if task complexity is low, and if repetitiveness is guaranteed. To think of an example, one might assume that, upon request, an associate formulates the content of a presentation to be given by their manager. At the end of their work day, the associate sends this content to an assistant at an offshore site (in a different time zone) for visualization, and, upon having completed the visualization task, the assistant then sends the slides to another site (in a different time zone) for proof-reading, this assistant then sends the final slides to the manager who needs to hold that presentation. Figure 6.7 visualizes this process.

When should one choose long-linked technology as the organizing principle (core technology) for managing how a virtual team transforms input into output?
Long-linked technology involves sequential task interdependence, due to the fixed sequence of tasks performed. The main coordination mechanisms are **rules, procedures**, and **schedules**. Because careful planning of tasks and scheduling of workers are imperative, long-linked technology is not well-suited for meeting the flexibility and discretion requirements of most types of global virtual team collaboration. The degree of control to be exercised and the required coordination efforts are too high to be achieved by means of ICTs, and there are no strategic considerations, despite, for instance, utilizing the advantages of different time zones for an even faster execution of simple and repetitive discrete tasks in a sequential order, such as preparing presentation files faster than could be done at a single location. Thus, long-linked technology is usually only suitable for the small portion of virtual team collaboration that is mundane and repetitive and related to execution.

6.6.3 Intensive Technologies

Intensive technologies are characterized by multi-directional workflows between mutually constitutive responsibilities (see Fig. 6.8). Any organization or team that uses intensive technology uses long-linked and mediating technologies as well: it is just that, in

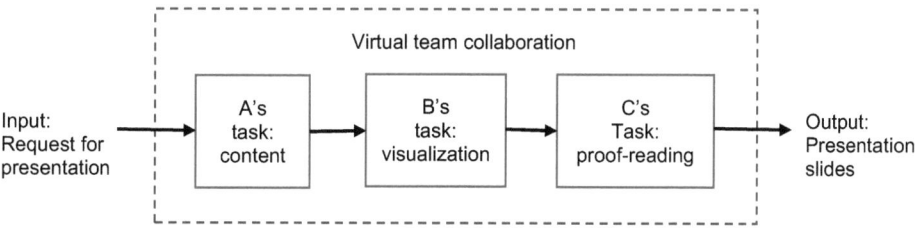

Fig. 6.7 Long-linked technologies: the case of preparing a presentation across time zones. *Source* own figure

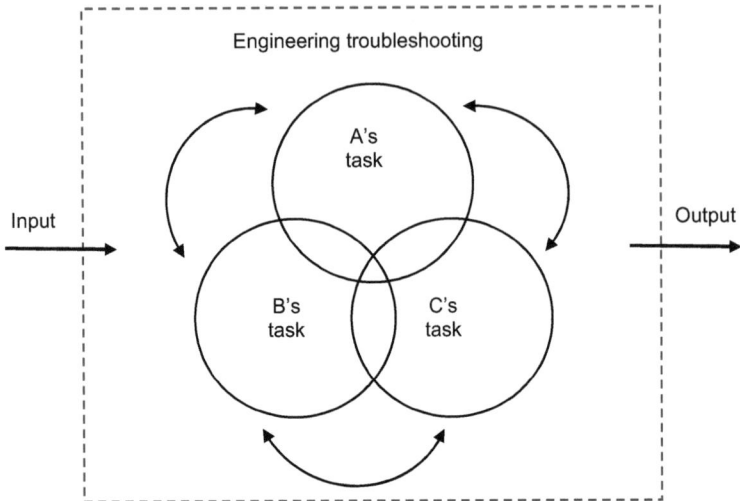

Fig. 6.8 Intensive technologies: the case of software troubleshooting. *Source* own figure

a certain situation, the intended outcome requires intensive technology and cannot be achieved solely by the means of the other two. For example, software engineering involves mediating and long-linked technologies. Yet, if a critical software, such as the steering software of a nuclear power plant ceases to function, a team of specialists need to work in parallel and in interaction to troubleshoot, as visualized in Fig. 6.8: at this point, intensive technology is employed.

When should one choose intensive technologies as the organizing principle (core technology) for managing how a virtual team transforms input into output?
Due to reciprocal task interdependence, intensive technologies require mutual cooperation and collaboration on team level. Centralized control and decision making, as well as fixed responsibilities are harmful to a team functioning by means of intensive technology, as everyone involved is dependent upon inputs and outputs from everyone else. If intensive technologies also involve technological actors, interface management is crucial to success. Those involved (humans and technology) furthermore need to give and receive feedback, and adjust to each other, as each unique situation requires. In order to facilitate these dynamics, team members must therefore be allowed to use discretion at work.

Thus, in order to ensure high performance collaboration in virtual teams, intensive technologies, due to their high coordination costs and efforts, are only to be used if less complex coordination mechanisms do not suffice. As mediating technologies are the simplest type of core technology, they should be used whenever possible. Long-linked technologies—which are difficult to implement and costly to control virtually—should only be used when absolutely necessary (over-scheduling and over-dependency need to be avoided) and for exploiting temporal advantages of virtual collaboration. Intensive technologies must be used whenever complex, unique, interdependent and knowledge-intensive task and responsibilities require it. Their usage automatically leads to multiple human-technology interfaces, rich ICTs and high collaborative complexity, which then implies that team members must possess (or be trained in) the required communicative competencies, technological expertise and self-organization skills.

> **Application 6.5: Core technologies of the global operations team**
>
> Consider the three main core technologies presented before:
>
> - Mediating technologies are characterized by pooled interdependence which only requires rules and procedures.
> - Long-linked technologies are characterized by sequential interdependence and thus require rules, procedures *and* scheduling.
> - Reciprocal interdependence in long-linked technologies require rules, procedures, scheduling *and* mutual adjustment.
>
> Based on this understanding:
>
> - Which core technology suits the global operations team of the opening case the most?
> - Would you choose only one or do you need a mixture of core technologies, e.g. depending on purpose, project status, task interdependence or team's lifecycle stage?
> - If so: for what purpose would you employ which core technology, and why? ◄

6.7 Should Teams Organize for Change or Stability, and How Much Bureaucracy is Required?

Depending on what organizations—and the people creating them—believe in and enact, some organizations seem more willing and able to change than others. There are three major approaches to the organizational transformation process that differ with regard to their understanding as to whether change would be necessary or desirable.

- The **technological imperative** (overview in Hatch, with Cunliffe, 2006) focusses on the inner-organizational transformation processes and describes the idea that an organization's inner core technology should determine its structural features (organization as machine). Scientific management (also known as 'Taylorism', see Taylor, 1911/2006), one application of this idea, maintains, for example, that there is one best way of running the production line, and environmental factors come second.

Organizations should not change what makes them excellent from this perspective, unless absolutely necessary.
- Conversely, **contingency theory** (overview in Hatch, with Cunliffe, 2006) maintains that the organization cannot be designed independently of the environment, from which it receives input and to which it delivers output, and for which it needs to be 'fit' (organization as organism). The main goal of contingency theory is to develop a formula for the best way to organize, that considers both the environment and the technology in use.
- **Sensemaking theory and enactment** (Weick, 1995) argues that organizations will only be successful if employees believe in them and create and align convincing 'mental maps' of what it means to work in this organization and why. This way, people make 'sense' out of the organizational past and present, and themselves in it, and they also act upon it ('enactment'), which then makes these ideas 'real' (organization as culture). Or, in other words: organization does not exist unless people create it in their minds and via their actions.

This then implies that one needs to take all three factors into account in virtual team collaboration when figuring out how to find the ideal stability-change ratio of the team.

Bureaucracy (based on Weber, 1947) is the prime example of a purely mechanistic organization (organization as machine). It is also an inevitable structural consequence of most organizations and emerges if organizations are large, rely upon recognized technical or functional expertise, or continue over a long period of time (e.g. governments). The idea of bureaucracy is to establish rules which are fair to all because they are independent of the person, to promote people on merit-based grounds, and to ensure reliable decision making. This way, it turns average people into competent administrators. However, it also tends to develop a life of its own and to hinder innovation, change and creativity by removing the individual from the organization. Therefore, bureaucracy should be avoided by small organizational units, such as virtual teams, and by those employing knowledge workers and relying on creativity. It is also never a good way of reacting to the environment and for implementing change. At the same time, bureaucracy keeps individual aims at personal power in check and ensures a minimum standard for all (e.g. performance norms for the virtual team against which each member is measured). Therefore, avoiding bureaucracy completely might also have severe negative consequences. Ultimately, all organizational structures are limited in the sense that they value the outcome of organization and internal stability more than processes of organizing and flexible reactions towards the organizational environment. Bureaucracy as a major impediment to change can be partially avoided by more organic designs, but is still prone to emerge due to sheer organizational size, which then encourages more mechanistic approaches to organizational structure.

> **Pause and reflect: Should work from home be organizationally supported or restricted?**

As the Munich-based research institute ifo finds based on a survey involving 9000 companies, almost a quarter of all employees in Germany worked from home at least partially in February 2024 (overview in Tagesschau, 2024). This proportion has remained fairly constant during the last two years. However, it is also reported that several large German companies, such as Volkswagen, Deutsche Bank, Telekom or SAP, prescribe that their employees work from the office at least three days. At Telekom, a higher physical presence is demanded from those in leadership positions (four days). According to ifo-expert Jean-Victor Alipour, on-site work and the alignment of core office hours strengthens knowledge transfer, group creativity and social relations. Therefore: should organizations restrict or support work-from-home, and when, how and for whom should they draw the line? ◄

6.8 Closing Part

6.8.1 Chapter Summary

This chapter has introduced and discussed the organizational design perspective on virtual team collaboration. Organization starts with people engaging in a coordinated effort with others to achieve a certain desired organizational end state or goal. Some of these interaction patterns then become organizational processes and structures, which result in the creation of identifiable organizational units to the outside. However, because organizations are embedded in changing environments, no organizational structure is set in stone, and organizations need to be designed for change as much as stability. In such ways, organization is a process (organizing), a principle (organization) and a specific outcome (*the* organization) which are mutually constitutive, and which need to be consciously configured. Organization serves its purpose of aligning tasks and people for achieving a larger goal if it is efficient and effective. This means that one has succeeded in finding and maintaining the ideal balance between differentiation and integration, and between collaboration and competition, and in minimizing the input required for the desired output. Because every organization is dependent upon several internal and external factors, it requires constant organizing and, if required, change.

Organizational design means to make such organizational choices consciously, and based on a patterned assessment of organizational reality and goals. Virtual team members and leaders in the role of organizational designers therefore need to be aware of the building blocks of organization, in relation to virtual team requirements. This way, they can make sure that design choices, such as mechanistic or organic types of collaboration, fit the team's purposes and needs. Or, in the case of existing virtual team collaboration, they can investigate whether the existing organizational processes and structures suffice or could be improved. Metaphors of organization make team members become aware of the organizational images they hold in their minds and, thus, enable them to move beyond such taken for granted implicit assumptions and to explicate them to others, for a better and more aware organizational design.

The ability to design organizational processes and structures follows from organizational awareness. Functional, divisional and matrix-structures are more or less suitable to certain types of virtual teams, with a matrix design generally being the most common and fitting. The key processes to be organized are the ways in which virtual teams transform inputs into outputs, and the means employed for doing so are referred to as 'organizational core technology'. Technology is a key actor in how transformation is achieved in the case of virtual team collaboration, and virtual teams therefore need to be understood as socio-technical systems of networks. Virtual team collaboration is also more dynamic than non-virtual team collaboration, and necessarily involves Information and Communication Technologies (ICTs), and both aspects need to be considered for organizational design. Three core technologies are available for organizing transformation—mediating, long-linked and intensive—and all have their advantages and disadvantages in how they differentiate and integrate human and non-human interfaces. This means that the choice must be made in relation to team characteristics. Virtual teams must organize for the ideal stability-change ratio and may not be overburdened by bureaucracy. By having engaged with these themes, you can now make more informed organizational design choices, thus influencing one of the key moderators of successful virtual team collaboration positively and in the most conducive manner.

6.8.2 Key Points

- Virtual team collaboration can be analysed and improved upon from an organizational design perspective.
- Organization involves processes of organizing and their outcome (organization) and builds entities (*the* organization).
- Organizational units, such as virtual teams, need to be designed for stability as much as for change.
- Organic organizational design is more conducive to virtual team collaboration than mechanistic organizational design.
- Different types of organizational structures are more or less suitable to virtual team collaboration.
- Organizational units transform inputs into outputs by means of core technologies.
- Human and non-human interfaces need to be organized and aligned in virtual team collaboration, understood as human-actor networks.
- Virtual teams may not be overburdened with bureaucracy.

6.8.3 Review Questions

1. What is organization, and what does it involve?
2. What are the building blocks of organization?
3. What is organizational design, and what is meant with virtual team members and leaders being in the role of organizational designers?
4. What characterizes mechanistic versus organic organizational design?
5. Which metaphors of organization can you briefly describe, and how are these relevant to (improving upon) virtual team collaboration?
6. Which key organizational structures do you know, and how is each of them more or less conducive to virtual team collaboration?
7. What is organizational transformation, and by means of which core technologies can it be achieved?
8. When and how are these core technologies useful to (which type of) virtual team collaboration?
9. What does actor-network theory tell you about virtual team collaboration, and why are these insights relevant?
10. What is bureaucracy, how does it emerge, and why can it be dangerous to virtual team collaboration?

6.8.4 Opening Case Revisited

The opening case of this chapter presented a global operations team which needs to collaborate strategically. With the full learning from this chapter in mind: Which are the key organizational requirements that team members need to keep in mind and implement for the team to perform?

Try to come up with the most nuanced and complete answer to this question, which also acknowledges different scenarios, e.g. of how the virtual team environment might develop, how customer demands might change or how technology might further develop.

6.8.5 Closing Activity

Choose any organizational effort you are presently engaged in, e.g. a student project, a sports activity or a type of work. The only requirement is that your example involves the need to collectively organize, that is: the goal must be larger than can be achieved by a single individual. Apply the learning from this chapter to your example: what is the best way to organize in this case? Make sure to consider:

- The three properties of organization: organizing as a process, organization as those parts of the process which are made permanent, and *the* organization as the entity resulting from both.
- The need to organize for stability as much as for change.
- The building blocks of organization and the configurative choices to be made.
- The need for awareness and to consider whether informed choices are being made.
- Organizational metaphors and their impact on how people (also: you) organize.
- Organizational process: how to transform input into output in the most effective and efficient ways. You need to define input and output in this given case as well as what the desired or required 'transformation' is in order to do so.
- How humans and non-human functions and roles interrelate, and the role and impact of technology.
- The requirement of not overburdening organization with bureaucracy.
- The need to find the ideal stability-change ratio of organization.
- If applicable: organizational structures and differentiating principles such as mechanistic and organic organization.

Based on your considerations, come up with a checklist: which organizational requirements are already fulfilled in the best possible way and what should be improved? If you can, discuss your findings with those with whom you collaborate in the given case and see whether and how this improves upon organizational reality.

Remark: When working on this task, be aware to keep bureaucracy to a minimum: do not over-organize and only focus on those aspects which are crucial and a 'must have'.

References

City University Hong Kong. (2023). *Global Operations Management*. Retrieved December 12, 2023, from https://www.cb.cityu.edu.hk/ms/bbagom/.

Cunliffe, A. (2012). *Organization Theory*. London: Sage.

Daft, R. L., & Lengel, R. H. (1984). Information richness: A new approach to managerial behavior and organizational design. *Research in Organizational Behavior, 6*, 191–233.

Hatch, M. J. (2011). *Organizations: A very short introduction*. Oxford University Press.

Hatch, M. J., & Cunliffe, A. (2006). *Organization theory—Modern, symbolic and postmodern perspectives*. Oxford University Press.

Kretschmer, C. (2024). Digitalisierung: Wie sich künstliche Intelligenz entwickeln wird. *Tagesschau January 07, 2024*. Retrieved January, 07, 2024 from: https://www.tagesschau.de/wirtschaft/digitales/kuenstliche-intelligenz-ausblick-100.html.

Latour, B. (1996). On actor-network theory: A few clarifications. *Soziale Welt, 47*(4), 369–381.

Mell, J. N., Jang, S., & Chai, S. (2021). Bridging temporal divides: Temporal brokerage in global teams and its impact on individual performance. *Organization Science, 32*(3), 731–751.

Morgan, G. (2006). *Images of organization*. Sage. (Original work published 1986).

Tagesschau. (2024). Arbeiten im Homeoffice weiterhin fest etabliert. *Tagesschau*. Retrieved March 01, 2024, from https://www.tagesschau.de/wirtschaft/arbeitsmarkt/homeoffice-umfrage-ifo-februar-100.html.

Taylor, F. W. (2006). *The principles of scientific management.* Cosimo Classics. (Original work published 1911)

Thompson, J. (1967). *Organization in action.* McGraw-Hill.

Troendle, S., & Schmidt, J. (2024). Künstliche Intelligenz im Straßenverkehr: KI warnt unterzuckerte Diabetiker beim Autofahren. *Tagesschau, February 21, 2024.* Retrieved February 21, 2024 from: https://www.tagesschau.de/wissen/gesundheit/ki-diabetes-100.html.

Weber, M. (1947). *The theory of social and economic organization* (A. M. Henderson, & T. Parsons, Trans.). Collier Macmillan Publishers.

Weick, K. (1995). *Sensemaking in organizations.* Sage.

Further Reading

Gibson, C.B. & Grushina, S.V. (2021), A tale of two teams: next generation strategies for increasing the effectiveness of global virtual teams. *Organizational Dynamics* 50(1), 100823. Retrieved May 1, 2024, from https://doi.org/10.1016/jorgdyn.2020.100823.

This article provides interesting insights into the organizational challenges related to global virtual teams. The title can potentially be read as an allusion to two works. First, to an organization studies classic, namely Barbara Czarniawska's (2017) A Tale of Three Cities on the challenges of public management and organization. This work is already an allusion to Charles Dicken's (1859) A Tale of Two Cities, from which the famous opening sentence "It was the best of times, it was the worst of times (…)" originates (which might also be of relevance for how people experience virtual team collaboration).

Digital Leadership and Virtual Team Collaboration: Options and Success Factors for Industry 4.0

7.1 Introduction

Leadership is one of the most relevant influential factors of virtual team collaboration. The key element of leadership in a team context lies in its motivational and guiding component, or, in other words: in its providing development, purpose and direction to others and oneself. For example, leaders guide followers to develop and use competencies and skills for achieving organizational goals, they direct followers to be motivated in alignment with larger goals, and they facilitate the usage of a variety of suitable methods, tools and processes by their followers. It is thus relevant to note that leadership emerges *between* people: one may only successfully 'lead' if others accept this claim and behave accordingly.

Despite being one of the most relevant aspects of managerial and professional practice, leadership is difficult to define conclusively. However, one can always see when leadership is lacking. One way of approaching leadership is thus by asking the question: what is it that leadership *does* for individuals, teams and organizations? It then becomes easy to define leadership, namely as those moderators that succeed in achieving the positive outcomes commonly associated with leadership. These are, for instance, influencing, facilitating, and organizing people into accomplishing a joint vision, purpose, or significant goal (Mendenhall et al., 2012). Leadership is an interpersonal and organizational process and practice from this perspective, not merely a single hierarchical position or an individual character trait. Leadership is also often global, and inevitably digital in the context of virtual team collaboration, that is: related to Information and Communication Technologies (ICTs) and aiming at utilizing the benefits of digitization.

Based on this outcome-oriented approach to leadership practice, this chapter discusses different approaches to leadership and summarizes those leadership concepts and practices that can be assumed to be most relevant to virtual team collaboration under Industry 4.0 conditions. After having read this chapter, you should know key leadership conceptualizations and qualities, and how they relate to successful virtual team collaboration, and you should be able to engage in informed leadership practices yourself, as a member of a virtual team.

Team	A small number of individuals who collaborate in a task and/or to reach a goal.
ICTs	Information and communication technologies.
Virtual Team Collaboration	Working together as a team by means of ICTs.
Leadership	Identifying and maintaining those higher-level moderators that succeed in achieving the intended positive outcomes of virtual team collaboration.
Industry 4.0	The intelligent networking of machines and processes in an industrial context that is supported by ICTs, and the developments which have created and are still creating this environment.

7.1.1 Learning Objectives

After having read this chapter, you should.

- Know what digital leadership involves.
- Understand and be able to apply the VUCA model which describes key challenges faced by leaders today.
- Understand the components of virtual team leadership in light of Industry 4.0 conditions.
- Know how transactional and transformational leadership differ from and complement each other in the context of virtual team collaboration.
- Understand key aspects of shared and distributed leadership in virtual team collaboration, and know when and how this style is required.
- Know what situational leadership is comprised of and why and how it is beneficial to virtual team development.
- Understand key leadership concepts as well as global leadership styles, and their respective strengths and weaknesses in facilitating virtual team collaboration.
- Be able to use leadership as a moderating factor for successful virtual team collaboration.

7.1.2 Opening case

> **Example**
>
> **Digital leadership**, also referred to as Leadership 4.0, is an in-vogue concept in contemporary managerial theory and practice. It is related to the conditions and requirements of the fourth industrial revolution (4IR), or **Industry 4.0**, understood as an

environment in which industries, in particular the manufacturing sector, are driven by big data, connectivity, virtual and augmented reality, data analytics, human-machine interaction, and improvement in artificial intelligence and robotics. The underlying disruptive, mainly digital developments of the business environment which have created and are still creating this environment are understood to be volatile, uncertain, complex and ambiguous (VUCA model, see Saleh & Watson, 2017). VUCA thus poses tremendous organizational and leadership challenges—but also the opportunity for transformation. Digital leadership refers to the competencies, skills and behaviour required for mastering the VUCA conditions of the fourth industrial revolution in order to achieve transformation (see also White et al., 2023).

According to Bennett and Lemoine (2014), these four components (Volatility, Uncertainty, Complexity and Ambiguity) can be differentiated with regard to two leadership questions, namely:

- How well can you predict the result of your actions?
  and
- How much do you know about the situation?

Under **volatile conditions**, there is knowledge, and the outcome of actions might be predicted: it is just the conditions that fluctuate, and one needs to react quickly. The best leadership options are either to go lean and react upon the situation, when changes occur (which is costly if the reaction is inadequate or insufficient) or to invest in being prepared (which is costly because one needs to hold reserve resources in stock). Example: rapid developments in the area of artificial intelligence and robotics which challenge existing business models.

Under **uncertain conditions**, there is some knowledge, but the consequences of one's actions are hard or impossible to predict. One thus needs to invest in acquiring further information. The best leadership option is to invest in learning as well as in learning structures and processes, such as networks or analytics, and thereby to improve upon existing systems. Example: a competitor has rolled out an innovative virtual meeting technology that challenges the organization's present technological set-up.

Under **complex conditions**, there are many interconnected parts and variables. This means that it is difficult to obtain knowledge about the situation. It might well be possible to predict the outcome of one's actions, once taken. However, the sheer amount of information required for acting might be overwhelming. The best leadership option is to learn, to build up resources and knowledge (or to bring in experts), and then to change and transform where required. Example: the need to achieve sustainability goals.

Under **ambiguous conditions**, knowledge is lacking and actions are difficult to predict. There are no precedents, and facing the unknown is experienced as overwhelming and emotionally challenging. The only leadership option in this situation is to experiment. Example: an overwhelming, unpredictable and threatening crisis, such as the COVID-19 pandemic, wherein no solution seems to be a 'good' one, and wherein each path of action also has negative consequences. The stated considerations are depicted by means of a table. ◄

VUCA Model	A model describing Industry 4.0 conditions as volatile, uncertain, complex and ambiguous.
Digital Leadership	The competencies, skills and behaviour required for mastering the VUCA conditions of Industry 4.0.

7.2 Evolution and Components of Virtual Team Leadership

Leadership is often presented as something that differs entirely from management or professional work. However, the distinction is not as clear-cut as many promoters of an exclusive 'leadership theory' might wish to suggest. Rather, and this is also the stance from which this text is written, leadership emerges from management and professional work, sometimes going beyond it.

Managers—as those business professionals who sometimes 'evolve' into leaders—are a group of people who try to organize and control a business, and managing involves all the activities which they engage in to reach this goal (Cunliffe, 2012). Management always takes place in relation to others, and this makes management—and leadership—an interpersonal, social activity. Or, in other words: leadership would be impossible without followership, and the question is thus what legitimizes managers to 'manage', and leaders to 'lead', in the eyes of others. According to Hendry (2013), one may observe three tendencies in management and leadership, namely rationalization, individualization and socialization.

- **Rationalization** refers to the assumption that management and leadership are about rational and impersonal choices and actions. This is the basis of bureaucratic management, that is: the leader as competent administrator and also as the 'best' expert who leads by setting a professional example.
- **Individualization** describes the assumption that management and leadership are about individual abilities and traits, sometimes even about having or not having a certain personality. This is the idea of the strong, charismatic leader who motivates and inspires others by sheer force of personality.
- **Socialization** refers to the assumption that management and leadership are about what happens between leaders and their followers, sometimes also about how groups of people together create 'leadership'.

Much of the daily business of management aims at rationalization, that is: objective and impartially 'right' decisions and actions. Think, for instance, of SWOT or PESTLE analyses or the Boston Consulting Group matrix: these are models rationalizing decision making via simplification. This approach gives the impression that one may control complex realities by means of predictable approaches. At the same time, management is never fully predictable: a large portion of it requires managers to 'cope with things' in the sense of unexpected situations, challenges or requirements. Furthermore, "reason (…) has a nasty habit of running out on us when things get really important" (Hendry, 2013, p. 5). It is often at this point, when direction and outcomes are unclear and when reason fails, that management becomes 'leadership', that is: a quality or practice that is more than mere administration or execution. Thus, while leadership is linked to management and professional work, it also goes beyond it. Furthermore, in particular in the context of interdisciplinary and professional virtual teams, leadership can also be exercised by a non-manager or by a collective; it is thus neither confined to the 'business people' formally in charge nor to a single individual.

If one looks at the history of management, one can see that that leadership—as a quality beyond routine administration and professional work—first became a requirement when organizations developed from mechanistic ('machine-like') into organic ('living' and 'cultural') entities, and when markets and customer requirements became more complex and fast-paced. Rethinking what organizations stand for was, amongst others, a result of changing employees' demands, namely the need to feel 'seen' and recognized at work and of employees' higher bargaining power. The stated market and business environment changes required that organizations meet more differentiated and complex demands, which again supported a less mechanistic organization of work and more fluid, interdisciplinary modes of collaboration (see Chap. 6). Finally, there is a general trend in post-industrialised societies towards knowledge-intensive work which requires mutual adjustment instead of strict schedules, rules and procedures: again, a reason for why rationalization of work in the sense of bureaucracy and routine does not suffice.

Conversely, in the 'old' world of work—with a hierarchical, bureaucratic and rather stable organization that prescribed work—it was only top management who set the direction for units led by individual managers, and leadership in the sense of establishing purpose and direction was thus limited to this small group. Alignment was mainly achieved through formal structures, such as protocols, manuals, job descriptions, and so on, and by a deep organizational culture that was shared by a fairly homogeneous group of long-term employees. The main task for managers/leaders was then to maintain the team that had been assigned to them and to guide them through occasional crises brought on by single isolated events. The focus was thus on bureaucratic management in the sense of Weber (1947): the competent administrator and the impersonal organization that, by means of rules and procedures, makes sure that performance never falls below a minimum standard and is objectively 'fair' to all.

When the organizational environment became more differentiated, globalized and fast-paced, management and leadership became less production- and more marketing-oriented. Thus, it became more common for top management to set performance targets (outputs) for units and leave it at the discretion of their subordinate managers how to direct the unit towards achieving these targets. Managers now also needed to motivate and inspire, and to encourage people to break out of their comfort zones and perform beyond themselves: they needed to act as 'leaders'. Consequently, the first leadership theories that emerged from the US-American context differentiated leadership from management. Or, as management guru Peter Drucker is reported to have said (also see Drucker, 2001): *"Management is doing things right; leadership is doing the right things."* The idea was that those who 'lead' establish direction, delegate work and motivate others by means of a combination of personal aura or charisma, sometimes also specific knowledge and skills. One could thus observe an individualization of leadership ('leadership as personality'), as opposed to the rationalization of management ('the competent administrator'). Furthermore, leadership requirements started to spread to other professions, as specialized disciplinary knowledge became more relevant in times of industrialization and digitalization.

▶ Rationalizing and individualizing leadership is insufficient for virtual team collaboration.

In today's globalized and virtualized world of work, organizations are less steered by clear, long-term and formalized rules, procedures and hierarchies. Rather, they are formed by short-lived collaborations and projects. Alignment, if possible at all, becomes difficult because of rapid organizational and environmental changes, more short-term, flexible and diverse teams of employment, and increased employee diversity. This then implies that 'teams', not 'individuals' are the basic unit of how organizations should excel: leadership as socialization. Because team-based organizing is less hierarchical and static than older organizational forms, it helps companies to react quickly towards a changing and complex environment, and to utilize the benefits of diversity (Zander et al., 2015). **Shared and distributed leadership** practices are essential to team-based organizing (Drogendijk et al., 2015).

The basis of shared and distributed leadership is team members' ability to lead themselves, also referred to as **self-leadership**. For instance, no single individual possesses the whole expertise for setting direction in an interdisciplinary team, and all team members are responsible for collective leadership to emerge.

To understand how self- and team-based leadership interrelate, Hendry's (2013) picture of the leader as a parent might be helpful: both are somewhat, but never fully, 'in charge', both lead by embodying actions and setting behavioural examples, both do so in light of unpredictable, evolving human beings with their own opinions and will power, and both face the disruptive and volatile influence of changing, ambiguous and complex boundary conditions. Therefore, much like 'family' emerges from the self-leadership,

7.2 Evolution and Components of Virtual Team Leadership

and the shared and distributed leadership of all involved, in light of context, situation and task, and as a deeply relational practice, so does 'virtual team collaboration'.

▶ Shared and distributed leadership is essential to virtual team collaboration. It is built from the self-leadership of all team members.

Digital leadership, as the final component of virtual team leadership, became a requirement when organizations started to seek out and consciously exploit advantages resulting from digitalization (see Chap. 2). It refers to the purposive or even strategic use of an organization's or team's digital assets for achieving strategic purposes or goals (Petry, 2018). Consequently, a digital leader is a person (or team) who is proactive in exploring how technology can help them in better reaching their goals and to adapt to a changing environment. Certain personality traits such as creativity, motivation, ambiguity tolerance and the ability to cope with uncertainty and frustration, are deemed indispensable for doing so (White et al., 2023). The final building block for virtual team leadership is thus digital proficiency and versatility, e.g. with regard to the usage of Information and Communication Technologies (ICTs), coupled with the motivation and ability to explore digital possibilities when facing the volatile, uncertain, complex and ambiguous disruptions brought about by the fourth industrial revolution (see opening case). What the digital and virtual context does to leadership is mainly that 'knowledge', 'control' and 'stability' are impossible to achieve: much like parents cannot fully understand, monitor or prescribe their children's digital behaviour, virtual team leadership simply needs to accept the conditions of volatility, uncertainty, complexity and ambiguity.

As Fig. 7.1 shows, virtual team leadership, as rooted in management, is comprised of three properties (bold), achieved by means of four channels (bottom), and exercised into four directions (italics). It may emerge and manifest in four shapes ('clouds'), namely individual, self-, shared/distributed and digital. Information and Communication Technologies are the means by which it is facilitated, under the general conditions of volatility, uncertainty, complexity and ambiguity.

Virtual team leadership manifests in **four shapes**. The difference between individual and self-leadership is that the first is exercised by the individual and directed towards others, and the second is exercised by the individual and directed towards oneself. Individual leadership is the 'traditional' leadership idea, whereas self-, shared and distributed and digital are required extensions in the context of virtual team collaboration.

The **three properties** of leadership are built upon each other. Routine administration and execution of tasks are not only managerial but also professional, for instance, related to other disciplines such as computer science or engineering. They form the basis of both leadership and everyday professional or managerial actions. Often, this part of the task is the one that is rationalized the most and executed by means of templates, procedures and software applications, such as the measurement of Key Performance Indicators (KPIs) or the tracking of status reports. However, when reason runs out, crisis management skills

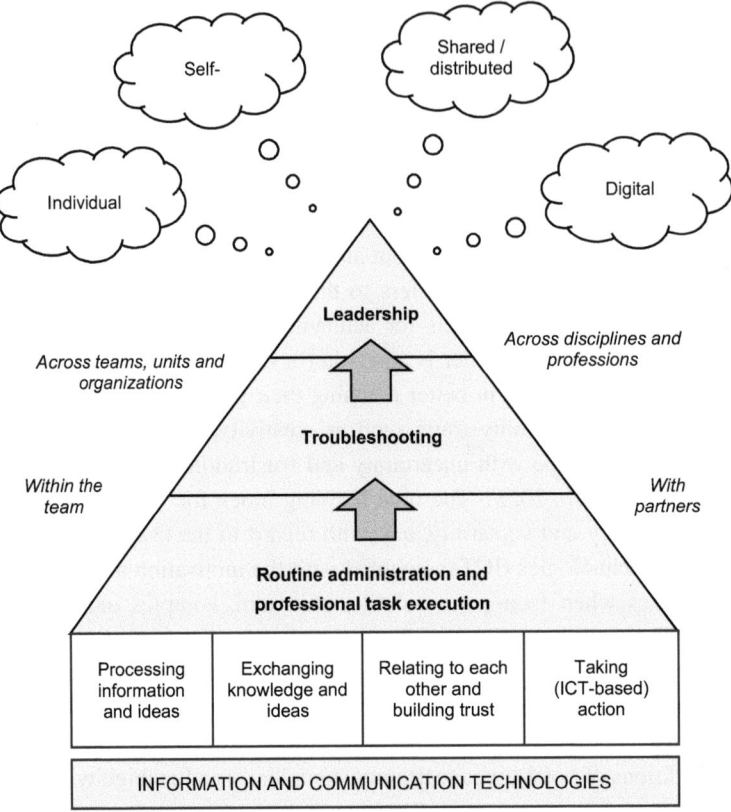

Fig. 7.1 provides a comprehensive overview on the components of virtual team leadership based on the previous considerations

('troubleshooting') need to take over, either on individual or social (team) levels, depending on the organizational form and the task at hand. For example, when the project is about to fail, known procedures do not provide conclusive advice, and, often, individuals then need to collaborate for finding solutions. Finally, leadership in its truest sense emerges whenever an individual or group needs to try out novel practices and processes that go beyond rational models and routine tasks, and the individual or collective comfort zones or what is already known.

Routine administration and professional execution, troubleshooting and leadership are achieved by means of **four channels**. These are:

- Processing information and ideas: the internal part of management and leadership that takes place inside people's heads.
- Exchanging knowledge and ideas: the interpersonal part of management in leadership in which—human and technological - actors find approaches and solutions together.

7.2 Evolution and Components of Virtual Team Leadership

- Relating to each other and building trust: the social and cultural part of management and leadership in which followership manifests and relations are built.
- Taking (ICT-based) action: the 'doing' part of management and leadership, which, in the case of virtual teams is largely based on Information and Communication Technologies, and which also involves digital means and solutions.

Finally, there are **four directions** of virtual team management and leadership, and, depending on the direction, different approaches and styles might be more conducive to high performance than others.

- First, management and leadership need to manifest within the team. This is the basis for the team to establish and maintain direction and common purpose.
- Secondly, management and leadership need to spread across teams, units and organizations, as the team itself is embedded in wider frameworks and often only temporary. This then requires team members to exploit their networks and to gather and spread information outside of the team, for instance, in order to gain organizational support for required investments into the team.
- Thirdly, management and leadership in virtual teams must cross the spheres of professions and disciplines, in particular in innovative and knowledge-intensive work which requires the expertise of different fields.
- Fourth, management and leadership in virtual teams is always enacted with partners, such as suppliers, distributors, customers or other organizations. The team cannot convert inputs into outputs as required without these partners and their support.

What remains unclear from this overview is how exactly these qualities of leadership, as emerging from management, shall be achieved. The next section delivers further insights into this question.

Application 7.1: Myself as contributing to virtual team leadership

Consider Fig. 7.1 which depicts the components of virtual team leadership:

- Where do you see your own strengths and weaknesses with regard to this model?
- Under which circumstances will your strengths result in potential opportunities for a virtual team?
- Under which circumstances will your weaknesses create threats for virtual team collaboration, and how might these threats be neutralized and remedied, e.g. by training and development or potentially also by complementary skills of other team members?
- Which specific challenges—or opportunities—are posed by the VUCA conditions of the Industry 4.0 (see Table in the Opening Case), and how well-equipped do you consider yourself with regard to them?

Table Opening Case 7 Leadership in light of volatility, uncertainty, complexity and ambiguity

		Knowledge about the situation	
		High	Low
Predictability of own actions	High	Volatility	Complexity
	Low	Uncertainty	Ambiguity

Source Own table

Exchange your findings with a fellow student or colleague whom you trust and seek their feedback:

- When and how does their assessment of your leadership qualities differ from your own?

Finally, reflect together:

- What have you now learned about the insight that virtual team leadership is based on self-leadership from which shared and distributed leadership emerges?
- What have you now learned about the specific digital requirements of virtual team leadership, and how to master them? ◄

7.3 Main Leadership Styles, and Their Pros and Cons for Virtual Team Collaboration

One needs to ask the question of how the implementation of leadership qualities is achieved based on the previous overview. One of the most common approaches in the literature is to differentiate leadership into styles and then to ask how effective and efficient these styles are, and under which circumstances. This is done with the full awareness that how leaders see themselves and how they behave is often a combination of styles (Hannah et al., 2009). Nonetheless, thinking about leadership in terms of distinct styles helps managers to make the overwhelming task of digital leadership 'manageable'. As each leadership style has its advantages and shortcomings, thinking about leadership in terms of styles also enables individuals and organizations to figure out what is presently lacking and, thus, take action that compensates for these shortcomings. As a starting point, transactional and transformational leadership are the two main styles to be differentiated and compared by the literature.

7.3.1 Transactional Leadership

Transactional leadership (Bass, 1985) as one of the earliest leadership styles is the most 'rational' and 'routine' option for establishing direction and ensuring performance. Transactional leaders set clear and specific goals, and those meeting these predefined goals are rewarded as announced (Parry, 2011). Conversely, ideas that do not fit existing plans and goals might not be rewarded by the transactional leader (Bryant, 2003). Since transactional leadership closely links goals with rewards (a rational, self-interest-based exchange), employees cannot be motivated to go beyond what is specified in their contract or bonus system (Parry, 2011). This means that transactional leadership can achieve expected commitment and performance but not go beyond it, and it might also struggle in instilling a 'team spirit' unless bonuses and rewards are reliably fixed on team levels. The main components of transactional leadership are contingent reward and management-by-exception (Bass, 1985; Bass & Riggio, 2006).

- **Contingent reward** is the essence of transactional leadership and describes that the leader must make clear what followers can expect to receive after achieving the predefined performance goals. Contingent rewards can be impersonal, like incentives and setting up goals, or personal, like recognition and praise (Yukl, 1999). Material rewards, such as bonuses, always imply transactional leadership.
- **Management by exception** involves active and passive management by exception (Hater & Bass, 1988). *Active* management by exception means to actively monitor followers and to intervene *before* a problem arises. If corrections are required, the leader then takes direct action. *Passive* management by exception means not to interfere as long as the original goal or plan is being followed: the leader interferes with critique and/or corrective actions only *after* mistakes have occurred or goals are not met.

7.3.2 Transformational Leadership

Transformational leaders stimulate and inspire team members to achieve extraordinary outcomes via aligning the objectives of individual team members, the leader, the team, and the organization into a 'vision'. Because transformational leadership also involves the idea of a higher moral cause embodied by the leader, it is similar to charismatic leadership and sometimes even equalled with it (Anderson & Sun, 2017). Unlike transactional leadership, transformational leadership can leverage exceptional commitment and can motivate followers to perform beyond expectations (Bass & Riggio, 2006). According to Bass (1999), transformational leaders achieve their goals via four means (four I's):

- **Idealised influence or charisma**: a leader influences a follower by achieving objectives and displaying a certain behaviour that is idealised by the follower. When a follower sees the leader achieving something that was thought to be impossible or difficult, the follower develops respect, sometimes admiration, for the leader, which convinces them to use their full potential to achieve the set objectives and contribute to the 'vision'.

- **Inspirational motivation**: a leader inspires a follower via a combination of intellectual stimulation and individualised consideration, and via setting a clear mission or objective for the follower.
- **Intellectual stimulation**: a leader pushes the follower into changing perspective on how to deal with problems, and on what needs to be achieved, and how.
- **Individualised consideration**: a leader pays attention to the needs and problems of each individual follower rather than treating every follower the same.

Transformational leadership has been used by celebrated political leaders like Mahatma Gandhi, John F. Kennedy and Nelson Mandela (Diaz-Saenz, 2011). Transformational leaders are typically very involving. However, occasionally, they may have to make unpopular decisions of their own, asserting their authority (Bass & Riggio, 2006). Bryant (2003) has found that transformational leaders inspire employees to higher levels of innovation and effectiveness. Two elements are key to the success of the transformational leadership style, namely the leader–follower relationship and the collective commitment.

7.3.3 Transformational and Transactional Leadership Compared

Transactional and transformational leadership have been said to have several characteristics in common. Transformational leadership also builds upon transactional leadership and adds to its effects (Bass, 1999; Howell & Avolio, 1993; Judge & Piccolo, 2004). Nonetheless, there are also differences between the two.

Bryant (2003) found that transactional leadership is more effective at exploiting knowledge by providing structures and systems for capturing knowledge. However, it does not promote creativity and the taking of initiative. Conversely, transformational leadership is more effective at creating and sharing knowledge (Bryant, 2003). Transactional leadership thus seems more appropriate to be utilized in stable environments, whereas transformational leadership may be applied during turbulence and under volatile conditions. Intrinsic motivation is capitalized upon only by transformational leadership (Bono & Judge, 2003), leading to increased effort and commitment from team members and resulting in performance beyond expectations, whereas the 'give-and-take' exchange that forms the basis of transactional leadership only leverages expected commitment and performance, and is not as effective in motivating team members (Bass & Riggio, 2006).

Application 7.2: Transactional and transformational digital leadership compared

As the opening case of this chapter suggests, digital leadership is related to four specific conditions of the fourth industrial revolution: volatility, uncertainty, complexity and ambiguity (VUCA, see Table of the Opening Case).

- Which strengths and weaknesses in addressing volatility, uncertainty, complexity and ambiguity, respectively, can you identify in the transactional and in the transformational leadership style, respectively?

Compare both styles with regard to all four VUCA components and come to a grounded conclusion of when to use which style, and why.

Next, if possible, relate your considerations to an organization, group or team that you are familiar with from your own experience:

- How ready is this organization, group or team in terms of their digital leadership qualities?
- What do you recommend to increase this organization's, group's or team's digital leadership readiness?—Make sure to remain realistic in your suggestions. ◄

7.4 Alternative and Complementary Leadership Styles for Virtual Team Collaboration

Adding to the discussion of transactional and transformational leadership, this section focuses on alternative styles that either seem particularly suited to virtual team collaboration or, alternatively, are found to be lacking for this purpose. It also pays attention to how certain styles might complement each other, based on the understanding that individuals and teams engage in leadership behaviour across styles, and the more reflexively they do so, the better they might 'lead' in the sense of achieving the desired outcomes in practice.

7.4.1 Pragmatic and Cognitive Leadership: Useful for Expert and Interdisciplinary Teams

Transformational leadership is **ideological** in the sense that it assumes that leaders base their behaviour on a 'vision'. A vision is a variety of persuasions that determine how people should behave and interact in order to reach an idealised situation or goal (Mumford & Strange, 2013). If transformational leaders overly impose their vision or focus too much on their own charismatic performance, they may thus lose sight of their followers' needs. Furthermore, strong charisma might not be suited to professions in which rationality and problem-solving abilities regardless of personality are valued, such as computer engineering.

In the case of expert teams, **cognitive** leadership (Fiedler et al., 1989) might thus be a better-fitting option. Cognitive leaders possess knowledge and/or experience in a specific field and contribute this knowledge to the team. They are perceptive and imaginative and use strategic thinking to draw a bigger picture. When aiming at finding solutions, they encourage participative decision making within the team (Bowers et al., 2017).

Pragmatic leadership (Mumford & van Doorn, 2001) is anti-ideological as well in the sense that relationships are less emotionally invested. Pragmatic leaders are problem-oriented and analyse present situations to find fitting solutions. They rely on professional followers with expert knowledge on how to solve problems at hand quickly. In contrast to the cognitive leader, the pragmatic leader does not need to be an expert themselves.

Both pragmatic and cognitive leadership are highly useful to technical and expert teams. Cognitive leadership seems more applicable to expert teams within a certain field or discipline (the leader uses their cognitive resources to contribute to working on the problem) whereas pragmatic leadership is more useful to interdisciplinary teams (no single individual can be the 'expert leader'). However, both styles require rather stable environments, as, otherwise, the 'expert leader' and/or the 'expert followers' cannot contribute their knowledge resources and solve problems as they occur. Thus, both styles might be limited under VUCA conditions, unless combined with other styles.

7.4.2 Servant and Authentic Leadership: A Means of Counterbalancing Ideology and Power

Transformational leadership incorporates many aspects of **servant** leadership, which describes the actions of leaders who combine their motivation to lead with the need to serve (van Dierendonck, 2011). Servant leaders empower and develop others; they are authentic and humble and see the best in others whom they then wish to develop further. However, they do not necessarily possess the charisma of a transformational leader which might even be an advantage when it comes to taking others' development first.

Pseudo-authentic leadership describes the negative potential of the (transformational, ideological or charismatic) leader to mislead followers using their visions (Bass & Steidlmeier, 1999). Another way of keeping the ideology of the transformational leader in check—besides servant leadership—is thus **authentic** leadership (Northouse, 2021). An authentic leader should be able to (1) understand themselves and how they appear to others through internalised reflection, (2) show their true self to others by being authentic, (3) analyse situations and other people's opinions for transparent decision making, and (4) guide their behaviour through their internal moral standards instead of relying on external influences.

When it comes to establishing a virtual team culture and climate that is inclusive and 'safe', given that team members are asked to learn and move beyond their comfort zones, both servant and authentic leadership thus seem particularly useful. However, due to their follower or 'self'-focus, respectively, both might also lose sight of the larger organizational interests and 'vision'.

7.4.3 Shared and Distributed Leadership: A Must-Have of Virtual Team Collaboration

Shared and distributed leadership refers to a situation in which several team members share the leadership role in a leadership network that influences team and individual actions and outcomes (Carson et al., 2007). These leaders direct, develop and motivate each other and other team members to achieve the team's goals. Often, their roles are situational and differentiated based on special competencies or skills: whenever a certain skill is needed, the team member possessing it steps forward, and then leads the team with their skill. Afterwards, they step back again, and let other members lead (Pearce & Conger, 2002). An internal team environment that facilitates shared and distributed leadership is based on three dimensions, namely shared purpose, social support, and voice (Carson et al., 2007).

- **Shared purpose:** team members have a common understanding of shared objectives and focus on reaching their collective goals.
- **Social support:** team members support each other emotionally and psychologically via recognition and praise of accomplishments and efforts.
- **Voice:** team members provide unsolicited and voluntary input on how the team acts and achieves its goals. Voice also encompasses initiative and the charismatic participation of team members; it requires an organizational structure that allows for both.

Based on the previous, shared and distributed leadership seems particularly helpful when it comes to navigating interdisciplinarity and the need for learning and innovative knowledge exchange in virtual team collaboration. It also seems a useful approach to mastering digital leadership under the conditions of volatility, uncertainty, complexity and ambiguity.

▶ Shared and distributed leadership requires shared purpose, social support and team members having voice.

7.4.4 Directive and Passive Leadership: Not Ideal for Virtual Team Collaboration

Directive and passive leadership are opposite approaches in many aspects. A **directive** leader has a strong opinion and image of what a team should and should not do. They clearly communicate what they want their followers to do and monitor the followers' tasks and the team outcomes. Directive leadership generally implies that the leader states a task without much room for discussion on their followers' side (Bowers et al., 2017). Directiveness can be divided into process and outcome directiveness (Peterson, 1997):

- **Process directiveness:** a leader influences and regulates the process of team decision making.
- **Outcome directiveness:** a leader defines or regulates the outcome of the team decision making.

Directive leadership is limited in the context of virtual team collaboration as it requires the leader to clearly 'see' their followers, and their needs, and to also 'know' direction better than them, which is seldom the case in diverse, distributed and interdisciplinary teams.

Passive leadership, which is also referred to as non-leadership, is a style that exists in practice but is obviously not a style that is recommended. It is composed of two behavioural principles, passive management by exception and laissez-faire. In both cases, the leader holds back and avoids active intervention.

- Passive management by exception is characterized by the idea that something that is not broken does not need to be fixed. This implies that leadership action is only required in extreme emergencies (Bass & Riggio, 2006).
- Laissez-faire leadership basically means that the leader lets followers do as they can and wish. It is often perceived as significant misconduct of a leader, because it signifies a lack of care, and of leaders not fulfilling the duties and responsibilities assigned to them (Vullinghs et al., 2020).

Passive leadership in virtual team collaboration, in particular in its laissez-faire variety, can be even more dangerous than directive leadership, as it fails to align and motivate the team, and as it cannot utilize the benefits of diversity and dispersion. Even passive management by exception is dangerous enough as, in a virtual environment, it is often unclear where and when problems occur, and some of them—such as individual team members' struggles with technology—might never surface on team level but still significantly harm virtual team processes and outputs. Furthermore, virtual team collaboration requires self-leadership, and this means that individual team members may not assume a passive role when it comes to how they self-organize, how they learn and how they approach and execute tasks. Passive self-leadership is thus highly harmful to the goal of a shared and distributed virtual team leadership. Rather, what is required is that individual team members provide constant feedback and voice their needs, knowledge, ideas and expertise to other team members.

> **Application 7.3: A full-range approach to virtual team leadership**
>
> As the opening case of this chapter suggests, digital leadership is related to four specific conditions of the fourth industrial revolution: volatility, uncertainty, complexity and ambiguity (VUCA, see Table of the Opening Case).

- Which strengths and weaknesses in addressing volatility, uncertainty, complexity and ambiguity, respectively, can you identify in the styles that were discussed in Sect. 7.4 of this chapter?

Next, if possible, relate your considerations to an organization, group or team that you are familiar with from own experience (you can use your example from Application 7.2):

- How would you suggest combining these additional styles with transactional and transformational leadership behaviour, respectively, for the best digital leadership performance in the given context? ◀

7.5 Recommendations for Leading Virtual Teams

The differentiation of leadership into styles requires the existence of behavioural templates ('how to normally do things as a leader') and of shared ideas of what differentiates 'outstanding leadership' from routine or even bad management. Both can only develop under rather stable circumstances. However, these stable circumstances often do not exist in the case of virtual team collaboration. Rather, in today's volatile organizational environment, teams might have to adjust practically overnight, with the COVID-19 pandemic being a striking example of such a phenomenon. The first question that arises in the context of virtual team collaboration is thus:

- How to lead virtual teams through changing circumstances, even crisis?

Secondly, virtual teams are often comprised of members from different fields and locations, and are furthermore even built from the purpose of utilizing the benefits of diversity and dispersion. Moreover, people's needs can change over time: beginners might become experts, and motivated team members might become disillusioned. This then brings about a second question:

- How to adjust virtual team leadership to changing individual requirements?

These two aspects, namely the changing virtual team environment with the potential need to lead through crisis, and the diverse requirements of those to be led are discussed in this section.

7.5.1 Leading Virtual Teams Through Change and Crisis

The need for change always poses a leadership problem because it challenges known procedures, skills and competencies. Addressing this problem under the VUCA conditions of the fourth industrial revolution becomes even more pressing. Underlying this dilemma is the organizational conflict between maintenance (technological imperative) and transformation (contingency theory), and the need to make sense out of both (see Chap. 6).

The technological imperative demands for stabilizing core organizational processes, e.g. of a virtual team, as much as possible so that members develop routine and expertise when collaborating. Technology, from this perspective, refers to all resources—human, technological and otherwise—that are employed by a team, unit or organization for achieving their purposes and goals (overview in Hatch, with Cunliffe, 2006). Consequently, if one has discovered an efficient and effective means of organizing work, one should not discard it at whim (because change will come at a cost). General examples of this insight are learning curves and economies of scale in production, and, in the context of virtual teams, the routine technological expertise of how to conduct virtual meetings that comes from experience. Changing 'what works well' will also make those involved feel disoriented and challenge their being knowledgeable and experienced.

However, because virtual team environments are volatile, uncertain, complex and ambiguous, teams and their performance are also contingent (that is: at least partially dependent) upon the environment in which they collaborate, from which they receive inputs and to which they deliver outputs. For instance, if user preferences change or richer ICTs become available at lower costs, companies need to rethink how they organize virtual work. This then not only requires actual changes in how work is organized but also for explaining these changes to those affected so that they maintain focus, motivation and orientation.

If VUCA conditions cumulate to crisis, managing the interrelations between maintenance, transformation and sensemaking becomes even more critical for success. The three elements of crisis are urgency, threat and uncertainty (Boin & t'Hart, 2007). Crises can be external, such as a pandemic or political upheaval, or internal, such as a failure in leadership, an internal moral dilemma, or an internal conflict (Bowers et al., 2017). Crises pose tremendous challenges, yet, can also bring about opportunity (Boin & t'Hart, 2007), with leadership being the crucial factor of how to turn crises into opportunities and transformation (Milburn et al., 1983). Yet, as a crisis comes with uncertainty and novelty, leaders face problems which have not occurred before. For example, ideally, crisis management is fast, effective and action-based. However, in reality, crisis management never goes smoothly and is often based on short-term solutions without planning for further crises (Rosenthal et al., 2001). Bhaduri (2019) thus suggests differentiating crisis leadership into phases, such as pre-crisis, crisis and post-crisis.

- Pre-crisis, the focus lies on detecting signals for crises and on preventing them, if still possible. In this phase, cognitive leadership might help in detecting crises, and a combination of transactional and directive leadership might help make the team act against internal crisis quickly.

- Teams in the crisis stage need to contain damage and work towards recovery. They need a varying degree of flexibility in order to do so, with both an internal and external focus. Team members need to take risks and to make decisions and communicate them., They may use a mix of transactional and transformational styles to do so.
- Post-crisis, team members then need to facilitate change and growth. This may be achieved by means of a transformational style.

However, as Hannah et al. (2009) argue, crises are always novel and unforeseen. Therefore, this is the situation when leaders need to work with those resources, abilities and skills which are at their disposal. The most relevant aspect here is to motivate the team to face crisis and to exemplify by one's own attitude and actions that crisis is manageable and might even have positive outcomes, such as learning, innovation or transformation. When leading oneself and others through crisis, one should nonetheless remain realistic and also explicate one's own struggles to others. This way, others do not feel misled and challenges and threats are clearly pointed out. As VUCA suggests, the task is not to already *know* how crisis shall be overcome but to instill the realistic belief that the team will manage, if everyone is motivated enough to *really* try. Being present, authentic and involved then makes the team more resilient against the VUCA conditions of the fourth industrial revolution. Crises also require a more relational approach to leadership: qualities such as empathy and compassion increase in relevance, as does the ability to coach others and make them learn (Bhaduri, 2019). Together, these insights then provide a conclusive answer to the first question, namely: how to lead virtual teams through changing circumstances, even crisis?

7.5.2 Situational Leadership: Rooting Leadership Practices in Followers' Needs

Situational leadership is an approach to leadership which bases a leader's behaviour on the lifecycle stage of their followers (Blanchard et al., 1993). There is no perfect leadership style from this perspective. Rather, leaders should adapt to the task and relations at hand (Thompson & Glasø, 2015). This approach fits virtual team realities and the VUCA conditions of Industry 4.0 very well. A virtual team, too, can be assumed to have a lifecycle, and is furthermore comprised of diverse and dispersed team members who have different needs and work under different conditions. Against this background, situational leadership helps to do individual needs justice while still keeping the team in mind. It can also build the basis for a shared and distributed leadership that is rooted in members' *actual* capabilities which remain hidden otherwise. According to Blanchard (2010), leaders should differentiate their followers into four types and then choose between four leadership approaches accordingly. The four follower types are:

- **The enthusiastic beginner**: a person with low competence but high commitment
- **The disillusioned learner**: a person with low to some competence and low commitment
- **The capable but cautious performer**: a person with moderate to high competence and variable levels of commitment (depending on how 'dangerous' the situation seems)
- **The self-reliant achiever**: a person with high competence and high commitment

Whereas the enthusiastic beginner requires direction, the disillusioned learner needs to be coached. The capable but cautious performer needs to be supported in taking the risk of acting and learning beyond their comfort zones, and the self-reliant achiever just requires that tasks and responsibilities are being delegated to them. Table 7.1 provides an overview.

Directing involves teaching required knowledge and skills and showing how to do the work and what good results should look like. According to Blanchard (2010), directing works best when coupled with a step-by-step plan for self-development, in which low-risk situations for initial learning are provided. However, the entry hurdle of how well one must be qualified and able to organize and lead oneself is already high in the context of virtual team collaboration: thus, such low-risk practices might not be available even to the enthusiastic beginner, e.g. when it comes to digital proficiency requirements. This then bears the danger that highly motivated but inexperienced team members might become disillusioned, for instance, with technology or with virtual collaboration.

Coaching provides a combination of direction and support, and is required when team members have become disillusioned learners. These team members have gained some competence, but they have lost their commitment as requirements were becoming harder than expected. Based on Blanchard (2010), leaders must thus provide praise and support, while closely monitoring for failure, to raise followers' confidence again which will then restore their commitment. In the context of virtual team collaboration, this style is best applied by partnering team members for mutual learning: e.g., in a global virtual team, one might partner a digitally versatile and confident team member who lacks international experience with a digitally less confident team member who is cross-culturally competent. Thus, coaching is best achieved via shared and distributed leadership.

Table 7.1 Overview of situational leadership

Observed follower's developmental level	Competence	Commitment	Required leadership behaviour
Enthusiastic beginner	Low	High	Directing
Disillusioned learner	Low to some	Low	Coaching
Capable but cautious performer	Moderate to high	Variable	Supporting
Self-reliant achiever	High		Delegating

Source own table

Supporting further develops those followers who have acquired a good level of skills but struggle with insecurity. According to Blanchard (2010) this type of follower is further developed by someone who listens to their concerns and suggestions, who supports their interactions, and who praises their work, but who also ask questions to expand the follower's thinking and encourage risk taking. As this style is collaborative and requires feedback in both directions, it is very well suited to the shared and distributed leadership practices envisaged for virtual team collaboration.

Delegating means to hand over the responsibility for decision making and problem solving to followers who are self-reliant achievers. According to Blanchard (2010), leaders should empower this follower type by allowing them and trusting them to act independently and to provide the resources for them to do so, thereby acknowledging their high levels of commitment and competence. Self-reliant achievers should furthermore be continuously challenged so that their abilities can grow. In the context of virtual team collaboration, this is then the ideal scenario of a competent team which leads, motivates and challenges themselves to even higher levels of performance.

Obviously, situational leadership as the solution to circumstantial volatility and team diversity only works if the leader (or, in the case of shared and distributed leadership: the team) succeeds in identifying their followers' developmental stage: situational leadership thus requires diagnostic skills. It also demands for the leader to be flexible in their approach, which implies that authenticity in the context of virtual team collaboration must be coupled with the versatility to relate to diverse individuals, as they require. Finally, situational leadership requires a partnership between leader and follower for achieving performance. It can thus never be based solely on directive leadership, and also limits transformation leadership in the sense that it provides limits to how visible the leaders' personality might be. In terms of vision, situational leadership thus combines pragmatic and ideological/charismatic leadership, and is particularly suited to shared and distributed practices. This then provides a conclusive answer to the second question, namely: how to adjust virtual team leadership to changing individual requirements?

▶ Situational leadership can make a virtual team grow and develop, but it only works if the leader or the team identify people's needs correctly.

7.5.3 Virtual Team Leadership: Summary and Best Practices

Based on the previous considerations, it has become evident that there is no single leadership style which solves all challenges of virtual team collaboration. However, because of certain characteristics of virtual team collaboration, some styles, or a combination of some, seem more suitable to achieving outcome than others. Table 7.2 provides an overview on relevant styles, and their pros and cons, also in relation to change and crisis, and to certain leader self-identities and followers' leadership expectations.

Table 7.2 Overview of leadership styles and their suitability for virtual team collaboration

Style	Key aspects	(Virtual team) advantages	(Virtual team) shortcomings
Transactional	▪ Contingent reward ▪ Active/passive management by exception	▪ Clear performance goals that are aligned with the organization ▪ Achievement-oriented ▪ Reliable give-and-take relations (rewards)	▪ Exchange-based, short-term relationship with leader ▪ Requires stable conditions ▪ Is limited to expected commitment and performance ▪ Lacks vision
Transformational	▪ Idealised influence (Charisma) ▪ Inspirational motivation ▪ Intellectual stimulation ▪ Individualised consideration	▪ Aligns people to vision ▪ Provides leading figure and positive energy to followers ▪ Might leverage exceptional commitment and performance beyond expectations ▪ Is highly motivational under difficult circumstances ▪ Suitable for digital leadership	▪ Leader as 'individual hero' who overshadows the team ▪ Potential power abuse by leader ▪ Only works if values are shared by followers ▪ Leader charisma might not be transferable via ICTs
Pragmatic	▪ Methodical problem-solving approach ▪ Knowledge-based ▪ Common sense ▪ Relying on elite (expert) followers	▪ Problem focus as vision ▪ Close observation and objective analysis ▪ Developing and implementing solutions at maximum profit and minimum cost ▪ Suitable for digital leadership	▪ Lack of higher vision ▪ Requires existence of shared 'common sense' in the team ▪ Leadership varies based on situation/problem and can thus be perceived as arbitrary
Cognitive	▪ Focus on leader's cognitive resources ▪ Leader has expertise in a specific field ▪ Perceptive ▪ Imaginative	▪ Strategic outlook ▪ Participative decision making ▪ (Team members') intelligence and/or experience are mobilized ▪ Suitable for analysing crisis ▪ Suitable for digital leadership	▪ Potential lack of empathy and interpersonal (soft-)skills ▪ Leader can only contribute if there are no cognitive blocks (like stress) ▪ Overly high cognitive demands

(continued)

7.5 Recommendations for Leading Virtual Teams

Table 7.2 (continued)

Style	Key aspects	(Virtual team) advantages	(Virtual team) shortcomings
Servant	- Leader with follower focus - Organisational goals are secondary to follower's growth	- Followers' needs are fulfilled - Relations and emotions are acknowledged (trust building) - Encourages ethical behaviour and reflexivity - Empowers followers	- Leader altruism seems utopian - Servant leadership might harm one's visibility in the team (own contribution is undervalued) - Lack of direction during crisis - Lack of vision
Authentic	- Self-awareness - Transparent relations - Regulating self through internalised moral standards - Reflecting upon self in front of others	- Displaying authentic self (strengths and weaknesses) and thus encouraging trust - Transparent actions - Others know where they stand - Diverse authenticities are possible: potentially inclusive	- Lack of objective definition or standard of morality might result in lack of orientation - Potential lack of alignment in times of crisis - Not suitable for all follower types
Shared/distributed	- Multiple leaders - Leaders step forward and back, as required - Leaders influence and complement each other - Mutual learning	- Meets demands of knowledge-intensive, innovative and interdisciplinary teams - Distributes leadership role - Uses benefits of diversity (e.g. if different leader self-identities complement each other)	- Might overwhelm cautious or inexperienced team members - Not suitable for beginners or disillusioned members - Might create conflicts with wider organizational vision or hierarchies
Directive	- Decisiveness - Clearly defined roles and expectations - Direct top-down communication - Monitoring	- Suitable for taking charge during pre-crisis stage - Provides direction to disillusioned or inexperienced team members - Suitable for early stages of digital leadership	- May result in groupthink (only one = leader's opinion counts) - Demotivates self-reliant follower - Not suitable for interdisciplinary or innovative teams - Not suitable for transformation

(continued)

Table 7.2 (continued)

Style	Key aspects	(Virtual team) advantages	(Virtual team) shortcomings
Passive	• Controlling only when mistakes surface (passive management by exception) *or* • No intervention at all (laissez-faire)	• Suitable for self-reliant achievers	• Problems remain 'hidden' • Lack of trust and alignment • Does not help navigate change and might even cause crisis • Does not fit all follower types • Not suitable for crisis and for assuming digital leadership
Situational	• Leadership behaviour is based on developmental level of follower	• Works also in diverse teams • Team members might coach and develop each other • Enables digital learning • Fits virtual team realities	• Might be perceived as unfair • Requires high interpersonal skills in assessing and meeting followers' needs • Potential lack of vision

Source own table

What seems certain is that a balanced combination of transactional and transformational leadership forms the basis of virtual team collaboration, and that passive leadership is almost never a good idea in virtual team collaboration, and that the benefits of directive leadership are limited mainly to pre-crisis analysis and preventive action, and to developing enthusiastic beginners. On the other end of the spectrum, shared and distributed leadership seems to be a must-have in virtual team collaboration. Situational leadership describes a way of developing team members' competence and commitment towards this goal. If team members then share and distribute leadership based on the respective self-identities which they personally feel comfortable with, team leadership is further strengthened. When doing so, each team member should pay attention to providing professional respect, to contribute, to engage in relationship- oriented behaviour and to display loyalty by means of public support for their team members.

> **Application 7.4: Digital leadership under VUCA conditions**
>
> As the opening case of this chapter suggests, digital leadership is related to four specific conditions of the fourth industrial revolution: volatility, uncertainty, complexity and ambiguity (VUCA, see Table of the Opening Case).
>
> - How can situational leadership contribute to managing the VUCA conditions of Industry 4.0, also concerning leading through change and crisis?
> - What are the shortcomings of situational leadership in light of the VUCA conditions of Industry 4.0, and by means of which alternative leadership styles might virtual team members and leaders complement for these shortcomings, in particular with regard to change and crisis?
> - Which leadership practices seems particularly well-suited to the VUCA conditions of Industry 4.0, and why? Or, in other words: which leadership practices does successful virtual team collaboration require under these conditions? ◄

7.6 Closing Part

7.6.1 Chapter Summary

This chapter has first provided an overview on the key leadership conditions of Industry 4.0, namely volatility, uncertainty, complexity and ambiguity, thus detailing the contemporary digital leadership challenges. After highlighting the evolution and components of virtual leadership today, it discussed transactional and transformational leadership in light of each other. Next, alternative and complementing styles such as pragmatic, cognitive, servant, authentic, shared and distributed, directive and passive leadership, were discussed with regard to their contribution to virtual team and digital leadership. From there, recommendations were drawn. The first recommendation focussed on how to lead virtual teams through change and crisis. Second, situational leadership was proposed as a way of acknowledging team members' different developmental needs. This led to a summary of recommendations and best practices so that you are now able to choose between different leadership-styles and to fit how you lead yourself and others to the situation and those involved (see Table 7.2).

7.6.2 Key Points

- The contemporary business environment, in particular Industry 4.0, is characterized by volatility, uncertainty, change and ambiguity, and digital leadership is an essential skill required for navigating such an environment.
- Virtual team leadership is built upon the usage of Information and Communciation Technologies; it involves three properties and four channels, targets four directions and manifests in four shapes (see Fig. 7.1).
- Transformational and transactional leadership are two main styles which complement each other for virtual team leadership.
- Pragmatic and cognitive leadership are useful for expert and interdisciplinary teams.
- Servant and authentic leadership are a means of counterbalancing ideology and power.
- Shared and distributed leadership are a must-have of virtual team collaboration.
- Directive and passive leadership are more harmful than useful for virtual team collaboration.
- Crisis leadership is part of the virtual team collaboration challenge.
- Situational leadership is a means of taking the developmental needs of virtual team members into account and for facilitating change and development.
- There is no single right or wrong virtual team leadership style; rather, best practice virtual team leadership requires situational leadership style choices (see Table 7.2).

7.6.3 Review Questions

1. What is virtual team leadership, and how has it evolved?
2. What are the components of virtual team leadership?
3. What are transactional and transformational leadership, respectively, and what are their advantages and disadvantages in light of each other and with regard to virtual team collaboration?
4. What are the benefits and limits of pragmatic and cognitive leadership in relation to virtual team collaboration?
5. What are the benefits and limits of servant and authentic leadership in relation to virtual team collaboration?

6. Why are shared and distributed leadership practices a must-have of virtual team collaboration, and how shall they be established and maintained?
7. Why does directed and passive leadership do more harm than good when applied to virtual team collaboration?
8. What is crisis leadership, how is it relevant to virtual team collaboration, and which styles does it require in which crisis phase?
9. What does situational leadership involve, and how is it helpful for learning, change and development in virtual team collaboration?
10. What does best practice virtual team leadership require (make sure to consider Fig. 7.1 and Table 7.2)?

7.6.4 Opening Case Revisited

Digital leadership is one of the in-vogue concepts of management theory and practice today. As this chapter suggested, digital leadership in virtual team collaboration is not rocket science. Rather, it is built from knowing how to structure a situation in terms of (1) how well one may predict the result of one's actions and of (2) how much one knows about the situation. This allows clustering conditions as volatile, uncertain, complex, ambiguous, or a combination thereof. Depending on the outcome of such clustering, one may then choose appropriate leadership styles, also in combination. When doing so, one needs to consider the components of virtual team leadership (Fig. 7.1), in particular, its four channels, its four directions and the four shapes which it might take. Essentially, rational and individual leadership does not suffice for virtual team collaboration, what is requires is shared and distributed leadership as a social practice and as emerging from individual and self-leadership. Virtual teams need to commit to performance norms in order to achieve this goal such as professional respect, contribution, affect and loyalty. The team should also reflect—individually and collectively—which member personality aligns the most with which collaborative challenges, and members should take up leadership tasks and responsibilities accordingly. This way, 'the best person for the job at hand' will step up when needed, and step down when another team member could do better. However, this then requires committing and adhering to the stated performance norms so that the team can grow together as joint leaders. Furthermore, those in a leadership role need to consider at which stage of development individual team members are: enthusiastic beginners require direction, disillusioned learners need to be coached, capable but cautious performers need to be supported and coached, and self-reliant achievers need to be trusted with tasks and responsibilities being delegated to them. Self-leadership, voicing one's needs and team level inputs are essentials for the full picture of team members' abilities and motivations to emerge: otherwise, opportunities cannot be given. In particular, this process is essential when leading the team through change and crisis.

Table Closing Activity 7 A personal leadership SWOT-Analysis

Personal strengths	Personal weaknesses
What are your strengths in a learning role? e.g. unique resources, know-how…	*What are your weaknesses in a leading role? e.g. lack of resources, missing know-how…*
Team opportunities	**Team threats**
How to turn these strengths into potential opportunities for a virtual team? e.g. tasks executed, goals achieved …	*How to prevent these weaknesses from becoming threats to a virtual team? e.g. tasks not executed, goals failed…*

Source Own table

Thus, digital leadership cannot be prescribed by means of a template: rather, it refers to a constant navigational process by those collaborating virtually, for mastering the specific challenges and for exploiting the specific opportunities which characterize this specific virtual team collaboration, under these specific boundary conditions.

7.6.5 Closing Activity

Consider yourself in a 'leading' role in a virtual team.

- What are your strengths?
- What are your weaknesses?
- How could your strengths be an opportunity to virtual team collaboration?
- How could your weaknesses be a threat to virtual team collaboration?
- Which configuration and collaboration choices will ensure that the team succeeds in exploiting the opportunity that potentially arises from your strengths?
- Which configuration and collaboration choices will ensure that the team overcomes the threat that that potentially arises from your weaknesses?

Write down your ideas about yourself, using the Table below.

Next, ask trusted fellow team members, students or co-workers how they perceive you in the role of a leader (strengths/weaknesses), the potential consequences, and how these consequences might be supported (opportunities) or prevented (threats).

Consider what you have learned from relating your self-perception to how others perceive you.

> **Link to practice: The leadership SWOT analysis as a virtual team building and team development activity**
>
> The leadership SWOT analysis is a team development activity for real life (virtual) team practice. Ideally, each team member fills in their own, personal leadership SWOT analysis, and then the team exchanges their profiles and provides feedback to

each other. If conducted on team level, then the ideal point in time would be at the late beginning of collaboration, at a point where team members had first interactions but in which the majority of responsibilities and tasks still needs to be allocated and executed.

Virtually, this requires a two-step process:

- First, all team members should send their SWOT profiles to each other (e.g. via e-mail, shared server et cetera), giving everyone enough time to go through the profiles independently and asynchronously.
- Next, rich ICTs should be used for virtual exchange and feedback, such as video conferencing tools.

The process of exchange and feedback should be facilitated by a person who pays attention that every profile receives the same time and attention. Additional tools (such as shared whiteboards or a chat) are helpful for providing feedback: they speed up the process, because they utilize a key advantage of ICT-supported communication: multiple modes of communication can be facilitated in parallel, and multiple people can send multiple communicative messages. This multiplicity of communication can then be looked at collectively, as an overview (e.g. everyone looks at the feedback results on the digital whiteboard), and be further clustered. It is also possible to provide virtual feedback anonymously, however, this possibility needs to be carefully assessed and weighed up with regard to its threats and opportunities. ◄

References

Anderson, M. H., & Sun, P. Y. T. (2017). Reviewing leadership styles: Overlaps and the need for a new 'full-range' theory. *International Journal of Management Reviews, 19*(1), 76–96.

Bass, B. M. (1985). *Leadership and performance beyond expectations*. Free Press.

Bass, B. M. (1999). Two decades of research and development in transformational leadership. *European Journal of Work and Organizational Psychology, 8*(1), 9–32.

Bass, B. M., & Riggio, R. E. (2006). *Transformational leadership* (2nd ed.). Lawrence Erlbaum.

Bass, B. M., & Steidlmeier, P. (1999). Ethics, character, and authentic transformational leadership behavior. *The Leadership Quarterly, 10*(2), 181–217.

Bennett, N., & Lemoine, G. J. (2014). What VUCA really means for you. *Harvard Business Review*. Retrieved January 1, 2024 from https://hbr.org/2014/01/what-vuca-really-means-for-you.

Bhaduri, R. M. (2019). Leveraging culture and leadership in crisis management. *European Journal of Training and Development, 43*(5/6), 554–569.

Blanchard, K. H., Zigarmi, D., & Nelson, R. B. (1993). Situational leadership after 25 years: A retrospective. *Journal of Leadership Studies, 1*(1), 21–36.

Blanchard, K. H. (2010). *Leading at a higher level: Blanchard on leadership and creating high performing organizations*. FT Press.

Boin, A., & 't Hart, P. (2007). The crisis approach. In H. Rodríguez, E. L. Quarantelli, R. R. Dynes, & W. A. Anderson (Eds.), *Handbook of disaster research* (pp. 42–54). Springer.

Bono, J. E., & Judge, T. A. (2003). Self-concordance at work: Toward understanding the motivational effects of transformational leaders. *Academy of Management Journal, 46*(5), 554–571.

Bowers, M. R., Hall, J. R., & Srinivasan, M. M. (2017). Organizational culture and leadership style: The missing combination for selecting the right leader for effective crisis management. *Business Horizons, 60*(4), 551–563.

Bryant, S. E. (2003). The role of transformational and transactional leadership in creating, sharing and exploiting organizational knowledge. *Journal of Leadership & Organizational Studies, 9*(4), 32–44.

Carson, J. B., Tesluk, P. E., & Marrone, J. A. (2007). Shared leadership in teams: An investigation of antecedent conditions and performance. *Academy of Management Journal, 50*(5), 1217–1234.

Cunliffe, A. (2012). *Organization theory*. Sage.

Diaz-Saenz, H. R. (2011). Transformational leadership. In A. Bryman (Ed.), *The Sage handbook of leadership* (pp. 299–310). Sage.

Drogendijk, R., van Tulder, R., & Verbeke, A. (2015). Introduction: Three organizational challenges for multinational enterprises. *Progress in international business research: The future of global organizing,* (Bd. 10, pp. 3–21). Emerald.

Drucker, P. F. (2001). *Essential drucker: 'The pre-eminent management thinker of our time'. Selections from the management works of Peter F. Drucker*. Taylor & Francis.

Fiedler, F. E., McGuire, M., & Richardson, M. (1989). The role of intelligence and experience in successful group performance. *Journal of Applied Sport Psychology, 1*(2), 132–149.

Hannah, S. T., Woolfolk, R. L., & Lord, R. G. (2009). Leader self-structure: A framework for positive leadership. *Journal of Organizational Behavior, 30*(2), 269–290.

Hatch, M. J., & Cunliffe, A. (2006). *Organization theory—Modern, symbolic and postmodern perspectives*. Oxford University Press.

Hater, J. J., & Bass, B. M. (1988). Superiors' evaluations and subordinates' perceptions of transformational and transactional leadership. *The Journal of Applied Psychology, 73*(4), 695–702.

Hendry, J. (2013). *Management: A very short introduction*. Oxford University Press.

Howell, J. M., & Avolio, B. J. (1993). Transformational leadership, transactional leadership, locus of control, and support for innovation: Key predictors of consolidated-business-unit performance. *The Journal of Applied Psychology, 78*(6), 891–902.

Judge, T. A., & Piccolo, R. F. (2004). Transformational and transactional leadership: A meta-analytic test of their relative validity. *The Journal of Applied Psychology, 89*(5), 755–768.

Mendenhall, M. E., Reiche, B. S., Bird, A., & Osland, J. S. (2012). Defining the "global" in global leadership. *Journal of World Business, 47*(4), 493–503.

Milburn, T. W., Schuler, R. S., & Watman, K. H. (1983). Organizational crisis. Part I: Definition and conceptualization. *Human Relations, 36*(12), 1141–1160.

Mumford, M. D., & Strange, J. M. (2013). Vision and mental models: The case of charismatic and ideological leadership. In M. D. Mumford & J. M. Strange (Eds.), *Transformational and charismatic leadership: The road ahead* (Vol. 5, pp. 125–158). Bingley.

Mumford, M. D., & van Doorn, J. R. (2001). The leadership of pragmatism. *The Leadership Quarterly, 12*(3), 279–309.

Northouse, P. G. (2021). *Leadership: Theory and practice*. Sage.

Parry, K. W. (2011). Leadership and organization theory. In A. Bryman (Ed.), *The SAGE handbook of leadership* (pp. 53–70). Sage.

Pearce, C. L., & Conger, J. A. (2002). *Shared leadership: Reframing the hows and whys of leadership*. Sage.

Peterson, R. S. (1997). A directive leadership style in group decision making can be both virtue and vice: Evidence from elite and experimental groups. *Journal of Personality and Social Psychology, 72*(5), 1107–1121.

Petry, T. (2018). Digital Leadership. In K. North, R. Maier, & O. Haas (Eds.), *Knowledge management in digital change. Progress in IS*. Springer.

Rosenthal, U., Boin, R. A., & Comfort, L. K. (2001). *Managing crises: Threats, dilemmas, opportunities*. Charles C. Thomas.

Saleh, A., & Watson, R. (2017). Business excellence in a volatile, uncertain, complex and ambiguous environment (BEVUCA). *The TQM Journal, 29*(5), 705–724.

Thompson, G., & Glasø, L. (2015). Situational leadership theory: A test from three perspectives. *Leadership & Organization Development Journal, 36*(5), 527–544.

van Dierendonck, D. (2011). Servant Leadership: A review and synthesis. *Journal of Management, 37*(4), 1228–1261.

Vullinghs, J. T., de Hoogh, A. H. B., den Hartog, D. N., & Boon, C. (2020). Ethical and passive leadership and their joint relationships with burnout via role clarity and role overload. *Journal of Business Ethics, 165*(4), 719–733.

Weber, M. (1947). *The Theory of Social and Economic Organization* (A. M. Henderson, & T. Parsons, Trans.). Collier Macmillan Publishers.

White, A., Wheelock, M., Canwell, A., & Smets, M. (2023). 6 key levers of a successful organizational transformation. *Harvard Business Review*. Retrieved January 1, 2024, from https://hbr.org/2023/05/6-key-levers-of-a-successful-organizational-transformation.

Yukl, G. A. (1999). An evaluation of conceptual weaknesses in transformational and charismatic leadership theories. *The Leadership Quarterly, 10*(2), 285–305.

Zander, L., Butler, C. L., Mockaitis, A. I., Herbert, K., Lauring, J., Mäkelä, K., Paunova, M., Umans, T., & Zetting, P. (2015). Team-based global organizations: The future of global organizing. In R. van Tulder, A. Verbeke, & R. Drogendijk (Eds.), *The future of global organizing. progress in international business research*, (Bd. 10, pp. 227–243). Emerald.

Further Reading

Mahadevan, J., & Steinmann, J. (2023). Cultural intelligence and COVID-induced virtual teams: Towards a conceptual framework for cross-cultural management studies. *International Journal of Cross Cultural Management, 23*(2), 317–337. Retrieved May 1, 2024, from https://doi.org/10.1177/14705958231188621.

This paper introduces and explains the concept of cultural intelligence as a relevant characteristic and success factor for virtual team leadership.

Cross-Cultural Management of Virtual Team Collaboration: Cultural Dimensions and Intercultural Competencies for Culturally Diverse Settings

8.1 Introduction

Many virtual teams today are characterized by cultural diversity. Some of this diversity originates from the country effect, that is: members' upbringing, education, professional training or work in different societal cultures. Cultural diversity can become an asset to the team because it might increase creativity and innovativeness—but only if difference does not result in misalignment and mistrust. Cross-cultural management is the interdisciplinary field of study that aims at leveraging the benefits of cultural diversity, as originating from differences in country cultures. However, as is the case for the 'culture as communication' perspective (see Chap. 5), managing country effects is only the starting point for developing collaborative cross-cultural management skills: the implications go beyond the country level and may also help to integrate cross-functional or interdisciplinary virtual teams.

First, this chapter provides a very brief overview on what cross-cultural management involves, and how it relates to virtual team collaboration. Next, it introduces the cultural dimensions of Hofstede (1980, 2001, 2010), Hofstede & Bond, 1988) and project GLOBE (House et al., 2004) as a relevant tool for investigating and, consequently, managing cross-cultural differences and cultural complexity. From there recommendations follow for managing cultural diversity in virtual teams. After having read this chapter, you should know key cultural dimensions, and how (not) to use them, and you should be aware that this knowledge is only the starting point, not the end goal, of the development of advanced intercultural competencies required for today's and tomorrow's virtual team collaboration.

Team	A small number of individuals who collaborate in a task and/or to reach a goal.
ICTs	Information and communication technologies.
Virtual team collaboration	Working together as a team by means of ICTs.
Cultural diversity	Multiple cultures being relevant to a situation, task, goal or purpose, which requires that difference be overcome and integrated for achieving the best possible process and outcome.
Cross-cultural management	The discipline that focusses on the interrelations between culture, management and organization, and seeks to develop people's competencies for managing situations that are characterized by cultural diversity.
Cultural dimensions	One introductory tool by means of which individuals and teams can assess and, consequently, manage cultural diversity in a situation.

8.1.1 Learning Objectives

After having read this chapter, you should

- Be aware of culture as a shared sense and way of 'how to normally do things' (around here, but not around there).
- Know key cultural dimensions and what they describe.
- Be able to use the GLOBE study for cross-cultural analyses and actions.
- Be able to identify relative differences in cultural dimension scores across countries.
- Know how to use cultural dimensions 'inside-out' to integrate virtual team collaboration.
- Be aware of intercultural competencies, and how to develop and apply them, as the ultimate challenge and long-term goal of any collaboration that is (also) characterized by cultural diversity of any kind.

8.1.2 Opening Case

> **Example**
>
> Zeynep, a German IT engineer, is the head of a global computer engineering team, in a German semiconductor company, with headquarters in Frankfurt and subsidiary sites in Bengaluru (India), Manchester (United Kingdom) and Sophia Antipolis (France). The corporate customer for which the team develops IT applications is

based in the USA, and a major sub-contractor is located in Xian (China). Because Zeynep has noticed difference in work styles and approaches across the different sub-teams, as well as differences between team, customer and subcontractor, she has contacted Human Resources (HR) who have commissioned an intercultural training event for the team. All team members meet at a business hotel in Bengaluru for this purpose. ◄

> **Background information: Intercultural Training**
> Intercultural training is a human resource development activity commissioned by the corporate HR function in order to train a specific group of people for working together across cultures and/or to prepare individuals or groups for working together with members of one or multiple other cultures. Usually, intercultural training is limited to one or two days and based on the assumption that those trained will transfer intercultural learning to their jobs afterwards.

8.2 What is Cross-Cultural Management, and How is It Relevant to Virtual Team Collaboration?

A practical and hands-on definition of culture for virtual team collaboration is "how we normally do things around here" (Deal & Kennedy, 1982). Individuals from different cultural backgrounds tend to collaborate and make decisions differently, and their verbal and non-verbal communication styles often differ (Gudykunst & Ting-Toomey, 1988). Not all 'differences' between countries are cultural, and not all cultural differences emerge from the country level—but some of them are, and these are often the initial focus of cross-cultural management.

▶ **Culture** Culture is 'how we normally do things around here' (but not 'around there').

Cross-cultural management is the discipline that studies the interrelations between culture, management and organization (Mahadevan, 2023). The goal of cross-cultural management is to provide individuals with a patterned and structured understanding of how culture is relevant at work, in order to enable them to manage a situation characterized by cultural diversity in more effective, appropriate and responsible ways (ibid.). In its original meaning, culture is the social dimension of human beings, that is: everything that people experience, learn, build, use, invent et cetera in relation to other people. Consequently, people in organizations are influenced by a wide range of cultural factors, such as departmental, regional, organizational, and societal cultures, but also by age, gender, professions, hierarchical position and tenure (Sackmann, 1997). Due to this complexity, culture cannot be managed in its entirety at work, and people and organizations have to find ways to operationalize culture (Mahadevan, 2017).

The challenge—also for Zeynep and her team—is to identify how exactly a larger influencing factor (societal culture), translated via several layers of organizational, professional and corporate cultures, manifests on individual and team levels. For example, Zeynep's team is also globally dispersed, as people work in different countries. However, dispersion is not a necessity for a team to be culturally diverse: it could also be that individuals from different countries work together at one location, and, because their work styles and expectations have been shaped by their upbringing or education in different countries, they bring these differences to the team: a case of cultural diversity without dispersion.

▶ Country cultures are not the only cultures that are relevant to virtual team collaboration, but they are a good starting point for figuring out how to make cultural diversity a team asset.

Leveraging the benefits of cultural diversity requires coming up with first hypotheses of how cross-cultural differences might influence collaboration for Zeynep and her team, and then testing this knowledge upon situations as they occur, in order to draw conclusions as the base of further actions from there: they need to **puzzle with culture** (overview in Mahadevan, 2017, 2023). Country cultures are a good starting point for doing so, and cultural dimensions, also referred to as cultural value orientations, are a suitable initial tool.

Cultural dimensions, also referred as cultural value orientations, describe selected, immaterial aspects of culture that are assumed to be universal, that is: to exist in all cultures (Leung & van de Vijver, 2008). They can be best understood as culturally-specific answers to universal human questions (Mahadevan, 2017). For example, it can be assumed that every group of people needs to organize themselves by means of hierarchies: a universal human question. However, how much difference in power (*power distance*, Hofstede, 1980) is accepted as 'normal'—that is: the culture-specific answer to this question—differs across groups. If one compiles a cross-cultural database on power distance as a universal aspect of culture, it will show different power distance scores for different cultures. One can then identify relative differences across cultures by comparing their understandings of 'normal power distance'. This way, a perceived or actual difference in behaviour, attitudes, expectations and motivations becomes tangible and less 'personal': it is easier for the team to overcome it.

▶ Cultural dimension scores are culture-specific answers to universal human questions.

The weakness of cultural dimensions is that they explain the complex realities of culture only by means of a few, selected, immaterial aspects. However, due to this same simplicity, cultural dimensions are also highly useful for coming up with first hypotheses of which culture-related root cause creates difference and, thus, potential conflict and negative divergence, in virtual team collaboration. They are the starting point, not the end goal of managing cultural diversity in global virtual team collaboration and beyond.

▶ Cultural dimensions highlight selected, universal cultural elements. They do not describe real cultures or individual behaviour. Cultural dimensions are a good start for mapping and integrating cultural differences in the team because of their simplicity and comparability.

The goal of successful cross-cultural management of virtual team collaboration is to come to a more integrated understanding of collaboration and communication practices in the team, based on the assumption that culturally diverse team members have culturally learned different ways of 'how to normally do things', and also seek the same behaviour in others. Cultural dimensions are the first tool for integrating culturally diverse behavioural templates and expectations. If used as cultural hypotheses—not as cultural realities—they can make interpersonal conflict—related to divergent answers to universal questions such as: how much hierarchy do we want and need in the team?—less personal. As a result, the team may move from negative divergence (conflict) to positive convergence (trust).

▶ Culture is 'how we normally do things around here'. Positively diverse teams have succeeded in creating an integrated team understanding of 'how to normally do things'.

Application 8.2: How things are normally done around here

Consider how things are normally done 'around here', that is: at work/at university, in the context in which you normally find yourself (your study program, your job, your profession). When doing so, consider expectations: how have you learned to see that another person of your study program or profession is competent, and what do others expect from you so that you exhibit being a 'good' student or professional 'around here'? Describe three aspects of 'how things are normally (expected to be) done around here'. Exchange with fellow students or professionals who know the context. You will have found culture if they agree that it is true that (one is expected) to 'normally do things like that around here' like this. ◀

8.3 Cross-Cultural Differences in Global Virtual Team Collaboration

This section introduces two major frameworks of cultural dimensions. The first two, the cultural dimensions of Geert Hofstede (Hofstede, 1980, 2001, 2010; Hofstede & Bond, 1988) and project GLOBE (House et al., 2004) build upon each other. They are related to general orientations of how expectations and behavioural templates of what a 'virtual team' is and how it should function might differ. Selected aspects of these frameworks will be applied to Zeynep's team in the following, in order to enable the team to 'puzzle with culture'.

8.3.1 The Hofstede Dimensions: First Ideas of 'What is a Team, and How Should It Function?'

During the intercultural training event, Zeynep and her team are firstly introduced to the cultural dimensions developed by Dutch researcher Geert Hofstede (1980).

> **Background information: The legacy of Geert Hofstede**
> Originally trained in mechanical engineering, Hofstede held professional and managerial jobs in several Dutch companies and did a part-time Ph.D. in Social Psychology, focussing on budget control. According to his own website (Hofstede, 2023b), he then founded and managed the Personnel Research Department of IBM Europe (1965–1971). It was at IBM when Hofstede conducted an employee survey and noticed that employees' responses seemed to differ across countries. He thus concluded that there was 'culture in management and business' and developed his first four cultural dimensions from there, published in 1980. Even though Hofstede relied on earlier conceptualizations of cultural dimensions, his 1980 book is generally accepted as the inception of **comparative cross-cultural management studies**, that is: an approach to culture that focusses on selected aspects of culture (cultural dimensions) which are measured and analysed their scores for large units of culture (nations or societies) by means of quantitative, statistical methods (Jackson, 2020).
>
> The first four of Hofstede's cultural dimensions, power distance, individualism vs. collectivism, masculinity vs. femininity, and uncertainty avoidance (see Table 8.1) are thus a direct result of his IBM study (Hofstede, 1980). Later, Hofstede updated his original 1980 findings with new data (Hofstede, 2001). This then also implies that the original database was limited to a single company, and there are some methodological concerns regarding the research outcome (House & Javidan, 2004; Javidan et al., 2004; Smith, 2006), for instance, as to how to differentiate organizational culture from societal culture (countries), given that the data origi-

8.3 Cross-Cultural Differences in Global Virtual Team Collaboration

Table 8.1 The cultural dimensions by Geert Hofstede

Dimension	Explanation	Virtual team example
Low vs. high power distance *(IBM study)*	The degree to which the community accepts and expects unequal distribution of power. In high power distance cultures, hierarchical structures are valued, whereas low power distance cultures rather strive for equality and power is more evenly distributed	The expectation that everyone voices opinions in the virtual team meeting (low) vs The expectation that this is the prerogative of management (high)
Individualism vs. Collectivism *(IBM study)*	The extent to which individuals prioritize their own interests over the interests of the collective. Individualistic cultures emphasize autonomy, personal freedom and individual achievements. In collectivist cultures, group harmony, cooperation, and loyalty to the community are prioritized	The expectation that team members should work at their own discretion and pace (individualism) vs The understanding that work processes and pace should be aligned (collectivism)
Masculinity vs. Femininity *(IBM study)*	This dimension reflects the gender-related distribution of roles and is also associated with gender-related values. In masculine cultures, there is a greater emphasis on assertiveness, competition, and success, often coupled with a higher proportion of men in roles of power. In feminine cultures, nurturing, quality of life, and cooperation are valued more, often coupled with a more gender-equal distribution of power roles	The idea that a team leader needs to be task-oriented, competitive, assertive and strong, not shying away from conflict (masculinity) vs The idea that to lead the team means to cooperate, integrate and emphatically motivate, also considering relations (femininity)
High vs. low uncertainty avoidance *(IBM study)*	The extent of a culture's tolerance for uncertainty and risk. Cultures with a high uncertainty avoidance prefer structured environments, rules and formal procedures to minimize unpredictability. Low uncertainty avoidance cultures tend to be more adaptable to change and innovation	The idea that virtual team collaboration needs to be structured and planned, to minimize unforeseen events (high) vs The idea that unforeseen events, also mistakes, are inevitable despite planning and should be embraced with a willingness to learn as they happen (low)

(continued)

Table 8.1 (continued)

Dimension	Explanation	Virtual team example
Long-term vs. Short-term orientation (*Chinese values survey*, Hofstede & Bond, 1988)	Long-term orientation implies that members of a culture pay attention to status differences and value seniority, have a strong work ethic and perseverance, and respect tradition Short-term orientation implies that members of a culture do not place high priority on status, try to postpone old age, are concerned with short-term results and aim for quick satisfaction of needs	The idea that established approaches, seniority, strong work-ethics and perseverance build long-term success (long-term) vs The idea that good team work is about immediate results and how people perform in this project (short-term)
Indulgence vs. Restraint (Hofstede, 2010)	This dimension reflects the degree of freedom and indulgence in human desires and impulses. Indulgent cultures allow gratification of the latter, whereas restrained cultures suppress gratification and regulate behaviour based on social norms	The idea that if one works hard, one may also expect the company to provide leisure opportunities or rewards (indulgence) vs The idea that good money, a secure job and self-motivation is reward enough (restraint)

Source Own figure, derived from Hofstede (1980, 2001, 2010; Hofstede & Bond, 1988)

nated from just one company (IBM). Becoming aware of a certain 'Western bias' in his data and building upon the work of Michael Bond's, Hofstede and Bond (1988) furthermore developed the dimension long-term- vs. short-term orientation. Hofstede and Bond (1988) try to take specific Confucian values into account with this dimension; they also refer to it as 'Confucian work dynamism'. In 2010, Hofstede introduced his sixth and last dimension, indulgence vs. restraint. He died in 2020. Summarizing Hofstede's legacy to cross-cultural management studies, Terence Jackson (2020, p. 3), editor-in-chief of the *International Journal of Cross-Cultural Management*, wrote:

> "Geert Hofstede was the first [cross-cultural] management scholar (…) who got himself heard (…). He did this mainly by keeping it simply, very simple. Not only was the concept of comparing nations on the basis of cultural dimensions easy to grasp, limiting the number of dimensions to four and then five and then six was easy to remember. (…) This simplicity came back to bite him, when later, after his theory became more mainstream, critics began to challenge his assumptions and methods. But this did not matter, as his achievement had already been registered. It helped considerably in launching an important subfield of study, cross-cultural management studies."

8.3 Cross-Cultural Differences in Global Virtual Team Collaboration

The Hofstede cultural dimensions, in their order of development, are depicted in Table 8.1.

The scores of the countries which are of interest to Zeynep and her team are depicted in Table 8.2.

What might the Hofstede cultural dimension scores *mean* for actual virtual team collaboration?

Cultural dimensions depict invisible, immaterial and 'broad' value orientations which do not mean anything unless 'puzzled with' in relation to a situation, task or team. When Zeynep engages in this process in order to come to first hypotheses of what to expect from the team, the following implications emerge.

According to the Hofstede database, Germany ranks lowest in **power distance** (35), and China the highest (80). This then suggests that the Chinese sub-contractor's teams are most likely more hierarchical than how Zeynep has learned to organize the team. In particular, the Chinese team members might not speak out freely when Zeynep asks for opinion in a virtual meeting, out of respect for power hierarchies, and it might be better if she talks one-to-one to her counterpart, the team leader, in order to get a clearer picture of what is going on in the Chinese sub-contractor's team. According to the power distance scores, there also seems to be a cross-cultural divide regarding which degree of power distance is commonly accepted as 'normal': Germany, the UK and the US all score in the 35–40 range, whereas France, India and China score between 68 and 80. This suggests that Zeynep may also make use of the bridge-building qualities of French

Table 8.2 Country scores according to the Hofstede dimensions

Country	Cultural dimension					
	Power Distance	Individualism	Masculinity	Uncertainty Avoidance	Long-Term Orientation	Indulgence
Germany	**35**	67	66	65	83	40
USA	40	**91**	62	46	**26**	68
United Kingdom	35	89	66	35	51	**69**
France	68	71	43	**86**	63	48
India	77	48	56	40	51	26
China	**80**	**20**	66	30	**87**	**24**

Explanation to score and visualization
- Scores range from 1 to 100. Highest and lowest country scores per dimension are marked **bold**
- Individualism: Scores below 50 indicate collectivism
- Masculinity: Scores below 50 indicate femininity
- Long-term orientation: Scores below 50 indicate short-term orientation
- Indulgence: Scores below 50 indicate restraint

Source Own figure, compiled from Hofstede (2023a, b)

team members who, being in the middle of both extremes, might be able to translate between both styles, and might furthermore know ways of how to integrate them.

When it comes to **individualism**, it is the UK (89) and the USA (91) that scores the highest, with Germany (67) and France being in the ideal bridge-building position (71) compared to the Indian team (48). Zeynep may thus assume that she will be able to integrate a more group-oriented work style and a more individual work style herself, except, maybe, for the Chinese subcontractor, as the score for China (20) is far away from what she is used to. Here, again, an Indian team member might provide advice.

All countries involved score moderately high on **masculinity** with the exception of France. The scores of Germany, the UK and China (all 66) suggest that values such as competition, achievement and success are relevant at work, and modesty, collaboration and quality of life are of less relevance. Scoring 48, France is the only country in which more 'feminine' values might be relevant in business. It has to be noted that the wording of this dimension is somewhat confusing, because it is not an automatic equation that men are more competitive and women are more caring (Emrich et al., 2004). Thus, this dimension is more a certain value orientation at work, not about how men and women actually *are*. However, it seems that more 'feminine' values at work promote a higher proportion of women's participation, most likely, because, then, the gender role expectation for men is not in contradiction to cultural traits associated with 'femininity'.

France (86) scores the highest on **uncertainty avoidance**, and China (30) the lowest, with Germany (65) occupying a middle position. This suggest that Zeynep will be able to mediate between a certain tendency towards flexibility, innovation and change (low uncertainty avoidance) and the wish to mediate the unpredictability of future events via planning (France).

Long-term orientation is the highest in China (87) and Germany (83) whereas the USA (26) are characterized by short-term orientation. This then suggests that Zeynep has learned a more long-term approach to work and needs to make sure that is actually suitable to the Americanized ways in which the tech business operates.

Indulgence is the highest in the UK (69) and the USA (68), whereas China (24) and India (26) are characterized by restraint. Germany (40) and France (48) are in the middle position, yet, more on the restraint side of the score. This then suggests that Zeynep will most likely be able to integrate between the indulgent idea that leisure opportunities and rewards should be an immediate consequence of hard work and the restrained expectation that one is self-motivated and, if not critiqued, is being praised enough and rewarded with long-term trust and stability.

Link to practice: Culturally-sensitive website design

How do differences in cultural dimension scores influence people's technological preferences? Lachner and colleagues (2018) analyse the effect for website design for one cultural dimension (power distance, according to the Hofstede scores) and two countries: Germany (Hofstede score: 35) and Vietnam (Hofstede score: 70). They created two website prototypes designed in light of lower and higher power distance preferences. For example, the language used was less or more formal, navigational structure involved less or more sub-hierarchies, and visual presentation was oriented towards higher equality or stratification. They found that their study participants (14 Germans and 14 Vietnamese) favoured the prototype which included culturally-sensitive design principles. ◄

How useful are the Hofstede cultural dimension scores for virtual team collaboration?

There is no doubt that the Hofstede dimensions are overly simplistic (Jackson, 2020). Yet, their contribution is to have made culture visible in management and organizations for the first time (ibid.). Nonetheless, there are three major methodological concerns associated with them, and Zeynep and her team have to be aware of these limitations so that the theories which they use do not become **stereotypes**. These stereotypes might be disguised as knowledge (cultural dimensions), but still, they remain stereotypes, just more 'sophisticated' ones (Osland & Bird, 2000). Stereotypes dressed in theory are one of the biggest dangers of intercultural training and corporate practices: it is not the theory that is sufficient or insufficient, rather, one has to understand what (not) to use cultural dimensions for (Mahadevan, 2017). Consequently, cultural dimensions may be a starting hypothesis, not the end point of cross-cultural learning.

Stereotype	A generalized, absolute and simplified belief about a group.
Sophisticating stereotyping	The process of coming to stereotypical understandings based on misused or misapplied theory.

The first, and strongest concern directed towards the Hofstede cultural dimensions, is that his approach equates broad value orientations (how culture 'should be') with the specific practice of what people do (how culture 'is'). However, what people say or wish they do, and what they *really* do tends to differ. Therefore, the relation between value orientation and behaviour is not a direct one, and the difference between the two needs to be taken into account.

Also, because of the narrow, non-representative initial database of the Hofstede studies (a single, Western company: IBM), organizational and societal cultures might have been confused with each other. A broader, more diverse data set might result in more representative findings.

Finally, because cross-cultural researchers, too, are influenced by culture, and because culture changes over time, the question is if 1960s (IBM organizational) culture is still relevant for the values and practice that characterize societal cultures today. For example, labelling a certain, assertive, management style as 'masculine', and a certain, collaborative, management style as 'feminine' when analysing employee responses at IBM in Western Europe might also be rooted in commonly held gender stereotypes of the place and time (Emrich et al., 2004). One might further wonder how many women were actually employed in a managerial or leading position at IBM in the 1960s, and whether professions at that time were not, in fact, differentiated across gender lines, with women being confined to clerical and office work (Mahadevan, 2017).

Thus, Zeynep and her team might turn to newer, more sophisticated comparative cross-cultural studies for insights. Inevitably, these studies will be more complex: it might not be that easy anymore to compare several countries at first glance. This then also brings the opportunity to come to more specific and differentiated insights. Project GLOBE is such a study.

8.3.2 The Cultural Dimensions of Project GLOBE: A More Sophisticated Framework

The so-called GLOBE (Global Leadership and Organizational Behaviour Effectiveness) study is the most recent large-scale comparative cross-cultural management study (House et al, 2004; Chhokar et al., 2007; House et al., 2004) which is still ongoing. The initial data for developing the GLOBE study cultural dimensions was collected by 170 scholars from various cultures through more than 17,000 interviews with middle managers from 62 countries in three industries (House et al, 2004). The database is thus much larger than the Hofstede database, and also more balanced in terms of industry and organizational cultures. However, it is also by now 'outdated' in the sense that data collection started in the 1990s.

Secondly, project GLOBE investigates cultural dimensions on two levels, namely **practices** ('as is') **and values** ('should be'). The intention was to uncover differences between reality and ideal. For example, there might be the ideal to be gender equal ('should be') in a certain culture, but at the same time, gender unequal practices ('as is') might prevail in this culture.

Also, because some countries were found to be culturally heterogeneous, some were split up into different 'societal cultures', such as French-speaking and English-speaking Canada. Others, like Germany, were split into West and East because of their separate history, and South Africa, due to its history of racial segregation, was split up into a 'White' and 'Black' sample. GLOBE thus considers societal cultures, not countries.

The GLOBE project can be accessed online at www.projectglobe.com (GLOBE, 2023a): open the website, choose the "The GLOBE Studies", and scroll to "visualizations of the 2004 study". This opens a map from which you can select a country of interest [last accessed 01 January 2024]. The way in which the GLOBE study cultural dimensions are presented online is that they are ranked on a scale from one to seven, based on whether the score for a certain dimension was very low (1), low (2) relatively low (3), medium (4), relatively high (5), high (6), and very high (7). In addition to specific country scores, GLOBE also presents the scores for the whole of the GLOBE societal cultures, both score range and average score. This means that one can also see which cultural dimension—value or practice—is deemed more important at work than others, across all cultures. GLOBE proposes **nine cultural dimensions** which are presented in Table 8.3.

The following changes compared to the Hofstede studies are noteworthy concerning the specific cultural dimensions:

- **Power distance** and **uncertainty avoidance** were found relevant and remained virtually unchanged.
- GLOBE could not confirm the presumed link of long-term orientation to Confucian values (Ashkanasy et al., 2004, pp. 282–342), yet, retained other aspects of this dimension (see Table 8.3) and renamed it **future orientation**.
- The Hofstede (1980) dimension 'collectivism' was critiqued for being a mixture of (1) external collective encouragement (**institutional collectivism**) and (2) the inner personal valuation of groups (**in-group collectivism**). Thus, each aspect was considered to be a separate dimension.
- Due to its confusing wording and potential gender bias, Hofstede's (1980) concept of masculinity versus femininity was split up into **assertiveness** (the expected business style) and the degree to which both genders are considered equally (**gender egalitarianism**).
- **Humane orientation** and **performance orientation** emerged as new dimensions.

Furthermore, GLOBE (House et al., 2004) identified four statistically relevant correlations which are not directly related to culture but nonetheless crucial for cross-cultural management.

- Firstly, the data suggests that **culture is an explanatory variable *only* if a country is sufficiently developed.** For instance, if child labour is prevalent in a country, this might have less to do with cultural value orientations and more with the sheer necessity to survive. Likewise, high performance orientation might be impossible to achieve and pursue if a country lacks the required infrastructure and the stable economy and political system necessary for enabling companies and individuals to perform.
- Secondly, there is a **gender bias in the data**: two out of three middle managers from which the data stems were men. Also, the mean score of the dimension Gender Egalitarianism is the lowest among all practice orientations, "indicating that GLOBE societies are reported to be male oriented" (Javidan et al., 2004, p. 31).
- Third, **women managers judged gender egalitarianism in their culture to be lower** than their male counterparts across all societal cultures studied.
- Together, two and three imply that all societal cultures studied are characterized by an imbalanced proportion of men and women in management, and that men—across all societal cultures—underestimate gender inequality compared to women (Emrich et al., 2004).

Table 8.3 Cultural dimensions according to project GLOBE

Dimension	Explanation	GLOBE average scores			
		Cultural practices		Cultural values	
Performance orientation	The degree to which a collective encourages and rewards group members for performance improvement and excellence	4.1	(0)	5.94	(++)
Assertiveness	The degree to which individuals are assertive, confrontational and aggressive in their relationships with others	4.14	(0)	3.82	(0)
Future orientation	The extent to which individuals engage in future-oriented behaviours such as delaying gratification, planning, and investing in the future	3.85	(0)	5.49	(+)
Humane orientation	The degree to which a collective encourages and rewards individuals for being fair, altruistic, generous, caring and kind to others	4.09	(0)	5.42	(+)
Institutional collectivism	The degree to which organizational and societal institutional practices encourage and reward collective distribution of resources and collective action	4.25	(0)	4.73	(+)
In-group collectivism	The degree to which individuals express pride, loyalty, and cohesiveness in their organizations or families	5.13	(+)	5.66	(++)
Gender egalitarianism	The degree to which a collective minimizes gender inequality	3.37	(-)	4.51	(+)
Power Distance	The extent to which the community accepts and endorses authority, power differences, and status privileges	5.17	(+)	2.75	(−)
Uncertainty avoidance	The extent to which a society, organization, or group relies on social norms, rules, and procedures to alleviate unpredictability of future events	4.16	(0)	4.62	(+)

Explanation to score and visualization
1 = very low; visualized as: (−−−)
2 = low; visualized as: (−−)
3 = relatively low; visualized as: (−)
4 = medium; visualized as: (0)
5 = relatively high; visualized as: (+)
6 = high; visualized as: (++)
7 = very high; visualized as: (+++)
Note: New or altered cultural dimensions (compared to Hofstede dimensions) are marked in **bold**
Source Own table, derived from GLOBE (2023a, 2024a)

According to project GLOBE data, in-group collectivism is the dimension in which GLOBE societal cultures differ the most (Javidan et al., 2004, pp. 31–32), and assertiveness the one with the least spread (ibid., p. 32). High power distance and "being somewhat male-orientated" is what most GLOBE cultures have in common (ibid., pp. 30–31).

There are also some links between certain cultural dimensions. For example, higher assertiveness often seems to be coupled with lower gender egalitarianism, suggesting that a more assertive style either advantages men over women or hinders men to assume roles and tasks which are thought of as being in contradiction with assertiveness, such as care work, flexible work arrangements or part-time occupation. It also seems that societal cultures have to decide how to 'care for others', either via rules and regulations (institutional collectivism) or via encouraging altruistic behaviour via humane orientations.

Table 8.3 also depicts general work-related implications beyond specific cultures with offering the absolute range and score of cultural dimensions across all GLOBE countries.

- First, the value scores of most cultural dimensions are higher than the practice scores: this suggests that it is more difficult to do things 'right' than to have an idea of what should be done: what people do and what they say they do, is different. This is the most striking for performance orientation and gender egalitarianism that score much higher on the value side: no one lives up to their own performance standard, and no culture succeeds in implementing the value of gender egalitarianism to the same degree.
- Second, the practice scores of some cultural dimensions, such as in-group collectivism and power distance are globally higher than, for example, gender egalitarianism and future orientation. Thus, team spirit and unequal distribution of power are more relevant to how work is done across cultures than ideas of gender inclusiveness and a long-term outlook. The first effect might be due to gender bias in the data (underrepresentation of women managers), the second might be due to the stated insight that underdevelopment limits behavioural scope, such as the ability to plan for the future.
- Third, the average for in-group collectivism is very high on the value side and also high in practice. Combined with the insight that the range for this dimension is the highest of all cultural dimensions (see e.g. GLOBE, 2023b, 2023c), this then means that the highest difference is experienced in this dimension: it is essential in a significant number of cultures, but virtually non-existent in a significant number of other cultures.

Keeping this in mind, Zeynep can now prepare for going to Bengaluru. Because the GLOBE study data is presented less simplistically than the Hofstede studies, she focusses on the comparison between Germany (West) and India first. Table 8.4 depicts the scores of these two societal cultures according to project GLOBE.

In Table 8.4, the column 'above' and 'below average' relates the specific country score to the average score across all GLOBE study countries. This puts the country score in relation to how valued a certain cultural orientation is in absolute terms, e.g. performance orientation is more valued in absolute terms on a global scale than future orientation. The highest deviation of the country score from the GLOBE average is marked in bold. For example, compared to the GLOBE average, the German score for in-group collectivism is below average in both the value and the practice dimension, and the Indian score, whilst considerably higher in both, is above average in the practice dimension and below average in the value dimension. Zeynep might thus expect a difference in the requirements concerning team spirit, yet, the difference is not the full range possible across all GLOBE countries.

> **Application 8.3: Cultural dimensions in how you are 'normally doing things'**

Revisit how you 'normally do, expect and are expected to do things around here' (Application 8.2) and reflect:

- Which cultural dimension orientations seem to underlie your behaviour?
- Does this behaviour reflect what is important to you (values)? If not: Why is there a difference between both?

Next, check out the respective cultural dimension score of the societal culture in which you attend university and/or work online: www.globeproject.com, go to "The GLOBE Studies", scroll to "visualizations of the 2004 study", which opens a map from which you can select a country of interest [last accessed 01 January 2024].

- Which value and practice scores are the average in this societal culture? If there is a gap between value and practice: What might this gap indicate?
- Does your own behaviour represent the business norm of this societal culture? Why (not)? Remark: consider alternative influences, such as age, profession, upbringing, lifestyle, country of origin, industry, department and so on to answer this question.
- Compare with fellow students and/or colleagues to establish what is shared and what is individual.

Remark: only consider the cultural dimensions scores on the website. The task is not to prove culture or come to 'true' conclusions but rather to offer plausible interpretations and a 'logic' that makes sense. ◄

Table 8.4 Societal cultures scores according to project GLOBE

Cultural dimension	Cultural practices ("as is")				Cultural values ("should be")			
	Germany (West)		India		Germany (West)		India	
Performance orientation	4.25 (0)	Above Average	4.25 (0)	Above Average	6.01 (++)	Above Average	6.05 (++)	Above Average
Assertiveness	4.55 (+)	Above Average	3.73 (0)	Below Average	3.09 (−)	Below Average	4.76 (+)	**Above Average**
Future orientation	4.27 (0)	Above Average	4.19 (0)	Above Average	4.85 (+)	Below Average	5.6 (++)	Above Average
Humane orientation	3.18 (−)	Below Average	4.57 (+)	Above Average	5.46 (+)	Average	5.28 (+)	Below Average
Institutional collectivism	3.79 (0)	Below Average	4.38 (0)	Above Average	4.82 (+)	Above Average	4.71 (+)	Average
In-group collectivism	4.02 (0)	**Below Average**	5.92 (++)	**Above Average**	5.18 (+)	Below Average	5.32 (+)	**Below Average**
Gender egalitarianism	3.10 (−)	Below Average	2.90 (−)	**Below Average**	4.89 (+)	**Above Average**	4.51 (+)	Average
Power Distance	5.25 (+)	Above Average	5.47 (+)	Above Average	2.54 (−)	Below Average	2.64 (−)	Below Average
Uncertainty avoidance	5.22 (+)	**Above Average**	4.15 (0)	Average	3.32 (−)	**Below Average**	4.73 (+)	Above Average

Explanation to score and visualization
1 = very low; visualized as: (− − −)
2 = low; visualized as: (− −)
3 = relatively low; visualized as: (−)
4 = medium; visualized as: (0)
5 = relatively high; visualized as: (+)
6 = high; visualized as: (+)
7 = very high; visualized as: (+++)
Note: The highest deviation from the GLOBE average is marked in **bold**
Source Own table, compiled from GLOBE (2024a, b)

8.4 Recommendations for Cross-Cultural Management and Global Leadership in Virtual Teams

Cultural dimensions describe selected universal and invisible aspects of culture (value orientations) which people are most likely not aware of. Cultural dimension scores for macro-units of culture (nations, societies) visualize relative differences in value orientations by means of quantitative methods. However, what remains tricky is to identify how value orientations translate into actual behaviour. Furthermore, cultural dimension scores never represent the whole variety of culture: they are merely an arithmetic mean compiled from the data analysed. In reality, culture is rooted in norms, that is: the shared ideas and ways of 'how to do things' in a situation that are internally heterogeneous—but also sufficiently homogeneous to be identifiable as such. It is thus important to differentiate between clear-cut cultural dimension scores and the somewhat 'fuzzy' norms underlying them, and to also never confuse an aggregated score with individual character traits. For instance, there are cultural dimension scores for Germany but it is not an automatic 'given' that Zeynep *must* represent them. Also, virtual team collaboration is a rather complex cultural scenario that—as all theories agree and as practical experience suggests—cannot be prescribed by means of rules.

Cultural dimension scores, and the relative differences across countries and societies which they visualize, are thus simply a hypothesis to be tested upon the situation: they are a starting point that make sense to unravel everything that is 'cultural' about the situation—they are not the solution to the problems occurring. Ultimately, the value of cultural dimensions depends on how the person applying them to a situation handles them: as stereotypes that *must* be true (which would be an insufficient approach) or as ideas that *might*—but do not have to—explain similarities and differences when and as they occur. Thus, the mindset and attitudes driving cross-culturally competent virtual team behaviour must go deeper than simply 'knowing' cultural dimension scores.

8.4.1 What Cultural Dimensions are Useful For

Like an iceberg, culture hides most of its deep layers, and only knowing visible contours of the iceberg is insufficient for circumnavigating it. Any culture-specific, inner logic that makes sense to the cultural insider is not visible to a cultural outsider. For example, a person who is trained in an assertive communicative style not only knows how to 'do' assertive communication but also (tacitly and implicitly) 'knows' why this style is positively influencing the situation, and how. However, from the outside, to a person not familiar with this style, this inside 'meaning' is not visible. People thus tend to interpret the behaviour of others based on how they would act in the same situation. For example, a person to whom a non-assertive style is culturally 'normal' is likely to perceive an assertive person as aggressive, and, in return, is likely to be perceived as 'wishy-washy' and unreliable themselves by the person trained in an assertive style. Knowledge of cultural dimensions thus helps to make differences in values, motivations and behavioural schemes tangible and 'real'. The first contribution of cultural dimensions is thus that they make conflict less personal and help move beyond subjective perceptions.

Culture as a 'way of how to normally do things (around here—but not there)' also involves the realization that 'what people do' *must make sense to them* (otherwise they would not do it). Yet, people are likely not to be aware of culture's imprint upon them: they often merely enact the 'script' that 'feels' familiar without being able to put what they do into words. Cultural dimensions give these implicit ideas and ways of how to normally do things around here a 'name tag', and people can then become aware of what underlies their behaviour and also explicate it to others. Thus, the second way in which cultural dimensions may be used is to use them as explanatory hypotheses for finding out what underlies one's own subjective motivations, expectations and behavioural schemes. Or, in simple terms: cultural dimensions help people to understand and explain, as far as is possible, the WHY behind WHAT they do.

Finally, cultural dimensions help people understand where their personal comfort zone ends. For instance, a person trained in an assertive communicative style is likely to use this style when something at work 'goes wrong': it is simply the approach that feels the 'safest' and the one that seems the most likely to deliver results. Likewise, a person used to in-group collectivism at work is likely to seek out others for solving the problems whereas a person to whom an individualist and 'sober' distribution of work is normal will not even imagine doing so. Whenever there is a problem or conflict, people are the most likely to withdraw to those cultural orientations that seem the safest— and these are often the cultural norms of the cultural context that is familiar to them. In simple words: A German/Indian/French team member is likely to behave the most 'German'/'Indian'/'French' when under stress or when the project is at risk of failure. This then implies: unfortunately, people orientate themselves towards divergent norms the most when this is the least appropriate and effective behaviour. Or, in other words: those involved would need to move beyond their respective cultural orientations for managing and overcoming conflict. Thus, a major contribution of cultural dimension underlying one's own behaviour is that one is better able to identify one's culturally instinctive behaviour when encountering negatively divergent dynamics, such as conflict, at work.

▶ Cultural dimensions make diversity conflict less personal and help increase cultural awareness. They help explicate one's own WHY behind the WHAT, and can be a first access point to the cultural orientations of others.

8.4.2 Cultural Dimensions as Part of the Global Virtual Team Configuration Challenge

Virtual team collaboration is characterized by both divergent and convergent processes. It is a key managerial task to promote positive dynamics, such as creativity (positively divergent) and trust (positively convergent), and to minimize negative ones, such as groupthink (a negative convergent process which mainly occurs in monocultural teams) and conflict (a negative divergent process which is likely to occur in multicultural teams).

Cultural dimensions need to be considered in light of the ideal convergence-divergence ratio to be achieved, which is specific to each global virtual team. For instance, low task interdependence can be managed by a clear hierarchy whereas high task interdependence requires mutual adjustment and a more collaborative leadership style. Thus, the impact of convergent and divergent team dynamics, and whether it is positive or negative emerges in relation to other team characteristics, such as task type and interrelatedness, the lifecycle stage of the team, the type of knowledge involved, and team members' technological and communicative requirements, knowledge and skills, and it is in this light that the potential impact of certain cultural dimension scores needs to be assessed. Furthermore, the Information and Communication Technologies (ICTs) which the team uses to collaborate need to be chosen according to the complexity of the message and the purpose of the task (Daft & Lengel, 1984). The more and more synchronous communication modes are enabled by an ICT, the richer it is. Virtual meetings enable video, audio and written interactions in real time (rich and synchronous), whereas e-mails only enable written communication and involve a time lag (lean and asynchronous). Together, these factors shape cross-cultural management requirements.

For example, a global research and development team charged with product innovation requires more positively divergent processes than a global operations team charged with execution and meeting set targets and fixed key performance indicators. The knowledge to be transferred in the global operations team, such as: how to measure product outcome or process efficiency, is fairly explicit. This knowledge can thus be put into manuals and schedules and does not pose much of a divergence risk. Thus, communication does not function as a means for further 'team building' and shared processes, databases and procedures might suffice for overcoming divergent approaches to it—e.g. higher or lower assertiveness or humane orientation.

Conversely, research and development require 'creative thinking' on the part of all team members, and it is not easy to put into words why one has come up with a creative idea or has found this specific solution to a novel problem—there is no schedule or manual for that. Creativity is therefore linked to tacit knowledge, that is: knowledge that is unique to a person, that is rooted in experience, and that cannot be easily explained to others. The required high divergence in creative thinking might then pose a risk to the team, as team members might grow further apart in the process if they fail to exchange the required knowledge by means of rich ICTs or, ideally sometimes also in person.

Thus, communication is also highly relational and a major means for building and maintaining trust: here, cross-cultural alignment is much more of a critical success factor.

The global operations team can split the task into separate individual tasks more easily whereas the research and development team would need to frequently exchange on ideas and to also develop them together. This then means that the global operation teams can do with less and leaner communicative interactions and lower in-group orientation whereas the research and development team needs to collaborate intensively and frequently by means of rich ICTs so that divergence does not impact the team negatively. Again, this then results in much higher cross-cultural alignment demands.

Also, communicative divergence *during rich communication* is something that should be consciously encouraged and supported in the research and development team: it fosters creativity and innovativeness and will help the team to think ahead and come up with a better product. Also, richer ICTs are much more conducive to cross-cultural alignment. For example, if one team member suddenly sends a very 'different' idea to all via a lean ICT (such as e-mail) or changes templates in the common database without the other team members understanding the rationale behind this action (and for this understanding, a richer communication channel should have been chosen), this might easily create mistrust in the team.

The major distortion factor for achieving the ideal divergence-/convergence ratio across all types of teams is power inequalities. These are most commonly rooted in language (different levels of proficiency, e.g. in the English language), position (e.g. corporate headquarters dominating collaboration) or knowledge (expertise being distributed unequally or not being shared). How to overcome such power effects, in particular with regard to global virtual team collaboration, will be highlighted in Chap. 9.

8.4.3 How to Do Reality Justice When Using Cultural Dimensions: Two Considerations

Culture refers to shared ideas and ways of 'how to normally do things'. This concept necessarily implies cultural diversity: how things are done 'around here' is not how things are done 'around there'. Cultural dimensions, as a tool for measuring objective differences across societal cultures, are a first entry point for deciphering these relative differences. However, this tool can only be helpful if those using it consider two requirements.

Firstly, the tricky task in a globalized and digitalized professional world is to identify where one culture ends and another one begins. Cross-cultural management researcher Geert Hofstede (1991, p. 5) has defined culture as the "the collective programming of the mind which distinguishes the members of one group or category of people from another". But: which 'group-related level' is the one creating perceived or actual differences across individuals and groups of people? (Mahadevan, 2023). For example, Zeynep, the virtual team leader of the opening case is a German citizen with Turkish ancestry. How 'German' is she, and as how 'German' will she be perceived, and which configurations of personal identity and societal culture will characterize her team members?

Nonetheless, despite societies being internally heterogeneous, the way in which the system 'functions' is something that often aligns people beyond their individual personalities: at work people are not 'who they are' but 'who they are expected to be'. Therefore, aspects such as how one is expected to perform as a team leader, how the organization functions and what it stands for, what work means to people and how they draw the line between work and life, might still differ between countries. Furthermore, professions are often global. Those team members sharing the same disciplinary background across their countries of residence or origin might feel and behave more alike than those from another profession. Organizational and departmental culture might be a convergent influence across team members' locations and cultures. Finally, culture is not static and, if Zeynep and the others build a team culture successfully, new, shared 'ways of doing things' will overcome initial differences.

Thus, one can never identify a certain root cause of why people's ways of doing things diverge, nor can one clearly identify the cultural level causing these effects. Or, in other words: the task is not to define Zeynep and her team in terms of culture but to use cultural dimensions as a first entry point for figuring out what actually creates different and similar ideas and ways of how to do things in this specific team. Cross-cultural management thus means to puzzle with culture 'inside-out', not with defining the cultural border.

▶   One needs to puzzle with culture 'inside-out', not define its borders in today's culturally complex, and digitalized and globalized world.

Secondly, a person using culture dimensions as an explanatory tool needs to make sure not to confuse objective and subjective culture. Whereas objective culture is clearly definable (the facts of the situation), subjective culture lies in the eye of the beholder, and insider and outsider perspective differ for these aspects of culture. For instance, there might be more levels of hierarchy at the Indian site compared to the USA: an objective cross-cultural difference. However, even if formal hierarchies are about the same, team members might 'live' and 'perceive' hierarchy differently: a subjective cross-cultural difference. Thus, Zeynep needs to both observe how team leaders like herself are placed in each site's hierarchies, and to consider what is expected of her as a team leader and how her actions might be perceived. Both differences are rooted in the cultural dimension of 'power distance', but the first refers to measurable facts and the second one to people's ideas about the situation, and a cross-culturally competent manager needs to differentiate between the two.

▶ **Objective culture** is clearly definable and facts-based. Conversely, **subjective culture** lies in the eye of the beholder; it necessarily involves insider and outsider perspective.

8.4.4 The Long-Term Goal of Developing Intercultural Competencies

Virtual team collaboration requires intercultural ('between-cultural') competencies, understood as the ability to influence a context characterized by cultural diversity effectively, appropriately and responsibly (Spitzberg & Chagnon, 2009; Mahadevan, 2023).

- Effectivity describes that one's actions have a desirable impact on the situation (what one does influences the situation to the better).
- Appropriateness describes that these actions also take other people involved and the immediate boundary conditions of the situation into account. For instance, whilst force or dominance might be effective, it is seldom appropriate in virtual team collaboration and elsewhere.
- Responsibility describes that one needs to measure one's actions against wider human standards, such as corporate sustainability, ethics or human rights.

For instance, when a company from a highly industrialized country oversees low-cost labour elsewhere, even workers there might actually want to work under unsafe conditions, for instance, when being compensated for it. The managerial decision to pay workers more so that they willingly work without minimum security standards is thus both effective and appropriate within the situation. However, it is not responsible. Also, skilled workers collaborating virtually as a team at a developing site might be permitted to spend 24-h non-stop at the offices, and workers might even want to do so to prove themselves in a highly competitive work environment. When going to Bangalore, a city that has been called the 'Silicon Valley' of India in which hundreds of companies compete for skilled IT personnel from all over the country, all of them aspiring to have a 'better life', Zeynep will certainly have to consider such wider questions of responsibility, beyond the immediate requirements of collaborating effectively and appropriately.

▶ **Intercultural competency** means to influence a context that is characterized by cultural diversity in a way that is effective, appropriate and responsible.

One problem with measuring intercultural competencies is that it is not clear which 'mindset' enables them. Or, in other words, intercultural competency only becomes visible when resulting in behaviour, such as more or less effective, appropriate and responsible words and actions. Thus, people might stereotype in their thoughts—but if they can deal with these feelings and move beyond them in their actions, they might still display highly interculturally competent behaviour. However, what they then lack is a truly 'global mindset' and, the more complex the situation becomes, the more likely it is that their non-global mindset will show. Simply changing one's behaviour thus only gets one so far: to the surface of culture as a set of 'rules' to be followed. For moving deeper, the interplay of five components is required (see Mahadevan & Steinmann, 2023). These are:

- **Emotional**: the ability to relate to others and to empathize with them, to cope with frustration and to tolerate the uncertainty and ambiguity of culturally diverse contexts.
- **Cognitive**: knowledge about cross-cultural differences, such as cultural dimensions, and the ability to hypothesize from the situation
- **Motivational**: the wish to also engage in difference and to learn from it, in light of the emotional challenges, and cognitive and behavioural requirements.
- **Meta-cognitive** (reflexive): the ability to hypothesize future intercultural (inter-) actions and, more importantly, to revisit prior intercultural (inter-) actions and to check whether one has achieved one's goals, and, if not to adjust one's goals and strategies
- **Behavioural**: the practice of putting the aforementioned components into concrete action, also: the constant seeking out of new intercultural experiences for further learning triggers.

These five components are mutually reinforcing and emerge from experience, that is: how a person lives through, deals with, reflects upon and prepares for situations and tasks that are characterized by cultural diversity. The development of such advanced intercultural competencies is thus the ultimate challenge to be faced by Zeynep and her team, beyond the ability to come to a first situational assessment via the application of cultural dimensions.

8.5 Closing Part

8.5.1 Chapter Summary

This chapter has introduced the tool of cultural dimensions as a first entry point for how to integrate divergent realities and perspectives in a global virtual team, and beyond. Culture can be defined as 'the shared ideas and ways of how people normally do things around here (but not there)', and it can be visualized by means of an iceberg. The benefits of cultural dimensions only emerge if those using them apply them in the right manner. Three considerations are essential for applying cultural dimensions in beneficial ways.

First, because culture, like an iceberg, is largely below the surface, people themselves might not be aware of what underlies their motivations, expectations and behaviours. Therefore, cross-cultural management learning is not only directed toward other cultures but builds awareness of what is in one's own cultural backpack, what glasses one wears when looking and acting upon a situation, and where one's own comfort zone ends. Or, in simple terms: the more you understand yourself, the more you can relate to others, and the more ways of managing a situation you learn from this experience, the more options for making the most appropriate and effective choice you have.

Secondly, 'what people do', and 'how they do it', must make sense to them—otherwise they would not do it, regardless of how 'strange' this behaviour might seem from the outside. The measuring rod for successful cross-cultural management is thus the ability and the wish to make oneself an 'insider' to another person's lived experiences. This requires not only a cognitive change of perspective, but also the emphatic motivation to relate to others and to question one's own normalities and 'logic'.

Thirdly, because virtual team collaboration is more complex than relative differences in country culture, one needs to understand culture 'inside-out', to unravel relative differences from the situation, and not to define cultural borders a priori. Or, in simple terms: the only thing that a (global) virtual team can be sure of is that team members come with some shared and some divergent ideas and ways of how to do things. They cannot be sure of where these similarities and differences emerge from: it could be country, region, profession, workplace, and many more aspects that have shaped and are continuously shaping their 'ways of doing things'. However, what they can be sure of is that relative differences in cultural orientations, once identified, will help them to make difference less personal, to relate to the other, become aware of their own ways of doing things, and to explain their own motivations to others.

This then enables team members and leaders to use cultural dimensions as a starting point for developing advanced intercultural competencies, as evidenced by the (increased) ability to influence situations characterized by cultural diversity effectively, appropriately and responsibly. This ability is built from the interplay of emotional, cognitive, motivational, meta-cognitive and behavioural capacities which are applied to actual experiences that are reflected upon.

▶ **Cross-cultural management skills** are built from the ability and motivation to relate to others and experience the world from their standpoints, coupled with cultural self-awareness. The goal is to develop more versatility and variety in how to approach a specific task or situation, and to make more conscious choices of which approach to employ. Five components need to come together for this ability to develop when experiencing and reflecting upon interactions characterized by cultural diversity.

8.5.2 Key Points

- Culture is 'how we normally do things around here' (but not 'around there')
- Cross-cultural management is the discipline that studies the interrelations between culture and management, with the goal of enabling individuals, teams and organizations to make cultural diversity a collaborative asset.

- Cross-cultural competencies describe the skills of successfully 'puzzling with culture', as evidenced by the ability to influence a situation characterized by cultural diversity more effectively, appropriately and responsibly.
- Cultural dimensions are selected, universal and immaterial aspects of culture by means of which relative difference in cultural orientations, expectations and interpretations may be deduced from experience.
- The Hofstede study is the first comparative cross-cultural management study which proposed the tool of cultural dimensions.
- Project GLOBE is the most relevant follower study of Hofstede, with a more differentiated approach to selected cultural dimensions and a larger database.
- Cultural dimensions are the starting point, but not the end goal, of cross-cultural management.
- Those applying cultural dimensions need to know what (not) to use them for, and how.
- Cultural dimensions might enable initial cross-cultural awareness, yet, the ultimate goal of cross-cultural management is the development of cross-cultural competencies.
- For the development of in-depth cross-cultural competencies, emotional, cognitive, motivational, meta-cognitive and behavioural capacities need to come together and be applied to actual experiences that are reflected upon.

8.5.3 Review Questions

1. What is culture, and why and how is cultural diversity a normality of virtual team collaboration?
2. What is cross-cultural management and what is its goal?
3. What is meant by selected, immaterial universal aspects of culture?
4. What is meant by 'relative difference' in cross-cultural management, and why is it that learning about another culture always implies learning about oneself?
5. What are cultural dimensions, and what are they (not) useful for?
6. Which key cultural dimensions can you name, and what do they describe?
7. What are intercultural competencies and how are they evidenced?
8. What does the development of intercultural competencies involve?

8.5.4 Opening Case Revisited

Zeynep and her team need to develop a functioning virtual mode of collaboration, and, for doing so, they need performance norms and trust. As Crisp and Jarvenpaa (2013) find, it is essential for trust development in global virtual teams that the performance norms that are set and monitored in the team are linked to those beliefs in each other that are initially held by the team members. This way, performance norms utilize the initial trust (swift trust) which members have in each other's performance and can thus support the building of later, more long-lasting trust, which then impacts positively upon team performance. Cultural awareness, rooted in the knowledge of cultural dimensions, is thus a double-edged sword: it can contribute or destroy this trust, depending on how this cross-cultural knowledge is handled and applied.

What should never be done is to use cultural dimensions prescriptively: as a way to tell team members how others *are* different—this will only destroy the initial trust people might have in each other, for example because they share a profession or work in the same organization. For instance, multinational companies training newly-formed global engineering teams often invest in intercultural training activities, that is: activities that shall make members aware of their cross-cultural differences. Yet, as Mahadevan (2011, 2017) finds, they might have the opposite effects. This is the case if the intercultural training activity overemphasizes the importance of cross-national differences in relation to other influencing factors, in particular, if there are already anxieties, e.g. fear of losing one's job due to transferring knowledge, in the team. In such cases, intercultural training does not create positive divergence, but rather pushes team members further apart, sometimes even destroying the 'swift trust' they might have had in each other. Or, in other words: had team members not received such training, they would have never doubted their being alike in their work approaches due to their shared professional identities in 'engineering'. Instead of increasing positive convergence in the team, an intercultural training activity that overemphasizes the importance of cross-national differences in relation to other influencing factors thus pushes the team further apart by questioning and, sometimes, destroying the initial professional trust that could have propelled the team forward.

Therefore, again, the usefulness of cultural dimensions depends on how they are used, also on team level. Instead of considering them to be 'truths' about their collaboration, the team should exchange on the cultural dimension scores of their respective societal cultures and hypothesize to what extent they might influence individual and team approaches and performance ideas (the idea of culture as 'doors within doors'). The team could also use cultural dimensions to reflect upon their own cultural backpacks and to better understand through which glasses they are likely to view and react upon specific situations, such as delays, insufficient quality or failure. Finally, the team could then make sure to prevent the hypothesized issues from happening and install 'fail-safe' mechanisms in their performance norms. For instance, how should one prevent and manage the likely incident of a German team member being assertive in their communication of project flaws, and an Indian team member not being able to handle such 'directness', which then might result in elusive project communication, which is again creating anxieties and trust issues for the German side, because it increases project uncertainty, that is likely not being handled well from the German side?

Thus, what Zeynep and her team should prepare for are hypothesized best-case and worst-case team scenarios due to a potential relative difference in cultural dimension scores and then check whether individual team member behaviour and the 'system' by which the project is run (schedules, procedures, organizational structures and hierarchies) is indicative of these relative differences. A good entry point for doing so is communication (see Chaps. 4 and 5), an everyday collaborative practice that makes differences in cultural value orientation the most visible. For example, communication styles can either be direct or indirect, explicit or implicit, and directed towards content or context—and if viewed in light of cultural dimensions, it becomes clear which cultural dimension is conducive to which communicative preference, and vice versa. Ultimately, what would benefit the team more is a long-term reflexive process of how culture impacts how things are done, beyond preparatory intercultural training (Mahadevan, 2014).

8.5.5 Closing Activity

Revisit the opening case and identify the worst-case collaborative scenarios in virtual team collaboration in this team. Or, in other words: where might virtual team collaboration 'go wrong' because of a relative difference in cultural dimension scores? Which performance norms could function as worst-case countermeasures for Zeynep and the team and secure the required minimum standard of collaboration? You might consider the properties and effects of virtual team communication to find a starting point for this activity (see Chaps. 4 and 5).

References

Ashkanasy, N., Gupta, V., Mayfield, M., & Trevor-Roberts, E. (2004). Future orientation. In R. House, P. Hanges, M. Javidan, & V. Gupta (Eds.), *Culture, leadership, and organizations—The GLOBE study of 62 societies* (pp. 282–342). Sage.
Chhokar, J. S., Brodbeck, F. C., & House, R. J. (Eds.). (2007). *Culture and leadership across the world: The GLOBE book of in-depth studies of 25 societies.* Lawrence Erlbaum.
Crisp, C. B., & Jarvenpaa, S. L. (2013). Swift trust in global virtual teams: Trusting beliefs and normative actions. *Journal of Personnel Psychology, 12*(1), 45–56.
Daft, R. L., & Lengel, R. H. (1984). Information richness: A new approach to managerial behavior and organizational design. *Research in Organizational Behavior, 6*, 191–233.
Deal, T. E., & Kennedy, A. A. (1982). *Corporate culture: The rites and rituals of corporate life.* Addison-Wesley.
Emrich, C. G., Denmark, F. L., & Den Hartog, D. N. (2004). Cross-cultural differences in gender egalitarianism: Implications for societies, organizations and leaders. In R. House, P. Hanges, M. Javidan, & V. Gupta (Eds.), *Culture, leadership, and organizations—The GLOBE study of 62 societies* (pp. 343–394). Sage.
GLOBE. (2023a). *Overview on GLOBE countries.* Retrieved November 1, 2023, from https://globeproject.com/results?page_id=country#country.
GLOBE. (2023b). *Country score: Germany.* Retrieved November 1, 2023, from https://globeproject.com/results/countries/DEU?menu=country#country.

GLOBE. (2023c). *Country score: India*. Retrieved November 1, 2023, from https://globeproject.com/results/countries/IND?menu=country#country.

GLOBE. (2024a). *Overview on GLOBE countries*. Retrieved November 1, 2023 from https://globeproject.com/results?page_id=country#country.

GLOBE. (2024b). *Leadership Styles*. Retrieved November 1, 2023, from https://globeproject.com/study_2004_2007?page_id=data#data.

Gudykunst, W. B., & Ting-Toomey, S. (1988). *Culture and interpersonal communication*. Sage.

Hofstede, G. H. (1980). *Culture's consequences: International differences in work related values*. Sage.

Hofstede, G. H. (1991). *Cultures and organizations: Software of the mind*. McGraw-Hill.

Hofstede, G. H. (2001). *Culture's consequences: Comparing values, behaviors, institutions and organizations across nations*. Sage.

Hofstede, G. H. (2010). *Cultures and organizations: Software for the mind*. McGraw-Hill.

Hofstede, G. H., & Bond, M. (1988). The Confucius connection: From cultural roots to economic growth. *Organizational Dynamics, 16*(4), 4–21.

Hofstede, G. H. (2023a). *Hofstede cultural dimension scores*. Retrieved September 5, 2023, from http://geert-hofstede.com/countries.html.

Hofstede, G. J. (2023b). *Geert Hofstede: Biography*. Retrieved October 31, 2023, from https://geerthofstede.com/geert-hofstede-biography/geert-hofstede-cv/.

House, R. J., & Javidan, M. (2004). Overview of GLOBE. In R. House, P. Hanges, M. Javidan, & V. Gupta (Eds.), *Culture, leadership, and organizations—The GLOBE study of 62 societies* (pp. 9–28). Sage.

House, R. J., Hanges, P., Javidan, M., & Gupta, V. (2004). *Culture, leadership, and organizations: The GLOBE study of 62 societies*. Sage.

Jackson, T. (2020). Editorial: The legacy of Geert Hofstede. *International Journal of Cross Cultural Management, 20*(1), 3–6.

Javidan, M., House, R., & Dorfman, W. (2004). A nontechnical summary of GLOBE Findings. In R. House, P. Hanges, M. Javidan, & V. Gupta (Eds.), *Culture, leadership, and organizations—The GLOBE study of 62 societies* (pp. 29–48). Sage.

Lachner, F., Nguyen, M.-A., & Butz, A. (2018) Culturally sensitive user interface design: A case study with German and Vietnamese users. In *Proceedings of the Second African Conference for Human Computer Interaction: Thriving Communities*. Retrieved July 31, 2022 from https://www.medien.ifi.lmu.de/pubdb/publications/pub/lachner2018africhi/lachner2018africhi.pdf.

Leung, K., & van de Vijver, F. J. R. (2008). Strategies for strengthening causal inferences in cross-cultural research: The consilience approach. *International Journal of Cross Cultural Management, 8*(2), 145–169.

Mahadevan, J. (2011). Engineering culture(s) across sites—Implications for cross-cultural management of emic meanings. In H. Primecz, L. Romani, & S. Sackmann (Eds.), *Cross-cultural management in practice: Culture and negotiated meaning* (pp. 156–174). E. Elgar.

Mahadevan, J. (2014). Intercultural engineering beyond stereotypes: Integrating diversity competencies into engineering education. *European Journal of Training and Development, 38*(7), 658–672.

Mahadevan, J. (2017). *A very short, fairly interesting and reasonably cheap book about cross-cultural management*. Sage.

Mahadevan, J. (2023). *Cross-cultural management: A contemporary approach*. Sage.

Mahadevan, J., & Steinmann, J. (2023). Cultural intelligence and COVID-induced virtual teams: Towards a conceptual framework for cross-cultural management studies. *International Journal of Cross Cultural Management, 23*(2), 317–337. Retrieved February 20, 2024, from https://doi.org/10.1177/14705958231188621.

Osland, J., & Bird, A. (2000). Beyond sophisticated stereotyping—Understanding cultural sensemaking in context. *Academy of Management Executive, 14*(1), 65–79.

Sackmann, S. A. (1997). Introduction. In S. A. Sackmann (Ed.), *Cultural complexity in organizations: Inherent contrasts and contradictions* (pp. 1–13). Sage.

Smith, P. (2006). When elephants fight, the grass gets trampled: The GLOBE and Hofstede projects. *Journal of International Business Studies, 37*, 915–921.

Spitzberg, B. H., & Changnon, G. (2009). Conceptualizing intercultural competence. In D. K. Deardorff (Ed.), *The Sage handbook of intercultural competence* (pp. 2–52). Sage.

Further Reading

Mahadevan, J. (2017). *A very short, fairly interesting and reasonably cheap book about cross-cultural management.* Sage.

Provides you with further insights into how to develop your cross-cultural management skills.

Osland, J., & Bird, A. (2000). Beyond sophisticated stereotyping—understanding cultural sensemaking in context. *Academy of Management Executive, 14*(1), 65–79.

Explains to you how to use cultural dimensions beyond sophisticated stereotyping.

9. Global Leadership and English Language Management in Virtual Team Collaboration: Considering Globalization, Digitalization and Power Effects

9.1 Introduction

Global virtual teams are a specific variety of virtual teams which are characterized by global dispersion and cross-national cultural diversity. They exploit technological and transportation cost advantages but face increased coordination and integration costs. For example, due to their global dispersion, they *must* rely on the extensive use of Information and Communication Technologies (ICTs). Often, there are power distortions to collaboration, such as negative effects brought about by unequal levels of English language proficiency. Thus, global virtual teams should only be formed if there are strategic or operational reasons which offset their increased diversity, dispersion and collaboration costs.

Global virtual team characteristics place additional requirements on team leaders. They also make it more difficult to implement the shared and distributed leadership style required for successful virtual team collaboration (Chap. 7). Furthermore, because global virtual teams mainly collaborate in the English language, communication Chap. 4) and integrating culture (Chap. 5) tends to be more difficult. The management of the English language is therefore another, crucial factor for successful virtual global team collaboration. In particular, the asymmetries originating from different levels of proficiency, need to be counter-balanced. English language management is also of relevance for non-global virtual teams for whom English is the major or an additional means of communication and collaboration.

Team	A small number of individuals who collaborate in a task and/or to reach a goal.
ICTs	Information and communication technologies.
Virtual team collaboration	Working together as a team by means of ICTs.

9.1.1 Learning Objectives

After having read this chapter, you should

- Know how to assess and configure diversity, dispersion and power dynamics in global virtual collaboration, also in relation to Information and Communication Technologies and in light of the global dimension of the digital transformation.
- Understand how virtual team collaboration can be a means of exploiting the advantages brought about by globalization and localization effects, such as standardization and differentiation, or the combination thereof.
- Be aware of glocalization as an integrative global virtual team strategy which aims at the best possible combination of globalization and localization advantages.
- Understand that global leadership must be culturally sensitive and know the culturally contingent leadership styles suggested by project GLOBE.
- Be able to reflect upon culturally contingent leadership orientations and expectations, and their effects, as described by project GLOBE scores.

9.1.2 Reading Requirements

You should have read Chaps. 3, 4, 7 and 8 of this book.

9.1.3 Opening Case

> **Example**
>
> Companies internationalize to gain access to suppliers, customers, partners, knowledge, components, materials and services abroad, and to utilize related advantages. **Global virtual teams** are a means for coordinating and executing international corporate activities without the need to physically move across locations. These are teams that are characterized by worldwide physical dispersion and cultural diversity on country level. They must rely extensively on Information and Communication Technologies (ICTs) for collaboration. The general advantage of collaborating virtually on a global level is that critical costs, such as transportation, travel or physical infrastructure are drastically reduced. However, as a downside, the team's geographic dispersion and country cultural diversity, as well as its extensive reliance on ICTs, result in additional coordination costs. There must be a convincing strategic or operational reason for engaging in virtual team collaboration to offset these costs. ◀

▶ **Global virtual teams** are virtual teams, often of strategic importance, that are distributed on a global scale and that enable companies to take advantage of some relevant aspect of the global business environment. The key characteristics of global virtual teams are their diversity and dispersion.

9.2 What Are Global Virtual Teams, and What Sets Them Apart?

9.2.1 Diversity, Dispersion, Power: Three Constitutive Factors of Global Virtual Teams

Global virtual teams are *always* characterized by three distinct factors, namely diversity, dispersion and power effects (Maznevski, 2012).

Diversity (*Who* is the team?) refers to the insight that global virtual teams work in different country-cultures and thus often experience cross-cultural differences (see Chap. 8). English is used as a shared common language of operations—a *lingua franca*—yet, it might be the first language of none of the team members.

Dispersion (*Where* is the team?) refers to the phenomenon that team members are geographically removed from each other. In a global business environment, this leads to the team operating across time zones, often allowing for 24/7-operations. Also, technological infrastructure and legal boundary conditions might differ across locations.

Diversity	Variations in team members' cultural characteristics, often as emerging from country cultures, to be assessed and utilized for higher performance of the team.
Dispersion	Team members' widespread geographical locations, to be assessed and utilized for higher performance of the team.

Power distortions are those negative collaboration effects that emerge from an unequal distribution of resources. The three major types of power distortions in global virtual team collaboration are related to language power (unequal levels of language proficiency, e.g. in the case of English), position power (hierarchy, location) and knowledge power (knowledge is unequally distributed or not shared across locations). Further examples are: the largest sub-team or the cultural majority dominates remote sub-teams or minority members, the technological infrastructure is better at some sites than at other sites: there is a pay gap between sites, and so on and so forth.

▶   Power distortions in global virtual team collaboration emerge from language power, position power, knowledge power, or a combination thereof.

The dispersion costs of virtual team collaboration ('the distance burden') are mainly structural and organizational. For example, it is the company which is largely responsible for substituting virtual teams with adequate means of technological collaboration and information exchange, and for selecting and further developing teams and team members with regard to their technological versatility and affinity. Sometimes, wider global, national and regional level factors such as a country's technological infrastructure also need to be considered. In any case, it is not the team and its members who need to bear the full burden of dispersion, beyond being willing to acquire technological versatility and in providing feedback concerning their training needs. The most notable exception is time planning which is a distance cost directly allocated to the team, e.g. how to conduct meetings, and manage availability and responsiveness across time zones.

Compared to the distance burden, the diversity costs of global virtual team collaboration (the 'culture burden') fall upon the team to a much larger extent: it is the team who have to become aware of diversity requirements, to develop the required cross-cultural management skills (see Chap. 8) and to create collaborative cultures through communicative awareness (see Chap. 5).

9.2.2 ICTs as Key Enabler of Global Virtual Team Collaboration

Global virtual team collaboration would be impossible without the global digital transformation. Commonly known drivers are the emergence and global adoption of the World Wide Web and related Information and Communications Technologies (ICTs). These developments drastically reduced communication, information and knowledge transfer costs and facilitated modes of collaboration that had been unimaginable before. For instance, e-mail exchange of information minimized response time, compared to postal mail. Companies then realized that it would be possible for employees at different corporate sites to strategize together, for example, concerning market entry decisions, global sourcing or product development, thus building better products and services, and enabling global adaptation and learning. However, global virtual teams also come at a cost to companies, as they are characterized by **increased coordination and integration costs:** to align people across organizational units, languages, cultures and time zones simply is very difficult. Choosing the right Information and Communication Technologies (ICTs) for the right kind of team dynamics is essential for global virtual team performance, as ICTs may support positive global virtual team dynamics and counteract the negative ones.

Together, synchronicity and number of communication modes determine the richness of an ICT (Media Richness Theory, Daft & Lengel, 1984). Media rich communication that is complex in terms of its task or relationship implications requires rich technologies. Conversely, mundane messages can easily be transmitted via lean ICTs. Confusing both either leads to oversimplification (the ICT is too lean for the communicative purpose) or overcomplication (the ICT is too rich for the communicative purpose). The ICT guideline is thus: **As lean as possible, and as rich as necessary**, considering both content (the task dimension) and context (the relationship dimension) of the communicative purposes. For further details see Chap. 3.

ICT preferences and usage in global virtual teams are also linked to members' cultural value orientations (Chap. 8) and the basic assumptions underlying how they communicate (Chap. 5). For example, as Martins and Schilpzand (2011) and Stahl and Maznevski (2021) find, in individualistic, more verbal and explicit country cultures characterized by low uncertainty avoidance (e.g., the United States), decision making is achieved by means of interaction and discussion. Consequently, the choice of comparably rich technologies is appropriate. Conversely, decision making in collectivist, non-verbal and implicit country cultures characterized by low uncertainty avoidance (e.g., China) involves indirect communication and conflict avoidance. Asynchronous, less rich communication media are more suitable for facilitating this process, as they allow for a longer response time and thus take pressure off the team members. In addition, these (mostly text-based) leaner ICTs can help to overcome language and cultural barriers as they enable simplified, non-confrontational processes of clarification and of asking questions.

> **Background information: where virtual and global meet**
> Gibson et al. (2014) conducted an extensive review of articles published on virtual teams between 2000 and 2013 in different disciplines (management, communication, psychology and information systems) and identify no less than 392 papers on virtuality (mainly understood as dependency on electronic communication and geographic dispersion of team members).
>
> The authors point out a major gap in the literature, namely that virtual teams are often also global teams and these two elements (the virtual and global characteristics of a team) need to be studied in intersection, as these elements interact and influence each other. After reviewing and presenting the most important findings of the articles dealing with virtual teams and global teams (global referring, for instance, to different cultural values, nationalities and demographic aspects of the team members), Gibson et al. (2014) discuss those eight articles which tackle both global and virtual aspects of a team.
>
> The authors explain why the interplay of global and virtual elements can have positive effects on efficiency and what can be done to mitigate the negative aspects of virtual team collaboration. For instance, leaders of global virtual teams are advised to create an environment where team members feel psychologically safe (p. 237) and enhance task-based trust (pp. 237–38). Special attention should be given not only to "objective assessments of virtuality or cultural differences in a team" (p. 239) but also to how members *perceive* those two factors.

9.2.3 The Need to Configure Global Virtual Team Dynamics

Global virtual team dynamics are characterized by the interrelations of divergent team processes, such as creativity and conflict, and convergent team processes like groupthink and trust (Maznevski, 2012). Groupthink describes the condition of a team operating within and being stuck in shared 'blind spots' of thought and action. Whereas creativity and trust are understood as beneficial, conflict and groupthink hinder team performance.

All dynamics are facilitated by ICTs, as the meta-level enabler of global virtual team collaboration (see Table 9.1).

As Table 9.1 suggests, global virtual team dynamics are not as simple as divergence only being negative, and convergence only being positive. For example, creativity—a positive divergent process—enlarges the team's scope of thought and action by letting team members' roam more freely and is more likely to emerge in newly formed and culturally diverse teams (Stahl & Maznevski, 2021). Conversely, culturally non-diverse and co-located teams are more prone to suffer from 'groupthink', a condition that is more prone to emerge in co-located, non-culturally diverse teams in the latter stages of their lifecycle (Maznevski, 2012).

Dispersion ('where is the team?') and diversity ('who is the team?') can therefore be both beneficial and harmful to teams—depending on how they are configured and moderated. For instance, time lags (a distance effect) enable global teams to work longer hours per day, yet, also complicate communication. Divergent approaches to work (a diversity effect) might result in more viewpoints on the same matter, thus contributing to the innovative potential of the team, yet, might also lead to mutual distrust, which, if this is the case, decreases team performance. How to configure and utilize global team diversity and dispersion in such ways that they are beneficial, and not harmful, to virtual team collaboration, is a key leadership challenge.

Part of the task is thus to figure out which factors constitute a risk to the required positive convergent-/divergent team dynamics. For instance, in the case of offshoring research and development to a low-cost country, headquarter employees charged with transferring knowledge overseas might not do so because they suspect being laid off after having transferred this knowledge. This means that power, team dynamics and people's needs, motivations and fears need to be assessed and handled in light of each other.

Furthermore, the wider organizational framework needs to support teams and team members in their configuration challenge (also see Chap. 6). For example, if there is one corporate site with 30 team members, and four additional locations with one team member each, the majority site (30 team members) is likely to dominate the other four minority sites, with diversity and dispersion advantages remaining unutilized. This is nothing the team can solve. Rather, the company has to make sure not to set up a global virtual team in such ways that its configuration and team member composition prevent the team from collaborating without power distortions. In simple terms: 30 team members at one

Table 9.1 Overview of key virtual team dynamics

	Positive	Negative
Convergent process	Trust	Groupthink
Divergent process	Creativity	Conflict
Meta-level process	ICT-based communication	

Source own table, based on Maznevski (2012), Stahl et al. (2010), Jimenez et al. (2017)

Table Application 9.1 Technologies for managing diversity, dispersion and power distortions

Technology	Helps manage	Contributes positively to virtual team collaboration because
Translation software	(linguistic) diversity; language power	Communication and, thus, understanding are improved
Shared server environment	(geographical/temporal) dispersion	All team members can access the required information, regardless of time zone difference and location
…	…	…

Source own figure

site and 1 team member each at 4 sites is not an organizational set-up that is conducive to high-performance collaboration. Therefore, the organization needs to rethink the strategic rationales and purposes of why this group of people needs to be a 'team'. It might then transpire, for instance, that it makes sense to limit the number of interaction partners from the majority site to a single spokesperson who functions as the interface between the majority site and the virtual team. This way, a more balanced global virtual team composition (5 members, one from each site) is achieved.

> **Application 9.1: Technologies for managing diversity, dispersion and power effects**
>
> Which technologies can support global virtual team collaboration? Consider both software and hardware solutions. Note these technologies in a Table Application 9.1. Next, revisit what you have learned about diversity, dispersion and power distortions in global virtual team collaboration. Which dynamic might be influenced positively by these technologies? Keep your insights for the further reading of this chapter. ◄

9.3 The Strategic Dimension of Global Virtual Team Collaboration

What sets a global virtual team apart except for ICT-reliance, country level diversity, worldwide dispersion and the need to counterbalance power distortions is the need for making a strategic contribution to how the company wishes to exploit digital opportunities (see Chap. 2) and internationalization advantages in a globalized business environment.

9.3.1 The Digital Transformation in a Global Perspective

There are three consecutive phases of how companies become more digital, and the completion of each phase is the prerequisite for entering the next phase (Verhoef et al., 2021):

- **Digitization:** the company changes from analogue to digital tasks, integrates IT to existing tasks and encodes analogue information in a digital format. Examples are: using SAP or virtual meeting technology instead of filling out files or meeting in person. Virtual team collaboration is beyond this phase.
- **Digitalization:** the company exploits digital technologies, such as ICTs, to enable novel modes of work and business. The inception of global virtual teams emerges from this phase.
- **Digital transformation:** the company changes its core business models and modes of work through digital technologies. For instance, the company is digitally transformed, if it applies what it has learned from global virtual team collaboration locally.

Digitalization is the prerequisite for internationalizing by means of digital modes, such as global virtual team collaboration. Digital transformation is a potential local result of global virtual team collaboration but also a further driver of corporate internationalization. Or in other words: whereas digitalization is a 'must', digital transformation is a 'can'.

9.3.2 Standardization and Differentiation Advantages in Globalization

Given that the company is sufficiently digitized, the major advantage of global virtual teams—instead of a non-virtual organization of work—is that the costs of physical travel are reduced and that the company can exploit advantages of other locations nonetheless. There are two interrelated but also conflicting advantages to be pursed, namely standardization and localization/differentiation.

Standardization enables companies to make use of **economies of scale** and exploit **learning curves**: for example, in production, costs per unit decrease and associated 'how-to' knowledge increases. In that sense, global virtual team collaboration is an opportunity for companies to integrate and streamline their products and operations internally. Access to more markets increases market knowledge and reduces the costs of every new market. Global virtual team collaboration is one means by which such a global presence may be achieved. This means: the more global a certain product or operation is, the more efficient it is. 'Global is better' in that sense.

9.3 The Strategic Dimension of Global Virtual Team Collaboration

Globalisation — The growing interdependence of economies, cultures, people, markets, and so on, but also the process by which organizations develop world-wide influence or start operating globally.

Standardization — Establishing and implementing consistent methods, procedures, and standardized and consistent methods, procedures and processes across an organization.

Economies of scale — The cost advantages 'per item' which companies experience when overall costs can be spread over a larger number of products, processes, procedures and so on.

Learning curves — The correlation between a person's performance on a task and the experience which they have on the task.

On the other hand, the better a single product is adapted to a single market, customer base or requirement, the more effective it is on that market. 'Local is better' in that sense and **localization** is the strategy to be pursued. From a single-product perspective, this requires **adaptation**—an otherwise standardized product (a certain model of a certain car brand) is adapted to a local market. From an overall product-portfolio perspective, this requires **differentiation**—products are differentiated based on certain delineations, such as cultural conventions or objective differences in national environments (such as left-hand traffic versus right-hand traffic). In that sense, companies wishing to employ global virtual teams in order to know local markets, products or partners better must also pay attention to how virtual team members are different—e.g. in terms their cultural diversity or their dispersed global locations. For example, a culturally diverse team might be better at linking a global company to many local requirements, because they can relate to more cultural contexts. Likewise, a dispersed team is closer to more markets and regions, and can thus bring in more and more different experiences and research on local preferences.

Localization — The strategy of adapting products, services, practices and strategies to meet the needs and preferences of specific local markets.

Differentiation — The diversity which results from locally adapted products, services, practices and strategies.

In summary, some factors push companies into the global sphere, and others pull them out of it again. Together, both effects are drivers of the digital transformation of which global virtual team collaboration is both a consequence and a part (see Fig. 9.1).

When implementing a global virtual team for strategic purposes, companies need to find the ideal ratio between economies of production (efficiency—global is better) and economies of adaptation (effectivity—local is better).

▶ **Global virtual teams** are virtual teams, often of strategic importance, that are distributed on a global scale and that enable companies to take advantage of some relevant aspect of the global business environment.

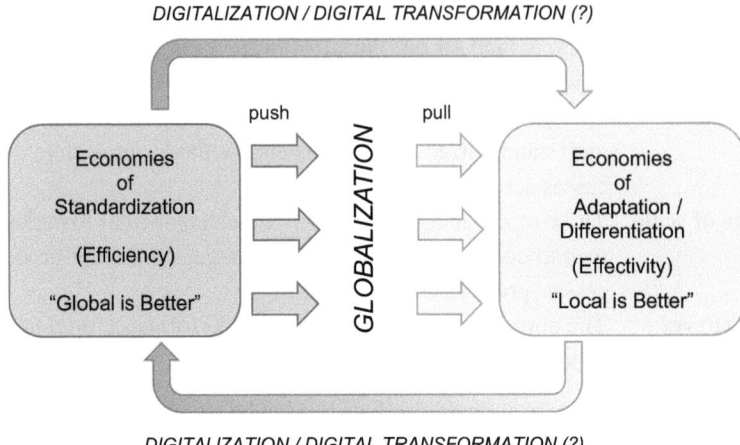

Fig. 9.1 Interrelated global and local drivers of the digital transformation. *Source* own figure

9.3.3 Glocalization as an Integrative Strategy

Companies that strategically combine the requirements of efficiency ('global is better') and effectiveness ('local is better') pursue a strategy of **glocalization.** For example, a company may standardise some products, services and parts of their value chain (see Fig. 9.2) to take advantages of economies of scale and exploit learning curves, and it might also adapt some other aspects of their business to customize their products and services for the variety of local customers now in reach. Car manufacturers, for instance, use platform technologies. This means that they build outwardly different brands and models from shared design, engineering and production sets—it is only the last, finishing stages, that make the cars 'different' in the eye of the customer. Pursuing a glocalization strategy related to global virtual team collaboration then implies that companies need to assess each part of their value chain separately, and to only implement global virtual teams when a combined global–local advantage may be identified.

▶ **Glocalization** The strategy and practice of combining and integrating global and local forces and requirements to achieve the best circumstantial 'fit'.

9.3.4 Corporate Internationalization Strategies and Their Digital Transformation Potential

Corporate international strategy can be classified into four types based on whether companies pursue globalization, localization and glocalization advantages (Bartlett & Gho-

9.3 The Strategic Dimension of Global Virtual Team Collaboration

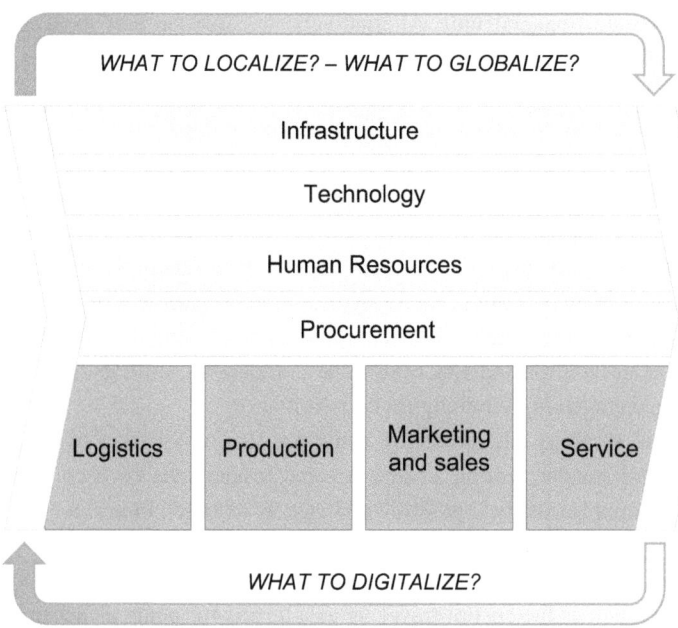

Fig. 9.2 Glocalization and digitalization in an exemplary value chain. *Source* own figure, based on Porter (1985)

shal, 1998), with an additional fifth, non-international type. When related to the digital transformation, companies may focus on:

- **Domestic** (or: non-international) **strategy**: the company is not international at all. There are no global virtual teams. The company may or may not be sufficiently digitalized and even be digitally transformed, yet, only in the domestic sphere.
- **International strategy**: the company neither exploits localization/differentiation or standardization advantages to a high degree. Such a company would not normally employ global virtual teams because there is no strategic or operational purpose that offset global virtual team costs. The company may or may not be sufficiently digitalized and even be digitally transformed, however, it has not yet linked the pursuit of digitalization advantages to internationalization strategy.
- **Multinational** (or: multi-domestic) **strategy**: the company exploits localization and differentiation advantages over standardization advantages. This then implies that each market and location is different, which often calls for local management to be in charge. If managers are being sent from elsewhere, they need to be physically present, and there is high local autonomy. Consequently, the company would only employ global virtual teams, if at all, for the small number of globally integrative functions, such as cost accounting. But even in this case, it could be that each location is organ-

ized as a separate financial unit. Alternatively, it could be that local knowledge is exchanged virtually, however, because of high local autonomy, this does not have to be the case. In summary, there are only a few reasons that could offset global virtual team costs related to coordination, ICT-based communication, diversity and dispersion. The company is sufficiently digitalized and could also be engaged in multi-local digital transformation.

- **Global strategy**: the company exploits standardization advantages over localization and differentiation advantages. This then implies that functions are centralized and that headquarter control is high. Therefore, headquarter staff is sent to lead local units, or these units are led remotely. Global virtual teams are mainly employed to centralize and integrate control and functions. The company is sufficiently digitalized and could also be engaged in global digital transformation.
- **Transnational strategy**: the company combines the exploitation of localization/differentiation and standardization advantages and investigates each corporate function or knowledge area for the best possible strategy, as depicted in Fig. 9.3. The company thus has a high strategic and operational reason for employing global virtual teams, for instance, as a means for reducing the costs of the required level of integration and collaboration, such as the cost of travel, or as a means for being closer to and learning from local markets and people, at comparably lower costs. The company is digitalized on a global level and engaged in a global–local digital transformation.

> **Link to practice: adapting working hours to match the requirements of a global workforce**
>
> Kossek et al. (2021) describe the case of a European oil company. Workers at one of its Asian worksites were found to prefer workdays starting at 3 PM until 9 AM, as this schedule allowed them to manage childcare responsibilities before work. Furthermore, this schedule increased the productive communication across time zone differences, as 3 PM for them equalled 9 AM at the European headquarters, leading to mutually convenient scheduling. Of course, this also brings about the question whether such a schedule is potentially exploitative (even if workers wish for it), as it also puts increased pressure on the offshore workers who completely adapt to headquarters' schedules *and* who now face a higher and more intensified work and care work load. As the example also shows, this strategy can only be implemented because of the availability of suitable ICTs which connect headquarters and offshore site. A glocalized collaborative strategy would require balancing out conflicting global–local interests to achieve the best possible 'fit' for as many interest groups as possible while also taking differences in bargaining power into account (low-cost workers are globally disadvantaged). ◄

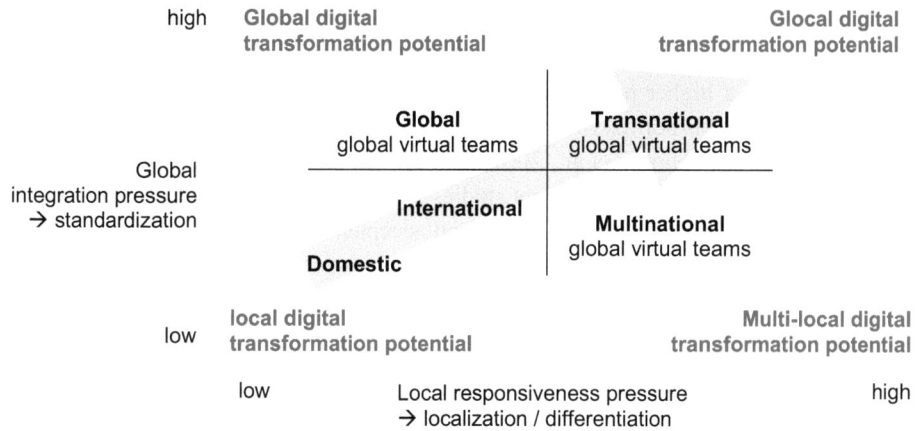

Fig. 9.3 The digital transformation potential of internationalization strategies. *Source* own figure, partly developed from Bartlett and Ghoshal (1998)

Application 9.2: Technologies for managing diversity, dispersion and power effects

Consider the types of corporate internationalization strategies.

- What are reasons for companies pursuing a multinational, global or transnational strategy, respectively, to invest in and implement in global virtual teams? Please also provide examples for global virtual team collaboration in each of the strategic orientations.
- What could be a reason for companies pursuing an international or domestic strategy to invest in global virtual teams? What kind of digital expertise or infrastructure would they need for implementing global virtual teams?
- Which internationalization problems cannot be solved by means of virtual team collaboration? ◄

9.4 Specifics of Global Virtual Team Leadership

Global virtual teams are those teams which are necessarily characterized by worldwide dispersion and cross-cultural differences on country level (see Chap. 8). Consequently, there are additional leadership requirements in these teams, such as the need to answer the question: which leadership style is culturally accepted in which country?

You are already aware of the concept of cultural dimensions, that is: divergent societal cultural value orientations that potentially underlie people's expectations, interpretations and actual behaviour (see Chap. 8). You are also aware of the fact that there are different leadership styles and that not all of them are equally conducive to virtual team collaboration (see Chap. 7). Both aspects seem interrelated. For example, research suggests that cultures with a higher performance orientation favour servant leadership more than cultures in which a higher power differential between leader and follower (high power distance) is accepted as normal (Mittal & Dorfman, 2012, p. 568).

Project GLOBE (Chhokar et al., 2007), one of the most extensive and still ongoing comparative cross-cultural management studies so far (see Chap. 8), has further explored the interrelations between country cultures and accepted leadership styles. The goal was to understand which leadership style was presumed to contribute to 'outstanding leadership' in which societal culture. First, the study clustered the cultural dimension data into leadership styles (see Table 9.2).

Next, the data was analysed to answer the question which of these leadership styles is thought of as contributing to 'outstanding leadership' in which societal culture (see overview at: www.globeproject.com: access the website, choose "The GLOBE Studies", scroll to "visualizations of the 2004 study". This opens a map from which you can select a country of interest [last accessed 01 January 2024]. Table 9.3 depicts the scores of five societal cultures, namely Germany (West), the USA, India, China and France. For instance, charismatic leadership in Germany (West) scores 5.84, meaning that it is assumed to 'contribute somewhat' to outstanding leadership in this country (++).

As Table 9.3 shows, some leadership styles are presumed to contribute more to outstanding leadership on a global level. For instance, charismatic leadership is perceived as contributing to outstanding leadership in all the five societal cultures whereas self-protective leadership is perceived neutrally at best. The difference for some leadership styles is only whether they contribute greatly, somewhat or slightly (charismatic, participative, team-oriented): they are perceived positively throughout. However, the spread is higher for some leadership styles with a related difference in judgement. For example,

Table 9.2 GLOBE leadership styles

Leadership style	Explanation
Charismatic	The ability to inspire, to motivate, and to expect high performance outcomes from others based on firmly held core values
Team-oriented	The ability to effectively build teams and implement a common purpose or goal among team members
Participative	The degree to which managers involve others in making and implementing decisions
Humane Oriented	The degree to which leaders are supportive and considerate but also includes compassion and generosity
Autonomous	The degree to which leaders are independent and individualistic
Self-protective	The degree to which leadership focuses on ensuring the safety and security of the individual and group through status enhancement and face saving

Source own table, based on data from GLOBE (2023)

9.4 Specifics of Global Virtual Team Leadership

Table 9.3 GLOBE leadership scores for Germany, USA, India, China and France

Leadership style	Contribution to "outstanding leadership"									
	Germany (West)		USA		India		China		France	
Charismatic	5.84	(++)	**6.12**	(++)	5.85	(++)	5.56	(++)	**4.93**	(+)
Team-oriented	5.49	(+)	5.8	(++)	5.72	(++)	5.57	(++)	**5.11**	(+)
Participative	5.88	(++)	**5.93**	(+)	**4.99**	(+)	5.04	(+)	5.9	(++)
Humane oriented	4.44	(0)	5.21	(+)	**5.26**	(+)	5.19	(+)	**3.82**	(0)
Autonomous	**4.30**	(0)	3.75	(0)	3.85	(0)	4.07	(0)	**3.32**	(−)
Self-protective	2.96	(−)	3.15	(−)	3.77	(0)	**3.80**	(0)	**2.81**	(−)

Explanation to score and visualization
1 = greatly inhibits; visualization: (− − − −)
2 = somewhat inhibits; visualization: (− −)
3 = slightly inhibits; visualization: (−)
4 = has no impact; visualization: (0)
5 = contributes slightly; visualization: (+)
6 = contributes somewhat; visualization: (++)
7 = contributes greatly; visualization: (+++)
Highest and lowest scores for a specific leadership style marked **bold**
Source own table, based on data from GLOBE (2024a, b, c, d, e)

humane-oriented leadership is perceived as contributing slightly to outstanding leadership in India, the USA and China, yet, is assumed to have no impact in France and Germany (West). Similarly, autonomous leadership is judged to be without impact in four of the societal cultures, except France, where it is assumed to slightly inhibit outstanding leadership.

It is also relevant to note that the GLOBE study scores were derived from data collected in *non-virtual settings*. As these aggregate scores on *societal cultural levels* (country culture), they also do not explain how individuals in the small and specific context of virtual teams behave. Therefore, scores only provide you with first hypotheses of what might influence team members' leadership expectations, including your own, which you then need to test for their applicability. For further advice on how to (not) use GLOBE study scores, see Chap. 8.

> **Application 9.3: GLOBE leadership styles in light of virtual team collaboration requirements**
>
> Successful global virtual team collaboration requires that members subsume their own, personal and task-related interests, under the overall team goals and act accordingly. This involves both divergent and convergent dynamics and the need to configure them positively, while using ICTs for collaboration. Based on Table 9.2, consider:
>
> - What might be the advantages and challenges of each GLOBE leadership style, if leadership needs to be exercised virtually and by means of ICT-based collaboration? Or, in other words: which GLOBE leadership styles seem to be more or less fitting to global virtual team requirements, and why?
>
> Next, imagine a global virtual team comprised of—an equal number of—members from Germany (West), India, China, France and the USA. Based on Table 9.3 scores, consider:
>
> - How might team members' expectations of how the team should be led differ?
> - Which conflicts might arise from the divergent perspectives?
> - Which synergies could emerge from the combination of the divergent perspectives, and how could one combine them?
> - Assume that team members know the GLOBE leadership styles and which are considered to contribute to 'outstanding leadership', and how, in their respective societal cultures. Should global virtual team members feel bound to the GLOBE leadership styles and scores, and why (not)? ◄

9.5 English Language Management in Virtual Team Collaboration

Most virtual team collaboration takes place in the English language. Statistically, English is the most widely used global language with approximately 1348 billion speakers in 2021. Only some 370 million of these were first-language users (Eberhard et al., 2021). English is not their first language for almost a billion speakers: a proportional relation that must be assumed to still exist in 2023 when the number of English language speakers has increased to around 1465 billion (Dyvik, 2023). The second most widespread language in 2021 was Mandarin Chinese. It had the largest number of first-language users (921 million) but only some 199 million speakers who do *not* use Mandarin Chinese as their first language (Eberhard et al., 2021): a reversed proportional relation. In contrast to Mandarin Chinese, English is therefore the global "chosen *foreign* language of communication" (Firth, 1996, p. 240, emphasis in the original). Consequently, a large portion of virtual team collaboration takes place at least partly in the English language.

9.5 English Language Management in Virtual Team Collaboration

Furthermore, English is the language of technology as well as of most of the ICTs which enable and mediate virtual team communication. English as a *lingua franca* (ELF) is the term most commonly used to describe that English has become the integrative working language for most of the global population.

9.5.1 Collaborative Challenges of English as a Lingua Franca Communication

The main rule of ELF communication is to convey the intended message and make oneself be understood. The challenges of ELF communication are manifold, as the proficiency and communicative scope of its speakers, as well as their underlying assumptions, are not aligned.

First, the level of proficiency of English as a *lingua franca* (ELF) speakers can vary greatly: ELF speakers include those from countries such as India or Nigeria in which English is the language of higher education, economic transaction, politics and national media. They might include those from small countries, such as the Netherlands and Denmark wherein another language is spoken, but wherein foreign language television shows and movies are not dubbed, and higher education involves a strong English language element. In other countries, such as France and Germany, English is indispensable at many workplaces but education and media content is in the national language. This then implies that German ELF speakers might be more limited to professional English, than, let's say, Swedish ELF speakers who are exposed to the English language in more parts of their daily lives and whose communicative scope is wider.

Second, professions and disciplines influence what people can and cannot express in the English language. For example, engineers, marketing specialists or medical doctors might very well be able to converse on task- and subject-related matters but not be able to engage in conversations concerning personal matters or other themes. Interdisciplinarity can distort this type of ELF communication.

Third, there are those virtual collaboration contexts wherein English is not spoken much but simply the language of work, documentation and data exchange. Software code, and its specifications and documentations, for example, are written in the English language regardless of the languages used and spoken in the development team. This means that, in some ELF contexts, speakers will converse on English language technical matters but frame them in another language. This specific type of ELF communication only works if both discipline and secondary language are shared.

Finally, those who speak English as their first language are also part of ELF. These use the language 'naturally' across all professional and relational spheres. This means that they do not know when they leave the shared sphere of professional communication and use styles, vocabulary and expressions unknown to other ELF speakers. For first-language users, it is therefore the most difficult to assess what to say and how, in order to convey the intended message and make themselves be understood. They are also more likely to misinterpret the communication of non-native ELF speakers who are often united by their shared understanding of what the limits of each other's communicative scopes are. For example, a speaker who uses ELF from a technical perspective as the means of professional exchange would not try to lighten the conversation by means of jokes, simply because they might not feel secure in joking in a foreign language wherein they cannot go 'anywhere' when communicating. Such restrictions do not apply for a native speaker—they might thus go there and then lose the other speakers.

9.5.2 English as *the* Global Language

What made English be adopted globally by so many speakers? One common explanation and the starting point of English language proliferation is the rise of the British Empire with its numerous overseas colonies. However, this only partly explains why English is (one of) the official language(s) in some former British colonies (Corradi, 2017) as the British, in contrast to, for instance, the French, followed a more liberal language policy in their colonies, encouraging "the use of indigenous languages in their colonial schools, in literature, and even occasionally in administration" (Michelman, 1995, p. 2018). Trade as a driving force is another explanation, as the British industrial revolution with its technical innovations certainly fuelled the expansion and the influence of the English language. Other reasons are the emergence of the United States of America (USA) as a superpower after World War II, demographic mobility, international markets, international political associations and advancements in communication technologies (Seidlhofer, 2011). Together, these developments gave the English language a status of dominance which is unprecedented in global history (Seidlhofer, 2011). This applies even to regions where English is not the first language of most of the population, such as in the Francophone Canadian province of Quebec (Chan, 2018).

But is English simply "the language of global success" (Neeley, 2017) or should one be concerned about its ever-growing influence (Chan, 2018; House, 2003) and protect the French language in Montreal and other local languages worldwide? Shams (2015) emphasizes that language is not just a mean of communication, but also contains values, beliefs and modes of thought. Therefore, some might be advantaged over others if "English […] is the [sole] language in which the fate of most of the world's millions is decided" (Phillipson, 1992, pp. 5–6). Furthermore, English is a political instrument of power. For example, the rulers of the Soviet Union tried to promote Russian in their sphere of influence, and Sir Richard Francis, director of the British Council, is quoted to have said "Britain's gold is not the North Sea oil but the English language" (Concise Oxford Companion to the English Language, 2019).

9.5.3 Language Power, Position Power and Expert Power in Virtual Team Collaboration

Power can be defined as "asymmetric control over valued resources in social relations" (Magee & Galinsky, 2008, p. 361). At work, English language proficiency may have become such a 'valued resource' by means of which some may control and influence how people collaborate more than others. Three types of power are relevant in virtual team collaboration:

- **Position power** describes the authority of the formal position holder (Harzing & Pudelko, 2013).
- **Expert power** is the power of competence and expertise which is not necessarily the same as position power. For instance, the most experienced engineer is listened to when a new technology is developed, due to their professional and task-related knowledge.
- **Language power** describes the advantages which individuals have because of their language skills, such as language proficiency advantages.

Language power can distort position power or expert power. For example, a person who is more fluent in the English language could be perceived as more eligible for promotion or as more competent, even though they are not. This might then challenge the authority of a position holder who is less fluent or undermine expertise. More proficient speakers might also act as informal 'language nodes' (Marschan-Piekkari et al., 1999a, b) or 'linking pins' (Harzing et al., 2011) who have privileged access to information and take on a range of intermediary roles such as gatekeepers, liaisons and translators for others with lower language proficiency. Conversely, employees lacking proficiency in the official corporate language are limited in their conversation abilities and may be excluded from critical exchanges of information (Fredriksson et al., 2006). They are less involved in decision making (Louhiala-Salminen et al., 2005) and often experience a loss of power within the organization (Luo & Shenkar, 2006).

> **Pause and reflect: does the English language hinder development?**
>
> Wangari Maathai specifically points out the 'Overuse of Foreign Languages' as one of the 'Bottlenecks to Development in Africa' in her speech at the Fourth United Nations World Women's Conference in Beijing (1995). She notes that:
>
> "At independence, many African States adopted imperial European languages as official languages and all official communication (in the mass media, courts, administration, education etc.) is conducted in those languages. […] People equate education and progress with the ability to speak and write in these languages, and entry into the job market, or upward social mobility, is virtually impossible without the ability to read and write in them. Yet, only a small number of the African elites speak and write fluently and competently in these languages,

even at the University level. [...] Insisting on foreign languages for universal functional literacy in Africa is tragic because literacy, use of own language and culture are very important in human development and in cultivating self-worth, self-confidence and self-pride." ◀

9.5.4 Overcoming Language Closures: A Virtual Team Checklist

Because of the interrelated effects of culture and identity, language and power, virtual teams have to become and be aware of the closure effects brought about by English as a lingua franca. A **closure effect** means that a privileged sphere is constructed which some cannot enter, for instance, because of language skills that are defined as inadequate by those with higher language power. The following checklist questions serve to overcome language closure and minimize distortions rooted in language power. Global virtual teams should consider:

- Which language barriers and language power distortions could potentially affect us negatively?
- How can we make sure that some members, perspectives and opinions do not simply dominate because of higher levels of language proficiency?
- Which collaborative mechanisms can we devise to overcome language barriers and language power distortions?
- How can we make sure that a competent expert who is less fluent in the English language can still sufficiently contribute to knowledge creation in the team?
- How can we make sure that a competent expert who is more fluent in the English language still takes the expertise of those who are less fluent into account?
- How can we support those in positions of power who are less fluent in the language?
- How can those in positions of power who are more fluent than others make sure that they do not exploit their language advantage?
- How can technology support any or all of the aforementioned processes?

Application 9.4: Myself as an ELF user

Consider what you now know about English as a lingua franca (ELF).

- When and how are you personally using ELF?

When looking back onto a relevant situation wherein you used ELF:

- How were you able to express yourself?
- Were there any misunderstandings, and why?
- Which differences in style, expression and choice of words did you notice compared to communication in your first language (which could also be English, but not ELF)?

Based on these considerations, reflect:

- Are you more advantaged or disadvantaged as an ELF speaker, and why?
- Which language barriers, if any, did you experience, and how can you overcome them?
- Which language power distortions did you experience or contribute to, and what is the impact of these power distortions on you and on those you communicated with?

With the emergence of Artificial Intelligence tools, please consider: How can technology and the information and communication technologies in use, support a virtual team in preventing and/or overcoming language barriers and language power distortions? ◄

9.6 Being a Virtual Team Leader on a Global Level

Global virtual teams are a specific variety of virtual teams which *must* be characterized by global dispersion and cross-cultural diversity. Members often have divergent leadership expectations and also tend to use ICTs differently, based on their underlying cultural value orientations and core cultural assumptions. This then poses three additional requirements on virtual team leaders, namely complexity, flow and presence (Mendenhall et al., 2012).

Complexity, the contextual dimension, describes the environment in which global leaders operate. It refers to the insight that the situation is never mono-dimensional or mono-causal. This implies that, whilst being first hypotheses to be tested upon the situation, the diversity configurations of the team might never be understood as objective, factual difference: they are just first entry point to the complex diversity configurations that are unique and specific to every global virtual team. If global team leaders succeed in thinking about the cultures of the team in a sufficiently complex manner, they will be able create a positive team vision and foster individual and collective growth beyond the limitations of culture-specific comfort zones.

Flow, the relational dimension, describes the boundary spanning activities and the information exchange via multiple ICTs and various types of channels that is required for high quality global virtual team collaboration. It refers to the insight that diversity configurations, such as the differences and commonalities depicted by means of cultural dimensions, necessarily change over time. For instance, if the team manages to engage in positive convergent and divergent processes while working together, then initial cross-cultural differences will dissolve. Boundary-spanning, that is: interacting and relating to each other across difference, is key to reaching this goal and, via reaching out across differences themselves and via integrating alternative styles and behavioural patterns into their 'ways of doing things', global team leaders can set an example for the team and thus encourage the whole team to become an organizational boundary-spanner.

Presence, the spatial-temporal dimension, describes the required degree of geographical co-location. It refers to how much those leading the team globally *must* physically move across geographical, cultural, and national boundaries. This decision should be based on how negatively the limitations of ICT-based collaboration, such as lower richness, manifests in the global virtual team, also in light of cross-cultural differences. For instance, based on the underlying cultural value orientations, decision making via leaner ICT-based communication might not work out for more humane-oriented team members, and this is when global team leaders must make the decision to be physically present in order to foster growth and inspire and motivate the team. Over time, this presence will become less important, as the team learns to manage complexity and establish boundary-spanning flows over time.

Furthermore, global team leaders need to be aware that there are different ideas of what constitutes 'outstanding leadership' in different societal cultures. One challenge that global leaders are likely to face is the **leadership power paradox**, which describes the situation when a global team leader acts in ways that are culturally preferred by some team members and perceived as a lack of leader competency or authority by others (Butler et al., 2012, p. 242). For example, delegating authority might be perceived as empowering by team members oriented towards low power distance, and as weak and indecisive by those oriented towards high power distance. Leaders stuck in a power paradox will remain ineffective unless they resolve it (Zander et al., 2012, p. 595).

Molinsky (2013) writes that global leadership requires "global dexterity", understood as "the ability to smoothly and successfully adapt how you act in a foreign setting—so that you are effective and appropriate in that setting without feeling that you are losing yourself in the process" (p. ix). One of Molinsky's anecdotes is that of an Italian manager working in India who is unable to motivate his employees. He knows that his employees are accustomed to a more authoritarian leadership style, but he would rather encourage his employees and give them more space to act. Slowly, he realises that he has to be more assertive if he wants deadlines to be met. Acting this insight out is going against his beliefs, but he is surprised to see that his assertiveness is actually appreciated., He develops higher leadership versatility, or: global dexterity via looking back onto himself from another cultural lens.

> **Link to practice: digital nomads as a novel phenomenon**
>
> There has been a steep increase in the number of so-called 'digital nomads', from 7.3 million people in 2019 to 17.3 million in 2023 in the United States of America alone (MBO Partners, 2023). In order to meet the rising demand for global remote work opportunities, more and more countries have introduced so called 'digital nomad visas', South Korea, for example launched a new visa in January 2024, which enables foreigners to stay in South Korea for up to two years, while maintaining a remote

position in their home country (Jung, 2023). This development thus has far-reaching consequences for global leadership, regarding the complexity, flow, presence and power effects to be considered and managed. ◄

Application 9.5: What kind of global leader does the team need?

In Application 9.3, you encountered a global virtual team that is comprised of—an equal number of—members from Germany (West), India, China, France and the USA. Assume that this team has a US-American team leader. Based on the information provided in Table 9.3 and the scores depicted in Table 9.3 scores, consider:

- What leadership style might the global team leader be the most trained in?
- What could be potential blind spots and strengths of this leadership style in a global virtual team environment?
- What kind of global dexterity does the global team leader need for integrating divergent demands?
- How can the global team leader avoid contradictions (power paradoxes)?
- What kind of leader should the global team leader be to fit to all team members? ◄

9.7 Closing Part

9.7.1 Chapter Summary

This chapter has highlighted the role and requirements of global leadership and English language management in virtual team collaboration, thus building upon and adding to your combined knowledge and skills from Chapt 3 (communication), Chap. 6 (digital leadership) and 7 (cross-cultural management). The first theme, global leadership, is specific to those teams that are characterized by global dispersion and multinational cultural diversity, so called global virtual teams. These teams *must* rely on Information and Communication Technologies (see Chap. 3), and, together, these effects place additional requirements on virtual team leaders, require culturally-sensitive leadership styles, and generally make it more difficult to implement the shared and distributed leadership practices required for best-practice virtual team collaboration. After having engaged with this chapter, you now understand the strategic dimension of global virtual team collaboration and how to contribute to strategy by means of global leadership practices that overcome dispersion, diversity and ICT-limitations. This will help you to configure global and non-global virtual team dynamics in more conducive ways. The English language, the second topic of the chapter, is not only the working language of global virtual teams, but also a means of collaboration for other types of teams. If mismanaged, the English language can distort competency and position power, result in language closures and hinder further team development. This chapter has enabled you to prevent and work against these negative effects and to configure the English language as a positive virtual team dynamic.

9.7.2 Key Points

- Diversity, dispersion and power are the three constitutive factors of global virtual teams.
- ICTs are a key enabler of global virtual team collaboration.
- Global virtual team dynamics need to be configured in a conducive manner, also in light of the global dimension of the digital transformation.
- Virtual team collaboration is a means of exploiting the advantages brought about by globalization and localization effects, such as standardization and differentiation, or the combination thereof.
- Glocalization is an integrative global virtual team strategy which aims at the best possible combination of globalization and localization advantages.
- Global leadership must be culturally sensitive, and as the GLOBE study suggests, different leadership styles are perceived as more or less competent and positive in different societal cultures.
- English as a lingua franca poses numerous challenges for virtual team collaboration, but, if managed well, also offers unique benefits and opportunities.
- If mismanaged, language power can distort expert and position power, and virtual teams and organizations need to prevent and work against these negative effects.

9.7.3 Review Questions

1. What are global virtual teams, and what sets them apart from other types of virtual teams?
2. Why and how are Information and Communication Technologies a key enabler of global virtual team collaboration?
3. What are key virtual team dynamics, and how should they be configured?
4. What does the strategic dimension of global virtual team collaboration involve?
5. What are standardization and differentiation advantages as brought about by globalization and localization effects, and how can global virtual team collaboration be a means of exploiting either one, or both?
6. Which leadership styles according to GLOBE can you name, and what do they describe?
7. Which leadership styles are assumed to contribute more or less to outstanding leadership in your country of residence and/or origin, and what does this tell you regarding your own leadership orientation in a global perspective?

8. What are the challenges, but also potential advantages, of English as a lingua franca, and why and how has English developed as *the* global language?
9. How can English as a lingua franca distort expert and position power, and what needs to be done (and by whom) for this not to happen?
10. How can one overcome language closures in virtual collaboration, and what needs to be done (and by whom) for achieving this goal?

9.7.4 Opening Case Revisited

You have already read Chap. 7 on digital leadership under Industry 4.0 conditions (see Chap. 7). Now, please integrate your learning and link the GLOBE leadership styles as defined in Table 9.2 and the country-specific scores for how they contribute to 'outstanding leadership' (Table 9.3) to (1) the requirements of digital leadership under industry 4.0 conditions. Based on what a certain style describes and how it scores:

- In which societal culture score do you identify the highest/lowest aptitude for digital leadership?
- In which societal culture score do you identify the highest/lowest aptitude for managing the VUCA conditions of Industry 4.0?
- In which societal culture score do you identify the highest/lowest aptitude for shared and distributed leadership practices?
- In which societal culture score do you identify the highest/lowest aptitude for developing the follower types of digital beginners/disillusioned learners/capable but cautious performers, and for delegating tasks and responsibilities to the follower type of self-reliant achievers?
- In which societal culture score do you identify the highest/lowest aptitude for leading virtual teams through change and crisis?
- Where do you find the scores inconclusive with regard to the aforementioned questions?
- What should be learned from your findings for global virtual team leadership?

9.7.5 Closing Activity

Language management, that is: the need to find a common language is another specific challenge of virtual team communication, particularly so if English is not team members' first language or if collaboration involves users from diverse English language backgrounds (English as a lingua franca, ELF). Language power can distort expert and position power in the team. By now, you are also aware of the properties of communication in virtual team collaboration (Chap. 4) and how deep cultural assumptions regarding relations, time and space are communicated (Chap. 5). Based on your combined knowledge of ELF and power, of the properties of communication and of how language communicates time, space and relations, answer the following questions:

- When and how does ELF complicate how well team members can reach an improved understanding of the five principles of communicative action (see Chap. 4), and what can be done about it?
- When and how does ELF complicate how well team members can acknowledge the four sides of communication (see Chap. 4), and what can be done about it?
- When and how does ELF complicate how well the team can integrate communicative context and content (see Chap. 4), and what can be done about it?
- When and how does ELF complicate how well team members can explicate their relations, space and time assumptions and expectations (the 'culture as communication' perspective by Hall (see Chap. 5), and what can be done about it?
- Which additional challenges related to communication and 'culture as communication' do you identify because of the use of ELF, and how should they be overcome by means of (global) virtual team configuration?

References

Bartlett, C. A., & Ghoshal, S. (1998). *Managing across borders: The transnational solution* (2nd ed.). Harvard Business School.

Butler, C. L., Zander, L., Mockaitis, A., & Sutton, C. (2012). The global leader as boundary spanner, bridge maker, and blender. *Industrial and Organizational Psychology, 5*(2), 240–243.

Chan, K. (2018). *Is the English language too powerful?* Retrieved March 17, 2021, from https://www.weforum.org/agenda/2018/11/is-english-too-powerful/.

Chhokar, J. S., Brodbeck, F. C., & House, R. J. (Eds.). (2007). *Culture and leadership across the world: The GLOBE book of in-depth studies of 25 societies*. Lawrence Erlbaum.

Concise Oxford Companion to the English Language. (2019). *The British Council*. Retrieved March 18, 2021, from https://www.encyclopedia.com/humanities/encyclopedias-almanacs-transcripts-and-maps/british-council.

Corradi, A. (2017). *The Linguistic Colonialism of English*. Retrieved March 15, 2021, from https://brownpoliticalreview.org/2017/04/linguistic-colonialism-english/.

Daft, R. L., & Lengel, R. H. (1984). Information richness: A new approach to managerial behavior and organizational design. *Research in Organizational Behavior, 6*, 191–233.

Dyvik, E. H. (2023). The most spoken languages worldwide 2023. *Statista*. Retrieved October 31, 2023, from https://www.statista.com/statistics/266808/the-most-spoken-languages-worldwide/.

Eberhard, D. M., Gary, F. S., & Charles, D. F. (Eds.). (2021). *Ethnologue: Languages of the World* (24th ed.). Retrieved October 31, 2023, from https://www.ethnologue.com/guides/most-spoken-languages.

Firth, A. (1996). The discursive accomplishments of normality: On 'lingua franca' English and conversation analysis. *Journal of Pragmatics, 26*, 237–259.

Fredriksson, R., Barner-Rasmussen, W., & Piekkari, R. (2006). The multinational corporation as a multilingual organization: The notion of a common corporate language. *Corporate Communications: An International Journal, 11*(4), 406–423.

Gibson, C. B., Huang, L., Kirkman, B. L., & Shapiro, D. L. (2014). Where global and virtual meet: The value of examining the intersection of these elements in twenty-first-century teams. *The Annual Review of Organizational Psychology and Organizational Behavior, 1*(1), 217–244.

GLOBE. (2023). *Leadership Styles*. Retrieved November 1, 2023, from https://globeproject.com/study_2004_2007?page_id=data#data.

GLOBE. (2024a). *Country score: Germany*. Retrieved January 1, 2024, from https://www.globeproject.com/results/countries/DEU%3Fmenu=list.html#list

GLOBE. (2024b). *Country score: India*. Retrieved January 1, 2024, from https://www.globeproject.com/results/countries/IND%3Fmenu=list.html#list.

GLOBE. (2024c). *Country score: USA*. Retrieved January 1, 2024, from https://www.globeproject.com/results/countries/USA%3Fmenu=list.html#list.

GLOBE. (2024d). *Country score: China*. Retrieved January 1, 2024, from https://www.globeproject.com/results/countries/CHN%3Fmenu=list.html#list.

GLOBE. (2024e). *Country score: France*. Retrieved January 1, 2024, from https://www.globeproject.com/results/countries/FRA%3Fmenu=list.html#list.

Harzing, A.-W., Köster, K., & Magner, U. (2011). Babel in business: The language barrier and its solutions in the HQ-subsidiary relationship. *Journal of World Business, 46*(3), 279–287.

Harzing, A.-W., & Pudelko, M. (2013). Language competencies, policies and practices in multinational corporations: A comprehensive review and comparison of Anglophone, Asian, Continental European and Nordic MNCs. *Journal of World Business, 48*(1), 87–97.

House, J. (2003). English as a lingua franca: A threat to multilingualism? *Journal of Sociolinguistics, 7*(4), 556–578.

Jimenez, A., Boehe, D. N., Taras, V., & Caprar, D. V. (2017). Working across boundaries: Current and future perspectives on global virtual teams. *Journal of International Management, 23*(4), 341–349.

Jung, M. (2023). Korea to launch new 'digital nomad' visa on Jan. 1. *The Korean Herald*. Retrieved February 12, 2024, from https://www.koreaherald.com/view.php?ud=20231229000516.

Kossek, E. E., Gettings, P., & Misra, K. (2021). The future of flexibility at work. *Harvard Business Review*. Retrieved February 16, 2024, from https://hbr.org/2021/09/the-future-of-flexibility-at-work.

Louhiala-Salminen, L., Charles, M., & Kankaanranta, A. (2005). English as a lingua franca in Nordic corporate mergers: Two case companies. *English for Specific Purposes, 24*(4), 401–422.

Luo, Y., & Shenkar, O. (2006). The multinational corporation as a multilingual community: Language and organization in a global context. *Journal of International Business Studies, 37*(3), 321–339.

Maathai, W. (1995, August 30). Bottlenecks to development in Africa [Conference presentation]. *4th UN World Women's Conference, Beijing, China*. Retrieved January 30, 2024, from https://www.greenbeltmovement.org/wangari-maathai/key-speeches-and-articles/bottleknecks-to-development-in-africa.

Magee, J. C., & Galinsky, A. D. (2008). Social hierarchy: The self-reinforcing nature of power and status. *Academy of Management Annals, 2*(1), 351–398.

Marschan-Piekkari, R., Welch, D. E., & Welch, L. S. (1999a). Adopting a common corporate language: IHRM implications?. *International Journal of Human Resource Management, 10*(3), 377–390.

Marschan-Piekkari, R., Welch, L. S., & Welch, D. E. (1999b). In the shadow: The impact of language on structure: Power and communication in the multinational. *International Business Review, 8*(4), 421–440.

Martins, L. L., & Schilpzand, M. C. (2011). Global virtual teams: Key developments, research gaps, and future directions. In A. Joshi, H. Liao, & J. J. Martocchio (Eds.), *Research in personnel and human resources management* (pp. 1–72). Emerald.

Maznevski, M. L. (2012). State of the art: Global teams. In M. C. Gertsen, A. –M.Søderberg, & M. Zølner (Eds.), *Global collaboration: Intercultural experiences and learning*. Palgrave Macmillan.

MBO Partners. (2023). Number of digital nomads in the United States from 2019 to 2023 (in millions) [Graph]. *Statista*. Retrieved February 12, 2024, from https://www.statista.com/statistics/1298313/number-digital-nomads-united-states/.

Mendenhall, M. E., Reiche, B. S., Bird, A., & Osland, J. S. (2012). Defining the "global" in global leadership. *Journal of World Business, 47*(4), 493–503.

Michelman, F. (1995). French and British colonial language policy: A comparative view of their impact on African literature. *Research in African Literatures, 26*(4), 216–225.

Mittal, R., & Dorfman, P. W. (2012). Servant leadership across cul tures. *Journal of World Business, 47*(4), 555–570. https://doi.org/10.1016/j.jwb.2012.01.009.

Molinsky, A. (2013). *Global dexterity*. Harvard Business Review Press.

Neely, T. (2017). *The language of global success*. Princeton University Press.

Phillipson, R. (1992). *Linguistic Imperialism*. Oxford University Press.

Porter, M. E. (1985). *Competitive advantage: Creating and sustaining superior performance*. Simon and Schuster.

Seidlhofer, B. (2011). *Understanding English as a Lingua Franca*. Oxford University Press.

Shams, S. (2015). Linguistic imperialism revisited: An analysis of the role of English in Bangladesh. *Crossings. A Journal of English Studies, 6*, 238–247.

Stahl, G. K., Mäkelä, K., Zander, L., & Maznevski, M. (2010). A look at the bright side of multicultural team diversity. *Scandinavian Journal of Management, 26*(4), 439–447.

Stahl, G. K., & Maznevski, M. L. (2021). Unraveling the effects of cultural diversity in teams: A retrospective of research on multicultural work groups and an agenda for future research. *Journal of International Business Studies, 52*, 4–22.

Verhoef, P. C., Broekhuizen, T., Bart, Y., Bhattacharya, A., Dong, J. Q., Fabian, N., & Haenlein, M. (2021). Digital transformation: A multidisciplinary reflection and research agenda. *Journal of Business Research, 122*, 889–901.

Zander, L., Mockaitis, A. I., & Butler, C. L. (2012). Leading global teams. *Journal of World Business, 47*(4), 592–603.

Further Reading

Selmer, J., Dickmann, M., Froese, F.J., Lauring, J., Reiche, B.S. & Shaffer, M. (2022). The potential of virtual global mobility: implications for practice and future research. *Journal of Global Mobility,* 10(1), 1–13. Retrieved May 1, 2024, from https://doi.org/10.1108/JGM-07-2021-0074.

This article sketches the contours of a new, virtual, managerial and professional world in which, for instance, people 'go to other countries' without actually changing location.

Change and Learning, Tacit Knowledge Management and Virtual Team Innovativeness Under BANI Conditions: The Role of Leadership, Organization and Technology

10.1 Introduction

Innovativeness, learning and change are crucial managerial and organizational challenges and, if mastered and further promoted, set successful teams and organizations apart, resulting in competitive advantages and more satisfied and motivated customers and employees. Innovation mainly manifests itself on team level, and change and learning are more crucial to virtual teams than to non-virtual teams. Whether virtual teams change and learn for higher innovativeness depends on the degree of organizational awareness and the underlying assumptions concerning change, on their leadership and knowledge creation processes and on their ability to overcome the technological unknown. This chapter brings these three factors—organization, leadership and technology—together to enable you to promote and contribute to virtual team learning, change, knowledge creating and innovativeness, as key prerequisites for success.

To this end, this chapter first discusses whether and, if so, under which circumstances virtual teams are more innovative than non-virtual teams. It then explains how to organize virtual team collaboration for innovation, learning and change, also providing you with details on the different perspectives on what constitutes change, and how it should be promoted, and their advantages and disadvantages for virtual team collaboration in light of each other. Generally, successful virtual team learning and change require exploration instead of exploitation, and integration instead of compromise, and this chapter explains why and how this is the case, and proposes the organizational change strategy of integration for higher innovativeness.

Next, the chapter outlines the leadership challenge of facilitating innovativeness and proposes the need for working towards safe belonging as a key leadership requirement under post-COVID-19 conditions, which are characterized by brittle systems, personal and organizational anxieties, and non-linear and incomprehensible problems (BANI

© The Author(s), under exclusive license to Springer Fachmedien Wiesbaden GmbH, part of Springer Nature 2024
J. Mahadevan, *Virtual Team Collaboration*, https://doi.org/10.1007/978-3-658-44969-8_10

model, see Cascio, 2020). Mastering BANI conditions on a team level requires exploring leader self-identities and promoting perceived virtual team membership via implementing team performance norms.

This chapter also highlights the role and issue of tacit knowledge creating and management for successful virtual team collaboration. Tacit knowledge, that is: the knowledge which stems from experience and of which people are largely unaware, and which cannot be put into words, is essential to virtual team collaboration, yet, very difficult to transport via Information and Communication Technologies (ICTs) that often force an incomplete conversion of tacit knowledge into explicit knowledge. Virtual teams should apply the SECI spiral for making sure that all of team members' tacit knowledges, for instance, their user experiences with technology, are converted to explicit knowledge (Nonaka & Takeuchi, 1995).

Finally, there is also the impact of technology and the need to integrate members' diverse user experiences with technologies (that are interconnected and learn from users in return) into a collective knowledge creation process. This requires that team members disclose what they hide or fear, and ask for feedback. The Johari window (Luft & Ingham, 1955) visualizes how such a process enables shared discoveries which minimize the technological unknown; it is a suitable method for further team development, learning and change.

After having engaged with the chapter you will be able to positively configure learning, change and innovativeness as key moderators of a best practice virtual team collaboration.

Team	A small number of individuals who collaborate in a task and/or to reach a goal.
ICTs	Information and communication technologies.
Virtual Team Collaboration	Working together as a team by means of ICTs.
Leadership	Identifying and maintaining those higher-level moderators that succeed in achieving the intended positive outcomes of virtual team collaboration.

10.1.1 Learning Objectives

After having read this chapter, you should

- Know the BANI model and what it implies for virtual team change, learning and innovativeness from a leadership, organizational and technological perspective.
- Be aware of the role of organizational choices in enabling learning and change and understand that virtual teams require explorational, not exploitative learning.
- Be able to apply the change strategy of integration.
- Know how to combine leader self-identities for higher resilience and adaptability.

- Understand the dangers of passivity originating from anxiety, and how to overcome it via virtual team performance norms that increase perceived membership.
- Know how to prevent tacit knowledge loss and promote tacit knowledge creation in virtual team collaboration by means of the SECI-spiral.
- Understand the technological dimension of virtual team change and learning, also in relation to user experiences and user interface design.
- Be able to apply the Johari window for increased individual and team awareness.

10.1.2 Reading Requirements

You should have read Chaps. 3 and 6 (Information and Communication Technologies, and organizing the collaboration of humans and technology), Chaps. 6 and 8 (digital and global leadership), and Chaps. 4 and 5 (establishing communication and collaborative cultures) of this book.

10.1.3 Opening Case

> **Example**
>
> The world of work has undergone drastic changes in recent years. The digital transformation, in particular, has created a business environment which is **volatile, uncertain, complex and ambiguous**. The so-called **VUCA model** describes these conditions (see Salch & Watson, 2017). VUCA is linked to the fourth industrial revolution (4IR), or **Industry 4.0,** which is driven by big data, connectivity, virtual and augmented reality, data analytics, human-machine interaction, and improvement in artificial intelligence and robotics. Most recent leadership theories thus focus on how to enable change and transformation under such conditions, and companies and their leaders are supposed to master risk taking and become and be more agile (White et al., 2023). Chapter 7 has focussed on the digital leadership qualities required under VUCA conditions.
>
> However, what happens, when crisis is no longer an exception but the new normal?
>
> On April 29, 2020, at the onset of the COVID-19 pandemic, futurologist Jamais Cascio proposed that we are *"facing the age of chaos"* (Cascio, 2020), and, announcing the obsoleteness of VUCA, proposed the **BANI model** for understanding the leadership challenges of the future. He described the human environment as increasingly **brittle, anxious, non-linear**, and **incomprehensible**. According to Cascio (2020):
>
> - Systems are **brittle**: they appear solid, until they are not anymore, and simply shatter.

- **Anxiety** describes people's sense of helplessness which can drive passivity, as every choice made seems potentially disastrous.
- The problems to be solved, such as battling COVID-19 infection rates or dealing with climate disruption, are **non-linear**, and thus seem to overwhelm people and systems.
- The challenges which are faced seem **incomprehensible**, despite best efforts.

Cascio argued that these are entirely different qualities which render VUCA-based leadership meaningless. For instance, while ambiguity, as brought about by VUCA, is a challenge, it can be nonetheless mastered. Conversely, incomprehensibility, as brought about by BANI, cannot be resolved: it remains incomprehensible.

Thus, what Cascio (2020) proposes is that organizations and leaders become aware that mastering present and future environments is about more than mastering risk taking and agility. Rather, it involves acknowledging people's emotional needs for belonging, enhancing resilience, adapting in responsible ways, and nurturing mindfulness, emotional awareness and transparency. But how can these wider goals be achieved? ◄

VUCA Model	A model describing current and future industrial conditions as volatile, uncertain, complex and ambiguous.
BANI Model	A model that describes the post-COVID-19 and future business environment as being characterized by brittle systems, people's anxieties, and non-linear and incomprehensible problems.

10.2 Are Virtual Teams More Innovative?

Innovation has become a critical means of competitive advantage for companies in a variety of industries because it allows organizations to diversify, adapt, and even reinvent themselves to match evolving market and technical conditions (Schoonhoven et al., 1990). Teams seem central to that endeavour. Edmondson (2002) argued that innovation inherently occurs at the team level because it requires learning behaviour, or transmission of knowledge bounded by tasks and opportunities that takes place through conversations among a limited number of interdependent people. These interactions are necessary because they enable individuals to combine different insights and institutionalize knowledge beyond what is known to a single team member (Nonaka & Takeuchi, 1995). Similarly, empirical research by Taggar (2002) suggested that team level innovation processes are needed to bring individual creativity into use. Even if individuals engage in innovation efforts and gain relevant insights, there is no organizational benefit without favourable group interactions, such as communication processes.

10.2 Are Virtual Teams More Innovative?

Given the fundamental nature of innovation and the potential for teams to contribute to it, organizations increasingly implement them for that purpose. Virtual teams, in particular, have been proclaimed as a promising design for integrating firms and are often established to take maximum advantage of innovation creating capabilities (Nonaka & Takeuchi, 1995). Organizations use designs that include some combination of geographic dispersion, electronic dependence, dynamic structure, or national diversity for virtual team collaboration, (also see Chap. 6).

Yet, these very characteristics also pose challenges that can be detrimental to innovation (Cramton, 2001; Kirkman et al., 2002, 2004; Sole & Edmondson, 2002). For example, geographically separated team members lack "mutual knowledge" of each other's lived experiences, which increases coordination problems in acquiring knowledge and resources (Cramton, 2001) (also see Chap. 9). Electronic dependence creates logistical and technological constraints that limit informal spontaneous interaction, hindering knowledge interpretation (DeSanctis & Monge, 1999) (also see Chap. 3). Full disclosure is often hampered in structurally dynamic teams by inexperience with the other party and lack of a shared history (Gibson & Cohen, 2003). When collaborators represent different national backgrounds, each of which has its own set of values, orientations, and priorities, this can detract the team from effective internal communication (Watson, et al., 1993) (also see Chap. 8). Accessing, combining, and applying knowledge relevant for innovation may thus be inherently problematic in teams characterized by these features. As a result, team members often struggle to understand each other and must resolve misinterpretations before they can truly innovate (Carlile, 2004; Dougherty, 1992) (also see Chap. 5).

Innovation A new product, method or idea, and the process of creating and using these.
Change To make or become different in some relevant way.
Learning The process by means of which individuals, teams, organizations, and so on, change.

Just bringing people with the required knowledge and skills together virtually thus provides no guarantee that they will be able to work effectively and innovate across contexts. The question is thus: *How do virtual teams learn and change, as required under BANI conditions, and which leadership and knowledge management practices can support their innovativeness?*

▶ Virtual teams can become drivers of innovation, but only if they master BANI conditions.

Application 10.1: When and how did you Learn?

Think back to any team work which you have been a part of.

- In which cases did you learn from others, and how did this learning take place?
- In which cases did you *not* learn from others, and why was this the case?
- In which cases would you describe a team process as 'innovative', and why? ◄

10.3 How to Organize Virtual Team Collaboration for Innovation, Learning and Change?

One needs to consider the impact which organizational choices have on virtual team innovation, learning and change in order to understand how virtual teams should master BANI conditions.

The main organizational principle of virtual team collaboration is to achieve and maintain a positive configuration of divergent-convergent dynamics in light of ICT conditions, team characteristics, task complexity and interdependence, and digital transformation requirements (see Chap. 2, the Five Factor Model). Both leadership and organizational design are moderators to influence team dynamics positively, and learning and transformation are a potential positive team outcome. Achieving them requires (1) organizational awareness, e.g. with regard to metaphors and bureaucracy (see Chap. 6), (2) a collective agreement of how to understand and approach learning and change and (3) an approach to leadership that facilitates learning.

Organization (see Chap. 6) is characterized by three properties, the so called **3Os** (Hatch, 2011):

- Processes of organizing.
- Organization as the abstract idea behind and the result of processes of organizing.
- *The* organization as a result of organization and processes of organizing.

Organizational design (Hatch, with Cunliffe, 2006) refers to those conscious choices made that steer how organization develops, for instance, as to whether a company has more or fewer levels of hierarchy. Because organization happens within potentially changing environments, those involved need to organize for change as much as for stability, and organizations need to find the right balance between adaptation and maintenance.

▶ Virtual teams need to organize for stability and change, and they need to find the right balance between maintenance and adaptation.

Generally, virtual team collaboration is more dynamic than non-virtual team collaboration, and this means that the change and learning requirements are higher than compared to non-virtual settings, and this why a high change awareness is required so that organizations can learn and transform, and also generate new knowledge in the process.

10.3.1 What is Learning, and how Should It be Implemented?

Learning is the means by which organizations change (also see Leavitt & March, 1988). Depending on what organizations—and the people creating them—believe in and do, their learning paths and to what extent they use this learning might differ. According to March (1991), there are two modes of organizational learning, namely exploitation and exploration:

- **Exploitation** means to use existing knowledge and resources in even better ways, for instance, by optimizing processes in the sense that one develops more sophisticated procedures to do the same things more efficiently. Exploitative learning may thus generate process innovations. However, it does not genuinely move beyond what is known to the organization, as it is too much focused on its inner workings (as the metaphor of 'organization as machine' suggests, see Chap. 6), sometimes also blinded by ideology (as the metaphor of 'organization as dark culture' suggests, see Chap. 6).
- **Exploration** means to combine and use knowledge and resources in unforeseen ways, for example by searching for benefits in previously unknown practices. Explorative learning may thus generate product innovations. An organization continuously 'searching' for new areas of learning in what was previously unknown is referred to as a **learning organization**. It is well-suited to adaptation and change (as the metaphor of 'organization as organism', potentially also as the 'brain' suggests, see Chap. 6).

What explorative learning does (and what exploitative learning does not do) is that it enables double-loop learning (Argyris & Schön, 1978). **Double-loop learning** means to learn from the outcomes of a previous learning cycle which then becomes an input for the next learning cycle. Conversely, **single-loop learning** means that one observes the consequences of previous actions to adjust future behaviour, thus preventing similar mistakes. For instance, if a certain line of software code proves to be faulty when the code is released, this mistake is corrected. Single-loop learning thus only solves problems as they manifest, yet, cannot explain why these problems occurred in the first place. Double-loop learning is achieved when specific incidents of faulty code are used to modify how future software development projects are specified in general. This means that learning as exploration can fundamentally change the organization, also in light of wider responsibilities such as sustainability or ethics, whereas learning as exploitation is performance-oriented in the narrow sense and only seeks to utilize existing resources and knowledge in even more efficient and effective ways. Virtual team collaboration can only be innovative, if the team engages in explorative learning.

10.3.2 What is Change, and how can it be Implemented?

Change is the result of organizational learning, and the organizational wish to change triggers further triggers learning. When it comes to implementing change, organizations can choose between a more mechanistic approach, and a more organic approach, depending on what manager and employees 'believe' organization is about (see Chap. 6). The mechanistic approach by Lewin (1951, 1958) argues that managers should implement change in three phases (see Fig. 10.1):

First, managers should **unfreeze** the organization by taking advantage of existing stress or dissatisfaction, or by reducing resistance through education concerning the need for change. Second, managers should enable **movement** by influencing the direction of change by altering reporting relations and reward systems, introducing a different managerial style or technology, et cetera. Third, managers should **refreeze** once a new balance is achieved and when the changes have been made permanent by means of new rules and procedures.

The underlying idea of change in this approach is that organizations run like a 'machine', and that change can be designed and steered by top management focussing on the inner workings of the organization (technological imperative). What this approach neglects is that organizations need to react quickly to environmental changes or new demands and should utilize novel environmental opportunities as they manifest (as the

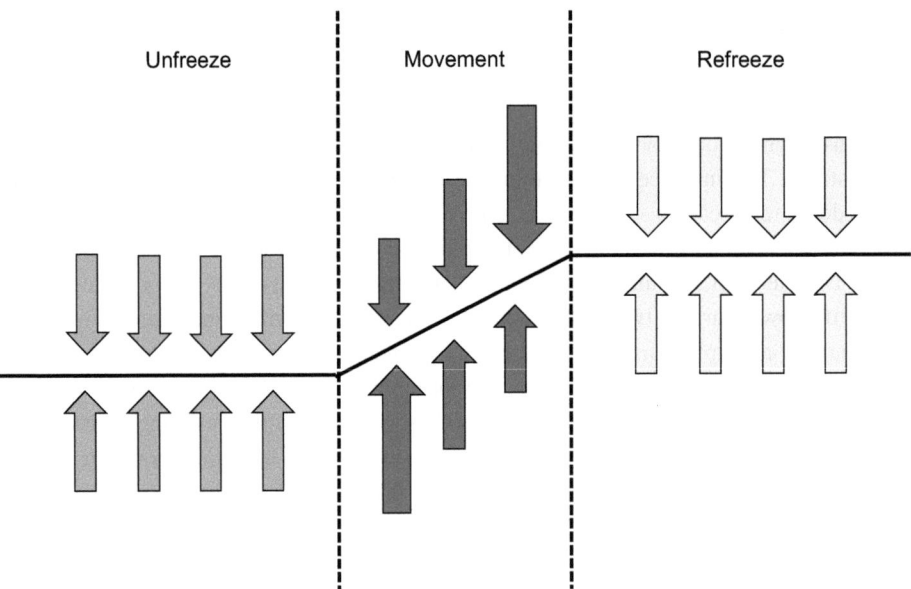

Fig. 10.1 Lewin's mechanistic model of organizational change. *Source* Hatch with Cunliffe, 2006, p. 309

organic approach proposes). Furthermore, the mechanistic approach stops at exploitative learning and does not do justice to people's emotional and social requirements in light of BANI. It presumes linear change (single-loop learning), and there is no feedback look from the last to the first phase, which means that the system fails to venture into the unknown: even VUCA requirements cannot be met by it. In summary, the mechanistic approach to change does not do the realities of virtual team collaboration justice. However, it is still often applied in practice, and this is a reason for why innovation by means of virtual team collaboration fails in corporate reality.

▶ The mechanistic approach to change is clearly insufficient from both VUCA and BANI perspectives. However, mechanistic change is still often done in corporate reality. It therefore is one of the major causes for innovation to fail in practice.

There are divergent perspectives of what needs to be learned or changed under VUCA conditions, and why and how, which—under BANI conditions—also have an overwhelming emotional quality. Also, virtual teams themselves are characterized by high levels of diversity or interdisciplinarity. Due to the combined effect of these external and internal conditions, change simply cannot be planned and steered by a selected group of managers who control its content, direction and desired outcome. To solve this dilemma, organization scholar Mary Parker Follett suggested the strategy of integration (Héon et al., 2017). She provides the following example (overview in Hatch, 2011, pp. 79–80): Imagine you are reading a book in the library. You need fresh air and would like to open a window. However, the person next to you has covered their desk with sheets of papers and manuscripts. They are afraid that you opening the window will allow the wind to throw their desk into disarray. You could now fight over the solution (only one person can win) or compromise (only open the window a little—which will cause you not much relief and still might bring some disarray to the other person—thus, neither is satisfied).

Follett recommends identifying the abstract needs of each person in this situation: what you desire is actually not opening the window, but fresh air. What the other person desires is not a closed window but an orderly desk. Unlike the specific actions, these abstract needs can then be integrated: namely, for instance, by opening a window in the adjacent room: this results in fresh air without direct gusts of wind to the room. This approach of identifying abstract patterns in concrete demands or actions in order to achieve integration seems particularly suitable for virtual team collaboration and conflict management. It is an explorative approach to learning which enables teams to revisit and expand their knowledge base (double-loop learning) which is deeply human and thus also allows for people's fears and anxieties to be overcome. In summary, the integration approach to change fits the requirement of 'a world of chaos' because it integrates people into a team and provides the team with a higher sense of agency and emotional resilience when facing overwhelming, incomprehensible and non-linear problems. Even if systems should crumble due to their brittleness, integration can still help to innovate from the experience.

▶ For innovative change, virtual teams should integrate, not compromise.

Application 10.2: Organizational Learning and Change in Virtual Team Collaboration

Assume that virtual team collaboration today takes place under BANI conditions.

- Under BANI conditions: How should a virtual team make sure that they learn, and in which ways should they learn? What are the risks of exploitative learning for virtual team collaboration, and why do cross-functional and interdisciplinary teams, in particular, need explorative learning?
- How might Follett's approach to integration be relevant to a virtual team's performance under BANI conditions?

When answering the previous questions, make sure to consider three levels of analysis: the virtual team, its corporate environment (the whole 'organization'), and the wider environment of the organization under BANI conditions. ◀

10.4 Facilitating Innovativeness: Leadership as Working Towards Safe Belonging During Crisis

Leadership under BANI conditions needs sentiment and emotional resilience, and it involves collective action for meeting overwhelming challenges. Virtual team members furthermore need a psychologically safe climate, and a sense of membership for achieving and sustaining innovativeness. Virtual team performance norms are a way towards reaching these goals.

10.4.1 Combining Leader Self-identities for Higher Resilience and Adaptability

As crises are always novel situations, in which both quick and long-term decision making is required, individuals and teams do not have a blueprint upon which to base their actions. Hannah et al. (2009) therefore suggest that leaders facing change and crisis combine multiple leader self-identities for effective action. In virtual team collaboration, these self-identities may also emerge from a combination of individuals, as shared and distributed leadership practices are an ideal way of enabling virtual team collaboration (see Chap. 7). Anderson and Sun (2017) propose five leader's self-identities that enable individual and teams to combine leadership styles for change and managing crises. These self-identities are:

- Visionary: a leader who is a futurist, with the ability to create a desired future
- Relational: a leader who is authentic, transparent, ethical and other-oriented
- Creative: a problem solving and intellectually stimulating leader
- Manager: an organiser who is task-oriented, who controls work and outcomes
- Community-oriented: a leader who contributes to the greater public good

If related to the requirement of leading virtual teams through change and crisis, one can see that a team member with a visionary leader self-identity is well suited to help transform the team. A relational personality might be very good at building trust, whereas a creative personality might explore the opportunities of digital leadership. Next, the team will also need a manager who organizes for reliability and stability, and a community-oriented leader who contributes altruistically and in a servant role.

The team should therefore reflect—individually and collectively—which member personality aligns the most with which leader self-identity (such as visionary, relational, creative, manager and community-oriented), and members should share and distribute leadership tasks and responsibilities accordingly. If team members consciously reflect upon their respective leader self-identities and what they might be useful for on team level, all might reach higher levels of performance, not only measured in terms of efficiency and effectiveness. Or, as Maznevski and DiStefano (2000, p. 195) put it: "Global leaders are team players", and this then means that, they take better care of the emotional needs of all team members in an increasingly chaotic and non-linear world (BANI) via combining the strengths of their respective leader self-identities.

10.4.2 Perceived Virtual Team Membership for Overcoming Passiveness

Due to the perceived brittleness of systems and the non-linearity and incomprehensibility of the problems to be solved, employees facing 'a world of chaos' might resort to passiveness when being overwhelmed by anxiety. This cannot be remedied by even better rational explanations, mechanistic approaches to change, exploitative learning or even a more motivational leadership. Rather, the requirement is that members feel that they 'belong' to the team and the organization, a concept referred to as Perceived Organizational Membership (POM, see Masterson & Stamper, 2003), and, this way, they may overcome anxiety.

Membership describes the belonging to or the affiliation in any social systems, such as a team, group, organization or sector of society (Bertolotti et al., 2015); it is characterized by some kind of sensed support or involvement (Bunderson, 2003). The affiliation of an employee with an employer is referred to as the organizational membership (e.g. Tsui et al., 1997).

Generally, the membership affiliation between the individual and the larger organization is weakened in virtual team collaboration, in particular when members work from home or from anywhere extensively. They then perceive themselves less as being members of a larger, abstract organization which has become more remote to their own experiences and identities at work. The only way to instill a sense of perceived organizational membership is related to the collaborative experiences which they have in their immediate surroundings, namely to strengthen the dimensions by means of which they perceive themselves as members of a virtual team. The concept proposed for leading virtual teams under BANI conditions—also in the sense of the team leading itself by means of shared and distributed practices—is thus 'perceived virtual team membership'. Based on the literature on POM, perceived virtual team membership can be assumed to involve three main elements, namely fulfilment, mattering and belonging (Shore & Coyle-Shapiro, 2003).

Need Fulfillment: According to McMillans and Chavis' (1986) research on group cohesion, social systems need to be perceived as rewarding in order to desire or maintain membership. The perception of being rewarded and recognized by the organization reflects the fulfilment of members' needs, as well as their belief of being valued as a member. Masterson and Stamper (2003) identify Person-Organization Fit (Kristof, 1996)—to be translated into: person-virtual team fit—and Psychological Contract (Rousseau, 1989, 1995) as the two factors through which need fulfilment is perceived by the individual employee, in this case: the individual virtual team member.

- **Person-virtual team fit** describes the compatibility of the virtual team and the individual member from the perspective of the team member. Often, these involve tacit elements such as basic assumptions that underlie communication and collaboration (see Chap. 5), cultural value orientations (see Chap. 8), or implicit, culture-specific leadership assumptions (see Chap. 9) of which the team member might not be aware but which influence their expectations, behaviour and perceptions nonetheless.
- The **psychological contract** describes the idea which the individual team member has in mind about why they work, what their work is about, and how they want to be rewarded by the virtual team. It is not the written contract. A perceived breach in psychological contract results in a loss of motivation and identification with the team.

Mattering refers to the perceived and observed evidence of the employee's importance and significance which the employee deduces from how the organization behaves towards them, for example, from how their work is valued and which kind of feedback and support they get. The feeling of mattering to the organization thus emerges from the perception of organizational support, in this case: **perception of virtual team support**. Members who feel valued and appreciated by the organization—in this case: the virtual team—are found to be actively contributing in return (McMillan & Chavis, 1986) and have a greater sense of membership (Masterson & Stamper, 2003).

Dimension of Belonging: Members of social systems—in this case: a virtual team—strive for affinity and a sense of belonging. McMillan and Chavis (1986) describe that individuals who make personal investments in the organization, in this case: the virtual team, feel a higher sense of belonging and ultimately perceive themselves as members more Organizations, such as virtual teams, need to provide an emotional component to membership for this investment to happen. (e.g. Filstad et al., 2019; Knapp et al., 2014). Three concepts are of relevance here, namely organizational—in this case: virtual team—identity, psychological ownership and perceived insider status.

- **Virtual team identity** describes several attributes that members perceive as central, distinctive and enduring to their organization (Knapp et al., 2014), in this case: the virtual team. Identification with this identity helps people to understand themselves and their own place in the world, and also places others in a shared context (Ashforth & Mael, 1989; Ashforth et al., 2008; Mael & Ashforth, 1992). Basically, what virtual team identity does is that it 'glues' team members together and also provides them with shared 'frames' of how to interpret collaboration and of how to behave.
- **Psychological ownership** describes a sense of possession over the organization (Vandewalle et al., 1995), in this case: the virtual team. Such ownership is developed when individuals perceive an intimate, close connection to and certain control over the subject (Pierce et al., 2001), in this case: virtual team collaboration. These claims can be both subjective (a perception), such as the perception of being 'heard' and being able to influence team decisions, and objective (factual), such as the ability to control technology.
- **Perceived insider status** represents an individual's sense of inclusion. Social systems, such as virtual teams, develop dynamics and group-specific characteristics and a shared understanding of how to recognize members (Masterson & Stamper, 2003). These properties can be either inclusive or exclusive for members. For instance, a virtual team demanding fixed working hours is more exclusive to those with caring commitments than a team allowing for the flexibilization of working hours.

Table 10.1 summarizes the Perceived Virtual Team Membership model.

The main challenge for instilling perceived virtual team membership is the diversity and dispersion of the team: when feeling remote to each other, it is difficult to achieve a sufficient sense of teamness and ensuing collaborative practice, and the leanness of ICTs further aggravate the issue. Thus, the recommendation is that virtual teams give themselves performance norms by means of which perceived virtual team membership is built and further strengthened.

10.4.3 Virtual Team Performance Norms for Increasing Perceived Virtual Team Membership

Liao (2017) proposes four virtual team performance norms. These are:

Table 10.1 The perceived virtual team membership model

Perceived Virtual Team Membership		
Need fulfilment	*Mattering*	*Belonging*
Person-Virtual Team Fit	Perceived Virtual Team Support	Virtual Team Identity
Psychological Contract		Psychological Ownership
		Perceived Insider Status

Source own figure, further developed from Masterson and Stamper (2003)

- **Professional respect**: by clarifying tasks and giving assistance to team members, team members gain trust and professional respect while helping others achieve their tasks.
- **Contribution:** team members' task-related behaviour positively influences other team members' willingness to contribute to work-oriented activities.
- **Affect:** the emotional bond between team members is facilitated and strengthened through team members' relationship-oriented behaviour.
- **Loyalty**: displaying public support for team members may increase team members' trust and enhance team members' loyalty towards those supporting them.

These four performance norms then create leadership building processes on team level, from which shared and distributed leadership practices may emerge. For example:

- The more team members engage in task- and relationship-oriented behaviour rooted in professional respect, contribution, affect and loyalty, the higher the quality of virtual collaboration.
- The higher the quality of virtual collaboration, the more team members share an understanding of each other's ideas and knowledge of what to do, and how to do it, and of who they are in the context of this team (shared mental models)
- The more mental models are shared and the higher the quality of virtual collaboration, the higher individual and collective trust levels and conflict resolution abilities.
- The more mental models are shared, the less harmful digital transformation is to the quality of virtual collaboration.
- The higher the quality of virtual collaboration, the clearer it becomes what to maintain and what to transform, and how to make sense of it, independent of technology.
- The higher the trust levels and conflict resolution abilities, the easier the implementation of shared and distributed leadership practices for managing change and crisis.

Once established, performance norms result in a positive leadership creating spiral that makes the team more resilient against the VUCA conditions of the fourth industrial revolution, and that also meets the BANI challenges of 'the age of chaos'. This then provides a conclusive answer to the first question, namely: how to lead virtual teams through changing circumstances, even crisis?

> **Application 10.3: Leadership as Enabling to Learn**
>
> Think back to a person who was in a leading role towards you (because of position, knowledge or expertise):
>
> - How did they enable you to learn?
> - Was the way in which they 'led' you also what you would have needed for the best possible learning experience? If not: what else would have been required?
> - Did you also *do* the learning actively, or, if not: what kept you in a passive role and how could you overcome passivity the next time?
>
> Imagine that you are in a leading role:
>
> - Which leader self-identities seem to fit your personality the most?
> - Will these leader self-identities enable others to learn? Why (not)?
> - Which leadership qualities would you still need to develop to enable others to learn? ◄

10.5 Knowledge Creation and Tacit Knowledge Management in Virtual Teams

Leadership is fundamental to the process of knowledge management, including the creation, distribution and exploitation of knowledge (Bryant, 2003). Virtual teams are typically more diverse, both in terms of their members and in terms of their divergent dynamics. Therefore, they potentially have access to a greater knowledge base than co-located teams. However, this knowledge must be exchanged by means of ICTs. Griffith et al. (2003) have assessed how the combination of virtual work and information technology may change the distribution of different types of knowledge across individuals, teams and the organization. They find that ICTs destabilize the relationship between organizations and employees when it comes to knowledge transfer. Therefore, it becomes more difficult to exchange tacit knowledge and to use individual members' knowledge for team level knowledge creation. This section presents an overview on the properties of knowledge and then proposes a way of how to create knowledge, namely by means of the SECI spiral (Nonaka & Takeuchi, 1995).

10.5.1 Knowledge Types in Relation to Knowledge Creation in Virtual Teams

When it comes to the question of how organizations can create knowledge, the following properties are relevant (see Nonaka & Takeuchi, 1995):

- Knowledge is justified true belief. This means that it is irrelevant whether the knowledge is objectively true or whether it is just subjectively believed to be true. For example, if a team member feels excluded in the team, this then becomes true knowledge from the person's side and influences their further expectations, behaviour and interpretations.
- Knowledge is the potential to define a situation in a way that permits skilful action or the actual skilful action. For instance, if a team member 'knows' that they have a solution to a problem, they will act upon it accordingly.
- Knowledge ranges from explicit to tacit along a continuum (Nonaka & Krogh, 2009).

The types of knowledge are highly relevant to virtual team collaboration.

- **Explicit knowledge**, the most visible of the three types of knowledges, is expressible, flexible and intentional. It is stored in media and is easily accessible, e.g. the answer to a quadratic equation. There is no room for knowledge confusion amongst 'knowing' individuals (e.g. those who have had maths at school), and virtual collaboration does not change this clarity of knowledge.
- **Implicit knowledge** has an implied meaning. The meaning of the knowledge could be expressed but is not, due to certain reasons, such as situational or cultural context. For example, depending on culturally learned assumptions underlying communication (see Chap. 5), some individuals might say 'maybe' to a question when the implied answer is 'no'. Due to the leanness of the ICTs used for virtual team collaboration (see Chap. 3), team members need to consciously explicate this implicit, context-bound knowledge as much as possible (see Chap. 4).
- **Tacit knowledge**, the most hidden of the three types of knowledges, is hardly expressible, automatic and unintentional. It is gained through personal experience and stored in people's heads. This knowledge cannot be expressed and cannot be consciously accessed, e.g. protecting the face instinctively when falling. Due to the leanness of the ICTs used for virtual team collaboration (see Chap. 3), tacit knowledge can hardly be transferred by digital means.

This implies that tacitness in relation to virtual team collaboration is a major root cause for knowledge loss, and even implicit knowledge is difficult to transfer. Because much of employees' knowledge is personal and rooted in experience (tacit), it is therefore a relevant leadership goal to make this knowledge accessible to the wider organization. This process is called **knowledge conversion**, and its goal is to create new knowledge which could not have emerged otherwise (**knowledge creation**).

Knowledge Conversion The constant conversion from tacit knowledge to explicit knowledge and vice versa.
Knowledge Creation The process of creating new knowledge, in this case: for the virtual team.

10.5.2 Tacit Knowledge Management and Knowledge Conversion by Means of the SECI Spiral

Tacit knowledge management uses conversion processes across the three types of knowledge (tacit, implicit, explicit) to expand the knowledge of the whole team or organization for higher innovativeness and, thus, competitive advantage. **The SECI model** (Nonaka & Takeuchi, 1995) which describes this process, consists of four phases which are connected by a constant conversion (**knowledge spiral**):

- **Socialisation** is the process of sharing experiences and therefore creating tacit knowledge. For example, virtual team members might discuss their experiences in using virtual meeting technologies. The required knowledge management action is that individuals **relate experience**. This way, individual tacit knowledge becomes shared tacit knowledge.
- **Externalisation** is the process of converting tacit knowledge to explicit knowledge and therefore articulating tacit knowledge to make it understandable and accessible. Metaphors or drawings are often used to form this process. For example, team members reflecting upon their virtual meeting tool experiences could refer to the tool as 'being slow as a snail' or visualize their user experiences by means of a shared whiteboard. The required knowledge management action is that individuals **explicate experience**. This way, individual tacit knowledge becomes individual explicit knowledge.
- **Combination** is the process of combining and exploiting explicit knowledge concepts to create a knowledge system. For example, one could deduce *the whole of* actual tool performance in light of *all* team members' tacit requirements (which are now shared through socialization and explicated through externalization) from the combined visualized and explicated experiences of virtual team members with the virtual meeting technology in use. The required knowledge management action is that individuals **connect explicit knowledge**. This way, individual explicit knowledge becomes shared explicit knowledge.
- **Internalisation** is the process of transferring explicit concepts into tacit knowledge by means of personal doings. For example, after team members have become aware of their combined virtual meeting tool experiences and requirements, they can then individually internalize what others have learned or need and consider these formerly

unknown requirements in their own actions. The required knowledge management action is that individuals **embody knowledge**. This way, shared explicit knowledge becomes (new) individual tacit knowledge.

After the completion of the four phases, the spiral begins anew, as team members can now make more and richer experiences and form new tacit knowledge based on the new explicit knowledge which they have internalized and apply to their actions. Figure 10.2 visualizes the SECI spiral and the knowledge conversion processes involved.

10.5.3 Recommendations for Preventing Tacit Knowledge Loss Because of ICT Limitations

Becoming aware of and utilizing tacit knowledge is even more relevant in virtual collaboration than in non-virtual collaboration. The reason for that is that many ICTs provide

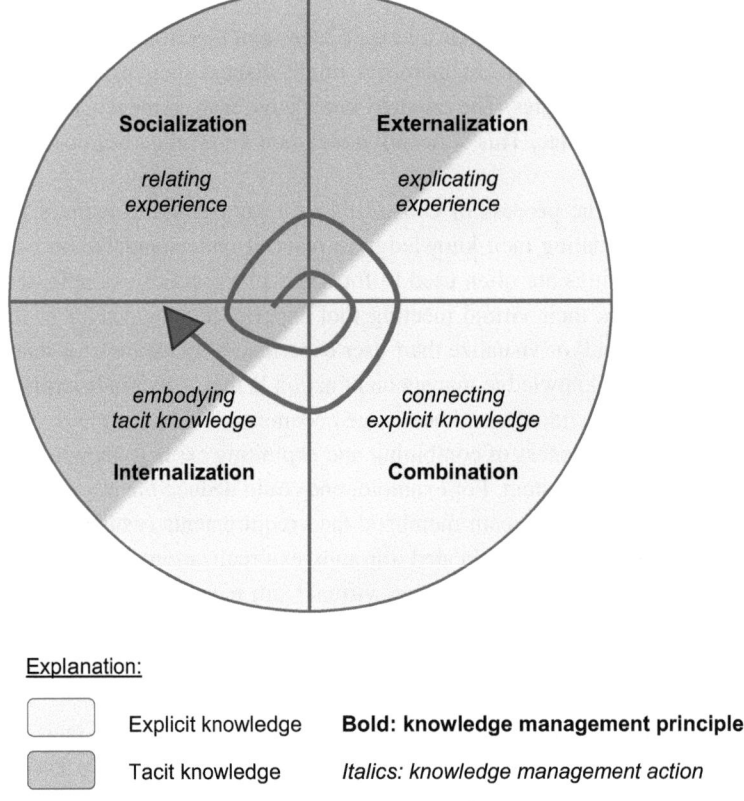

Fig. 10.2 Tacit knowledge management by means of employing the SECI spiral. *Source* own figure

functionalities that enable teams to structure their tasks more easily, to analyse team processes, and to store team knowledge and information. This means that ICTs support the "declarative nature of explicit knowledge" (Griffith et al., 2003, p. 271). Virtual teams therefore find themselves forced to transform tacit knowledge into more explicit forms in order to transmit knowledge to their team. However, if this happens, tacit knowledge uses its richness: other team members can no longer 'see' how the knowledge is 'done' and what it 'meant'. For example, written documents with a continuous copytext transport much more context information than presentation slides with bullet points. Therefore, presentation slides enable execution (what to do) but not purposive thinking or strategic considerations (why and how to do). Translated to virtual team collaboration, this implies that ICTs often over-simplify knowledge by forcing a tacit-to-explicit knowledge conversion that is incomplete. Conversely, the SECI spiral is a way in which most of the individual tacit knowledge is utilized on team level.

To be more certain that knowledge conversion by means of the SECI spiral does not result in knowledge losses, the following actions proposed by Griffith et al. (2003) are helpful. Virtual teams should

- Verbalize rules, terminology, and descriptions.
- Provide team members with experience building opportunities, such as experiences with technologies and tasks, which are then shared.
- Provide team members with access to tools that support highly interdependent work.
- Create and consciously develop **communities of practice** that is: exchange networks in which team members exchange on their work practice and approaches. Communities of practice (Bourdieu, 1977) are those who are united by a 'shared way of doing things' based on a shared implicit and/or tacit knowledge reservoir which stems from what they do. For example, computer engineers are united by their being trained in the same theories and their acting upon hard and software in certain ways.
- Develop strategies and technologies that support **transactive memory** (Wegner, 1986), that is: a knowledge system in which no single member knows everything but in which all (or: as many as possible) know who knows what and how their own expertise relates to the knowledge of the other members. The key to building transactive memory is thus to picture knowledge as a space, such as a 'town', in which all team members live in certain houses. Transactive memory means to understand who lives where and which road one needs to take to get from one's own house to another person's house.
- Develop strategies and technologies that support the transfer of tacit knowledge.
- Focus on the continuous and ongoing development of individual level tacit knowledge.

When supported by the four performance norms proposed for virtual team collaboration (Liao, 2017), namely professional respect, contribution, affect and loyalty, these proposed actions can serve as a guideline for leaders on how to manage knowledge in virtual teams. Figure 10.3 visualizes the combined process.

> **Application 10.4: Knowledge Conversion in Virtual Team Collaboration**
>
> Think of knowledge that is stored in your personal experience and interactions with technology, such as: how to play a certain video game, how to use a certain smart phone application or how to navigate a certain social media platform. Talk to at least one person who plays the same video game, uses the same smart phone application or navigates the same social media platform. Find out which new knowledge emerges between the two of you and consider how this new knowledge could be useful for a larger group of video gamers, application users or social media users. Also, figure out which steps you would need to take to 'formalize' this knowledge from experience, e.g. how you could write it down so that a third party will understand it. ◄

10.6 The Technological Dimension of Virtual Team Learning and Change

By nature, virtual team collaboration is mediated by technology (Chap. 3), and how humans interact with technology, and how these interfaces are designed, is thus highly relevant for learning, innovation and change. Also, the virtual team is connected to the internet and each other via numerous devices, and many technologies in use are part of larger systems. Consequently, Tim Ryan, the chairman of PwC, stated in an interview with Jacob Morgan (2020b, p. 26) that "[…] what made a great leader 50 years ago or

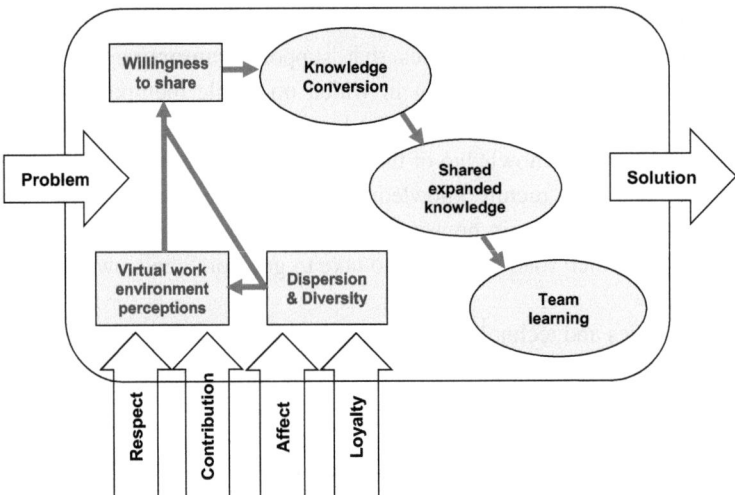

Fig. 10.3 Knowledge conversion in virtual teams. *Source* own figure

25 years ago will not likely make a great leader 10 years from now". Among the reasons that determine what leadership will look like in the future, are artificial intelligence and the advancement of technology, as well as the pace of change (Morgan, 2020a). How well leaders are able to deal with these factors is therefore of paramount importance of what people's lives will look like in the future. This section provides an overview of the technological dimension of virtual team collaboration and proposes the Johari window (Luft & Ingham, 1955) as a suitable method for overcoming technological blind spots.

10.6.1 Towards an Internet of Things?

The first particularity of today's technology, objects and devices is that they are often interconnected. For instance, when using any collaborative technology, there is a high likelihood that, by doing this, a virtual team will also provide the tool or artificial intelligence (AI) with user information which the tool or AI will then use for further learning and technological development. This means that systems are embedded in wider systems (**embedded systems**).

In totality, people are thus surrounded by objects, technologies and devices which are connected to the internet, such as wearables, smart fridges, smart vehicles, cars and homes, the so-called **Internet of Things** (IoT). Office buildings or entire cities use such solutions (e.g. smart bins, smart utility meters, smart grids, etc.) to optimize energy consumption, to address public safety issues or transportation problems, and many more. Smart objects, technologies and devices are furthermore interconnected to other embedded systems to form so called **Cyber-Physical Systems**. Together, this interconnectedness and knowledge exchange brings about technological learning cycles which then change the objects, technologies and devices with whom users interact. Table 10.2 contains some definitions of IoT.

One can most likely start speaking of an IoT from the moment on when the number of "things or objects" (technical actors) surpassed the number of human actors connected to the internet (Evans, 2011, p. 2), and this happened somewhere between 2008–2009 (Evans, 2011, p. 3). Cisco's (2020) *Annual Internet Report* forecasts growth rates of the internet users, of the devices connected to the internet, of the Machine-to-Machine (M2M) connections and an increase in fixed and mobile broadband speed. As early as in 2011, Dave Evans, chief technologist and futorologist for Cisco had argued that the IoT "will change everything—including ourselves" (Evans, 2011, p. 2).

For example, smart leak sensors, smart bulbs, smart thermostats aim at saving energy and money. Companies cut costs and enhance manufacturing productivity with the help of smart adaptable assembly lines (ElMaraghy & ElMaraghy, 2016). The advances in sensor technology simplify the monitoring of air and water quality or radiation (Ullo & Sinha, 2020), and satellite technology and thermal alert systems can detect volcanic activity before eruption (Schmidt, 2004). Consequently, authorities and policy makers can look for optimal solutions or react faster to environmental challenges based on real-

Table 10.2 Relevant definitions of the internet of things

Definition	Source
"Objects with computing devices in them that are able to connect to each other and exchange data using the internet"	Cambridge Dictionary (n.d.)
"The network of physical objects that contain embedded technology to communicate and sense or interact with their internal states or the external environment"	Gartner (n.d.)
"A network of objects (such as sensors and actuators) that can capture data autonomously and self-configure intelligently based on physical world events, allowing these systems to become active participants in various public, commercial, scientific, and personal processes"	Gates (2017)
"*Systems* that contain *ubiquitous 'everyday' objects* […] that are accessible through the Internet and equipped with *sensing, storing, and processing capabilities* that allow these objects to *understand their environments*; contain *identifying and networking capabilities* that allow them to *communicate information about themselves*; involve *object-object, object-person, and person-person communication*; and make autonomous decisions"	Van Deursen and Mossberger (2018, p. 125) *(emphasis in the original)*

Source own table

time information and historical data. The benefits and possibilities of the IoT seem endless, and with the emergence of Artificial Intelligence, such as AI assistants who mimic social interactions, one can even speak of a Social Internet of Things (SIoT) (Firouzi et al., 2020). Cisco (2013) had also proposed the expression Internet of Everything (IoE), which includes not only things, but also people, processes and data.

As with other developments, the IoT has its dark sides, too. Ziegeldorf et al. (2013) raise awareness on the threats that IoT carries with regard to users' privacy: tracking, localization, profiling, inventory attacks, etc. Van Deursen and Mossberger (2018) are sceptical that the IoT is beneficial to all stakeholders and show how it actually can increase inequality due to a skill divide and a lack of similar usage opportunities. Computerizing everything can have many advantages, but the effects of security breaches can be catastrophic as shown by Bruce Schneier in his 2018 book "Click here to kill everybody". Bridle (2018) presents many dangers originating from technological developments and he emphasizes the need for all individuals to engage critically with technology, to question its purpose and to gain "technological literacy". Whether technology will bring the "end of the future" as Bridle's (2018) book title might suggest, can be doubted, but his words deserve attention: "We know more and more about the world, while being less and less able to do anything about it" (p. 186). Thus, technology as an actor might add to the BANI conditions as experienced by humans.

Internet of Things The phenomenon that more 'things' than humans are interconnected in the world wide web.
Embedded Systems Systems, such as software, which are part of larger systems (software-hardware combinations).
Cyber-Physical Systems Embedded systems which are interconnected, e.g. via the internet.

10.6.2 Designing Human—Machine Interfaces for Virtual Team Collaboration

Most people at work interact with computers on a daily basis (human-computer interaction—HCI) via user interfaces (UIs). Virtual team collaboration would be unfathomable and impossible without well-functioning UIs. **Usability engineering**, the art and craft of designing UIs, needs to consider a combination of universal, cultural and individual factors, as well as objective regulations and subjective interpretations, to let users interact with technology intuitively, efficiently and effectively (Marcus, 2006). It is part of the organizational design challenge for virtual team collaboration and can help reduce human anxiety and passivity.

Usability engineering places the user at the center of the software development efforts, so that the resulting user interfaces can be "readily comprehended, quickly learned, and reliably operated" (Butler, 1996, p. 53). Moreover, there are also international standards (e.g. ISO 9241 or ISO 13407), which provide guidelines and information on design principles, ergonomic requirements, etc. The principles and practices by means of which the interface between humans and technology should be configured is referred to as **user-interface design**.

Technology as related to learning and innovativeness also has a cultural component (Marcus, 2006). Cultural dimensions (see Chap. 8) and basic underlying assumptions, such as those concerning context, relations, space and time (Chap. 5), are likely to influence user experiences, and this influence should be considered when user interfaces are designed. For example, Callahan (2005) investigated the relationship between country culture and interface design. She presents examples about the different perception of colours and icons, language and translation issues or the way the information is structured in different cultures. Some elements are critical with that regard (e.g. the language), while others (e.g. the meaning of a colour in a certain culture) may have little impact on the interaction at the user interface. Lachner et al. (2018) created website prototypes, a visual user interface. These were designed to visualize more or less hierarchy through variations in navigation structure, visual presentation and language. The researchers showed the websites to study participants from Germany and Vietnam. The result was that participants favoured different website designs in line with the power distance orientation in their country. Heimgärtner (2019, p. 156) comes up with a "toolbox for intercultural user interface design". The toolbox encompasses cultural dimensions (e.g. uncertainty avoidance), intercultural variables (e.g. language), user interface characteristics (e.g. layout, appearance preferences), information about the HCI (e.g. frequency of interaction, information density, navigational preferences). When combined, they result in a culture dependent HCI model (see pp. 159–160).

User Interface   The part of a technology, device or system with which a user interacts.
User-Interface Design   The art and craft of designing user interfaces.
Usability Engineering   Designing technology for its being used by humans.

Link to Practice: Cortana by Microsoft

When developing the AI assistant Cortana, Microsoft's developers took variations in cultural value orientations (cultural dimensions) and underlying cultural assumptions into account so that Cortana's perceived personality matches user expectations (Ash, 2015). Depending on the language of the user, Cortana will, for example, phrase questions in a more direct (low context) or more indirect (high context) manner. The AI will also change the emotional quality of verbal expressions and use or not use certain types of humour, based on culture-specific norms (ibid.). ◄

10.6.3 The Johari Window

As a team learning and development tool, the Johari window (Luft & Ingham, 1955) is a visual representation of what a team member knows about themselves, and of what others know about the individual team member. Its purpose is to increase the totality of knowledge in a team, and to also develop self-awareness and trust, by engaging in self-disclosure and feedback processes across individuals in a team. The model can, for example, increase the technological awareness of those engaged in virtual team collaboration, for instance, as related to user interface experiences or as related to the anxieties which people might have with regard to technology, and how to use it. The model was developed by American psychologists Joseph Luft and Harry Ingham, and the name 'Johari' originates from a combination of their first names. It visualizes how knowledge is interpersonally created and further enhanced in a team.

As Fig. 10.4 shows, the Johari window divides knowledge into four areas:

- Area 1: What is known to oneself and to others: this is the open area, or knowledge arena: everyone knows this in the team. The knowledge creation goal is to maximize this area in relation to the other areas.

10.6 The Technological Dimension of Virtual Team Learning and Change

- Area 2: What is unknown to oneself but known by the others, such as unconscious traits of which the individual is unaware but which others observe in interaction. This is the blind area in the sense of a personal 'blind spot'.
- Area 3: What is known to oneself but what one wishes to hide from the others, such as struggles, anxieties, failures or shortcomings. This is the hidden area (others cannot see it), also known as the façade.
- Area 4: What neither individuals nor the team know. This is the unknown area which, from a learning perspective, is the key zone of 'exploration', namely the zone that leads to innovation and transformation (see Sect. 10.3.3).

To maximize Area 1 and to discover what is unknown (Area 4), requires the following processes:

- Area 1 → Area 2: Individuals should ask others for feedback, and others should also offer feedback. Shared performance norms (see Sect. 10.4.3) help stabilize this process.
- Area 1 → Area 3: Individuals should disclose themselves to the team. This, of course, requires trust, because the individual is exposed to the team. Shared performance norms (see Sect. 10.4.3) help stabilize this process.

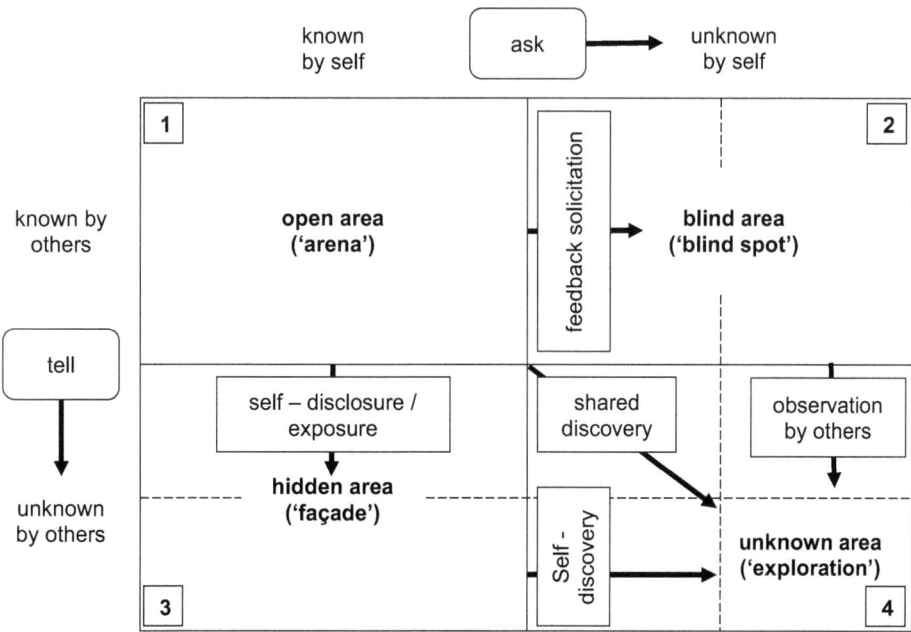

Fig. 10.4 The Johari window for virtual team learning and knowledge enhancement. *Source* own figure, based on Luft and Ingham (1955)

- Area 2 → Area 4: Self-disclosure and -exposure initiate a process of self-discovery: the individual realizes what else they are capable of, how they can further learn, and in what other ways they can contribute to change and innovativeness. This way, the unknown team area is reduced. For instance, team members might develop their leader self-identities through this process.
- Area 3 → Area 4: Asking and providing feedback leads to an improvement of feedback skills, expertise and knowledge which increases the scope and relevance of the observations made by others. This way, the unknown team area is reduced. For example, team members develop their leader self-identities by this process and can then better know when to step up and take a leading role as part of the shared and distributed leadership practices of the team.
- Area 4 → Area 4: Shared discoveries of the team emerge from the combination of the observation by others and the self-discovery of the individual, such as a better overview on who is capable of what and who needs what kind of relational support.

Because individual human-technology interactions are invisible to other team members and because virtual team collaboration is more dispersed, divergent and remote, it is more difficult to establish team level awareness, relations and knowledge. The Johari window is therefore also a good tool for reducing what the team does not *know* about how members use and interact with technology.

Application 10.5: Exploring the Technological Unknown

Take the example of a technology, application or device which you use often or even on a daily basis. Based on your understanding of the knowledge creation processes depicted by the Johari window, engage in the following activity and answer the following questions:

- What is it that you know about how you use this technology, application or device that you do not tell others (for whatever reasons)? What hinders you to disclose this part of you?
- Ask others about how you use this technology, application or device. What can you learn from what they tell you?
- Combine both insights: What have you discovered about your own technology usage, and what will be the effects on others and yourself, if you implement this learning in your further user practices. ◄

10.7 Closing Part

10.7.1 Chapter Summary

Innovation manifests on team level, and change and learning are more crucial to virtual teams than to non-virtual teams. Whether virtual teams change and learn for higher innovativeness depends on the degree of organizational awareness and the underlying assumptions concerning change, on their leadership and knowledge creation processes and on their ability to overcome the technological unknown. As Chap. 6 suggests, metaphors of organization can be a way of increasing such awareness. Companies must also keep in mind not to overburden a virtual team with bureaucracy so that the team's ability to learn, change and be innovative remains uncompromised (see Chap. 6). Generally, successful virtual team learning requires exploration instead of exploitation, and integration instead of compromise. Leadership is essential for enabling teams to learn. This requires exploring leader self-identities and establishing perceived virtual team membership via implementing team performance norms on team level. Tacit knowledge is essential to virtual team collaboration, yet, very difficult to transport via ICTs which often force its incomplete conversion into explicit knowledge. Virtual teams should apply the SECI spiral in order to make sure that all of team members' tacit knowledge, for instance, their user experiences with technology, are converted to explicit knowledge. Finally, there is also the impact of technology and the need to integrate members' diverse user experiences with technologies (that are interconnected and learn from users in return) into a collective knowledge creation process. This requires that team members disclose what they hide or fear, and ask for feedback. The Johari window visualizes how such a process enables shared discoveries that minimize the technological unknown.

10.7.2 Key Points

- The BANI model describes post-COVID realities; it has deep implications for virtual team change, learning and innovativeness.
- Virtual teams require explorational, not exploitative learning.
- Innovation requires integration, not compromise.
- Leader self-identities may be combined for higher resilience and adaptability.
- Passivity originating from anxiety endangers virtual team collaboration; it can be overcome via virtual team performance norms that increase perceived membership.
- The SECI spiral is a means for preventing tacit knowledge loss needs and promoting tacit knowledge creation in virtual team collaboration.
- The technological dimension of virtual team change and learning is essential to innovativeness.
- The Johari window can be applied to increase individual and virtual team awareness.

10.7.3 Review Questions

1. What does the BANI model describe, and how it is relevant to virtual team collaboration?
2. What approaches to learning do you know and how do they differ from each other regarding their effects on virtual team collaboration?
3. Which approaches to change do you know, and how do they differ from each other regarding their effects on virtual team collaboration?
4. Which leader self-identities do you know, and what is the relation between leader self-identity and team resilience and adaptability?
5. What is perceived virtual team membership, and how does it interrelate with the passiveness that can emerge from the anxieties described by the BANI model?
6. What are the main knowledge types that are relevant at work?
7. Which knowledge types can be transferred more or less successfully in virtual team collaboration?
8. What is the SECI spiral, which knowledge conversion processes does it involve, and why and how should it be applied to virtual team collaboration?
9. How should human-machine interfaces be designed for change and learning in virtual team collaboration?
10. What is purpose of the Johari window, how does it work, and why is it relevant to virtual team collaboration?

10.7.4 Opening Case Revisited

Performance has been defined as a combination of people's abilities and motivation, and the opportunities given to them. However, people might feel anxiety which then leads to passiveness under current BANI conditions, that is: not doing anything at all anymore, because every choice seems insufficient and could even trigger a turn for the worse. Such passiveness has disastrous effects on virtual team collaboration. In particular, shared and distributed leadership can only work if team members are able and motivated enough to adhere to the team's performance norms and if they are given the opportunities to contribute to the team's self-organization. Please answer the following questions against this background:

- Which emotional competencies do people need to perform under BANI conditions, and how could the team support these qualities?
- How can the team and its members acknowledge anxiety while not letting it take over?
- How can shared and distributed leadership overcome people's sense of passiveness?

- Which of these qualities do you believe that you possess and which ones would you need to develop?
- Do you feel that you have been adequately trained for leadership under BANI conditions? Why (not), and what kind of additional support, if any, would you need?

In summary, please consider the novel emotional and relational requirements of shared and distributed leadership when 'facing a world of chaos' and assess how well prepared you personally are for this scenario.

10.7.5 Closing Activity

Technology, as it has developed until now, is highly useful for virtual team collaboration but might also contribute to brittleness, anxiety, non-linearity and incomprehensiveness (BANI).

- How is technology as experienced by users also potentially brittle, what are the consequences for virtual team collaboration, and what should virtual teams do about it?
- What are people's anxieties associated with technology under BANI conditions and how can they overcome these anxieties individually or collectively in virtual team collaboration?
- What could create technological passivity under BANI conditions, and what needs to be done to overcome it (individually or collectively) in virtual team collaboration?
- In what ways is technology a 'non-linear problem' to be solved by individuals and teams? How should they approach this problem in virtual collaboration?
- In what ways does technology contribute to incomprehensibility, what are the consequences for virtual team collaboration, and what should individuals and teams do about it?

The goal of this activity is to increase your own technological awareness, with regard to how you interact with and use technology and also how you experience and feel about this interaction. This way, you will come to a more differentiated understanding as to how technology is part of work and the world in general, and this means that you will enter virtual team collaboration with less knowledge limitations and 'blind spots'.

References

Anderson, M. H., & Sun, P. Y. T. (2017). Reviewing leadership styles: Overlaps and the need for a new 'full-range' theory. *International Journal of Management Reviews, 19*(1), 76–96.

Argyris, C., & Schön, D. (1978). *Organizational learning: A theory of action perspective*. Addison-Wesley.

Ash, M. (2015, July 20). Cortana brings cultural savviness to new markets. *Windows Experience Blog.* https://blogs.windows.com/windowsexperience/2015/07/20/cortana-brings-cultural-savviness-to-new-markets/. Accessed 20 Feb 2024.

Ashforth, B. E., & Mael, F. (1989). Social identity theory and the organization. *The Academy of Management Review, 14*(1), 20–39.

Ashforth, B. E., Harrison, S. H., & Corley, K. G. (2008). Identification in organizations: An examination of four fundamental questions. *Journal of Management, 34*(3), 325–374.

Bertolotti, F., Mattarelli, E., Vignoli, M., & Macrì, D. M. (2015). Exploring the relationship between multiple team membership and team performance: The role of social networks and collaborative technology. *Research Policy, 44*(4), 911–924.

Bourdieu, P. (1977). *Outline of a theory of practice.* Cambridge University Press.

Bridle, J. (2018). *New dark age. Technology and the end of the future.* Verso Books.

Bryant, S. E. (2003). The role of transformational and transactional leadership in creating, sharing and exploiting organizational knowledge. *Journal of Leadership & Organizational Studies, 9*(4), 32–44.

Bunderson, J. S. (2003). Team member functional background and involvement in management teams: Direct effects and the moderating role of power centralization. *Academy of Management Journal, 46*(4), 458–474.

Butler, K. A. (1996). Usability engineering turns 10. *Interactions, 3*(1), 58–75.

Callahan, E. (2005). Interface design and culture. *Annual Review of Information Science and Technology, 39*(1), 255–310.

Cambridge Dictionary. (n.d). The internet of things. In *Dictionary.Cambridge.org.* https://dictionary.cambridge.org/dictionary/english/internet-of-things?q=Internet+of+things. Accessed 23 June 2021.

Carlile, P. R. (2004). Transferring, translating, and transforming: An integrative framework for managing knowledge across boundaries. *Organization Science, 15*(5), 555–568.

Cascio, J. (2020). *Facing the age of Chaos.* Medium. https://medium.com/@cascio/facing-the-age-of-chaos-b00687b1f51d. Accessed 1 Jan 2024.

Cisco. (2013). *The Internet of Everything: Cisco IoE Value Index Study* [PDF file]. https://www.cisco.com/c/dam/en_us/about/business-insights/docs/ioe-value-index-faq.pdf. Accessed 23 June 2021.

Cisco. (2020, March 9). *Cisco Annual Internet Report (2018–2023) White Paper.* https://www.cisco.com/c/en/us/solutions/collateral/executive-perspectives/annual-internet-report/white-paper-c11-741490.html. Accessed 20 Feb 2024.

Cramton, C. D. (2001). The mutual knowledge problem and its consequences for dispersed collaboration. *Organization Science, 12*(3), 346–371.

DeSanctis, G., & Monge, P. (1999). Introduction to the special issue: Communication processes for virtual organizations. *Organization Science, 10*(6), 693–703.

Dougherty, D. (1992). Interpretive barriers to successful product innovation in large firms. *Organization Science, 3*(2), 179–202.

Edmondson, A. C. (2002). The local and variegated nature of learning in organizations: A group-level perspective. *Organization Science, 13*(2), 128–146.

ElMaraghy, H., & ElMaraghy, W. (2016). Smart Adaptable Assembly Systems. *Procedia CIRP, 44*, 4–13. https://doi.org/10.1016/j.procir.2016.04.107. Accessed 1 May 2024.

Evans, D. (2011, April). *The Internet of Things. How the Next Evolution of the Internet is Changing Everything* [PDF file]. https://www.cisco.com/c/dam/en_us/about/ac79/docs/innov/IoT_IBSG_0411FINAL.pdf. Accessed 21 June 2021.

Filstad, C., Traavik, L. E. M., & Gorli, M. (2019). Belonging at work: The experiences, representations and meanings of belonging. *The Journal of Workplace Learning, 31*(2), 116–142.

References

Firouzi, F., Farahani, B., Weinberger, M., DePace, G. & Aliee, F. S. (2020). IoT fundamentals: Definitions, architectures, challenges, and promises. In F. Firouzi, K. Chakrabarty & S. Nassif (Eds.), *Intelligent Internet of Things. From Device to Fog and Cloud* (pp. 3–50). Springer.

Gartner. (n.d.). Internet of Things (iot). In *Gartner Glossary*, https://www.gartner.com/en/information-technology/glossary/internet-of-things. Accessed 24 June 2021.

Gates, M. (2017, November 9). IoT glossary: 55 terms you need to know. In *DZone*. https://dzone.com/articles/iot-glossary-terms-you-need-to-know. Accessed 20 Feb 2024.

Gibson, C. B., & Cohen, S. G. (2003). *Virtual teams that work: Creating conditions for virtual collaboration effectiveness*. Jossey-Bass.

Griffith, T. L., Sawyer, J. E., & Neale, M. A. (2003). Virtualness and knowledge in teams: Managing the love triangle of organizations, individuals, and information technology. *MIS Quarterly, 27*(2), 265–287.

Hannah, S. T., Woolfolk, R. L., & Lord, R. G. (2009). Leader self-structure: A framework for positive leadership. *Journal of Organizational Behavior, 30*(2), 269–290.

Hatch, M. J. (2011). *Organizations: A very short introduction*. Oxford University Press.

Hatch, M. J., & Cunliffe, A. (2006). *Organization theory—Modern, symbolic and postmodern perspectives*. Oxford University Press.

Heimgärtner, R. (2019). Towards a toolbox for intercultural user interface design. In H. Plácido Silva, A. Jimenez Ramirez, A. Holzinger, L. Constantine, & M. Helfert (Eds.), *Proceedings of the 3rd International Conference on Computer-Human Interaction Research and Applications* (pp. 156–163). https://doi.org/10.5220/0008345201560163. Accessed 1 May 2024.

Héon, F. H., Damart, S., & Nelson, L. A. T. (2017). Mary Parker Follett: Change in the paradigm of integration. In D. B. Szabla, W. A. Pasmore, M. A. Barnes, & A. N. Gipson (Eds.), *The palgrave handbook of organizational change thinkers* (pp. 1–22). Springer.

Kirkman, B. L., Rosen, B., Gibson, C. B., Tesluk, P. E., & McPherson, S. O. (2002). Five challenges to virtual team success: lessons from Sabre, Inc. *Academy of Management Perspectives, 16*(3), 67–79.

Kirkman, B. L., Rosen, B., Tesluk, P. E., & Gibson, C. B. (2004). The impact of team empowerment on virtual team performance: The moderating role of face-to-face interaction. *Academy of Management Journal, 47*(2), 175–192.

Knapp, J. R., Smith, B. R., & Sprinkle, T. A. (2014). Clarifying the relational ties of organizational belonging: understanding the roles of perceived insider status, psychological ownership, and organizational identification. *Journal of Leadership & Organizational Studies, 21*(3), 273–285.

Kristof, A. L. (1996). Person-organization fit: An integrative review of its conceptualizations, measurements and implications. *Personnel Psychology, 49*(1), 1–49.

Lachner, F., Nguyen, M.-A., & Butz, A. (2018). Culturally sensitive user interface design: A case study with German and vietnamese users. In H. Winschiers-Theophilus, I. van Zyl, N. Goagoses, D. Singh Jat, E. G. Belay, R. Orji, & A. Peters (Eds.), *Proceedings of the Second African Conference for Human Computer Interaction: Thriving Communities* (pp. 1–12).

Leavitt, B., & March, J. (1988). Organizational learning. *Annual Review of Sociology, 14*, 319–340.

Lewin, K. (1951). *Field theory in social science*. Harper & Row.

Lewin, K. (1958). Group decisions and social change. In E. E. Maccobby, T. M. Newcomb, & E. L. Hartley (Eds.), *Readings in social psychology* (pp. 459–473). Holt, Rinehart & Winston.

Liao, C. (2017). Leadership in virtual teams: A multilevel perspective. *Human Resource Management Review, 27*(4), 648–659.

Luft, J., & Ingham, H. (1955). The Johari window: A graphic model for interpersonal relations. Western Training Laboratory in Group Development, University of California.

Mael, F., & Ashforth, B. E. (1992). Alumni and their alma mater: A partial test of the reformulated model of organizational identification. *Journal of Organizational Behavior, 13*(2), 103–123.

March, J. G. (1991). Exploration and exploitation in organizational learning. *Organization Science, 2*(1), 71–87.

Marcus, A. (2006). Cross-Cultural user-experience design. In D. Barker-Plummer, R. Cox & N. Swoboda (Eds.), *Proceedings of the 4th international conference on Diagrammatic Representation and Inference (Diagrams'06)* (pp. 16–24). Springer.

Masterson, S. S., & Stamper, C. L. (2003). Perceived organizational membership: An aggregate framework representing the employee-organization relationship. *Journal of Organizational Behavior, 24*(5), 473–490.

Maznevski, M. L., & Distefano, J. J. (2000). Global leaders are team players: Developing global leaders through membership on global teams. *Human Resource Management, 39*(2–3), 195–208.

McMillan D. W., & Chavis D. M. (1986). Sense of Community: A definition and theory. *Journal of Community Psychology, 14*(1), 6–23.

Morgan, J. (2020a, February 10). 140 CEOs on: What it will take to be a leader in 2030 [Audio podcast episode]. In: *Great Leadership with Jacob Morgan. The Future Organisation.* https://thefutureorganization.com/140-ceos-on-what-it-will-take-to-be-a-leader-in-2030/. Accessed 20 Feb 2024

Morgan, J. (2020b). *The future leader: 9 Skills and mindsets to succeed in the next decade.* Wiley.

Nonaka, I., & Takeuchi, H. (1995). *The knowledge-creating company: How Japanese companies create the dynamics of innovation.* Oxford University Press.

Nonaka, I., & Von Krogh, G. (2009). Tacit knowledge and knowledge conversion: Controversy and advancement in organizational knowledge creation theory. *Organization Science, 20*(3), 635–652.

Pierce, J. L., Kostova, T., & Dirks, K. T. (2001). Toward a theory of psychological ownership in organizations. *The Academy of Management Review, 26*(2), 298–310.

Rousseau, D. M. (1989). Psychological and implied contracts in organizations. *Employee Responsibilities and Rights Journal, 2*(2), 121–139.

Rousseau, D. (1995). *Psychological contracts in organizations: Understanding written and unwritten agreements.* Sage.

Saleh, A., & Watson, R. (2017). Business excellence in a volatile, uncertain, complex and ambiguous environment (BEVUCA). *The TQM Journal, 29*(5), 705–724.

Schmidt, L. J. (2004, February 16). *Sensing Remote Volcanoes.* Earth Data. https://earthdata.nasa.gov/learn/sensing-our-planet/sensing-remote-volcanoes. Accessed 20 Feb 2024.

Schneier, B. (2018). *Click here to kill everybody. Security and survival in a hyper-connected world.* Norton & Company.

Schoonhoven, C. B., Eisenhardt, K. M., & Lyman, K. (1990). Speeding products to market: Waiting time to first product introduction in new firms. *Administrative Science Quarterly, 35,* 177–207.

Shore, L. M., & Coyle-Shapiro, J.A.-M. (2003). New developments in the employee-organization relationship. *Journal of Organizational Behavior, 24*(5), 443–450.

Sole, D., & Edmondson, A. (2002). Situated knowledge and learning in dispersed teams. *British Journal of Management, 13*(Supp.), 17–34.

Taggar, S. (2002). Individual creativity and group ability to utilize individual creative resources: A multilevel model. *Academy of Management Journal, 45*(2), 315–330.

Tsui, A. S., Pearce, J. L., Porter, L. W., & Tripoli, A. M. (1997). Alternative approaches to the employee-organization relationship: Does investment in employees pay off? *Academy of Management Journal, 40*(5), 1089–1121.

Ullo, S. L., & Sinha, G. R. (2020). Advances in smart environment monitoring systems using IoT and sensors. *Sensors, 20*(11), 3113.

Vandewalle, D., Van Dyne, L., & Kostova, T. (1995). Psychological ownership: An empirical examination of its consequences. *Group & Organization Management, 20*(2), 210–226.

Van Deursen, A. J. A. M., & Mossberger, K. (2018). Anything for anyone? A new digital divide in internet-of-things skills. *Policy and Internet, 10*(2), 122–140.

Watson, W. E., Kumar, K., & Michaelsen, L. K. (1993). Cultural diversity's impact on interaction process and performance: Comparing homogeneous and diverse task groups. *Academy of Management Journal, 36*(3), 590–602.

Wegner, D. M. (1986). Transactive memory: A contemporary analysis of the group mind. In B. Mullen & G. R. Goethals (Eds.), *Theories of group behavior* (pp. 185–205). Springer.

White, A., Wheelock, M., Canwell, A., & Smets, M. (2023). *6 Key Levers of a Successful Organizational Transformation*. Harvard Business Review. https://hbr.org/2023/05/6-key-levers-of-a-successful-organizational-transformation. Accessed 1 Jan 2024.

Ziegeldorf, J. H., Morchon, O. G., & Wehrle, K. (2013). Privacy in the internet of things: Threats and challenges. *Security and Communication Networks, 7*(12), 2728–2742.

Further Reading

Morrison-Smith, S. & Ruiz, J. (2020). Challenges and barriers in virtual teams: a literature review. *SN Applied Sciences 2*, 1096. https://doi.org/10.1007/s42452-020-2801-5. Accessed 1 May 2024.

This article provides an overview on the existing literature regarding the challenges and barriers in virtual teams. Most findings and their leadership implications can be interpreted in light of the VUCA conditions of Industry 4.0, but you could also draw wider BANI implications.

Digital Ethics, Artificial Intelligence, and Responsible Research and Innovation: Sustainable and Inclusive Virtual Team Collaboration for a Better Future

11.1 Introduction

From a narrow, managerialist view, virtual teams are employed to utilize business advantages such as lower costs or higher innovation. However, from a wider, human, perspective, virtual team collaboration also contributes to how 'the world evolves' in general. Therefore, one may identify wider goals of virtual team collaboration, such as the need to contribute to a more sustainable development or to work towards a more inclusive workplace for all. This is particularly relevant for those teams engaged in technological development and innovation. It requires that these teams, and their individual members, consider questions of responsibility and ethics, also in relation to technological advancement, Artificial Intelligence (AI) and human-machine interactions. Nuclear fusion, for example, is a ground-breaking scientific achievement which produces virtually no carbon emissions and delivers more energy than other sources and little waste (van de Poel, 2011). Yet, it has also brought about a potentially devastating arsenal of global weaponry, and leaks of nuclear waste, as in Chernobyl and Fukushima, which have caused long-term, widespread damage to society (Corkhill & Hyatt, 2018).

To address such issues at the intersections of technology (natural sciences) and human development (society), also on a global scale, this chapter first outlines the wider goals of virtual team collaboration, such as sustainability, responsibility and ethics. Next, it introduces the principles of responsible research and innovation, as a way to be more certain that one has considered the wider requirements when assessing the consequences of technology. Technological assessment, as a crucial virtual team responsibility, is discussed by means of the Collingridge Dilemma. This model (Collingridge, 1980) describes how those who develop technology might be able to foresee its future consequences. From there follows a discussion of the ethics of digital and human-machine collaboration, and the ethics of Artificial Intelligence. These issues are illustrated by means of two examples, namely robots in care and autonomous driving. Each of the aforementioned sections are concluded with recommendations to facilitate the ultimate goal of this chapter—and this book—namely to enable individual team members to make more responsible, sustainable and ethical virtual collaboration choices when navigating the impact of technology and their own role in bringing it about.

Team	A small number of individuals who collaborate in a task and/or to reach a goal.
ICTs	Information and communication technologies.
Virtual Team Collaboration	Working together as a team by means of ICTs.

11.1.1 Learning Objectives

After having read this chapter, you should

- Understand the wider requirements of virtual team collaboration, such as sustainability, responsibility and ethics, also in relation to digital technology and artificial intelligence.
- Be familiar with the concept of sustainable development that requires considering ecology (planet), society (planet) and economy (profit) in such ways that the life opportunities of future generations remain uncompromised.
- Understand the diversity demand of working towards inclusiveness and ensuring equality and/or equity in the light of relevant differences between team members.
- Know the ethical principles relevant to the responsible creation and usage of artificial intelligence and digital technology, and how to apply them
- Understand the responsible research and innovation framework as an attempt of aligning and engaging multiple stakeholders in joint efforts for creating a science and technology that benefits society, economy and ecology.
- Be familiar with the Collingridge dilemma that describes that humans cannot foresee the consequences of technology and science, in particular not the unintended ones.
- Know ways of technological assessment, in particular those that involve multiple stakeholders, as a relevant approach to handling the Collingridge dilemma.

11.1.2 Opening Case

> **Example**
>
> As technology advances, autonomous vehicles, also known as self-driving cars, are brought further into the public spotlight. Autonomous vehicles can operate without a human driver through the use of various sensors, cameras, and other technologies to navigate their environment. The development of autonomous cars has been driven

11.1 Introduction

by a desire to improve safety and increase efficiency and accessibility (Hansson et al., 2021; Stilgoe & Mladenovic, 2022). Proponents argue that autonomous vehicles could lead to a significant reduction in the number of accidents caused by human error, as well as a decrease in traffic congestion and air pollution (Stilgoe & Mladenovic, 2022).

According to international norms, there are six levels of vehicle autonomy to be differentiated (Landolt & Dähler, 2022). On Level 0, humans drive on their own; on Levels 1 and 2, the human driver is supported by driver assistant systems, such as speed control systems keeping inter-car distance (Level 1) or lanes (Level 2). From Level 3 onwards, the car starts checking and evaluating driving conditions on its own and independently executes complex functions such as changing lanes. From Level 4 onwards, the car is permanently self-steering, in certain areas and under certain conditions. Level 5 describes fully automated driving during which humans are confined to the role of passenger. Ethical implications multiply with increasing autonomy (see Figure).

Increased technological autonomy → multiplicity of ethical implications

Levels 0-1	Levels 2-3	Levels 4-5
Driver controls the car. No (Level 0) or minimal (Level 1) supportive technology	Automated functions such as acceleration and steering. Driver has to be active (and, on Level 2, must monitor conditions constantly) and be able to control the car.	Vehicle can execute all driving functions independently (on Level 4: under certain conditions). On Level 5, the car acts driverless.
Non- to minimally-automated	Assess and evaluate results	Implement solutions

← Increased human involvement

Figure Opening Case 11 Levels of vehicle autonomy. *Source* own figure

Automated driver assistant systems on Levels 2–3 are mandatory for newly built road vehicles in the European Union (European Commission, 2024) from July 2024 onwards. Features include intelligent speed assistance, reversing detection with camera or sensors, attention warning in case of driver drowsiness or distraction, event data recorders, cybersecurity and an emergency stop signal; additional features like lane-keeping systems and automated braking are required for cars and vans (ibid). The rationale behind it is to increase motor vehicle safety, as involving the safety of vehicle occupants and of vulnerable road users.

However, despite the potential benefits of driver assistant systems there are also concerns about the safety and ethics of autonomous vehicles. Since autonomous vehicles are designed to operate without human intervention by using advanced sensors, machine learning algorithms and artificial intelligence to make decisions in real time, the ethical implications are multifaceted (Hansson et al., 2021; Nyholm & Smids, 2016).

At the centre of the ethical discussion lie dilemma-like scenarios, which raise the question how autonomous vehicles should be programmed to react in scenarios in which accidents are unavoidable (Lukovics et al., 2020; Nyholm & Smids, 2016). One of the most significant challenges is determining who is responsible when the car is involved in an accident or other incident. The responsibility could either fall on the manufacturer, the programmer, or the vehicle owner (Bonnefon et al., 2016). Another ethical issue is how autonomous vehicles should prioritize different outcomes when faced with a "no-win situation". If, for example, the vehicle is about to crash into a pedestrian and an accident becomes unavoidable, should the car be programmed to prioritize the safety of the pedestrian or the safety of the vehicle's occupants?

The ethical considerations of autonomous vehicles also extend to issues of privacy and security. As self-driving cars collect and transmit vast amounts of data, concerns arise about how that data is used and who has access to it. Finally, there is also a risk of cyber-attacks that could compromise the safety of the vehicles and their passengers. For example, terrorists and other criminals could hack into a vehicle and make it crash (Hansson et al., 2021). Therefore:

Which moral principles should serve as a basis for the further development of autonomous vehicles, and how should autonomous driving technologies be regulated? ◂

11.2 The Wider Requirements of Virtual Team Collaboration

11.2.1 Sustainability as a Measuring Rod for Virtual Team Collaboration

As the opening case exemplifies, science and technology can never be developed independently of society: they have human, and sometimes also ecological, implications. Likewise, the technologies employed in virtual team collaboration change how people live, which resources are depleted and replenished, and how profitable business evolves at large.

Sustainability refers to the understanding that the needs of future generations, as well as their being free to choose their lifestyles, are not compromised by meeting the needs of the present (Brundtland, 1987). The term was first coined and further defined in 1987, in a report of the United Nations (UN) World Commission on Environment and Development entitled "our common future". Led by Gro Harlem Brundtland, the report later became known as the "Brundtland report". Subsequent global, national and corporate

11.2 The Wider Requirements of Virtual Team Collaboration

sustainable development goals, and how to achieve them, were deduced from it. For example, the trend towards e-mobility is also driven by the insight that fossil energy is not environmentally friendly and that reserves will run out eventually. Seeking to reduce fuel consumption by means of assisted or autonomous driving is then one measure towards a more sustainable development.

In its present definition, sustainability involves three pillars, also referred to as "3Ps", namely **P**eople (society), **P**rofit (economy) and **P**lanet (ecology). This then implies, for example, that an e-car to be developed by a virtual team, needs to be socially responsible (people), economically profitable (profit) and environmentally friendly (planet). This demand also refers to corporate sourcing and sales chains. For example, the lithium, cobalt and nickel used for building car batteries need to be mined in an ecologically friendly way and those employed in mining may not work in unsafe conditions depriving them of their health (people). Finally, the profits made may not only benefit present generations. For example, nowadays, an e-car is also assessed with regard to its **carbon footprint**, that is: the amount of carbon dioxide (CO_2) associated with it. This includes direct emissions (e.g., fossil fuel combustion in manufacturing) as well as indirect emissions (e.g., emissions required to produce the electricity to manufacture the car). Other greenhouse gases, such as methane, nitrous oxide, or chlorofluorocarbons (CFCs), are also often included in the carbon footprint (see Eckley Selin, 2024).

Virtual team collaboration is more sustainable in certain aspects per definition, as it might reduce the carbon footprint of commuting to work (planet). On the other hand, it also enables new modes of work, such as work-from-home or work-from-anywhere which might make it more difficult for people to distance themselves from work and result in increased (self-) exploitation (people). Whether team members find it more or less difficult to integrate work and life in sustainable and healthy ways, ultimately depends on the ways in which team processes are configured and whether team inputs and outputs are oriented towards effectiveness, efficiency and responsibility goals.

11.2.2 The Starting Point: From Shareholder to Stakeholder Value

Orienting virtual team collaboration towards sustainability, responsibility and ethics starts with the insight that virtual teams are always embedded in wider systems, such as social, economic and technological systems, or a combination thereof. For example, a company is a socio-economic system, and a corporate chat program is a socio-technical system. Systems are a combination of interrelated parts which, as a whole, are too complex in order for a single individual or single part of the system to be aware of the system as a whole or to foresee the systemic consequences of partial actions, modifications or changes. Multiple systems are embedded into each other in most cases. Part of the systemic challenge of virtual team collaboration is thus to define which systems a team is part of, contributes to and is responsible for. Two concepts have been proposed for measuring outcome, namely the narrow, performance-oriented concept of shareholder value, and the wider, sustainability- and responsibility-oriented concept of stakeholder value.

Shareholders are those who have invested money in a certain business or operations. **Shareholder value** describes the narrow, performance-oriented business concept that companies seek to maximize the return on investment of those who have invested money in the company. From this perspective, a team charged with developing a new e-car performs well if the car can be manufactured and sold on profitable terms.

Stakeholders are those groups who have an interest in a certain business or operations. Relevant stakeholders are, for example, low-cost workers, society, the environment, local communities, or consumers. From this perspective, business operations, such as building a new e-car, need to be measured against the wider societal, economic and ecological needs of maximizing **stakeholder value**, such as the requirement not to exploit local environments or global workers. A way of maximizing stakeholder value is to internalize external costs which are not considered by a company focussing on shareholder value. For example, a company polluting a lake nearby with sewage water from e-car production does not normally take the costs into account, for example, local fishers not being able to catch enough fish. Charging companies for such external costs in some ways, for example, via taxes or emission rules, is thus a way to make those who have caused the costs (the company) pay for them.

> **Background Information: The Circular Economy**
> The concept of a **circular economy** has been proposed as one model for how to reconfigure business operations in more ecological ways. The circular economy is "a model of production and consumption, which involves sharing, leasing, reusing, repairing, refurbishing and recycling existing materials and products as long as possible" (European Parliament, 2024). The practical goal is to extend product lifecycles so that waste is reduced to a minimum. Ideally, it would imply that everything is reused, and that production and consumption become fully circular. As a conceptualization, the circular economy might thus help a virtual team to become more sustainable in their operations. **Circular economy engineering** is the specific way of implementing this goal. Coupled with green controlling, it addresses both the planet and profit dimension of sustainability, which, per definition, should then also improve upon the working conditions of those involved in the value chain (people).

11.2.3 The Diversity Responsibility of Inclusive Virtual Team Collaboration

Addressing the people dimension of sustainability, the concept of **diversity** is a business concept that has gained in relevance in recent years and will further do so in the years to

11.2 The Wider Requirements of Virtual Team Collaboration

come. On a very generic level, diversity combines the insight that people are *different* in certain relevant ways, e.g. with regard to culture, age, gender, ethnicity, profession, and so on, with the need of everyone having to be *included,* e.g. in a purpose, team or organization, for higher fairness and sometimes also higher outcomes at work (see Charta der Vielfalt, 2024). The background to this argument is the insight that some individuals are historically or systemically privileged or disadvantaged because of certain diversity characteristics and thus are not judged based on their abilities and performance at work but based on the perceived status of the group into which they are categorized. For example, in many societies it used to be (and potentially still is) more likely to attend university or enter the ranks of higher management because of social class: Those whose parents already know 'how to behave' and 'who to be' have a head start in terms of how they are perceived, over those who are 'new' to these spheres. This then contradicts the business idea of meritocracy upon which 'fairness' at work is based, namely the idea that the employee who is more capable and performs better will be promoted over others (Castilla & Benard, 2010).

The goal of the difference-inclusion relations described by the term diversity is higher *equality or equity*. Equality refers more to giving people equal opportunities whereas equity refers more to people's equal opportunity to participate, and both are used when defining and managing diversity. Sometimes, creating a level playing field means to overcome bias and treat everyone equally, sometimes, it requires supporting some employees more than others to ensure equity, as in the case of a visually impaired employee who needs special equipment or conditions for being able to perform as well as a visually non-impaired employee in virtual collaboration. Together, these three terms—*difference, equality/equity* and *inclusion*—describe the work-related phenomenon of *diversity*; the best possible ('fairest') configuration of their interrelations is the envisaged outcome of managing diversity at work.

Why is mastering diversity an integral part of successful virtual team collaboration?

First, virtual teams are characterized by difference in multiple relevant ways: Members might differ in terms of discipline, profession, location, workplace conditions, cultures, whether they work from home or not, how technologically motivated and skilled they are, how they integrate work and life, and many more. These virtual team-related factors come on top on general diversity categories that shape how people experience work and life and are perceived by others, such as age, gender and gender identity, world view and religion, race, ethnicity, nationality, ability, and sexual orientation and identity. Diversity complexity in virtual team collaboration is thus much higher than in non-virtual team collaboration.

Second, virtual team collaboration requires more active trust building than non-virtual team collaboration. Because virtual teams necessarily collaborate via Information and Communication Technologies (ICTs), their experiences of each other are leaner. It is then more difficult to relate to each other and to build trust which, due to ICT leanness, is more relevant for a virtual team to perform well. Inclusive team cultures need to be built and maintained as a counter-measure. Addressing relevant diversity in conducive ways is therefore more crucial to virtual team performance than to non-virtual team performance.

Also, virtual teams are characterized by higher dispersion in many ways, which then multiplies the 'difference' which they experience. For instance, because most virtual teams are employed for interdisciplinary or cross-functional tasks, no single team member possesses full knowledge or expertise. Team members also work from different locations and much of what they know and do is 'hidden' to others. Therefore, team members need to share and distribute key leadership functions such as learning, delegation and motivation amongst each other for the overall team to achieve its goals: They need to counterbalance their experiences of 'difference' by means of inclusive actions.

Consequently, diversity is not a luxury item of virtual team collaboration: it is one of the major constitutive factors of what makes a successful team.

11.2.4 What are Virtual Teams and Their Individual Members Responsible for?

One might argue that single teams, always being placed in wider organizational frameworks and systems, do not have the agency to define their own goals. However, such an approach neglects the fact that most virtual teams are charged with knowledge-intensive, white-collar work, often in industrialized and high income countries, and that some of them, in particular global virtual teams, are even of strategic importance: they have the power to make decisions that change how their business affects weaker, more removed stakeholders. For example, a single programmer responsible for one part of an e-car's autonomous driving system, is free to make decisions when programming their part of the system. When foreseeing the driving system's functionality, it is thus relevant that they not only focus on when and how the technology is profitable in cost-related terms but also whether the technology is to the wider good of those using it—now and in the future.

For example, the raw materials to manufacture PCs and other technological equipment might be linked to the unsustainable mining of rare earths and other materials, and the low-cost workers manufacturing or refurbishing said equipment might work under inhumane or unsafe conditions. No individual team member and no single team can determine how the global economy impacts upon these stakeholders and resources in positive or negative ways. However, every individual team member *contributes* to this configuration. Virtual team members, and their team processes, are therefore both products and producers of the wider systems they are a part of and are thus not free of responsibility: Together, their actions *make* the global economy.

Responsibility means to acknowledge the consequences of one's actions, also for others, and to take them into account in the sense that one tries to foresee the negative consequences of one's actions before engaging in them. For example, a responsible team management takes team members' physical and psychological health into account and prevents over-exploitation. Or, on a wider level, companies need to acknowledge their responsibility for human well-being at large: if intensity, quantity and pace of work leave no time and energy for care work, then either humanity will cease to reproduce (in order to work) or qualified potential workers will not seek employment in order to do care work.

Corporate social responsibility (CSR) encompasses the economic, legal, ethical and philanthropic expectation that societies have of organizations (Carroll, 1979). The specific understanding and the drivers of CSR might differ depending on region, country and community. According to Visser (2011), the most important 'glocal' drivers of CSR are cultural tradition, political reform, socio-economic priorities, governance gaps and crisis response. This means that teams and organizations wishing to pursue CSR goals should not simply execute what society, politics or legal requirements demand but also ask themselves which ideas and measurements of CSR are sustainable. For instance, what sustainable development goals and which responsibility criteria should disciplines such as electrical engineering or computer programming be measured against?

When asking this question, it is important to note that responsibility and sustainability, which are often seen as an obstacle to efficient and effective return on investments, are not always in contradiction to performance in the narrow sense. For example, as argued by Porter and van der Linde (1995), the relations between the three pillars of sustainability are not necessarily a trade-off, in which an increased effort to achieve, for example, environmental sustainability, inherently will come at the cost of, for example, the economic sustainability of a company's profits. Rather, if one takes a more long-term outlook, both can be mutually enriching. For example, innovations triggered by environmental regulations may not only advance the ecology but also increase corporate productivity which, in the long run, leads to more, not less, economic competitiveness. Also, regulatory frameworks often support the integration of business and wider human goals. For example, in Horizon 2020—the most important framework program for research and innovation in the European Union (EU)—the priority of research and innovation lies on mastering grand challenges, such as climate change or the demographic shift (European Commission, 2011). Responsibility and sustainability therefore provide virtual teams and organizations with a measuring rod for the last phase of the digital transformation (see Chap. 2), namely an answer to the question of how new modes of work and business might be beneficial to societies, long-term development and the planet at large. Taking responsibility for these wider aspects of one's work is part of the contemporary management and professional challenge, also on the level of teams.

Link to Practice: The Need for Inclusive and Fair Facial Recognition Software

Facial recognition software is an example of a technology that calls for responsible development. The software used needs to be trained for recognizing facial features and, if the training data used for development is biased or lacks diversity, the algorithms used can result in unequal outcomes for individuals with different skin colours.

For example, if the algorithm has mainly been trained on data from lighter-skinned individuals, it may struggle to accurately recognize people with darker skin tones. Buolamwini and Gebru (2018) identified these effects for three facial-analysis programs from major technology companies. They found gender as well as skin-type bias: The software´s error rates were never over 0.8% for light-skinned men, but up to 34.7% for dark-skinned women. Along with other studies (e.g. Raji & Buolamwini, 2023; Rhue, 2018), this proves that facial recognition software development suffers from biases, in this case: a combined gender and racial bias, and those developing these technologies need to work towards higher inclusiveness and user fairness. ◀

Of course, virtual team collaboration takes place in more or less 'ethical' organizational environments. Therefore, teams also have to pay attention to those influencing factors which make it so much harder to establish team ethics, and inclusive and responsible collaboration practices. Commonly known root causes for unethical behaviour are:

- An **organizational culture** that emphasizes business over ethics.
- A **decision making process** that does not incorporate ethics: at a certain point, the question of ethics has to be part of the project-plan, the team's checklist or the formal mechanisms and procedures.
- **Personal ethics**: Team members and leaders who are neither guided by an own moral compass nor seek to further develop this compass.
- **Unrealistic performance goals** which put team members and leaders under pressure and lead to a conflict between business goals and ethics as well as their own moral compass.
- A **leadership** which does not set an ethical example for followers.

As this list suggests, ethics in practice are always a combination of organizational system and structure, what is done by most and what individuals and teams seek to achieve. Simply saying that one cannot change the system is too easy an answer, however, it is also true that not every unethical system can be changed (easily). The matter of ethics is further complicated in virtual team collaboration by the need to reflect upon technology, and how it is used and applied.

Application 11.1: What is Diversity, and How do Equity and Inclusion Affect Me and Others?

Research the Charta der Vielfalt (Diversity Charter, https://www.charta-der-vielfalt.de/en/) online.

- What is it, and what does it involve?
- What is the difference between equality and equity?—Explain with the help of examples.

- How is inclusion relevant to people at work, you yourself included? Explain with the help of examples.

Write down your insights and exchange with others. If you find that others have found a similar or different relevance of the Charta der Vielfalt and/or understand key terms and diversity goals similarly or differently: what could be reasons for this being the case? ◄

11.3 The Ethics of Digital Collaboration and Artificial Intelligence

11.3.1 Ethical Principle of Digital Collaboration

Digital media and social networks allow for new forms of digital collaboration and global connectivity which are not without risks (Gohl, 2015; Müller, 2022). **Ethics of digital collaboration** are those moral principles which have been proposed for guiding the responsible use of digital technologies and communication tools (Belliger & Krieger, 2022). They involve considerations regarding technology use, data privacy, security, social impact, and how information is constructed in the digital world, e.g. in terms of its reliability (Becker et al., 2023; Burr et al., 2020). There are furthermore digital ethics for particular areas like 'the ethics of AI', 'data ethics' or 'robot ethics' (Müller, 2022). The general purpose of digital ethics is not only to describe the present, but also to also anticipate future developments. Figure 11.1 highlights the major principles of the ethics of digital collaboration.

As Fig. 11.1 visualizes, ethical considerations for digital collaboration include several key aspects.

- **Privacy and safeguarding data security**. The security of digital systems needs to be ensured to protect sensitive information from unauthorized access, theft or misuse (Ess, 2009; Himma & Tavani, 2008). According to the European Data Protection Supervisor (EDPS), the right to data protection may seem to be key to regulating the digitalized world, yet, there are many further ethical challenges, such as digital discrimination (see section ethics of AI).
- **Transparency in decision making and processes**. This is crucial to maintaining transparency regarding the use of digital tools and technologies (Belliger & Krieger, 2022; Floridi, 2019). Algorithmic transparency and accountability also connect to the freedom of access, which can nowadays be considered a fundamental ethical principle, similar to freedom of speech and the press (EDPS, 2018).
- **Fairness and Equality**, as new forms of algorithmic discrimination pose a risk to the equality of opportunity. For example, when hiring is done by means of an AI, this AI matches new applicants to the criteria of previous applicants to establish 'fit'

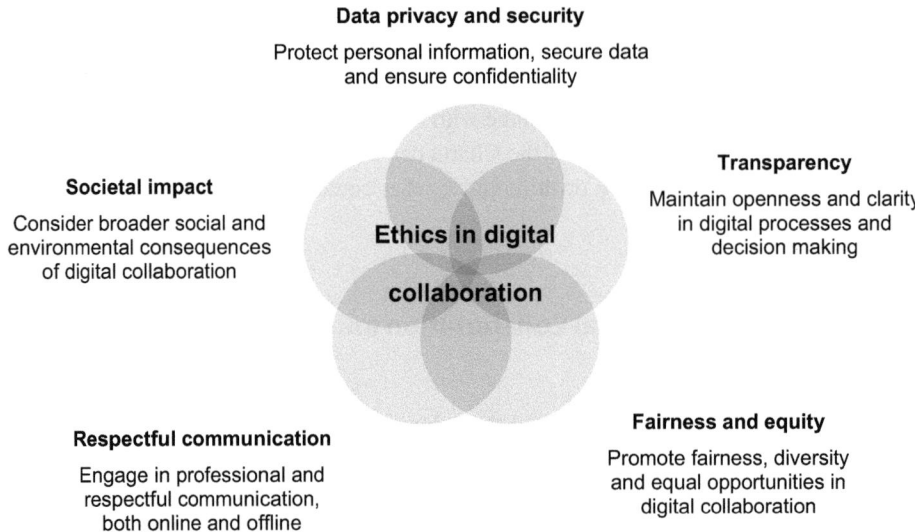

Fig. 11.1 Key principles of ethics in digital collaboration. *Source* own figure

and might come up with potentially discriminatory items such as 'active soccer club member' as an indicator for 'team player at work' which then advantages able-bodied applicants over others. Therefore, eliminating discriminatory practices or biases in collaboration based on gender, race, religion, sexual orientation, or other characteristics are a key aspect of digital ethics (Becker et al., 2023; Criado & Such, 2019; Floridi, 2019).

- Fostering **respectful and inclusive communication** is another key principle. This is established by means of 'netiquettes' for using digital communication tools (Kurtzberg, 2014; Morrison-Smith & Ruiz, 2020).
- Finally, when using digital collaboration technologies, their **broader societal impact** should also be considered. This includes efforts in e.g. minimizing negative impacts on the environment or society (Belliger & Krieger, 2022).

By adhering to ethical principles in digital collaboration, individuals and organizations can harness the full potential of digital collaboration while upholding fundamental values like integrity, trust, respect, and fairness. Ethical digital collaboration therefore ensures a responsible and respectful engagement with the digital work landscape and contributes to a more equitable and sustainable society.

Application 11.2: Digital Ethics for Virtual Team Collaboration

Form groups of three to five students. Imagine you need to work together as a virtual team: Create a set of rules and guidelines for working together and rank them in order of perceived importance. The key principles illustrated in Fig. 11.1 may help to guide you through this task. Take notes on your discussion process and its outcome. Afterwards, share your thoughts in class and compare your process and outcome with the other groups. ◄

11.3.2 The Ethical Principles of Artificial Intelligence

Artificial Intelligence (AI) is believed to offer a variety of potential advantages, such as reducing costs, and minimizing human error and risk. However, AI also brings about various ethical concerns (Stahl et al., 2023), such as the ones raised by the development of autonomous vehicles, as described in the opening case. Furthermore, several studies show that AI does not work equally for every individual, which undermines its accuracy (Fernández-Martínez & Fernández, 2020). This can result in **digital discrimination**, that is: a situation in which users are treated unfairly, unethically or simply differently based on how their personal data and characteristics (e.g. income, education, gender, age, ethnicity or religion) are automatically processed by an algorithm (Criado & Such, 2019; O'Neil, 2016). For example, emotional recognition software may not consider different intonations or expressions of emotions across cultures (Fernández-Martínez & Fernández, 2020). Furthermore, since a user is not able to engage in a discussion with the AI as they could with a human interlocutor, an asymmetrical communicative relationship evolves (also see Chap. 4), with the user being confined to the standard set within the technology (Royakkers et al., 2018; Spahn, 2012).

> **Link to Practice: The Gender Bias of Artificial Intelligence**
>
> AIs need to be trained with data, and this can lead to bias, for example, when the AI makes hiring decisions (Criado & Such, 2019). This issue is exemplified by a hiring algorithm by Amazon, which (in its test mode) discriminated against women by assigning lower scores to resumes of women when ranking candidates. The reason was purely technological: since the algorithm had been trained on data of current top performers, of which the majority were male, female attributes were underscored (Hunkenschroer & Luetge, 2022; Stahl et al., 2023). ◄

Biases can impact upon the interaction at any technological state. Next to bias in the training data, Yarger et al. (2020) named two other factors that may lead to biases, such as bias in the model design principles and bias in the feature selection. An example for a biased design is a job platform that focuses only on who is most likely to click on the job ad. Consequently, stereotypes can be perpetuated, as proven by a study revealing that targeted ads on Facebook for supermarket cashier positions were displayed to an audience composed of 85% women (Bogen, 2019). To prevent discrimination, moral value dimensions need to integrated into AI development at all stages (Dignum, 2018). The UNE-

SCO therefore concludes that addressing bias in AI requires a multi-faceted approach. Firstly, it is essential to ensure that the training data is diverse, representative, and free from bias. Furthermore, transparency and accountability in design and implementation of AI systems are crucial. Regular audits and evaluations of AI tools to identify and reduce any biases are recommended (UNESCO, 2022). Figure 11.2 provides an overview on the ethical principles of AI.

Different **regulatory frameworks** have been put in place for promoting the ethical principles of AI (Stahl et al., 2023). Within the European Union (EU), the "Artificial Intelligence Act" came into effect in 2021 (European Parliament, 2023a, b). It covers aspects like transparency, accountability, safety, and fundamental rights. For example, the use of AI for evaluating individuals based on their social behaviour or personality traits, if leading to discrimination, is prohibited (Tagesschau, 2022). In May 2023, the European Parliament followed up with an update of the AI act: The rules to ensure a human-centric and ethical approach to AI development prohibit AI practices that pose high risks to people's safety or involve discriminatory uses. High risk AI areas were expanded to include health, safety, fundamental rights, environment, and political campaigns. However, the regulations also support AI innovation by providing exemptions for research activities and open-source licenses (European Parliament, 2023a, b). Another notable regulatory framework includes UNESCO's "Recommendation on the Ethics of AI", which aims at providing a universal framework of values, principles and actions to guide the formulation of national legislation or policies regarding AI, consistent with international law. It has been adopted by 193 countries as of November 2021 (UNESCO, 2022).

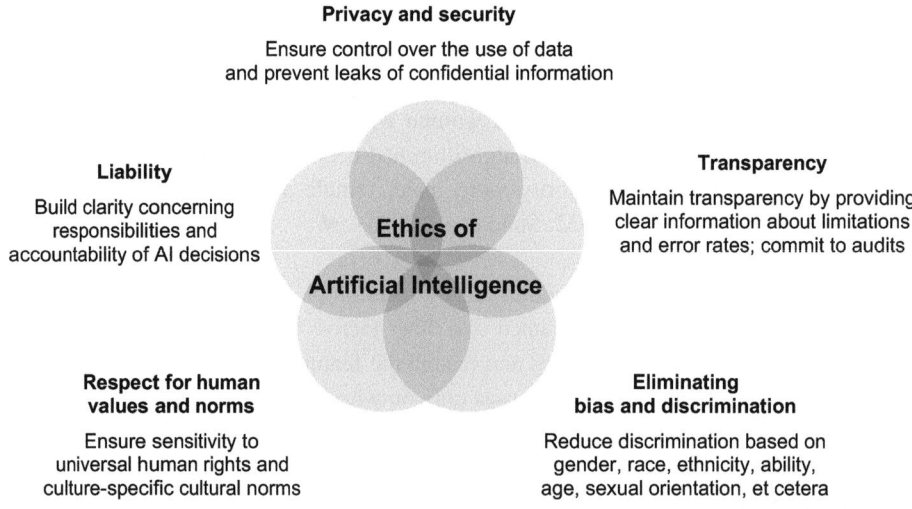

Fig. 11.2 Key principles of the ethics of artificial intelligence. *Source* own figure

> **Application 11.3: The Ethical Issues of Artificial Intelligence**
>
> The practical examples in this chapter have presented ethical issues associated with gender and racial biases in AI. Gather in small groups and think about:
>
> - Which other real-life case examples of ethical issues associated with Artificial Intelligence have you heard of and/or can you imagine?
> - Which rules or technological advancements would be needed to avoid these issues?
>
> Take notes on your discussion process and its outcome. Afterwards, share your thoughts in class and compare your process and outcome to the other groups. ◄

11.4 Responsible Research and Innovation

11.4.1 What is Responsible Research and Innovation, and Why do we Need it?

The concept of Responsible Research and Innovation (RRI) is relatively new. After having appeared at the beginning of the twenty-first century, it was adopted by the European Union a few years later (Blok & Lemmens, 2015; Declich et al., 2022; Fisher & Rip, 2013). The roots of RRI are multidisciplinary, but the definition by Von Schomberg (2013, p. 63) is the most widely accepted one. RRI is a "transparent, interactive process by which societal actors and innovators become mutually responsive to each other with a view to [ethical] acceptability, sustainability and societal desirability of the innovation process and its marketable product (…)". From this perspective, responsible innovation not only provides solutions concerning innovation outcomes, but also considers innovation processes (Stilgoe et al., 2013; van der Duin, 2019). The definition implies that RRI assigns an important role to the cooperation of innovation stakeholders (European Commission, 2011). The main goal of the public engagement with RRI is to better manage the relations between science (technology) and society (humans) (Declich et al., 2022). Figure 11.3 provides an overview on the RRI framework.

As Fig. 11.3 shows, RRI is a proactive and interdisciplinary approach that integrates the natural and social sciences to handle innovation challenges responsibly. It explicitly requires integrating ethical, social and environmental considerations into daily research & innovation (R&I) decisions and to share information on technological development in a transparent manner. RRI is mainly relevant with regard to emerging technologies such as nanotechnology, synthetic biology, Information and Communication Technologies (ICT) and neurotechnology. (Srinivas, 2022), the future consequences of which cannot yet been foreseen. Debates about an inadequate integration of RRI include, for instance, controversies around nuclear power and genetically modified agriculture (Lukovics, et al., 2020). In the case of autonomous vehicles, too, an in-depth consideration of algo-

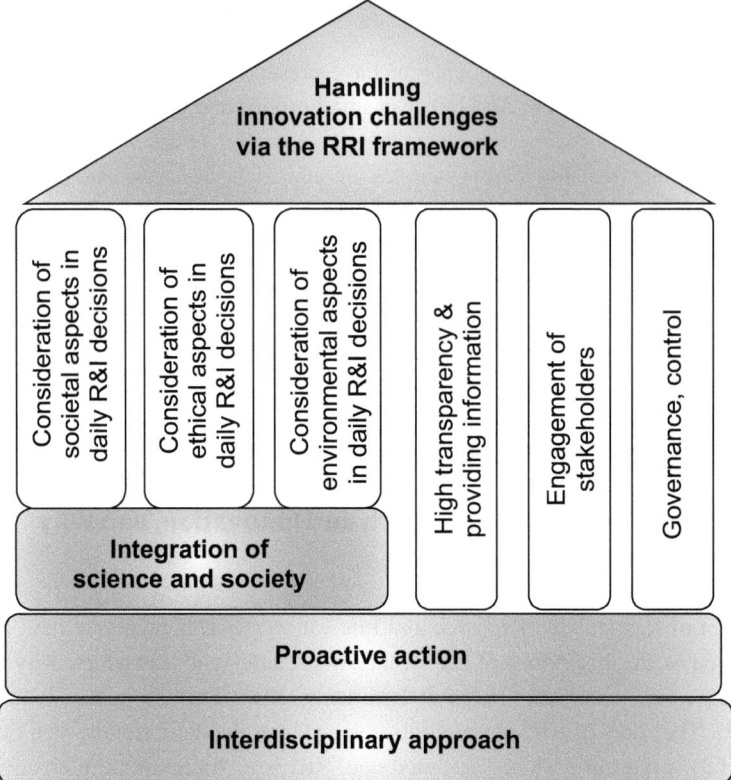

Fig. 11.3 The rationale, pillars and outcomes of the RRI framework. *Source* own figure, based on Lukovics et al. (2020)

rithmic morality, continuous dialogue and ethical reflection among stakeholders are of utmost importance: It is the only way to guarantee that technology is created and implemented in a manner that maximizes benefits while minimizing potential harm (Bonnefon et al., 2016).

11.4.2 Stakeholder Engagement as a Crucial Process

Stakeholder engagement is key to responsible innovation (Koops, 2015; von Schomberg, 2013), as cross-sector partnerships are likely to lead to the most innovative and responsible solutions (Eweje, 2007). Relevant stakeholders are, for example, educators, policy makers, researchers, business and industry, and civil society organizations. The six key areas for which the European Commission (2011) has identified a relevant contribution by science to society or, in other words: a scientific responsibility to meet societal

11.4 Responsible Research and Innovation

demands, are: public engagement, gender equality, scientific education, ethics in science (understood as adherence to basic human rights and ethical standards of the EU), open science (to ensure the availability of innovation to everyone), and governance. To promote advancements in these areas, stakeholders should anticipate each other's actions, strive for diversity and inclusion, be transparent and mutually responsive (Stilgoe et al., 2013; Wittrock et al., 2021), and work towards the reduction of information asymmetries (Blok & Lemmens, 2015). Figure 11.4 visualizes this understanding.

The application of RRI is difficult to achieve in practice due to conflicting stakeholder world views and interests. Also, as Blok and Lemmens (2015) find, the required transparency and mutual responsiveness among stakeholders may be called naïve, since, for example, competitive advantage is *based* on the very information asymmetries which RRI seeks to reduce. Taking a more positive view, Lukovics et al (2020) argue that RRI will not be able to solve all challenges automatically, but *could* be effective if the active processual participation of all stakeholders is ensured: Ultimately, RRI is what all stakeholders make of it, as RRI means to integrate wider responsibilities into one's daily R&I decisions by asking how the innovation process might affect society and its stakeholders.

Relating back to the opening case, Table 11.1 illustrates how the development of autonomous cars can become more responsible by applying the previously identified RRI key elements. Obviously, this is a very simplified depiction, but it can nonetheless help increase awareness and develop more responsible R&I practices.

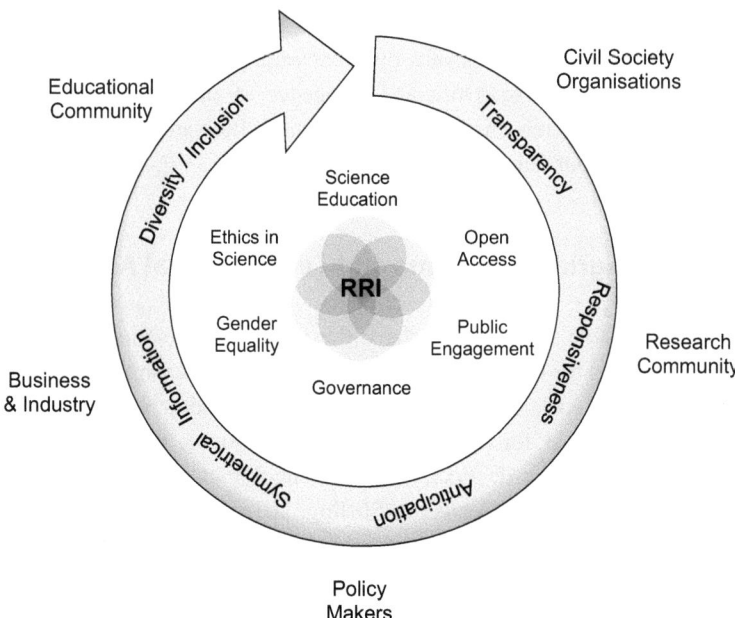

Fig. 11.4 RRI as a multi-stakeholder collaboration process. *Source* own figure

Table 11.1 Managing the challenges of autonomous driving via the RRI framework

Stakeholder implications of self-driving cars	RRI key areas and recommended actions
• Societal division	**Public Engagement, Gender Equality** Considerations of societal aspects in daily decisions by innovators
• Lack of information and trust in automation • Fear of technological failures	**Scientific Education, Open Access** High levels of transparency, education of the public as well as of the scientific community
• Uncertainty of medium & long-term impact on the environment	**Public engagement & ethics** Considerations of environmental aspects in daily decisions by innovators and in supply chains
• The "decisions" of cars in emergency situations • Interaction with other traffic partners	**Ethics** Considerations of ethical aspects in daily decisions by innovators
• Immaturity of the regulatory environment • Uncertainty regarding legal liability	**Government** Governance, control and further development of legal aspects

Source own figure, based on Lukovics et al. (2020)

> **Application 11.4: Managing Challenges in Innovation Through RRI**
>
> Form groups of three to five students. Discuss stakeholder implications, RRI key areas and recommended actions of a different example than autonomous cars based on Table 11.1. You may use Artificial Intelligence as an example, or come up with your own idea. Provide reasons for your decisions. Afterwards, share your thoughts in class and compare your outcome to the other groups. ◄

11.5 The Collingridge Dilemma and Technological Assessment

Being hardly predictable, technologies have the potential to "seriously impact society, for the good as well as for the bad" (van de Poel, 2016). For example, smartphone technology has unexpected social impacts such as smartphone addiction, the encouragement of (cyber-)bullying or a risk for mental health issues in young adults (Gowthami & Venkatakrishnakumar, 2016; van de Poel, 2011). Technological error is therefore an unavoidable part of being human (Genusa & Stirling, 2018) and thus a major challenge of responsible technological innovation.

11.5.1 The Collingridge Dilemma

The **Collingridge dilemma**, also known as the "dilemma of control" (Kudina & Verbeek, 2019; Genusa & Stirling, 2018) describes the problem of trying to control the impact of technology on society. It is named after David Collingridge, who first articulated it in his book *The Social Control of Technology* in 1980. According to Collingridge (1980), "attempting to control a technology is difficult (…) because during its early stages, when it can be controlled, not enough can be known about its harmful social consequences to warrant controlling its development; but by the time these consequences are apparent, control has become costly and slow". In other words, the problem consists of how to make decisions during an innovation process without it either being too early for its consequences to be known or too late to guide the development into a desirable direction (Köhler & Som, 2014; Kudina & Verbeek, 2019; Shelley-Egan & Davies, 2013). During the later stages of a technology's lifecycle it becomes increasingly difficult to control the impact of technology on society, since the variety of options decreases as society adapts to the technology or even becomes dependent on it. This societal dependence upon technology is referred to as socio-economic lock-in effect or **entrenchment** (Köhler & Som, 2014). For example, most moral dilemmas associated with autonomous vehicles exist because it is too early for the technological consequences to be known. Conversely, the further development of the nuclear fusion reactor can no longer be guided into alternative directions because society, economy, investment and infrastructure are already 'locked in'.

> **Practical Example: The 3D Printer**
>
> The 3D printer as a technological innovation was intended to make life easier by being able to print small three-dimensional plastic objects at home. It later turned out that also medical equipment and other, highly useful objects, could be printed in 3D at much lower costs, with tremendous sustainable development benefits, for example, for lower-income countries. Open access to the technology, that is: having the blueprints available on the internet, is highly relevant for these applications, as also suggested by the Responsible Research and Innovation (RRI) framework (see Sect. 11.4). However, in 2013, there was also the first shot fired by a gun printed by a 3D-printer in the US (Walther, 2015). This illustrates the implication of the Collingridge dilemma—once a file is out for a few days, it is available online forever (Walther, 2015) and the misuse can hardly be tackled anymore. At the same time, not making the technology accessible would also impede its unforeseen beneficial usages, such as the printing of medical equipment. ◄

There are both information and power problems associated with the Collingridge dilemma: the impact of technology cannot be easily predicted until the technology is extensively developed and widely used. However, control or change is difficult when the technology has become irreversible entrenched. A related problem is the so-called **pacing effect**, which describes the insight that technological development is usually faster-paced than the development of policy, and that technology tends to be developed or made available prior to policy being in place. For example, the technologies of autonomous vehicles developed earlier and faster than the principles and policies regulating them. Figure 11.5 visualizes the Collingridge dilemma, the associated pacing effect, and the combined consequences over time.

> **Application 11.5: Transferring the Collingridge Dilemma to Current Innovations**
>
> Think about a current innovation in technology which is still at the beginning of its 'lifecycle'. (One possible example could be the use of AI tools for research, knowledge gathering or learning, such as open access chat or translation tools.
>
> - Which negative societal impacts could possibly arise when the innovation has been widely accepted and entrenched in society?
> - Which measures could be taken now in order to prevent these possible dangers from happening?
>
> Discuss in small groups and take notes on your discussion process and its outcome. Afterwards, share your thoughts in class and compare your process and outcome to the other groups. ◀

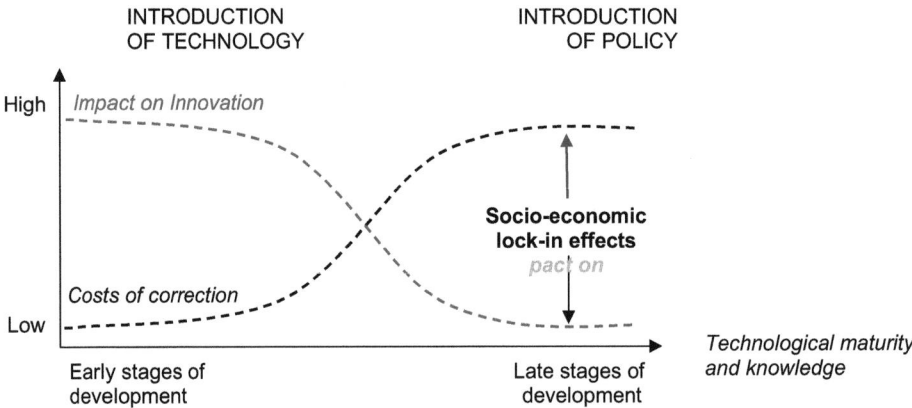

Fig. 11.5 The Collingridge dilemma, pacing effects, and consequences over time. *Source* own illustration, based on Malanowski (2017)

11.5.2 Technological Assessment as a Way of Handling the Collingridge Dilemma

Technological Assessment (TA) is a concept that was first developed in the United States in the late 1960's, when largescale technological adoption started to (noticeably) affect society (Berloznik & van Langenhove, 1998; Tran, 2007; van der Duin, 2019). Technological Assessment is a way of handling the Collingridge Dilemma. It describes a systematic attempt to foresee and evaluate the unintended, indirect or delayed societal consequences of technological introduction, modification or extension (Braun, 2005; Gloede, 2007; Banta, 2009). Relevant contemporary applications are, for example, information technology, hydrogen technologies, nuclear technology, molecular nanotechnology, pharmacology, organ transplants, gene technology, artificial intelligence, and the World Wide Web. TA is based on two convictions: Firstly, that new developments and discoveries by the scientific community are relevant for the whole world rather than just for the scientists themselves, and secondly, that technological progress can never be free of ethical implications (Banta, 2009). Besides assessing the effects, consequences and risks of a technology, TA also wishes to provide forecasts for strategic planning, for example, in order to minimize negative pacing effects, such as safety regulations lagging behind the technologies of autonomous vehicles. Ideally, TA is related to all three sustainability pillars (people, planet profit), thus taking social, economic *and* ecological criteria into account (Henriksen, 1997; Mazurkiewicz et al., 2015). Figure 11.6 provides a generalized overview on the three main phases of a TA process.

In practice, one may discern different modes of Technical Assessment. They differ with regard to which stakeholders they involve, and how. In other words, the main differentiation is the extent to which the TA is conducted within a Responsible Research & Innovation (RRI) framework that considers science as interrelated with society or whether the TA is limited to solely or mainly to the field of science.

- The "traditional" concept is the **expert TA**, wherein the assessment is carried out by experts. Input from stakeholders and other actors is included only via written statements, documents and interviews. This is insufficient from an RRI perspective.
- Adding to the previous, **participatory TA (pTA)** also involves the input of social actors as stakeholders of RRI. pTA methods e.g. include focus groups, scenario workshops and consensus conferences (Van Eijndhoven, 1997).
- **Constructive TA (CTA)** aims at addressing social issues around technology via involving users in the development and innovation process. Often, the focus is on technology design (Konrad et al., 2017; Schot & Rip, 1997), and there is a link to the human-technology interaction which lies at the heart of virtual team collaboration (see Chap. 10).
- Lastly, **parliamentary TA (PTA)** involves TA activities that provides scientific policy advice to parliament as a key policy maker and stakeholder of regulations and public

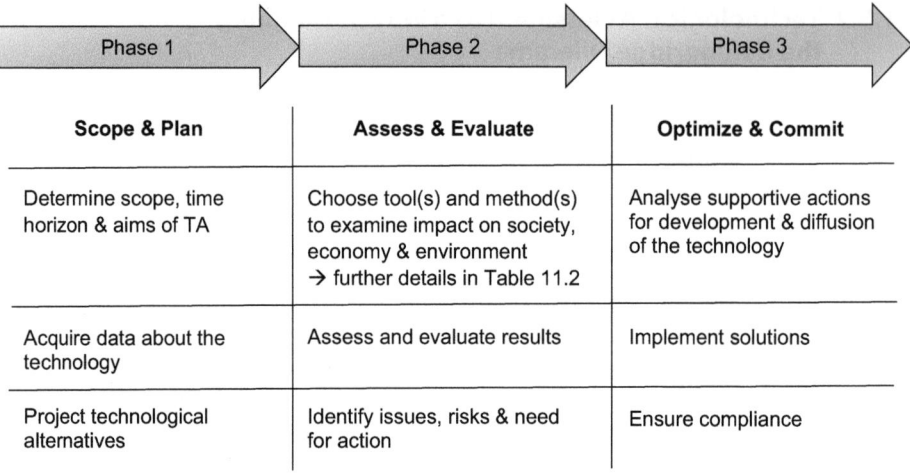

Fig. 11.6 The three main phases of the technological assessment process. *Source* own figure

engagement (Nentwich, 2016). For example, in Germany, the Office of Technology Assessment at the German Parliament has existed since 1990 (Grunwald et al., 2012).

There is wide range of tools and method for conducting TA in practice, in particular during Phase 2 (see Fig. 11.6). The most relevant ones are presented in Table 11.2.

Application 11.5: Conducting a Theoretical Technological Assessment

Form groups of three to five students. Using the example of autonomous vehicles, plan how a (simplified) technological assessment could be conducted. Consider the following aspects for this:

- Which tools and methods would you choose for the TA, and why?
- Which issues do you expect to arise?
- Which supportive actions for a socially, environmentally and economically beneficial development of autonomous vehicles can you think of?

Note your discussion process and its outcome. Afterwards, share your thoughts in class and compare your process and outcome to the other groups. ◄

Table 11.2 Tools and methods for technological assessment

Tool	Exemplary methods
Economic analysis	• Cost benefit analysis • Return on investment • Breakeven point analysis
Decision analysis	• Scoring model • Group decision support systems, e.g. Delphi
Systems analysis	• Simulation modelling & analysis • Systems optimization techniques
Technology forecasting	• Trend extrapolation • Probabilistic methods
Information monitoring	• Literature reviews • Electronic database, Internet
Technical performance assessment	• Statistical analysis • Trial use periods
Risk assessment	• Simulation modelling and analysis
Market analysis	• Market push/pull analysis • Surveys/Questionnaires
Externalities/Impact analysis	• Business environment analysis • Life cycle analysis

Source own figure, derived from Henriksen (1997) and Tran (2007)

11.6 Closing Part

11.6.1 Chapter Summary

This chapter has discussed the wider requirements of virtual team collaboration. These involve the need to contribute to a sustainable development, to collaborate inclusively and ensure the equity of diverse team members, and to engage in responsible research and innovation. For these wider goals to be achieved, team members and leaders need to develop a sense of ethics, work towards a more ethical and responsible organization, leadership and business system, and to also apply ethical considerations to digital technology, artificial intelligence and human-technology interactions. A key element is the understanding of how to handle the Collingridge dilemma which describes how humans can never fully control technology, particularly not its unintended consequences. Nonetheless, there are various modes of technological assessment which can minimize the issue and those which view science and technology in relation to society, economy, ecology and politics and involve multiple stakeholders are the most promising for handling the Collingridge dilemma responsibly. After having engaged with this chapter, you have brought your virtual team collaboration skills to the next level of an inclusive, responsible and sustainable development, and you know how to contribute to these wider human and technological goals in your everyday work life. To complete this learning cycle, you could now read the previous chapters of this book again, applying what you now know to be the ultimate considerations and goals of virtual team collaboration for a better future.

> **Pause and Reflect: Where will the Evolution of Artificial Intelligence go?**
>
> Where will the ongoing AI revolution bring us to? Andreas Dengel, managing director of the German Research Centre for Artificial Intelligence (DFKI), forecasts the following evolution (Kretschmer, 2024): He names financial accounting and biotechnology as high potential applications. AI could be used, for instance, to trace money laundering or test medical agents. Dengel also expects AI to become sustainable, that is: to be able to function and learn without the vast amounts of energy currently required, but also to be increasingly applied to questions of sustainability. Climate research could be one application area. Furthermore, Dengel finds that AI tools become more integrated into other applications or interconnected with numerous tools, and he also forecasts an increased AI multi-modality, or, in other words: an increased richness of the virtual worlds created by means of AI. Facing this future: How will *you* make use of AI, and how will your lived experiences be shaped by it, perhaps even involuntarily? ◄

11.6.2 Key Points

- Technological change and digital transformation involve wider questions of responsibility, sustainability and ethics.
- From a wider perspective, stakeholder value, not shareholder value, is relevant to virtual team collaboration.
- Sustainable development requires considering ecology (planet), society (planet) and economy (profit) in such ways that the life opportunities of future generations remain uncompromised.
- Diversity means to work towards inclusiveness and to ensure equality and/or equity in the light of difference.
- The responsible creation and usage of artificial intelligence and digital technology require the development and application of ethical principles.
- The responsible research and innovation framework is an attempt of aligning and engaging multiple stakeholders in joint efforts for creating a science and technology that benefits society, economy and ecology.
- The Collingridge dilemma describes that humans cannot foresee the consequences of technology and science, in particular not the unintended ones.
- Technological assessment is a way of handling the Collingridge dilemma, albeit an incomplete one.

11.6.3 Review Questions

1. Why and how is sustainability a measuring rod for virtual team collaboration?
2. What is circular economy engineering, and how is it related to the need for a sustainable development which also underlies virtual team collaboration?
3. What is the diversity responsibility of virtual team collaboration, and how is it related to the need for a sustainable development?
4. In summary: What are virtual teams and their individual members responsible for?
5. What is meant by the ethics of digital collaboration, and why and how are these relevant to a sustainable development in general and to virtual team collaboration in particular?
6. What is meant by the ethics of artificial intelligence, and why and how are these relevant to a sustainable development in general and to virtual team collaboration in particular?
7. What is the responsible research and innovation framework, what are its rationale, pillars and intended outcomes, and which issues does it attempt to handle and improve upon?
8. Why and how is stakeholder engagement crucial to a responsible, inclusive and sustainable virtual team collaboration?
9. Which issues are described by means of the Collingridge Dilemma, and how is the concept, and the insights emerging from it, relevant to virtual team collaboration?
10. Which types of Technological Assessment do you know, and which seem more or less useful for a responsible, inclusive and sustainable development, and why?

Opening Case Revisited

The opening case has introduced ethical dilemmas associated with self-driving cars. In pairs of two, first conduct research in your country of residence and/or relevant supra-national unit (e.g. the European Union). Find out how driver assistance systems are regulated in the relevant country or supra-national unit. Next, create a visual (e.g. a mind map) that connects your research to the following concepts:

- Responsible Research and Innovation
- The Collingridge Dilemma
- Technology Assessment

Make sure to consider this chapter's content when doing so.

Afterwards, share your thoughts in class and compare your outcome with the other groups.

Closing Activity: Is Technology Good or Bad?

Group with at least three other students, ideally more. Organize a public debate on the question: '**Is technology good or bad?**' Imagine that this question is discussed in parliament or any other decision making body. An equal number of you will speak for technology (technology is good), and against technology (technology is bad). Each of you has five minutes, and, in each round, a pro speaker should be followed by a con speaker, until everyone has put forward their arguments.

Draw lots in order to assign speakers, including yourself, to the pro or con side. When you engage in this activity, it is relevant that you do proper research in advance, in order to come up with relevant arguments for your side of the coin, and that you also back up your speech with notes and visualizations, e.g. slides, to be shown to the audience. Apply knowledge from this chapter to develop and make your point. Assume that social media is a part of technology and make sure to define what you mean by 'technology' when putting forward your argument. Research the internet for exemplary videos on the so called "Oxbridge Debate" in order to understand how such a debate might evolve and how an argument should be put forward.

Prior to the speakers presenting their arguments, let the audience vote on whether technology is good or bad from a cross-cultural perspective. Afterwards, let the audience vote again. Both times, note the outcome and reflect upon it and the potential difference between the pre- and post-activity vote.

References

Banta, D. (2009). What is technology assessment? *International Journal of Technology Assessment in Health Care, 25*(S1), 7–9.

Becker, S. J., Nemat, A. T., Lucas, S., Heinitz, R. M., Klevesath, M., & Charton, J. E. (2023). A code of digital ethics: Laying the foundation for digital ethics in a science and technology company. *AI & Society, 38*(6), 2629–2639.

Belliger, A., & Krieger, D. J. (2022). New directions in digital ethics. *IKF Institute for Communication & Leadership.* IKF.

Berloznik, R., & Van Langenhove, L. (1998). Integration of technology assessment in R&D management practices. *Technological Forecasting & Social Change, 58*(1), 23–33.

Blok, V., & Lemmens, P. (2015). The emerging concept of responsible innovation. Three reasons why it is questionable and calls for a radical transformation of the concept of innovation. In B.-J. Koops, I., Oosterlaken, H., Romijn, T., Swierstra, & J. van den Hoven, (Eds.), *Responsible Innovation 2: Concepts, Approaches, and Applications* (pp. 19–35). Springer.

Bogen, M. (2019, May 6). All the ways hiring algorithms can introduce bias. *Harvard Business Review.* https://hbr.org/2019/05/all-the-ways-hiring-algorithms-can-introduce-bias. Accessed 20 Feb 2024.

Bonnefon, J. F., Shariff, A., & Rahwan, I. (2016). The social dilemma of autonomous vehicles. *Science, 352*(6293), 1573–1576.

Braun, E. (2005). *Technology in context: Technology assessment for managers.* Routledge.

Brundtland, G. H. (1987). *Report of the World Commission on environment and development: "Our common future"* [PDF file]. https://sustainabledevelopment.un.org/content/documents/5987our-common-future.pdf. Accessed 20 Feb 2024.

Buolamwini, J., & Gebru, T. (2018). Gender shades: Intersectional accuracy disparities in commercial gender classification. *Proceedings of Machine Learning Research, 81*, 1–15.

Burr, C., Taddeo, M., & Floridi, L. (2020). The ethics of digital well-being: A thematic review. *Science and Engineering Ethics, 26*(4), 2313–2343.

Carroll, A. B. (1979). A three-dimensional conceptual model of corporate social performance. *Academy of Management Review, 4*(4), 497–505.

Castilla, E. J., & Benard, S. (2010). The paradox of meritocracy in organizations. *Administrative Science Quarterly, 55*(4), 543–676.

Charta der Vielfalt [*Diversity Charter*]. (2024). https://www.charta-der-vielfalt.de/en/. Accessed 20 Feb 2024

Collingridge, D. (1980). *The social control of technology*. St. Martin's Press.

Corkhill, C., & Hyatt, N. (2018). *Nuclear waste management*. IOP Publishing.

Criado, N., & Such, J. (2019). Digital discrimination. In K. Yeung & M. Lodge (Eds.), *Algorithmic regulation* (pp. 82–97). Oxford University Press.

Declich, G., Berliri, M., & Alfonsi, A. (2022). Responsible research and innovation (RRI) and research ethics. In D. O'Mathúna & R. Iphofen (Eds.), *Ethics, integrity and policymaking: The value of the case study* (pp. 13–28). Springer.

Dignum, V. (2018). Ethics in artificial intelligence: Introduction to the special issue. *Ethics and Information Technology, 20*(1), 1–3.

Eckley Selin, N. (2024). *Carbon footprint*. Encyclopaedia Britannica. https://www.britannica.com/science/carbon-footprint. Accessed 20 Feb 2024.

Ess, C. (2009). *Digital media ethics*. Polity Books.

European Commission. (2011, November 30). *Horizon 2020—The Framework Programme for Research and Innovation (2014–2020)* (Proposal COM2011). https://eur-lex.europa.eu/LexUriServ/LexUriServ.do?uri=COM:2011:0808:FIN:en:PDF. Accessed 20 Feb 2024.

European Commission. (2024). *Vehicle Safety and Automated/Connected Vehicles*. https://single-market-economy.ec.europa.eu/sectors/automotive-industry/vehicle-safety-and-automatedconnected-vehicles_en. Accessed 20 Feb 2024.

European Parliament. (2023a, May 11). *AI Act: A Step Closer to the First Rules on Artificial Intelligence*. https://www.europarl.europa.eu/news/en/press-room/20230505IPR84904/ai-act-a-step-closer-to-the-first-rules-on-artificial-intelligence. Accessed 20 Feb 2024.

European Parliament. (2023b, May 24). *Circular Economy: Definition, Importance and Benefits*. https://www.europarl.europa.eu/news/en/headlines/economy/20151201STO05603/circular-economy-definition-importance-and-benefits. Accessed 20 Feb 2024.

European Parliament. (2024) Circular Economy: Definition, Importance and Benefits. Retrieved August 1, 2024, from https://www.europarl.europa.eu/topics/en/article/20151201STO05603/circular-economy-definition-importanc-eand-benefits

Eweje, G. (2007). Strategic partnerships between MNEs and civil society: The post-WSSD perspectives. *Sustainable Development, 15*(1), 15–27.

Fernández-Martínez, C., & Fernández, A. (2020). AI and recruiting software: Ethical and legal implications. *Paladyn Journal of Behavioral Robotics, Intelligent Agents, and Artificial Intelligence, 11*(1), 199–216.

Fisher, E., & Rip, A. (2013). Responsible innovation: Multi-level dynamics and soft intervention practices. In R. Owen, J. Bessant, & M. Heintz (Eds.), *Responsible Innovation: Managing the Responsible Emergence of Science and Innovation in Society* (pp. 165–183). John Wiley & Sons.

Floridi, L. (2019). Translating principles into practices of digital ethics: Five risks of being unethical. *Philosophy & Technology, 32*(2), 185–193.

Genus, A., & Stirling, A. (2018). Collingridge and the dilemma of control: Towards responsible and accountable innovation. *Research Policy, 47*(1), 61–69.

Gloede, F. (2007). Unfolgsame Folgen: Begründungen und Implikationen der Fokussierung auf Nebenfolgen bei TA. *TATuP—Zeitschrift für Technikfolgenabschätzung in Theorie und Praxis, 16*(1), 45–54.

Gohl, C. (2015). Ethik der digitalen Kollaboration. In M., Friedrichsen, & R., Kohn (Eds.), *Digitale Politikvermittlung* (pp. 215–230). Springer.

Gowthami, S., & Kumar, S. V. K. (2016). Impact of smartphone: A pilot study on positive and negative effects. *International Journal of Scientific Engineering and Applied Science, 2*(3), 473–478.

Grunwald, A., Revermann, C., & Sauter A. (Eds.). (2012). *Wissen für das Parlament. 20 Jahre Technikfolgenabschätzung am Deutschen Bundestag.* Nomos, Edition Sigma.

Hansson, S. O., Belin, M. -Å., & Lundgren, B. (2021). Self-driving vehicles—An ethical overview. *Philosophy & Technology, 34*(4), 1383–1408.

Henriksen, A. D. P. (1997). A technology assessment primer for management of technology. *International Journal of Technology Management, 13*(5–6), 615–638.

Himma, K., & Tavani, H. (Eds.). (2008). *The Handbook of information and computer ethics.* Wiley.

Hunkenschroer, A. L., & Luetge, C. (2022). Ethics of AI-enabled recruiting and selection: A review and research agenda. *Journal of Business Ethics, 178*(4), 977–1007.

Köhler, A. R., & Som, C. (2014). Risk preventative innovation strategies for emerging technologies the cases of nano-textiles and smart textiles. *Technovation, 34*(8), 420–430.

Konrad, K., Rip, A., & Greiving-Stimberg, V. C. S. (2017). Constructive technology assessment—STS for and with technology actors. *EASST Review, 36*(3), 13–19.

Koops, B.-J. (2015). The concepts, approaches, and applications of responsible innovation. In B.-J. Koops, I. Oosterlaken, H. Romijn, T. Swierstra, & J. van den Hoven (Eds.), *Responsible innovation 2: Concepts, approaches, and applications* (pp. 1–15). Springer.

Kretschmer, C. (2024). Digitalisierung: Wie sich künstliche Intelligenz entwickeln wird. *Tagesschau January 07, 2024.* https://www.tagesschau.de/wirtschaft/digitales/kuenstliche-intelligenz-ausblick-100.html. Accessed 7 Jan 2024.

Kudina, O., & Verbeek, P.-P. (2019). Ethics from within: Google glass, the Collingridge dilemma, and the mediated value of privacy. *Science, Technology, & Human Values, 44*(2), 291–314.

Kurtzberg, T. R. (2014). *Virtual teams: Mastering communication and collaboration in the digital age.* Bloomsbury.

Landolt, H., & Dähler, M. (Eds.). (2022). *Jahrbuch zum Strassenverkehrsrecht.* DIKE.

Lukovics, M., Zuti, B., Fisher, E., & Kézy, B. (2020). Autonomous cars and responsible innovation. In A. Kosztopulosz & E. Kuruczleki (Eds.), *The challenges of analyzing social and economic processes in the 21st century* (pp. 19–34). University of Szeged.

Malanowski, N., & Krug, C. (2017). Digitalisierung in der Industrie im Spiegel der prospektiven Technikgestaltung. In M. Vassiliadis (Ed.), *Digitalisierung und Industrie 4.0—Technik allein reicht nicht* (pp. 67–94). Industriegewerkschaft Bergbau, Chemie, Energie.

Mazurkiewicz, A., Belina, B., Poteralska, B., Giesko, T., & Karsznia, W. (2015). Universal methodology for the innovative technologies assessment. *Proceedings of the 10th European Conference on Innovation and Entrepreneurship* (pp. 458–467).

Morrison-Smith, S., & Ruiz, J. (2020). Challenges and barriers in virtual teams: a literature review. *SN Applied Sciences, 2*(6).

References

Müller, V. (2022). The history of digital ethics. In C. Véliz (Ed.), *Oxford handbook of digital ethics* (pp. 3–19). Oxford University Press.

Nentwich, M.F. (2016). Parliamentary technology assessment institutions and practices. a systematic comparison of 15 members of the EPTA network. *ITA-manu:script* 16-02. https://epub.oeaw.ac.at/0xc1aa5576_0x00345db6.pdf. . Accessed 20 Feb 2024.

Nyholm, S., & Smids, J. (2016). The ethics of accident-algorithms for self-driving cars: An applied trolley problem? *Ethical Theory and Moral Practice, 19*(5), 1275–1289.

O'Neil, C. (2016). *Weapons of math destruction: How big data increases inequality and threatens democracy*. Crown Publishing Group.

Porter, M. E., & Van der Linde, C. (1995). Green and competitive: Ending the stale-mate. *Harvard Business Review, 33*, 119–134.

Raji, I.D., & Buolamwini, J. (2023). Actionable auditing revisited: Investigating the impact of publicly naming biased performance results of commercial AI products. *Proceedings of the 2019 AAAI/ACM Conference on AI, Ethics, and Society* (pp. 429–435).

Rhue, L. (2018, December 6). Racial influence on automated perceptions of emotions. *Social Science Research Network SSRN*. https://doi.org/10.2139/ssrn.3281765. Accessed 20 Feb 2024.

Royakkers, L., Timmer, J., Kool, L., & Van Est, R. (2018). Societal and ethical issues of digitization. *Ethics and Information Technology, 20*, 127–142.

Schot, J., & Rip, A. (1997). The past and future of constructive technology assessment. *Technological Forecasting and Social Change, 54*(2–3), 251–268.

Shelley-Egan, C., & Davies, S. R. (2013). Nano-industry operationalizations of "responsibility": Charting diversity in the enactment of responsibility. *The Review of Policy Research, 30*(5), 588–604.

Spahn, A. (2012). And lead us (not) into persuasion…? persuasive technology and the ethics of communication. *Science and Engineering Ethics, 18*(4), 633–650.

Srinivas, K. R. (2022). Responsible research and innovation in India: A case for contextualization and mutual learning. In D. O'Mathúna & R. Iphofen (Eds.), *Ethics, integrity and policymaking: The value of the case study* (pp. 29–48). Springer.

Stahl, B. C., Schroeder, D., & Rodrigues, R. (2023). *Ethics of artificial intelligence: Case studies and options for addressing ethical challenges* (1st ed.). Springer.

Stilgoe, J., & Mladenović, M. (2022). The politics of autonomous vehicles. *Humanities & Social Sciences Communications, 9*(1), 1–6.

Stilgoe, J., Owen, R., & Macnaghten, P. (2013). Developing a framework for responsible innovation. *Research Policy, 42*(9), 1568–1580.

Tagesschau. (2022, December 6). Erstmals Regeln für Künstliche Intelligenz. Press release. https://www.tagesschau.de/ausland/europa/eu-kuenstliche-intelligenz-101.html. Accessed 20 Feb 2024.

Tran, T.A. (2007). Review of methods and tools applied in technology assessment literature. *Portland International Conference on Management of Engineering & Technology (PICMET '07 – 2007)* (pp. 1651–1660). IEEE. https://doi.org/10.1109/PICMET.2007.4349490. Accessed 1 May 2024.

UNESCO. (2022). *The Ethics of Artificial Intelligence*. https://www.unesco.org/en/artificial-intelligence/recommendation-ethics. Accessed 20 Feb 2024.

van de Poel, I. (2011). Nuclear energy as a social experiment. *Ethics, Policy & Environment, 14*(3), 285–290.

van de Poel, I. (2016). An ethical framework for evaluating experimental technology. *Science and Engineering Ethics, 22*(3), 667–686.

van der Duin, P. (2019). Toward "responsible foresight": Developing futures that enable matching future technologies with societal demands. *World Futures Review, 11*(1), 69–79.

Van Eijndhoven, J. C. M. (1997). Technology assessment: Product or process? *Technological Forecasting & Social Change, 54*(2), 269–286.

Visser, W. (2011). *The age of responsibility: CSR 2.0 and the new DNA of business*. Wiley.

von Schomberg, R. (2013). A vision of responsible research and innovation. In R. Owen, J. Bessant, & M. Heintz (Eds.), *Responsible innovation: Managing the responsible emergence of science and innovation in society* (pp. 51–74). Wiley.

Walther, G. (2015). Printing insecurity? The security implications of 3D-printing of weapons. *Science and Engineering Ethics, 21*(6), 1435–1445.

Wittrock, C., Forsberg, E. M., Pols, A., Macnaghten, P., & Ludwig, D. (2021). *Implementing responsible research and innovation: Organisational and national conditions*. Springer.

Yarger, L., Cobb Payton, F., & Neupane, B. (2020). Algorithmic equity in the hiring of underrepresented IT job candidates. *Online Information Review, 44*(2), 383–395.

Further Reading

Stahl, B. C., Schroeder, D., & Rodrigues, R. (2023). *Ethics of artificial intelligence: Case studies and options for addressing ethical challenges* (1st ed.). Springer.

This book provides an overview of the ethics of Artificial Intelligence, with wide-ranging implications for the wider responsibilities of virtual team collaboration.

MIX
Papier aus verantwortungsvollen Quellen
Paper from responsible sources
FSC® C105338

If you have any concerns about our products,
you can contact us on
ProductSafety@springernature.com

In case Publisher is established outside the EU,
the EU authorized representative is:
**Springer Nature Customer Service Center GmbH
Europaplatz 3, 69115 Heidelberg, Germany**

Printed by Libri Plureos GmbH
in Hamburg, Germany